A Dangerous Parting

A Dangerous Parting

The Beheading of John the Baptist in Early
Christian Memory

Nathan L. Shedd

BAYLOR UNIVERSITY PRESS

© 2021 by Baylor University Press
Waco, Texas 76798

All Rights Reserved. No part of this publication may be reproduced, stored in a retrieval system, or transmitted, in any form or by any means, electronic, mechanical, photocopying, recording, or otherwise, without the prior permission in writing of Baylor University Press.

Cover and book design by Kasey McBeath
Cover image: Caimi Antonio, Salomè the Daughter of Herodias (Salomè figlia di Erodiade), 19th century, oil on canvas, 118 x 93 cm. Academy Collection, Brera, Milan, Lombardy, Italy. Mondadori Portfolio/Electa/Sergio Anelli / Bridgeman Images.

Library of Congress Cataloging-in-Publication Data

Names: Shedd, Nathan L., author.
Title: A dangerous parting : the beheading of John the Baptist in early Christian memory / Nathan L. Shedd.
Description: Waco : Baylor University Press, 2021. | Includes bibliographical references and index. | Summary: "Traces early Christian interpretations of the story of John the Baptist's death by means of memory theory and reception theory, arguing that early Christians used John's beheading to justify hostility toward Jews"-- Provided by publisher.
Identifiers: LCCN 2021022761 (print) | LCCN 2021022762 (ebook) | ISBN 9781481315227 (hardcover) | ISBN 9781481317139 (pdf) | ISBN 9781481315241 (epub)
Subjects: LCSH: John, the Baptist, Saint. | Church history--Primitive and early church, ca. 30-600. | Collective memory. | Beheading. | Antisemitism.
Classification: LCC BS2456 .S48 2021 (print) | LCC BS2456 (ebook) | DDC 232.9/4--dc23
LC record available at https://lccn.loc.gov/2021022761
LC ebook record available at https://lccn.loc.gov/2021022762

Printed in the United States of America on acid-free paper with a minimum of thirty percent recycled content.

For Kristen

Contents

Acknowledgments   ix

   Introduction   1
   A History of Violence

1   **Violence Exposed**   25
   Social Memory Theory and the Negotiation of Trauma

2   **Cultures of Violence**   57
   Beheading in the Ancient World

3   **Contesting Violence**   83
   John's Beheading and Degradation in the Gospel of Mark

4   **The Violence of Memory**   129
   Christian Identity via Anti-Jewish Polemic

   Conclusion   165
   Reading beyond Violence

Bibliography   175
Index of Modern Authors   205
Index of Primary Sources   210

Acknowledgments

Although my name occupies the slot of author on this book, I am fully aware that my work would not have been possible without the guidance, encouragement, and critical feedback that conditioned its inception, various iterations, and final materialization. I am grateful for this system of support that structured its completion. As this book constitutes a revision of my PhD thesis completed at the Centre for the Social Scientific Study of the Bible at St. Mary's University (Twickenham, London), I would like to express my gratitude to my doctoral supervisors, Chris Keith and James Crossley. To Chris, thank you for your constant commitment to forming me as a researcher and professional colleague. The effort and attention to detail that you give to your students is of epic proportions. I am honored to have been one. To James, thank you for always being available to meet over a pint to discuss various drafts of particular chapters. Your constant pursuit in prodding me to push the bounds of my knowledge made this work much more interesting than it would have been had I ignored your suggestions. I am likewise honored to have been one of your students.

Several friends and colleagues left their mark on this study through their feedback and inspiration. Sarah Rollens, Rafael Rodríguez, Kelly Murphy, Grace Emmett, Justin Daneshmand, Brandon Massey, and Michelle Fletcher all carefully read various portions of this study or some of my research underlying it. Scott Robertson deserves a shiny medal (I would make you one myself, but you know how terrible I am at crafts) for combing through every page in search of error and unclear sentence structure. I sorely miss riding the 281 to visit you and Dani for game night at your former flat in Teddington. I want to convey a special thanks to the team at Baylor University Press—Cade Jarrell, Jenny Hunt, Kasey McBeath, Michelle McCaig, David Aycock, and Madeline Barbier—for providing a home for this manuscript and helping sculpt its final shape. I am deeply thankful especially for Cade Jarrell, who kept an open, clear, and professional line of communication from the proposal stage to the various stages of production. To the anonymous peer reviewers, your insight was incisive and spot-on—I hope you will be proud of the end result. To my Shedd, Collins, and Wooden family members, thank you for your perpetual love and support. Finally, I dedicate this work to my spouse, Kristen, who has endured my intellectual processes (read: terribly annoying bad habits), including an unhealthy sleeping schedule, a penchant for divided attention, and general selfishness. If Scott deserves a shiny medal, you deserve two bedazzled ones—because you win.

Introduction

A History of Violence

> Immediately, the king ordered the executioner
> to bring [John the Baptist's] head.
> Having departed, he beheaded him in the prison
> and brought his head on a platter and gave it to the girl;
> and the girl gave it to her mother.
> When his disciples heard,
> they came and took his body and placed it in a tomb.[1]
>
> There is no understanding without memory,
> no existence without tradition.[2]

In the final year of his life (192 C.E.), the Roman Emperor Commodus participated in the gladiatorial games at the amphitheater;[3] a peridrome was constructed therein for Commodus. From the spatial distance this structure provided, he would release arrows and heave spears at an array of wild animals, avoiding the danger inherent in close proximity to them. Although the ancient historian Herodian indicates that this safe separation did not showcase Commodus' "manliness" (ἀνδρεία), he admits that it demonstrated the emperor's "marksmanship" (or "the good aim of his hand" [τὸ εὔστοχον τῆς χειρὸς αὐτοῦ]), for his projectiles did not miss; his blows were always fatal. Commodus' exceptional marksmanship was typified on one occasion in particular when he managed to decapitate swift-footed ostriches with his specialized

---

[1] Mark 6:27–29. All translations of primary sources are my own unless otherwise indicated.
[2] Jan Assmann, *Religion and Cultural Memory*, trans. Rodney Livingstone (Stanford: Stanford University Press, 2006), 27.
[3] Herodian, *Hist. Emp.* 1.15.1–15.

"crescent-shaped" arrowheads.⁴ Like the proverbial chicken, the ostriches continued to run swiftly even after their heads had been cut off.

According to a different account, after killing and cutting off one ostrich's head, Commodus approached Dio Cassius and some other senators while grasping the bird's severed head in his left hand and elevating his blood-soaked sword in his right.⁵ (Word, moreover, had spread beforehand that Commodus wanted to shoot his bow at some audience members in the amphitheater.) Dio reports that in that moment Commodus "said nothing" (εἶπε οὐδέν) but instead "motioned (ἐκίνησεν) his own head with a partial grin" thereby "showing that he will do this same thing to us [senators] also."⁶ The senators' initial reaction to this spectacle consisted not of distress but rather of laughter.⁷ They avoided lethal repercussions for their jocular response because, as Dio claims, their own type of bodily motion prevailed: Dio grabbed foliage from his wreath to chew on and convinced the other senators to do likewise. The idea was that "by means of the steady motion (κινήσει) of the mouth" they might "conceal the proof of [their] laughter."⁸ Despite Dio's insistence that he and the senators were not overtaken by distress, in his narrative introduction of the episode he identifies Commodus' display as one reason they feared they might be killed.⁹

I make reference to these twin accounts of decapitated ostriches to underscore a fundamental recognition underlying my analysis throughout this book: *deliberately severed heads are manifestations of social and cultural location and thus serve as vehicles of communication as they are localized.* To elaborate:

> There is nothing natural about decapitation. The deliberate separation of a head from its body is exclusively cultural. Not only is decapitation exclusively cultural, but it is also the first sign of the symbolic processes that mark our species as distinctively human or at least hominid. Decapitation as we now know it resembles other forms of violence. . . . Unlike other forms of violence, however, decapitation, defined as the deliberate separation of a head from its body, does not occur outside human culture. Natural decapitations are by-products or accidents.¹⁰

---

[4] Herodian, *Hist. Emp.* 1.15.5–6 (Whittaker, LCL).
[5] Dio Cassius, *Hist. rom.* 73.21.1–2.
[6] Dio Cassius, *Hist. rom.* 73.21.2.
[7] See Mary Beard, *Laughter in Ancient Rome: On Joking, Tickling, and Cracking Up* (Berkeley: University of California Press, 2014).
[8] Dio Cassius, *Hist. rom.* 73.21.2.
[9] Dio Cassius, *Hist. rom.* 73.21.1
[10] Regina Janes, *Losing Our Heads: Beheadings in Literature and Culture* (New York: New York University Press, 2005), 2.

Localizing Beheading

Ancient accounts of beheading are the sites of localized negotiations of society, politics, and culture. This is a book about one such account and its commemorative negotiation across time: John the Baptist's beheading in the Gospels and their early reception. Most readers are likely already familiar with the general contours of the tale of John's death. The Baptist's rebuke of Antipas' marriage to Herodias spurs Herodias to seek John's demise. She finds her opportunity during Antipas' birthday banquet when Antipas, upon witnessing Herodias' daughter dance before him and his banquet guests, swears to give the daughter whatever she desires. Goaded by her mother, the daughter makes her macabre request, which is quickly fulfilled: the head of John the Baptist on a platter. The story is inherently captivating, as it contains elements that tend to pique our curiosity: power struggles, gender stereotypes, at least a hint of eroticism, and graphic violence.

This last element occupies my attention in this book. As I will demonstrate, interpreters have not fully appreciated the communicative impact of the violence of John's death in the Gospels and in the Gospels' early reception. This underappreciation is quite unfortunate not only because NT scholars are, contrariwise, quick to recognize the crucial importance of understanding Jesus' death in light of ancient scripts of crucifixion, but also because the account of John's decapitation practically begs readers to interpret John's death in light of the discourse of beheading. The earliest written portrayal of John's death (Mark 6:14–29) *fixates* on the bodily violence applied to John's person during Herod's birthday banquet:

- Herodias compels her daughter to ask Herod for John's "head" (κεφαλήν, 6:24)
- The girl requests Herod to give her "on a platter, the head (κεφαλήν) of John the Baptist" (6:25)
- Herod obliges and orders an executioner to deliver John's "head" (κεφαλήν, 6:27)
- The executioner "beheads" (ἀπεκεφάλισεν) John in prison (6:27)
- The executioner brings "his head (κεφαλήν) on a platter" (6:28)
- Herod (or the executioner) delivers "it [the head]" (αὐτήν) to the girl (6:28)
- The girl "gives it [the head]" (αὐτήν) to Herodias (6:28)
- John's head is then separated from its body's entombment—John's disciples take his "body" (πτῶμα) and entomb "it [the body]" (αὐτό, 6:29)

Mark 6:17–29 employs thirteen finite verbs to describe the desired or implemented action taken with respect to John's whole person, bodiless head, or headless body. Mark's introduction of the story, moreover, portrays Herod contemplating the bodily violence of John's death ("He whom I beheaded [ἀπεκεφάλισα], John, has been raised," 6:16).

In light of the intense focus this tradition places on narratively displaying the manipulation of John's severed head as it is transferred from person to person, and then intersecting this display with the observation of John's headless burial and the hint of John's revivification, it would be nearly miraculous if these features did not convey anything for Mark or Mark's early reception. Why, though, is a cut-off head so compelling as a hermeneutical vantage point?

As suggested above, a bodiless head, as a manifestation of location, reflects the inherited ideologies, conceptual frameworks, identity, and vices and virtues of a present social and cultural network. Those who make an effort to separate a head from its body stimulate the conceptual and commemorative synapses of a given context. Those who perceive or construct an image of the severed head conceptualize that head in language comprehensible to and valuable for their present. As one sociologist avers: "We cannot be oriented by a past in which we fail to see ourselves."[11] To state the matter rather ironically: as it is framed to embody a given present, the disembodied head mediates meaning that matters in the present.[12] As we will see, the head, separated from its body by whatever deliberate means, compels those who perceive or remember such an image to render it intelligible, to negotiate its potential resonances.[13]

So, what is the communicative impact of a head being unnaturally severed from its body? In the example above, for Herodian, the emperor's beheading of ostriches in tandem with (1) the speed of the birds, (2) their continued

---

[11] Barry Schwartz, *Abraham Lincoln and the Forge of National Memory* (Chicago: University of Chicago Press, 2000), 18.

[12] The irony extends to the entirety of my book as well. Although I seek to emphasize how the Gospels and certain early receptions of the Gospels embody John the Baptist's beheading in terms of *their* social and cultural locations, I nevertheless do so in language (mostly American English) and in conceptual frameworks (social memory theory) comprehensible in *my* present location (the academic study of religion). In so doing, the images of John the Baptist's head that I portray are inevitably reconfigured to reflect my social and cultural location. Simultaneously, as these images manifest my present, they also function as vehicles of communication that convey what matters for my readership. This manifestation of my present horizon does not mean that I run roughshod over the historical materials inherited from the past; it is rather the unavoidable consequence of the fact that the past can only ever be approached from the vantage point of the present. Irony, in this case, is not a counterargument. To think that one can approach the past sans present manipulation would show a lack of self-awareness. On approaching the past via social memory theory and on the present significance of studying the beheading of John the Baptist, keep reading.

[13] Of course, the move to render violence intelligible does not necessitate that portrayals are always or completely successful in doing so. As I will show in chapter 3, for example, the Gospel of Mark's image of John's beheading contains an essential ambiguity that opens up a number of plausible understandings.

sprint even after their decollation (which implies the birds were in motion as Commodus aimed his arrows), but also (3) Commodus' safe distance from the animals, negotiates Commodus' political identity as a credible imperial ruler in two ways. On the one hand, this display reinforces Commodus' reputation as an incomparable marksman. On the other hand, the safe distance does not provide Commodus an opportunity to perform his masculinity. This account, therefore, qualifies Herodian's later statement that Commodus' general conduct was almost entirely unfitting for a man of his imperial station except for his characteristic "manliness" (ἀνδρείας) and "marksmanship" (εὐστοχίας).[14] The decapitated birds' episode qualifies this assessment by explicitly denying that the beheadings showcased the first of these characteristics (manliness). In effect, Commodus' marksmanship is embraced, his manliness acknowledged but relativized, and all his other conduct deemed unsuitable for a figure of his stature. The beheaded ostriches serve as an essential component of reconfiguring Commodus' local (i.e., Roman) political identity in this way.

For Dio Cassius, the emperor's public exhibition of the severed ostrich head in front of the senators helped communicate a message specific in space and time. Although Commodus could speak and chose not to ("he said nothing" [εἶπε οὐδέν]), the bodiless ostrich head incapable of literal speech itself—framed in conjunction with the blood-spattered sword, the parting of Commodus' lips into a grin, and the report spread beforehand that Commodus wanted to shoot audience members in the amphitheater—stimulates Dio's (and the other senators') perceptual cognition. Dio registers this spectacle as a threat against their lives ("he [Commodus] will do this same thing to us [senators] also"). The severed head reflected and marked their identity: they were, or rather would be, the beheaded ostrich.

But Dio further complicates this image with laughter.[15] He insists that he did not react in sheer terror ("for laughter—but not distress—took us") even as he acknowledges that Commodus' foreboding message was readily understood. As Beard cogently argues: "To say 'I found this funny' or, even better, 'I had to conceal my laughter, else I would have been put to death' simultaneously indicts and ridicules the tyrant while casting the writer as a down-to-earth, genial observer not taken in by the ruler's cruel but empty posturing."[16] Whether Dio's stifled laughter consisted of elements of mockery at the absurdness of displaying a decapitated ostrich head, covert defiance of threatened imperial oppression, or careful trepidation, his contextual framing

---

[14] Herodian, *Hist. Emp.* 1.15.7
[15] Laughter, as Beard (*Laughter in Ancient Rome*, 7) rightly insists, is not always comical, but raises "interpretive dilemmas." On the various ways commentators have understood Dio's laughter in this episode, see Beard, *Laughter in Ancient Rome*, 5–8.
[16] Beard, *Laughter in Ancient Rome*, 7–8.

of the severed ostrich head nevertheless functions to accentuate Commodus as a tyrant while dissociating himself from said tyrant. This dissociation was an advantageous maneuver to make since, by the time this account was written (just two decades after the event described), Commodus' tyrant-like reputation was recognized across the social spectrum.[17]

To reiterate, a deliberately severed head is a manifestation of individual and collective location and, simultaneously, a vehicle of communication for society and culture. Images of beheading and the beheaded are shaped by the contours of present frameworks of conceptualization even as they shape and reinforce ideology and identity. Much like the Roman senators who saw their own heads in the bird's head, a severed head can mark and distinguish between collectives.[18] It can highlight an individual's skillset suitable for an ancient Roman emperor. Or it can frame that skillset as implicit mockery if it is the only conduct that an emperor has consistently working in their favor. Or it can even showcase an emperor's behavior as tyrant-like. Disassembled heads are able to frighten, inspire laughter, threaten, and isolate valued or marginalized behavior.[19] But all of these connections are contingent upon conceptual processes and cultural schemes of reference where the image of the head is framed and localized. This process of localization is what we shall consider in relation to John's beheading.

The Beheading of John the Baptist

That severed heads function as conduits of meaning only as they are localized in a given context underscores the importance of critically examining the beheading of John the Baptist in light of the ideological scripts of beheading in existence in the ancient world. Despite the account's attention on guiding readers to focus on John's severed head, the beheading itself receives far too little attention

---

[17] Beard, *Laughter in Ancient Rome*, 7. See also Herodian, *Hist. Emp.* 1.15.7, whose note that Commodus "was still quite popular with the mob" at the time he beheaded ostriches insinuates that this popularity would wane.

[18] Nearly Headless Nick would agree. In the literary world of *Harry Potter*, Sir Nicholas de Mimsy-Porpington, one of the ghosts who resides at Hogwarts and is nicknamed Nearly Headless Nick after his death because his neck was not fully severed from its body (he was struck with a blunt axe forty-five times), grumbles at his exclusion from the headless huntsmen. Nick is unable to join the group of huntsmen because that collective "can only accept huntsmen whose heads have parted company with their bodies." Thus, in this imaginative social structure, the completely severed head marks the entry requirement for group connectivity, whereas even less than an inch of epidermal residue marks one's exclusion from group belonging. See J. K. Rowling, *Harry Potter and the Chamber of Secrets*, illustrated by Jim Kay (London: Bloomsbury, 2016), 96.

[19] One need look no further than King Joffrey's public display of—spoiler alert—Ned Stark's severed head on a spike in HBO's epic *Game of Thrones*. When Joffrey shows Lady Sansa her father's spiked head, the image is a source of distress for Sansa and, in turn, schadenfreude for the king.

by NT scholars who study this figure.[20] To be sure, the Baptist is an intriguing person to study in many respects, and scholarship has concentrated, fittingly, on various facets of his life, including: his infancy and youth;[21] his possible connection to the Essenes (and relatedly the Qumran community);[22] his social identity as a prophet;[23] the register and meaning of his water immersion;[24] and his

---

[20] One exception is the brilliant study by Ross S. Kraemer, "Implicating Herodias and Her Daughter in the Death of John the Baptizer: A (Christian) Theological Strategy?" *JBL* 125 (2006): 321–49, whose arguments I engage in chapter 3.

[21] See, e.g., A. S. Geyser, "The Youth of John the Baptist: A Deduction from the Break in the Parallel Account of the Lucan Infancy Story," *NovT* 1 (1956): 70–75; Paul Winter, "The Proto-Source of Luke I," *NovT* 1 (1956): 184–99; Raymond E. Brown, *The Birth of the Messiah: A Commentary on the Infancy Narratives in Matthew and Luke* (Garden City, N.Y.: Doubleday, 1977); Stephen Farris, *The Hymns of Luke's Infancy Narratives: Their Origin, Meaning, and Significance*, JSNTSup 9 (Sheffield: JSOT Press, 1993).

[22] See, e.g., W. H. Brownlee, "A Comparison of the Covenanters of the Dead Sea Scrolls with Pre-Christian Jewish Sects," *BA* 13 (1950): 50–72; Geyser, "Youth of John the Baptist"; W. H. Brownlee, "John the Baptist in the New Light of Ancient Scrolls," in *The Scrolls and the New Testament*, ed. K. Stendahl (London: SCM, 1958), 33–53, 252–56; Jean Daniélou, *The Dead Sea Scrolls and Primitive Christianity* (Baltimore: Helicon, 1958); Jean Steinmann, *Saint John the Baptist and the Desert Tradition*, trans. Michael Boyes (London: Longmans, 1958), esp. 49–79; Charles H. Scobie, *John the Baptist* (London: SCM, 1964), 58–59; Otto Betz, "Was John the Baptist an Essene?" *BRev* 6 (1990): 18–25; Hershel Shanks, "Understanding the Dead Sea Scrolls," in *Was John the Baptist an Essene?* ed. Otto Betz (New York: Random House, 1992), 205–16; Joan E. Taylor, "John the Baptist and the Essenes," *JJS* 47 (1996): 256–85; Joan E. Taylor, "John the Baptist," in *The Eerdmans Dictionary of Early Judaism*, ed. John J. Collins and Daniel C. Harlow (Grand Rapids: Eerdmans, 2010), 819–21; Hartmut Stegemann, *The Library of Qumran: On the Essenes, Qumran, John the Baptist, and Jesus* (Grand Rapids: Eerdmans, 1998); J. I. H. McDonald, "What Did You Go Out to See? John the Baptist, the Scrolls and Late Second Temple Judaism," in *The Dead Sea Scrolls in Their Historical Context*, ed. T. H. Lim et al. (Edinburgh: T&T Clark, 2000), 53–64. For a recent study that argues that John once belonged to the Qumran community, see Joel Marcus, *John the Baptist in History and Theology* (Columbia: University of South Carolina Press, 2018), 27–45.

[23] See, e.g., Richard A. Horsley and John S. Hanson, *Bandits, Prophets and Messiahs: Popular Movements in the Time of Jesus* (Minneapolis: Winston, 1985), 135–89; Robert Webb, *John the Baptizer and Prophet: A Socio-Historical Study*, JSNTSup 62 (Sheffield: Sheffield Academic Press, 1991), esp. 219–378; Michael Tilly, *Johannes der Täufer und die Biographie der Propheten: Die synoptische Täuferüberlieferung und das jüdische Prophetenbild zur Zeit des Täufers*, BWANT 7 (Stuttgart: Kohlhammer, 1994); Joan E. Taylor, *The Immerser: John the Baptist within Second Temple Judaism* (Grand Rapids: Eerdmans, 1997), 101–54; David E. Aune, *Prophecy in Early Christianity and the Ancient Mediterranean World* (Eugene, Ore.: Wipf & Stock, 2003), 129–32.

[24] See, e.g., Ernst Lohmeyer, *Johannes der Täufer* (Göttingen: Vandenhoeck & Ruprecht, 1932), 67–81; Webb, *Baptizer and Prophet*, 95–216; Taylor, *Immerser*, 49–100; James D. G. Dunn, *Christianity in the Making*, vol. 1: *Jesus Remembered* (Grand Rapids: Eerdmans, 2003), 355–79; Daniel W. McManigal, *A Baptism of Judgment in the Fire of the Holy Spirit: John's Eschatological Proclamation in Matthew 3*, LNTS 595 (London: T&T Clark, 2019); Benjamin Snyder, *Ritual Purity and the Origin of John's Βάπτισμα Μετανοίας*, WUNT II (Tübingen: Mohr Siebeck, forthcoming).

8 A Dangerous Parting

relationship with Jesus of Nazareth.[25] And, of course, his execution. However, research on John's death has been typically driven by three questions not directly focused on the communicative power of John's actual beheading.

Question One: Time

One question is that of time (or "When did John die?"). This issue primarily involves consideration of the specific dating of John's death (the year it happened), and secondarily the chronological ordering of John's and Jesus' deaths (who died first). Many chroniclers date John's death between 28/29 C.E. and 37 C.E. by appealing to the temporal parameters set forth in Luke 3:1–3 and Josephus' *Ant.* 18.116–119. In the former text,

---

[25] See, e.g., Maurice Goguel, *Au seuil de l'Évangile: Jean-Baptiste*, Bibliothèque Historique 40 (Paris: Payot, 1928), 235–57; John A. T. Robinson, *Twelve New Testament Studies*, SBT (London: SCM, 1962), 28–52; Scobie, *John the Baptist*, 142–62; Jürgen Becker, *Johannes der Täufer und Jesus von Nazareth*, BibSN 63 (Neukirchen-Vluyn: Neukirchener Verlag, 1972); Morton Scott Enslin, "John and Jesus," *ZNW* 66 (1975): 1–18; Pierson Parker, "Jesus, John the Baptist, and the Herods," *PRSt* 8 (1981): 4–11; Paul W. Hollenbach, "The Conversion of Jesus: From Jesus the Baptizer to Jesus the Healer," *ANRW* 2.25.1:196–219; William B. Badke, "Was Jesus a Disciple of John?" *EvQ* 62 (1990): 195–204; Jerome Murphy-O'Connor, "John the Baptist and Jesus: History and Hypotheses," *NTS* 36 (1990): 361–66; Knut Backhaus, *Die "Jüngerkreise" des Täufers Johannes: Eine Studie zu den religionsgeschichtlichen Ursprüngen des Christentums*, Paderborner Theologische Studien 19 (Paderborn: Schöningh, 1991), 22–112; John P. Meier, *A Marginal Jew: Rethinking the Historical Jesus*, vol. 2: *Mentor, Message, and Miracles*, ABRL (New York: Doubleday, 1994), 116–30; Robert Webb, "John the Baptist and His Relationship to Jesus," in *Studying the Historical Jesus: Evaluations of the State of Current Research*, ed. Bruce Chilton and Craig A. Evans, NTTS 19 (Leiden: Brill, 1994), 179–229; Laurent Guyénot, "A New Perspective on John the Baptist's Failure to Support Jesus," *Journal of Unification Studies* 1 (1997): 71–92; John W. Pryor, "John the Baptist and Jesus: Tradition and Text in John 3.25," *JSNT* 66 (1997): 15–26; Dale C. Allison, *Jesus of Nazareth: Millenarian Prophet* (Minneapolis: Fortress, 1998), esp. 39–106; Bruce Chilton, "Friends and Enemies," in *The Cambridge Companion to Jesus*, ed. Markus Bockmuehl (Cambridge: Cambridge University Press, 2001), 72–86; Dale C. Allison, "The Continuity between John and Jesus," *JSHJ* 1 (2003): 6–27; Dunn, *Christianity in the Making*, 1:348–55; Daniel S. Dapaah, *The Relationship between John the Baptist and Jesus of Nazareth: A Critical Study* (Lanham, Md.: University Press of America, 2005); Graham H. Twelftree, "Jesus the Baptist," *JSHJ* 7 (2009): 103–25; Dale C. Allison, *Constructing Jesus: Memory, Imagination, and History* (Grand Rapids: Baker Academic, 2010); Maurice Casey, *Jesus of Nazareth: An Independent Historian's Account of His Life and Teaching* (London: T&T Clark, 2010), 171–97, 282–83; Max Aplin, "Was Jesus Ever a Disciple of John the Baptist? A Historical Study" (PhD thesis, University of Edinburgh, 2011); Roberto Martínez, *The Question of John the Baptist and Jesus' Indictment of the Religious Leaders: A Critical Analysis of Luke 7:18–35* (Cambridge: James Clarke, 2011); Joan E. Taylor and Federico Adinolfi, "John the Baptist and Jesus the Baptist: A Narrative Critical Approach," *JSHJ* 10 (2012): 247–84; Federico Adinolfi, "Gesù continuatore di Giovanni. Studio storico-esegetico sulla relazione tra Gesù di Nazaret e Giovanni il Battista" (PhD thesis, University of Bologna, 2014).

Luke indicates that John the Baptist emerged on the public scene in the fifteenth year of emperor Tiberius' reign (c. 27–29 C.E.). In the latter text, Josephus observes that some Jews interpreted the military defeat of Herod Antipas (c. 34–36 C.E.) by the Nabataean king Aretas as divine retribution for Antipas' execution of the Baptist, whose death Josephus relays as a narrative "flashback." If John was still alive by 27 C.E. but dead by 37 C.E. as these sources suggest, then these parameters enable scholars to approximate or pinpoint a more precise date within this range. Joan Taylor, for example, squeezes a tighter date range for John's death to c. 28–34 C.E. by observing that Mark 6:22 does not portray Herodias' daughter as married to Philip yet, whom she married sometime before his death in 34 C.E.[26] Taylor also insists that John "must have been executed . . . before 37 [when Pontius Pilate was deposed]" because "[o]bviously, Jesus was killed after John."[27] Others have tried unraveling the assumption that Jesus must have died before John, such as Schenk.[28] Still others have reached reticent

---

[26] Taylor, *Immerser*, 257. Cf. Josephus, *Ant.* 18.136–137.

[27] Taylor, *Immerser*, 257. See also Harold W. Hoehner, *Herod Antipas* (Grand Rapids: Zondervan, 1980), 125, who argues that Luke 3:1 requires the death of John to "have occurred between A.D. 28 and 32." Hoehner, however, observes that Josephus makes "it [seem] that John's death occurred not much before the defeat of Antipas' army by Aretas in A.D. 36" (p. 125). Rather than proposing a late date for John's death, however, he argues that a late date proposal is "an inference from Josephus that the Baptist's death must have occurred very shortly before the time of Antipas' defeat by Aretas" (p. 126). According to this reasoning, Josephus' account does not set a strict parameter on the date of John's death; it only indicates that John's death occurred at an indefinite time before Antipas' defeat by Aretas. Likewise, Gerd Theissen and Annette Merz (*The Historical Jesus: A Comprehensive Guide*, trans. John Bowden [London: SCM, 1998], 197) assign John's death to "an indefinite time before the defeat of Herod Antipas by the Nabataean king Aretas in 36 CE." Their rationale is that since the Baptist emerged during the fifteenth year of Tiberius' reign (28 C.E.), then John probably died early in 30 C.E.; consequently, John died "even before Jesus" (pp. 197–98 [quotation, p. 198]).

[28] Wolfgang Schenk, "Gefangenschaft und Tod des Täufers Erwägungen zur Chronologie und ihren Konsequenzen," *NTS* 29 (1983): 453–83. Schenk dates Antipas' defeat by Aretas to 36 C.E. This late date allows him to remain open to the idea that John may have outlived Jesus by four or five years. He reasons with respect to *Ant.* 18.116–119 in this way: "The interpretation of the defeat of Antipas as divine rehabilitation/restoration for the executed Baptist points at narrow, factual, and chronological coherences. This elimination of a disturber hardly allows [us] to reckon/calculate that Antipas had arrested him several years prior and then left [him] incarcerated" (p. 463; translation mine). Put otherwise, Schenk suggests that the populace's interpretation of Antipas' defeat necessitates that John died in close proximity to 36 C.E. and was not in fact arrested many years earlier (Mark 1:14; 6:14; Matt 11:12/Luke 7:16). Against this idea see Hoehner, *Antipas*, 126, n. 1; Theissen and Merz, *Historical Jesus*, 89–90; Ulrich B. Müller, *Johannes der Täufer: Jüdischer Prophet und Wegbereiter Jesu*, BG 6 (Leipzig: Evangelische Verlagsanstalt, 2002), 79–82; Marcus, *John the Baptist in History and Theology*, 124.

conclusions on pinpointing the date of John's death.²⁹ And one scholar has even assigned John's death to the early 20s C.E.³⁰

Question Two: "Historical Accuracy"

A second query energizing scholarly discourse is the convoluted issue of "historical accuracy." The term "historical accuracy" is intrinsically vague, but I use it here to capture a set of three interrelated questions at work in scholarly discussions: historicity ("What actually happened and why?"), primitivity ("What was the tradition's prehistory?"), and plausibility ("Is the story anachronistic *or* informed about the social and political conditions of early first-century Galilee?"). For example, Roger Aus argues that Antipas' oath to give up to half of his kingdom (Mark 6:23) "has nothing to do with historical reality," but it rather "derives from the Esther narrative," and most ostensibly from the first targum of Esther 5:3 where Ahasuerus offers Esther half of his kingdom.³¹ This and the apparent presence of other cultural tropes in Mark 6:17-29 lead Aus to doubt its historicity.³² Further, some interpreters doubt

---

²⁹ E. P. Sanders, *The Historical Figure of Jesus* (London: Penguin, 1993), 287-90; Kraemer, "Implicating Herodias," 327-30, 340.

³⁰ See Chilton, "Friends and Enemies"; idem, "John the Baptist: His Immersion and His Death," in *Dimensions of Baptism: Biblical and Theological Studies*, ed. Stanley E. Porter and Anthony R. Cross (Sheffield: Sheffield Academic Press, 2002), 25-44; idem, "John the Baptist," in *The Routledge Encyclopedia of the Historical Jesus*, ed. Craig A. Evans (New York: Routledge, 2008), 339-42. Cf. idem, "John the Purifier," in *Jesus in Context: Temple, Purity, and Restoration*, ed. Bruce Chilton and Craig A. Evans (Leiden: Brill, 1997), 203-20.

³¹ Roger Aus, *Water into Wine and the Beheading of John the Baptist: Early Jewish-Christian Interpretation of Esther 1 in John 2.1-11 and Mark 6.17-29*, BJS 150 (Atlanta: Scholars Press, 1988), 55-56 (quotations, p. 55). Similarly, Joachim Gnilka, "Das Martyrium Johannes' des Täufers (Mk 6, 17-29)," in *Orientierung an Jesus: Zur Theologie der Synoptiker*, ed. P. Hoffmann, Norbert Brox, and Wilhelm Pesch (Freiburg: Herder, 1973), 78-92; Gerd Theissen, *The Gospels in Context: Social and Political History in the Synoptic Tradition* (Minneapolis: Fortress, 1991), 86; Taylor, *Immerser*, 246; James G. Crossley, "History from the Margins: The Death of John the Baptist," in *Writing History, Constructing Religion*, ed. James G. Crossley and Christian Karner (Aldershot: Ashgate, 2005), 148; Taylor, "John the Baptist," 821; Marcus, *John the Baptist in History and Theology*, 99.

³² Aus, *Water into Wine*, 73: "There was no birthday banquet of a 'King' Herod Antipas, no dancing of a 'little girl' Salome before drunken men, no head dripping of blood brought in on a platter." See also Martin Dibelius, *Die urchristliche Überlieferung von Johannes dem Täufer* (Göttingen: Vandenhoeck & Ruprecht, 1911), 79 (translation mine), who argues that the dance of the girl and the king's promise to her are based on "saying motifs" and thus fit "in the palace of a fairy-tale king than in the court of Antipas." Scholars also argue that Mark 6:17-29 is crafted out of Elijanic tropes. For this reason, Catherine M. Murphy, *John the Baptist: Prophet of Purity for a New Age* (Collegeville, Minn.: Liturgical Press, 2003), 72-73, argues that it does not pass the criterion of discontinuity. For the parallels between Mark's account and the Elijah-Ahab-Jezebel conflict, see, e.g., David M. Hoffeditz and Gary E. Yates, "Femme Fatale Redux: Intertextual Connection to the Elijah/Jezebel Narratives in Mark 6:14-29," *BBR* 15 (2005): 199-221; M. Eugene Boring, *Mark: A Commentary*,

the historicity of most of Mark's account based on Mark's dubious knowledge of the Herodian dynasty in particular. For instance, pointing out that it was Herodias' daughter, Salome, who married Antipas' brother Philip (Josephus, *Ant.* 18.136–137) and not Herodias herself (Mark 6:17),[33] Meier poses an *a fortiori* interrogative argument: "If Mark can be so wrong about the basic familial relationships that are the driving engine of the plot of his story about John's execution, why should we credit the rest of the story as historical?"[34] One page

---

NTL (Louisville: Westminster John Knox, 2006), 178. For Greco-Roman parallels see, e.g., Rudolf Bultmann, *History of the Synoptic Tradition*, trans. John Marsh (Oxford: Basil Blackwell, 1963), 301, n. 5; Joel Marcus, *Mark 1–8: A New Translation with Introduction and Commentary*, AB 27 (New York: Doubleday, 2000), 402. Cf. Charles H. Talbert, *Matthew*, Paideia (Grand Rapids: Baker Academic, 2010), 183. Alternatively, Scobie (*John the Baptist*, 180, n. 1) contends that the similarities between John's death and the stories of Elijah and Esther "are not close enough to warrant the conclusion that the New Testament story is a pure fiction." Although Scobie reveals that he questions the precision or the amount of the parallels, his phraseology implies that he would conclude John's execution story as some sort of literary creation had the parallels aligned more considerably.

[33] Matthew 14:3 likewise mentions that Herodias was the wife of Philip. Josephus (*Ant.* 18.109, 136) indicates that Herodias was married to "Herod" (Antipas' half-brother) before she married Antipas. Josephus claims that Herodias and Herod had a daughter named Salome who married Philip the tetrarch before his death in 33/34 C.E. (Salome would remarry and have three sons with Aristobolus [*Ant.* 18.136–137]). The difficulty lies in the observation that no ancient source indicates that "Herod" whom Herodias married was also named "Philip." If Mark and Matthew both have Philip "the tetrarch" in view (neither explicitly identifies him as "tetrarch"), then this is incompatible with Josephus, who clearly identifies Philip the tetrarch as the husband of Salome, not Herodias. Codex Bezae (D) at Matt 14:3 omits the name "Philip" to read that Herodias was married to Antipas' brother. The codex thus portrays the familial relationship similarly to Josephus' portrayal. Likewise, Luke 3:19 refers to Herodias' former husband as merely Antipas' brother. Adding to this complexity is the name of the dancing "daughter" in Mark 6:17–29. Some manuscripts at Mark 6:22 (e.g., ℵ, B, D, L) indicate that this figure was Antipas' daughter and named Herodias (like her mother). If Mark understands this daughter to be born of Antipas and Herodias (cf. 6:24), then this comes into tension with Josephus. Josephus does not indicate that Antipas and Herodias had any children together. Other manuscripts at Mark 6:22 (e.g., A, C) indicate that the girl is Herodias' daughter and also named Herodias ("her daughter, Herodias" [θυγατρὸς αὐτῆς τῆς Ἡρῳδιάδος]). This also presents problems in relation to Josephus. He indicates that "Salome" was the name of Herodias' daughter from Herodias' previous marriage (*Ant.* 18.136–137). Still other manuscripts at Mark 6:22 (e.g., 205) are grammatically ambiguous in their reading: θυγατρὸς τῆς Ἡρῳδιάδος. The genitive τῆς Ἡρῳδιάδος could be rendered appositionally ("the daughter, *that is, Herodias*") or as a genitive of relationship ("the daughter *of Herodias*"). This same grammatical ambiguity with respect to the genitive case is also at work in the manuscripts (again, e.g., ℵ, B, D, L) that read θυγατρὸς αὐτοῦ Ἡρῳδιάδος ("his daughter, that is, Herodias" or "his daughter of [i.e., whom he had with] Herodias"). Finally, Matt 14:6 does not explicitly name the daughter but refers to her as "the daughter of Herodias" (ἡ θυγάτηρ τῆς Ἡρῳδιάδος). See further Marcus, *Mark 1–8*, 396.

[34] Meier, *Marginal Jew*, 2:172.

earlier Meier even declares: "The Marcan account contains little of historical worth, even with reference to the historical John."[35]

Question Three: Meaning

The third major question is that of function ("What does John's death mean?").[36] Several arguments have been offered in this regard. One idea is that the Markan account intends "to brand" Antipas and his court, as Gnilka puts it.[37] But debate rages as to whether Mark is sympathetic to Antipas—who wants to protect John, is entrapped by an oath, and is grief-stricken—or disparaging of the Herodian court (Antipas, Herodias, and the dancing daughter) altogether.[38] This debate includes consideration of the parallel account in Matt 14:1–12 and goes back centuries, as interpreters have varyingly estimated the figures' inner character,[39] or have attached

---

[35] Meier, *Marginal Jew*, 2:171.

[36] To state the obvious, the question of function poses itself differently to scholars who approach the Synoptic Gospels with different critical methodologies. For example, the early form critics tended to conceptualize the role of the synoptic writers in the composition of the Gospels primarily as mere collectors or editors of isolated (anonymous) units of tradition. See Martin Dibelius, *From Tradition to Gospel*, trans. Bertram Lee Woolf, The Library of Theological Translations (Cambridge: James Clarke, 1971), 3. Cf. Vincent Taylor, *The Formation of the Gospel Tradition* (London: Macmillan, 1933), 1–43. Consequently, the orientation of their method was principally focused on tradition-historical matters (e.g., tracing the origin and development of units of tradition). See, e.g., Bultmann, *History of the Synoptic Tradition*, 6. Dibelius (*From Tradition to Gospel*, 1), however, maintained that, in addition to penetrating into a period previous to the written Gospels, a further objective of *Formgeschichte* was "to make clear the intention and real interest of the earliest tradition."

[37] Joachim Gnilka, *Das Evangelium nach Markus*, 5th ed., EKK (Neukirchen-Vluyn: Neukirchener Verlag, 1998), 1:246 (translation mine).

[38] See William D. Davies and Dale C. Allison, *A Critical and Exegetical Commentary on the Gospel According to Saint Matthew*, ICC (London: T&T Clark, 1988), 2:465; Meier, *Marginal Jew*, 2:173; Abraham Smith, "Tyranny Exposed: Mark's Typological Characterization of Herod Antipas (Mark 6:14–29)," *BibInt* 14 (2006): 259–93; R. Alan Culpepper, "Mark 6:17–29 in Its Narrative Context: Kingdoms in Conflict," in *Mark as Story: Retrospect and Prospect*, ed. Kelly R. Iverson and Christopher W. Skinner, SBLRBS 65 (Atlanta: Society of Biblical Literature, 2011), 145–63; Adela Yarbro Collins, *Mark: A Commentary*, Hermeneia (Minneapolis: Fortress, 2007), 313; Crossley, "History from the Margins," 147–61.

[39] In the mid-fourth century, Hilary of Poitiers (*Comm. Matt.* 14.7–8) viewed Antipas as an analogue to Israel, whose unbelief led to lustfulness. Later in the same century, Jerome (*Comm. Matt.* 14.9 [Scheck, FC]) suggested that Antipas' fidelity to his oath reveals his impiety "under the pretext of piety." Jerome does not take at face value Antipas' supposed grief at the daughter's request in Matt 14:9. He argued that Antipas "was hiding his true thoughts" and thus "feigning sadness in his countenance, while he had joy in his heart" (*Comm. Matt.* 14.9 [Scheck, FC]). See also Jerome's previous comments regarding Matt 14:7: "I do not excuse Herod by saying that he committed murder reluctantly and against his will on account of the oath. For he perhaps took the oath *in order to create the conditions for this future occasion*" (*Comm. Matt.* 14.7 [Scheck, FC; italics added]). In the early fifth century, Augustine (*Serm.* 307.1) regarded Herodias as more wicked than Antipas, referring

normative significance to their actions.⁴⁰ Historically, in addition to these anti-Herodian readings, the most frequently offered interpretation of John's death is that it literally foreshadows or anticipates Jesus' demise. Steinmann describes John's death as a "martyrdom" designed to "prefigure the passion of the servant of Yahweh."⁴¹ A decade later in his commentary on Mark, E. Schweitzer entitled his discussion of Mark 6:14–29, "The Destiny of the Baptist as Prophetic of the Destiny of Jesus."⁴² The language of Steinmann and Schweitzer is typical in scholarship.⁴³ A final interpretation

---

to her as "[t]hat detestable woman" (trans. Edmund Hill, in *Sermons* [306–340A], ed. John E. Rotelle, The Works of Saint Augustine: A Translation for the 21st Century 3/9 [Hyde Park, N.Y.: New City Press, 1994]). In contradistinction to Jerome, Augustine viewed Antipas as having a more positive inclination toward John ("Herod loved John") (*Serm.* 307.1 [Hill, *Sermons*]). Antipas, according to Augustine, was torn between his lust for Herodias and his reverence for the Baptist until he positioned himself—via his oath—in a situation where he had to make a decision between two evil choices. John Calvin, *Commentary on a Harmony of the Evangelists, Matthew, Mark, and Luke*, trans. Rev. William Pringle (Grand Rapids: Baker, 2005), 222–23, observes the dissonance between the Markan and Matthean portrayals of Antipas' disposition toward John (Mark 6:20, 26; Matt 14:5, 9). He attempts to harmonize the depictions by positing an elaborate sequence. Antipas progresses from someone unwilling to put John to death, to someone willing but unable to do so, and finally to someone with an insufficient disposition to commit murder, of whom Herodias took advantage in her scheme to strike down the Baptist.

⁴⁰ In his letter to Amphilochius, Basil (*Letters* 199.29 [Way, FC]) draws attention to Antipas' "wickedness under a pretext of piety" as substantiation for his prohibitions against making oaths and keeping wicked oaths already sworn. Appealing to Herodias' and Antipas' involvement in John's death, Ambrose (*Concerning Virgins* 3.5.25–3.6.31) pleads to women to teach their daughters modesty and to men to avoid banquets. John Chrysostom (*Hom. Matt.* 48 [quotation, 48.5; *NPNF*¹ 10:299]) too employs both Antipas and Herodias as examples of the dangers of oaths, dancing, and banquets. Like Augustine, he especially views Herodias as the most wicked character: "But albeit [Antipas] was so wicked, that base woman was more wicked than all of them, both the damsel and the tyrant"; "Let us weep for Herodias, and for them that imitate her" (Chrysostom, *Hom. Matt.* 48.8 [*NPNF*¹ 10:301]). Finally, Harriet Beecher Stowe, Euphemia Johnson Richmond, Mrs. Donaldson, and Margaret Black all appeal to Herodias or Salome as negative examples to dissuade the misuse of power among women. See Marion Ann Taylor and Heather E. Weir, eds., *Women in the Story of Jesus: The Gospels through the Eyes of Nineteenth-Century Female Biblical Interpreters* (Grand Rapids: Eerdmans, 2016), 163–76.

⁴¹ Steinmann, *Saint John the Baptist and the Desert Tradition*, 99.

⁴² Eduard Schweizer, *The Good News According to Mark* (Atlanta: John Knox, 1970), 131.

⁴³ See, e.g., A. E. J. Rawlinson, *St Mark* (London: Methuen, 1925), 83; C. E. B. Cranfield, *The Gospel According to Saint Mark*, CGTC (Cambridge: Cambridge University Press, 1959), 208–9; Walter Wink, *John the Baptist in the Gospel Tradition*, SNTSMS 7 (Cambridge: Cambridge University Press, 1968), 17, 86; Willi Marxsen, *Mark the Evangelist: Studies on the Redaction History of the Gospel*, trans. Roy A. Harrisville (Nashville: Abingdon, 1969), 40; William L. Lane, *The Gospel According to Mark*, NICNT (Grand Rapids: Eerdmans, 1974), 215, 223; Morna D. Hooker, *The Gospel According to Saint Mark* (London: Black and Peabody, 1991), 158–59; Davies and Allison, *Saint Matthew*, 2:476; Janice C. Anderson, *Matthew's Narrative Web: Over, and Over, and Over Again*, JSNTSup 91 (Sheffield: JSOT Press, 1994), 83–90; Marcus, *Mark 1–8*, 397–404; R. T. France, *The Gospel of Mark*, NIGTC (Grand Rapids: Eerdmans, 2002), 257; Mark McVann, "The 'Passion' of John the Baptist and

posits that the story of John's death in Mark 6:17–29 functions to show that Jesus cannot be the resurrected John the Baptist (Mark 6:14, 16): "The point is that people with their own speculations were not coming up with the notion that Jesus was Messiah or Lord, and in a biography this story about the Baptist is crucial, for it clears up once and for all that Jesus is not John."[44]

A Fourth Question: Memory

When did John die? *What* actually happened and *why*? And *what* did it mean? Although these questions have been the object of detailed investigation, the sociological question of *how* John's *beheading* mediates meaning in its present actualization has not received the attention it deserves. This question is significant not only because attending to the sociology of meaning-making opens up new pathways of understanding the potential resonances of John's death. It is also significant because the question of the sociology of John's beheading is really a question about memory and reception—a query that takes seriously the communicative impact of the past in a given present.

Benefits of a Social Memory Approach

In this book, my aim is to reexamine the beheading of John the Baptist in light of the theoretical contours of social memory. In chapter 1, I will introduce social memory theory and its import for studying narrations of violence more fully. Sufficient for previewing the significance of my study here at the outset is the rudimentary recognition that social memory theory is an interdisciplinary theoretical framework whose theorists study the intersection of the inherited past and the present in individual and collective articulations of the past, especially as such articulations relate to society and culture. Thus, *how* John's *beheading* serves as a vehicle of communication in its various present verbalizations is a question that social memory theory is capable of conceptualizing and structuring. As Schwartz claims: "How the past is symbolized and how it functions as a mediator of meaning are questions that go to the heart of collective memory."[45]

Jesus before Pilate: Mark's Warnings about Kings and Governors," *BTB* 38 (2008): 152–57; Christos Karakolis, "Narrative Funktion und christologische Bedeutung der markinischen Erzählung vom Tod Johannes des Täufers (Mk 6:14–29)," *NovT* 52 (2010): esp. 146–52; Rivka Nir, *The First Christian Believer: In Search of John the Baptist* (Sheffield: Sheffield Phoenix Press, 2019), 231–57.

[44] Ben Witherington, *The Gospel of Mark: A Socio-Rhetorical Commentary* (Grand Rapids: Eerdmans, 2001), 214 (italics added). Witherington, however, does not detail how John's beheading itself contributes to his interpretation. A small handful of other interpreters do consider the beheading itself as dispelling the rumors of Jesus' identity as John *redivivus* (e.g., Kraemer, "Implicating Herodias," esp. 341–42). I will return to this line of argumentation in detail in chapter 3.

[45] Schwartz, *Abraham Lincoln*, 17.

The benefits and significance of approaching John's beheading from the vantage point of this theoretical framework are manifold. Of course, social memory theory has its limitations. And so, it is necessary first to highlight what it does not do before we can clarify what it does do. As a modern framework, social memory theory does not generate new evidence about John's beheading.[46] The primary data on our desks and screens remain the same unless archaeologists are to unearth new discoveries. With respect to the first century C.E., this means that Mark 6:14–29 is the point of departure in interpreting John's beheading.[47] Further, social memory theory does not represent a singular approach to historiography. For decades in NT scholarship, social memory theory has predominantly been applied to historical Jesus research in a bid to redefine how or if historians can construct the Jesus of Nazareth "behind" the Gospels.[48] But social memory theory can also be useful as a heuristic tool in another respect, as I will explain below. The theory, moreover, when applied to ancient history, does not forego historical-contextual analysis of the ancient world.

Reinforcing the Need to Understand the Violence of John's Beheading

Instead, social memory theory acknowledges that any given present articulation of the past reflects the frameworks of conceptualization available to that present social and cultural location. The past is always remade in the image of a present context because the past can only be approached and verbalized within a particular social and cultural matrix. In reference to Mark's memory of John's death, therefore, this theory does not forego but rather *reinforces* the necessity of engaging the cultural scripts of beheading in existence in Mark's ancient Mediterranean milieu if we are to have any chance at approximating the communicative potential of Mark's image of John's severed head (which again Mark seems to emphasize).

Accordingly, in chapter 2 I will argue that the severing of a head comprised a degrading form of somatic violence that could interrupt proper burial and impact the victim beyond death—in life in the hereafter—by rendering their body broken in such a way that it is incapable of revivification or resurrection. This understanding of beheading, in turn, opens up new ways of understanding John's beheading in Mark 6:14–29. Hence, in chapter 3, I agree with Kraemer

---

[46] Cf. John S. Kloppenborg, *Christ's Associations: Connecting and Belonging in the Ancient City* (New Haven: Yale University Press, 2019), 5, who makes a similar point in relation to employing ancient associations heuristically in comparison in early Christ-assemblies.

[47] I exclude Josephus' *Ant.* 18.116–119 from my analysis because Josephus does not focus on the specific mode of John's execution or the postmortem public display of John's body, only that Herod Antipas executed the Baptist.

[48] Thus, NT memory theorists led the charge in dismantling the criteriological approach in historical Jesus studies, as I will observe in chapter 1.

who notices that "the body of John is desecrated in a manner that makes it impossible to resurrect it."[49] But her deployment of this insight—where she insists that the story of John's desecration in 6:17-29 is designed to refute the idea that Jesus might be the resurrected John (6:14-16)—is not the only connection that early recipients might have made.[50] Undoubtedly, it is certainly plausible that Antipas' comment in 6:16 ("John, whom I beheaded, has been raised.") can be translated as a question ("Has John, whom I beheaded, been raised?") *suspicious* of the populace's view recorded in 6:14 that Jesus is the revived John; for Herod is privy to the fact that John was executed in such a way that made this conjecture impossible (6:17-29).

But Antipas' comment in 6:16 can be comprehended equally plausibly as a *genuine* question ("Has John, whom I beheaded, [indeed] been raised?") or a declarative statement ("John, whom I beheaded, has been raised.") that entertains not only the possibility that Jesus *was* the resurrected John the Baptist, but alternatively also the notion that Jesus managed to raise the beheaded Baptist from the dead. From this latter perspective, the degradation of John's body beyond death—with his head separated from his body in burial—serves to underline the impressive prestige Antipas afforded to Jesus' miraculous activity, which already included reviving the dead (Mark 5:21-24, 35-43). Antipas not only thinks Jesus can revive the dead, but also the decapitated dead. Underlying this portrayal, moreover, is perhaps a sense of mockery, where Mark implicitly ridicules a political ruler who considers the ludicrous notion of a beheaded man coming back to life or perhaps mockery in the sense that Herod is shown fearful of the repercussions from John for his improper (partial) burial. Understanding the cultural contours of beheading, therefore, helps us navigate the potential legitimate resonances Mark's portrayal could invoke depending on what connections different readers make.

A Move toward Reception

Not only does social memory theory recognize that images of the past are constructed in terms available to the present, it also concentrates on how any articulation of the past is the product of a complex interrelationship between the reception of the past in the present and the present sociocultural circumstances that activate recollection in the first place. Individuals and collectives invoke their salient past to solidify social bonds and reinforce boundary demarcations in their present horizons.[51] The present's mobilization of the apical past is essential to the formation and preservation of collective identities

---

[49] Kraemer, "Implicating Herodias," 341.
[50] Kraemer, "Implicating Herodias," 341.
[51] Bruce Lincoln, *Discourse and the Construction of Society: Comparative Studies of Myth, Ritual, and Classification* (Oxford: Oxford University Press, 1989), 20.

(tribes, families, nations, religious groups, etc.). As the past can be approached only from the perspective of the ever-shifting horizon of the present, significant social memories are in constant fluctuation. In this regard, the salient past resembles "moving pictures," to borrow Capps' metaphor.[52] Archetypal memories thus iteratively shape—and are repeatedly (re)shaped in—the present, as they are re-*present*ed. Because an interpreter's view of the past is always in motion (by virtue of their coterminous relationship with the present), history is not merely about a static image of the "actual past." Nor is historiography only about the reconstruction of originating stimuli of the past. History must also be about the reverberations of the past in multiple presents. Historians, consequently, must give attention to dynamic temporalities, not merely stationary time.[53] Put otherwise, scholars must offer an account of the reception of the past in its previous presents.[54]

In this vein, this book reflects recent developments in social memory and theories of history that have shifted away from historical positivism.[55] I do not, in other words, join Meier's futile attempt at uncovering an objective past that discards Mark's account as containing "little of historical worth, even with reference to the historical John" due to its apparent inaccuracy.[56] In his study on the historical Jesus, Keith cogently showed that the historical Jesus was likely a person capable of producing both accurate and inaccurate impressions of his reading and writing skills.[57] By analogy, we could remind ourselves that Mark's account of John's beheading, even if "inaccurate," could tell us something valuable about John's reputation. But more relevant for my purposes in this work, Mark's account of John's beheading, whether "accurate" or "inaccurate," contains much of "historical worth" precisely because it exists as a historical artifact itself and helped generate a subsequent reception history.

In this study, therefore, we will focus not only on how John's severed head mediates meaning in the Gospels, but will also see how it serves as a vehicle of

[52] Walter H. Capps, *Religious Studies: The Making of a Discipline* (Minneapolis: Fortress, 1995), 343.
[53] Jeffrey K. Olick, Vered Vinitzky-Seroussi, and Daniel Levy, introduction to *The Collective Memory Reader*, ed. Jeffrey K. Olick, Vered Vinitzky-Seroussi, and Daniel Levy (Oxford: Oxford University Press, 2011), 37.
[54] Similarly, Markus Bockmuehl, *Seeing the Word: Refocusing New Testament Study*, STI (Grand Rapids: Baker Academic, 2006), 168: "Because history is about effects and consequences as much as it is about the causes and conditions, an account of its impact and aftermath is indeed an integral part of all good historiography."
[55] For a recent overview of such shifts, see Chris Keith, Helen K. Bond, Christine Jacobi, and Jens Schröter, introduction to *The Reception of Jesus in the First Three Centuries*, ed. Chris Keith, Helen K. Bond, Christine Jacobi, and Jens Schröter (London: T&T Clark, 2020), 1:xv–xxvii.
[56] Meier, *Marginal Jew*, 2:171.
[57] Chris Keith, *Jesus' Literacy: Scribal Culture and the Teacher from Galilee*, LNTS 413 (London: T&T Clark, 2011).

communication in its early reception history. Particularly since the time Ulrich Luz began publishing his four-volume commentary on Matthew in the series Evangelisch-Katholischer Kommentar zum Neuen Testament, an explosion of "reception" publications has surfaced in biblical scholarship.[58] As Joynes rightly evaluates, reception history is no longer "*terra incognita*" as Bockmuehl had previously described it in 1995.[59] Although reception history captivates much scholarly interest, the reception of John's beheading has received little analysis by NT scholars. As I explained above, scholarship on John's death has predominantly focused on three different types of questions. But I do not mean to suggest that scholars have paid no attention to the post-history of John's death. In

[58] See, e.g., Ulrich Luz, *Das Evangelium Nach Matthäus*, 4 vols., EKKNT (Zürich/ Neukirchen-Vluyn: Benziger/Neukirchener, 1985–2002); Markus Bockmuehl, "A Commentator's Approach to the 'Effective History' of Philippians," *JSNT* 60 (1995): 57–88; Gregory L. Blomquist, "Patristic Reception of a Lukan Healing Account: A Contribution to a Socio-Rhetorical Response to Willi Braun's Feasting and Social Rhetoric in Luke 14," in *Healing in Religion and Society from Hippocrates to the Puritans*, ed. J. Kevin Coyle and Steven C. Muir (Lewiston, N.Y.: Mellen, 1999), 105–34; David Paul Parris, *Reception Theory and Biblical Hermeneutics*, Princeton Theological Monograph Series 107 (Eugene, Ore.: Pickwick, 2009), esp. 202–74; Christine E. Joynes, "The Sound of Silence: Interpreting Mark 16:1–8 through the Centuries," *Int* 65 (2011): 18–29; J. Christopher Edwards, *The Ransom Logion in Mark and Matthew*, WUNT 327 (Tübingen: Mohr Siebeck, 2012); Robert Evans, *Reception History, Tradition and Biblical Interpretation: Gadamer and Jauss in Current Practice*, Scriptural Traces 4; LNTS 510 (London: T&T Clark, 2014); Carol Hebron, *Judas Iscariot: Damned or Redeemed? A Critical Examination of the Portrayal of Judas in Jesus Films (1902–2014)*, Scriptural Traces 4; LNTS 510 (London: T&T Clark, 2016); Kengo Akiyama, *The Love of Neighbour in Ancient Judaism: The Reception of Leviticus 19:18 in the Hebrew Bible, the Septuagint, the Book of Jubilees, the Dead Sea Scrolls, and the New Testament*, AGJU 105 (Leiden: Brill, 2018); James G. Crossley, *Cults, Martyrs, and Good Samaritans: Religion in Contemporary English Political Discourse* (London: Pluto, 2018); Alison M. Jack, *The Prodigal Son in English and American Literature: Five Hundred Years of Literary Homecomings*, Biblical Refigurations (Oxford: Oxford University Press, 2019). These works represent just the tip of the iceberg of scholarly research on the reception of the Bible. In 2002, Christopher Rowland and Christine Joynes founded Oxford University's *Centre for Reception History of the Bible*. For a report on the Centre's activity since its inception, see Christine E. Joynes, "Changing Horizons: Reflections on a Decade at Oxford University's Centre for Reception History of the Bible," *JBRec* 1 (2014): 161–71. By my count, sixteen volumes have emerged in the *Blackwell Bible Commentary* series, a series chiefly dedicated to the reception of the Bible in literature, music, art, politics, etc. The appearance of the *Encyclopedia of the Bible and its Reception*, the *Journal of the Bible and Its Reception*, Bloomsbury's annual volume in their *Biblical Reception* series, the 2018 launch of the *Visual Commentary on Scripture* online project (funded by a $2 million USD donation by billionaires Roberta and Howard Ahmanson), and the 2020 coedited reference volumes dedicated to the reception of Jesus in the first three centuries (Keith, Bond, Jacobi, and Schröter, *Reception of Jesus in the First Three Centuries*) all attest to this burgeoning area of inquiry. Interest in the influence of the NT, of course, predates this explosion of interest. See, e.g., Ernst von Dobschütz, "Bible in the Church," ed. James Hastings, *Encyclopaedia of Religion and Ethics* (Edinburgh: T&T Clark, 1909), 2:579–615.

[59] Joynes, "Changing Horizons," 168, quoting Bockmuehl, "Commentator's Approach," 60.

his 2001 monograph, Hartmann included a brief treatment of samples of the reception of Mark 6:14–29, including in the nineteenth-century paintings of Gustave Moreau.[60] In 2013, Neginsky studied the reception of Salome in texts, iconography, paintings, sculptures, poetry, etc., especially from the fourth century through the Middle Ages, Renaissance, and nineteenth century.[61] In her 2015 article, Stichele includes an analysis of the fifteenth-century artist Giovanni di Paolo's six panels on the life and death of John the Baptist.[62] And, in her 2017 essay, Joynes performs an analysis of the reception of Mark 6:14-29 in Hinrik Funhof's late fifteenth-century painting *The Feast of Herod*.[63] Clearly, scholarship has focused on the afterlife of John's death to an extent. However, what these studies illustrate is that when scholars focus on the reception of John's death, the selection of texts and artifacts under investigation often encompasses an expanse of one or two millennia. There is a notable lack of emphasis on the reception of John's death in the second and third centuries in particular. For example, the volume dedicated to the Gospel of Mark in the *Ancient Christian Commentary on Scripture* series concentrates mostly on interpreters from the fourth century onwards in regards to Mark 6:14–29.[64] A similar focus is apparent in Luz' analysis of Matthew 14:1–12.[65] In Neginsky's study on the reception of Salome, she notably claims: "a religious and theological interest in [Salome] came only in the fourth century."[66] In a section entitled "Wirkungsgeschichte," Gnilka discusses the critical tone against Herod that Calvin and Luther hold in their discussions of John's death.[67] The present study, therefore, steps into this lacuna by analyzing the reception history of John's beheading in the first three centuries.

Drawing attention to second- and third-century commemorations of John's beheading is significant because, as we will see, John's beheading became the locus of early "Christian" expressions of identity during a critical phase of the

---

[60] Michael Hartmann, *Der Tod Johannes des Täufers: Eine exegetische und rezeptionsgeschichtliche Studie auf dem Hintergrund narrativer, intertextueller und kulturanthropologischer Zugänge*, SBB 45 (Stuttgart: Verlag Katholisches Bibelwerk, 2001), 356–64.

[61] Rosina Neginsky, *Salome: The Image of a Woman Who Never Was* (Newcastle upon Tyne: Cambridge Scholars Publishing, 2013).

[62] Caroline Vander Stichele, "The Head of John and Its Reception or How to Conceptualize 'Reception History,'" in *Reception History and Biblical Studies: Theory and Practice*, ed. Emma England and William John Lyons, Scriptural Traces 6, LHBOTS 615 (London: T&T Clark, 2015), 79–93.

[63] Christine E. Joynes, "The Reception of the Bible and Its Significance," in *Scripture and Its Interpretation: A Global, Ecumenical Introduction to the Bible*, ed. Michael J. Gorman (Grand Rapids: Baker Academic, 2017), esp. 160–63.

[64] Thomas C. Oden and Christopher A. Hall, eds., *Mark*, ACCS 2 (Downers Grove: InterVarsity Press, 1998), 82–88.

[65] Ulrich Luz, *Matthew 8–20*, Hermeneia (Minneapolis: Fortress, 2001), 308–9.

[66] Neginsky, *Salome*, 23.

[67] Gnilka, *Markus*, 1:252–53. Gnilka briefly notes the reception of the populace's identification of Jesus as John (Mark 6:14) in Origen before proceeding to Erasmus and Calvin.

development of "Christianity" in relation to "Judaism." Inscribed on John's severed head are localized early articulations of the so-called "Parting of the Ways." To preview one example for the moment, Justin Martyr in his *Dialogue with Trypho* activates the idea of John's severed head on a platter—which for Justin proves that John was Elijah—to combat the adoptionistic Christology of his Christian rivals. Justin is careful to assign John this Elijanic identity without lending credence to the additional notion that John, as Elijah, anointed (i.e., adopted) Jesus as the Christ. Justin then *aligns* his competitors' ideology with Jewish ideology (which held that Elijah would anoint the Christ). But this articulation of ideological difference takes anti-Jewish turns in that Justin makes denigrating Jewish ideology an essential component of establishing the superiority of his own version of Christian identity over competing versions. By looking at the early reception of John's beheading, therefore, we will see that John's severed head was the locus of early Christian articulations of boundary demarcation, albeit in a negative anti-Jewish way.

A Heuristic Framework for Studying Violence

In addition to shifting the theoretical focus of historiography to the reception of the past in the present, social memory theory also provides a heuristic framework for analyzing the reception of bodily violence. Whereas prior appropriations of social memory theory in NT studies have primarily focused on the methodological repercussions of the theory for historical Jesus research, I will show in this study that social memory also offers a heuristic grid at an analytical level for studying accounts of violence. I will set forth the contours of this framework in the next chapter more substantially. But at the heart of this framework is the awareness that traditions of somatic violence are sites of *contestation* in commemorative activity. Identity is readily negotiated around such narratives of violence, as many instances of bodily mutilation seem to possess an intrinsic gravitational pull in this direction.[68] Those who harness violence in commemorative processes often contest the degrading potential of bodily mutilation so that the symbolically freighted violence organizes perpetrators and victims into heroes or villains, thereby mapping moral configurations and group demarcations.

But memories of violence can also become invisibly violent.[69] The commemorative resonances of a violent past carry along in their wake—and

[68] See, e.g., Steven D. Brown, Matthew Allen, and Paula Reavey, "Remembering 7/7: The Collective Shaping of Survivors' Personal Memories of the 2005 London Bombing," in *Routledge International Handbook of Memory Studies*, ed. Anna Lisa Tota and Trever Hagen (London: Routledge, 2016), 428–41. For further examples and discussion, see chapter 1.

[69] Throughout this book, I employ the metaphor of "invisible violence" to describe (1) other forms of violence besides bodily harm and (2) the social conditions that structure and enable violent conflict. Specifically, I use the term in reference to "anti-Jewishness" to

thus inscribe in shifting present horizons—the social conditions (e.g., moral configurations, group estrangements) that help enable violence. As Lincoln notes, invoking a figure from the past in present moments of recollection often involves evoking "a correlated social group."[70] This correlation between the past and the present holds the dangerous capacity to recreate violence as opposing group identities in the present are separately infused with the moral and behavioral colorations of the past. In this way, "powerful collective memories—whether real or concocted—can be at the root of wars, prejudice, nationalism, and cultural identities."[71]

The tradition of John's beheading constituted a "powerful" social memory. My main argument in this book is that the early reception history of John's beheading is characterized by a dangerous synchroneity. On the one hand, the memory of John's beheading is the site of commemorative contestations over the degrading potential of John's bodily mutilation. For instance, the Gospel of Mark acknowledges the degrading potential of John's beheading by stressing features of his decapitation that typically highlight the emasculation of the victim, such as the public display of the severed head and the separation of the head from its body's burial. But Mark counterbalances these features by bringing them into tension with other narrative elements that enhance Jesus' prestige and that characterize John and Herod Antipas as positive and negative figures, respectively.

More specifically, in chapter 3 I demonstrate that Mark contests the degrading script of John's beheading in three ways. First, Mark keys John's beheading to Jesus' crucifixion, infusing their deaths with the same moral configuration, so that they are mutually affecting and exonerating. Second, much like the ostrich beheadings discussed above, Mark's picture of John's beheading negotiates Herod's identity as a credible masculine ruler. Antipas affirms John's masculinity: "Herod knew him [John] [to be] a righteous and holy man (ἄνδρα) and protected him" (6:20). Herod's apologetic posture toward John, however, *sharpens* the portrayal of Herod as a unmasculine "king" who ultimately fails to watch over John and instead is controlled by Herodias, without self-awareness of this external control. In Mark's portrayal, Antipas is never shown to be cognizant (1) that it was Herodias who concocted the daughter's request for John's head and (2) that it was Herodias who ended up possessing

---

highlight the inherent *dangerousness* of anti-Jewish ideology as an enabler of violent conflict. See further chapter 1.

[70] Lincoln, *Discourse and the Construction of Society*, 20. Although Lincoln makes this assertion to claim that this correlation can enable the "reawaken[ing]" of group "affinity," his discussion presumes that it can also recreate "estrangement" and "hostility."

[71] James W. Pennebaker, introduction to *Collective Memory of Political Events: Social Psychological Perspectives*, ed. James W. Pennebaker, Dario Paez, and Bernard Rimé (New York: Psychology Press, 1997), vii.

John's severed head. In these regards, Antipas only has an interchange with the daughter and the executioner:

- Request for John's Head (6:24–27): Herodias → Daughter → Antipas → Executioner
- Delivery of John's Head (6:27–28): Executioner → Antipas → Daughter → Herodias

Rather than John's beheading highlighting John as a degraded, emasculated man, therefore, the public spectacle of his severed head displays Antipas' ignorance, lack of control, and political inefficacy. Third, the framing of John's beheading in Mark's narrative serves to enhance Jesus' reputation as a prestigious miracle worker since Herod, in response to Jesus' growing fame, considers the impossible scenario in Mark 6:16 that the beheaded John the Baptist "has been revived [by Jesus]."[72]

On the other hand, however, as the memory of John's beheading is activated in the social context of early "Jewish-Christian relations," the degradation of his severed head is contested in anti-Jewish directions. In this respect, the memory of John's beheading itself becomes invisibly violent. On this matter in chapter 4, I concentrate on Justin Martyr's *Dialogue with Trypho* and Origen's *Commentary on Matthew* because they show clearly how later readers could rhetorically capitalize on the tradition's negative characterization of the Herodian court. Justin's contestation of John's beheading takes anti-Jewish turns in two ways. First, he keys Antipas' actions to contemporary second-century non-Christian Jews. In effect, he constructs and perpetuates a cultural system of contemporary non-Christian Jews as those who kill God's prophets. He also appeals to this system to structure and justify the violence refugee Jews are experiencing in his milieu. Second, as aforementioned, John's severed head on a platter forms a key component of Justin constructing his own version of Christian identity at the expense of Jewish ideology. Consequently, Justin perpetuates a pattern of thinking that makes a negative Jewish foil essential to Christian expressions of identity.

Origen's contestation of John's beheading also redeploys the tradition in anti-Jewish directions. Similar to Justin's commemorative maneuver of aligning Herod to his contemporary social framework, Origen allegorically disseminates an image of the Herodian court who beheaded John as reflective of contemporary Jewish behavior and status. Herod, Herodias, the

---

[72] To portray Herod as doubting the efficacy of beheading may reveal a hint of Markan mockery in that Herod almost inexplicably considers that John overcame a method of death designed to violate the integrity of the body in perpetuity. On the ambiguity of Mark 6:16 in relation to 6:17–29, see further chapter 3.

dancing girl, and even the banquet guests at Herod's birthday celebration all function as symbols of contemporary Jews. These figures' moral grit, their actions, and the consequences their actions incur are emblematic of the character and status of the present Jewish people. I show the contours of these maneuvers by means of a sweeping analysis of four passages in *Comm. Matt.* 10.21–22. Through his allegorical mode of discourse, Origen harnesses the inherited past of John's death to construct a cultural schematic of contemporary non-Christian Jews as incapable of correct teaching, since they are the beheaders of prophets/prophecy. However, even though John's beheading serves to indict contemporary Jews for their maltreatment of true teaching and prophecy, John the Baptist is not left completely unscathed in Origen's activation of the tradition. For Origen, the broken, beheaded body of John the Baptist alongside Jesus' unbroken body is a template that registers non-Christian Jews and Christians, respectively, in a hierarchical relationship, with the former occupying the inferior slot. Christians possess a whole Jesus and "the [gift] greater entirely than [the gift of prophecy]" (*Comm. Matt.* 10.22). Jews, however, despise prophecy since they beheaded it; their unbelief in Jesus is just another instance of them decapitating the prophets. The gift of prophecy, therefore, is absent among them. Etched on John's beheaded body, in other words, is a reflection of the Jews' charismatic inferiority to Christians.

Final Remarks

For professional researchers and students, I hope that my study will demonstrate the capacity of social memory theory to conceptualize and address problems outside historical Jesus research, particularly those problems confronting the historian who focuses on the reception of the past in the present. In the preface of his 2018 monograph, *John the Baptist in History and Theology*, Marcus rightly recognizes that "John the Baptist was a key figure in the parting of the ways."[73] He proceeds to confess, however, that he does not know "how to make the parting-of-the-ways project gel into a book" and so he "wrote this book" instead.[74] In light of our analysis of the inherited past of John's severed head in early constructions of Jewish and Christian difference, I propose that social memory theory offers a helpful way to navigate this tumultuous terrain. Further, our emphasis on understanding ancient scripts of beheading shows the potential for discourses on the body to be a hermeneutical vantage point for understanding ancient group boundary demarcations, gendered ethical configurations, and political rhetoric.

---

[73] Marcus, *John the Baptist in History and Theology*, ix.
[74] Marcus, *John the Baptist in History and Theology*, ix.

And finally, I hope that teachers and students of religion—who occupy spaces of power from lectern to pulpit *and* seat—will see the importance of contemplating the ethics *of reading* ancient texts. Disseminating knowledge in conjunction with reading texts from the past—especially texts that are often deemed sacred or that are frequently esteemed as authoritative for properly understanding sacred texts—is not an innocuous exercise, but a process that constructs social formations, ideological patterns of thinking, and cultural frameworks of living. Although it is often perceived as such, violence is almost never non-contingent: it is almost always socially, ideologically, and culturally structured and conditioned. In view of our analysis in chapter 4 of the anti-Jewish directions that John's beheading takes in the works of Justin Martyr and Origen, I hope that teachers and students will be more equipped to identify ideological patterns of thought and cultural schematics that have had and continue to have an invisibly violent impact on the lived experiences of Jews. In the conclusion of this book, moreover, I offer one particular strategy for how we can actively contribute to the dismantling of harmful social constructs that anti-Jewishness represents. We should be under no obligation to recreate cultural patterns that cause harm. I hope readers will close this book with a sense of responsibility and willingness to look for ways to construct identity positively, without caricaturing Jews to get there.

1
Violence Exposed

Social Memory Theory and the Negotiation of Trauma

> Every encounter with tradition that takes place within historical consciousness involves the experience of a tension between the text and the present.[1]
>
> Collective memory continuously negotiates between available historical records and current social and political agendas.[2]

Social memory provides a heuristic analytical framework for investigating traditions of bodily violence that are freighted with symbolic potential (such as beheading). Fleshing out the contours of this analytical framework constitutes my primary focus in this chapter. Although social memory theory should not be equated with an "exegetical method,"[3] I set forth four features of social memory in the following pages that are heuristically valuable in probing the reception of John's violent end: identity formation, interpretive keying, the violence of memory, and commemorative contestation.

---

[1] Hans-Georg Gadamer, *Truth and Method*, trans. Joel Weinsheimer and Donald G. Marshall (London: Bloomsbury Academic, 2013), 317.

[2] Yael Zerubavel, *Recovered Roots: Collective Memory and the Making of Israeli National Tradition* (Chicago: University of Chicago Press, 1995), 5.

[3] According to Sandra Hübenthal ("Social and Cultural Memory in Biblical Exegesis: The Quest for an Adequate Application," in *Cultural Memory in Biblical Exegesis*, ed. Pernille Carstens, Trine Bjornung Hasselbach, and Niels Peter Lemche, PHSC 17 [Piscataway, N.J.: Gorgias Press, 2012], 196), biblical scholarship "has a backlog to work off when it comes to understanding and using social memory theory." She reaches two conclusions. The first conclusion is that social memory theory needs to be brought to bear on biblical studies more fully than it has in the past. The second conclusion is that the need exists to explain what the theory has to offer at the exegetical level in particular.

I describe these features as a *heuristic* analytical framework because they provide the historian with a useful tool to compare the tradition of John's violent death with the memories of violence in contemporary cross-cultural contexts. In his recent monograph on comparing the sociology of early Christ-assemblies to ancient associations (e.g., occupational guilds), Kloppenborg explains: "To claim that comparison is a heuristic practice is to say that it enables us to 'discover'—*heuriskein* means 'to find or discover'—possible understandings in the lesser known object."[4] In a similar manner, engaging the interdisciplinary research on memory and violence—an area in which our knowledge is relatively high—enables us to probe the sociological dimensions, and thus communicative impact, of the lesser-known phenomenon: John's beheading. In other words, social memory theory informs our intellectual curiosity (that is, our imagination), allowing us to notice interpretive potentialities that we might otherwise overlook. Exploiting this theory, then, is an advantageous (and for this scholar at least, a necessary) maneuver to make if we are even to attempt to approximate how John's beheading served as a vehicle of communication in a crucial period of the development of "Christianity" and "Judaism."[5] Before discussing the four features of this interpretive framework, however, it is necessary first to introduce social memory theory, its emergence in NT scholarship, and its relationship to reception history.

What Is Social Memory Theory?

Social memory theory is an interdisciplinary area of inquiry whose theorists study the social and cultural dimensions of individual and collective articulations of the inherited past in the present.[6] Although the interdisciplinary theory

---

[4] John S. Kloppenborg, *Christ's Associations: Connecting and Belonging in the Ancient City* (New Haven: Yale University Press, 2019), 5.

[5] For memory theory to be a useful heuristic tool in studying the early reception history of John's beheading, we do not need to assume that the primary data in these centuries belong to identical literary genres or are instances of eyewitness or living reminiscences of the past. Origen's *Commentary on Matthew*, for example, is not an instance of "eyewitness/living recollection," nor does the allegorist articulate his image of the past regarding John's beheading in the same way as the Gospel of Mark or Justin Martyr. Social memory encompasses *any* articulation of the past in a given present, regardless of genre, medium, hermeneutical method, or distance from an originating event. The theory encompasses these because all articulations of the past draw upon social and collective frameworks to bring the past to bear on the present. Thus, for the theory to be useful as a heuristic device, all we need is that the primary sources under investigation embody an interrelationship between the inherited past (no matter how fanciful) and a present social context (no matter how limited our access to that social context might be). From this vantage point, it is appropriate to utilize this heuristic framework to approach Origen's allegorical interpretation of the Gospel of Matthew: Origen's allegorical method still represents the reception of Jesus tradition about John in the present, adapting—albeit creatively—past images to meet his contemporary rhetorical needs.

[6] Barry Schwartz, "Iconography and Collective Memory: Lincoln's Image in the American Mind," *Sociological Quarterly* 32 (1991): 302, defines "collective memory" as "a

now consists of a sizeable makeup of practitioners,[7] social memory theory—in large measure—traces its roots back to the French sociologist Maurice Halbwachs, who in 1925 published his seminal work on the social frameworks of memory.[8] For Halbwachs, all instances of remembrance, including individual recollections, are triggered by and localized in group identities (e.g., families, religious groups, social classes) to which the rememberer(s) belongs in the present.[9] Because of these "social frameworks" that encompass recall, "the past is not preserved but is reconstructed on the basis of the present."[10] Thus, Halbwachs argues against a perspective of memory that views recollection as simply

---

metaphor that formulates society's retention and loss of information about its past in the familiar terms of individual remembering and forgetting." On the similarities and differences between the terms "social memory," "collective memory," and "cultural memory" in critical discourse, see especially Sandra Hübenthal, "Social and Cultural Memory in Biblical Exegesis," 175-99. Since all three terms share a common interest in the social frameworks of memory, this study will utilize the term "social memory" to refer to individual or group memory localized in a given present. For helpful introductions to the theory, see Paul Connerton, *How Societies Remember* (Cambridge: Cambridge University Press, 1989); Barbara Misztal, *Theories of Social Remembering* (Maidenhead: Open University Press, 1990); James Fentress and Chris Wickham, *Social Memory*, New Perspectives on the Past (Oxford: Blackwell, 1992); Jeffrey Olick and Joyce Robins, "Social Memory Studies: From 'Collective Memory' to the Historical Sociology of Mnemonic Practices," *Annual Review of Sociology* 24 (1998): 105-40; Astrid Erll and Ansgar Nünning, eds., *Cultural Memory Studies: An International and Interdisciplinary Handbook*, Media and Cultural Memory 8 (Berlin: de Gruyter, 2008); Jeffrey K. Olick, Vered Vinitzky-Seroussi, and Daniel Levy, introduction to *The Collective Memory Reader*, ed. Jeffrey K. Olick, Vered Vinitzky-Seroussi, and Daniel Levy (Oxford: Oxford University Press, 2011), 3-62. See also Susannah Radstone, ed., *Memory and Methodology* (Oxford: Berg, 2000); Geoffrey Cubitt, *History and Memory* (Manchester: Manchester University Press, 2007).

[7] Olick and Robins, "Social Memory Studies," 106, describe social memory studies as "a nonparadigmatic, transdisciplinary, centerless enterprise."

[8] Maurice Halbwachs, *Les cadres sociaux de la mémoire* (Paris: Librarie Félix Alcan, 1925). Astrid Erll ("Cultural Memory Studies: An Introduction," in Erll and Nünning, *Cultural Memory Studies*, 8) considers it unquestionable that Halbwachs' "studies of *mémoire collective* have emerged as the foundational texts of today's memory studies." Similarly, Jeffrey K. Olick (*In the House of the Hangman: The Agonies of German Defeat, 1943-1949* [Chicago: University of Chicago Press, 2005], 336) refers to Halbwachs as the "founding father of the sociology of collective memory." Fentress and Wickham (*Social Memory*, ix) too describe Halbwachs as "the first theorist" of collective memory. The study of memory, including its social aspects, however, predates the French sociologist. For examples, see Olick, Vinitzky-Seroussi, and Levy, "Introduction."

[9] Maurice Halbwachs, *On Collective Memory*, ed. and trans. Lewis A. Coser (Chicago: University of Chicago Press, 1992), 37-40. See Olick, Vinitzky-Seroussi, and Levy, introduction to *Collective Memory Reader*, 19. Anthony Le Donne ("Theological Memory Distortion in the Jesus Tradition," in *Memory and Remembrance in the Bible and Antiquity*, ed. Stephen C. Barton, Loren T. Stuckenbruck, and Benjamin G. Wold, WUNT 212 [Tübingen: Mohr Siebeck, 2007], 164) reminds us, "This is why amnesia patients are often advised to return to a familiar environment for recovery. External environments prompt the memories required to operate within them."

[10] Halbwachs, *On Collective Memory*, 40.

replicating the past as such. Instead, he advocates for a view that understands recollection as embedded within the language and ideas one appropriates by virtue of existing within a social matrix. Coser, therefore, is correct when he claims that Halbwachs construed the relationship between the past and the present as one where "the past is a social construction mainly, if not wholly, shaped by the concerns of the present."[11]

The recognition of memory as a social construct is axiomatic for memory theorists. In 1932, seven years after Halbwachs' publication of *Les cadres sociaux de la mémoire*, psychologist Bartlett argued that recollection is enabled by the construction of "schemata."[12] For Bartlett, "schemata" are structures of memory that individuals inherit by virtue of their connection to the past:

> [Remembering] is thus hardly ever really exact, even in the most rudimentary cases of rote recapitulation.... [This imprecision is] an effect of the organism's capacity to turn round upon its own "schemata," and is directly a function of consciousness.... So, since many "schemata" are built of common materials, the images and words that mark some of their salient features are in constant, but explicable, change. They, too, are a device made possible by the appearance, or discovery, of consciousness, and without them no genuine long-distance remembering would be possible.[13]

Bartlett was skeptical of the notion that collectivities possessed a literal mental capacity to recall, but was receptive to Halbwachs' idea that an individual's membership in a social group stimulated and conditioned an individual's recollection.[14] Recently, Schwartz has argued that individuals do not remember the past in isolation but "they do so with and against others situated in different groups and through the knowledge and symbols that predecessors and contemporaries transmit to them."[15]

The recognition that commemorative activity bears the marks of the present context in which recollection takes place, however, captures only "half the truth" of memory, as one memory theorist puts it.[16] Schudson argues that the

---

[11] Lewis A. Coser, "Introduction: Maurice Halbwachs 1877–1945," in Halbwachs, *On Collective Memory*, 25.

[12] Frederic C. Bartlett, *Remembering: A Study in Experimental and Social Psychology* (Cambridge: Cambridge University Press, 1932).

[13] Bartlett, *Remembering*, 213–14.

[14] Bartlett, *Remembering*, 294–96.

[15] Barry Schwartz, "Where There's Smoke, There's Fire: Memory and History," in *Memory and Identity in Ancient Judaism and Early Christianity: A Conversation with Barry Schwartz*, ed. Tom Thatcher, SemeiaSt 78 (Atlanta: SBL Press, 2014), 9.

[16] Michael Schudson, "The Present in the Past versus the Past in the Present," *Communication* 11 (1989): 113; Barry Schwartz, *Abraham Lincoln and the Forge of National Memory* (Chicago: University of Chicago Press, 2000), 25.

past is under certain circumstances resistant to present manipulation.[17] He maintains, for instance, that traumatic pasts often force themselves upon the present as events that must be remembered.[18] I would add that certain individual and cultural traumas can force themselves upon the present as events that must, for whatever reason, be repressed.[19]

Like Schudson, Schwartz contends that the past constrains the degree of present manipulation of the past. In reference to the Gospels, he writes: "No successful historical writer, however, is free to create any conversation he or she likes; the writer must construct talk that readers find plausibly motivated, consistent with the subject's actions, and hence objectively possible."[20] In this light, it is quite possible for an individual or collective entity to recall erroneously the words of a historical figure's speech and yet still capture an "accurate" initial impression of that figure's message. Conversely, as different aspects of a record are selectively emphasized, suppressed, or varyingly contextualized, it is quite possible for an exact transcription of a figure's actual words to obscure considerably the essence of the speaker's originating message.[21]

Importantly, therefore, Schwartz does not regress to what Casey categorizes as a "photographic paradigm" or "passivist" view of memory where the "remembering subject" replicates the past with minimal manipulation.[22] Schwartz does not deny that social institutions, differing economic statuses, or competing power structures distort our narrations of the past.[23] He affirms that "[r]ecollection of the past is an active, constructive process, not a simple matter of retrieving information. To remember is to place a part of the past in the service of conceptions and needs of the present."[24] Nor does he emphasize exclusively the instrumentality of memory for advancing present ideologies. Rather, as another theorist observes, Schwartz critiques an "overemphasis"

---

[17] Schudson, "Present in the Past."
[18] Schudson, "Present in the Past," esp. 109–10.
[19] See, e.g., Janet Jacobs, "The Memorial at Srebrenica: Gender and the Social Meanings of Collective Memory in Bosnia-Herzegovina," *Memory Studies* 14 (2017): 423–39.
[20] Schwartz, "Where There's Smoke, There's Fire," 9. See also Le Donne, "Theological Memory Distortion in the Jesus Tradition," 166: "In order for images associated with the past to make sense in the present state of mind, the localization process must reinforce memories with plausibility and integrity."
[21] Cf. Chris Keith, *Jesus' Literacy: Scribal Culture and the Teacher from Galilee*, LNTS 413 (London: T&T Clark, 2011), 64, who argues that the historical Jesus was likely someone capable of producing both accurate and inaccurate memories of himself.
[22] Edward S. Casey, *Remembering: A Phenomenological Study* (Bloomington: Indiana University Press, 1987), 269.
[23] Cf. Le Donne, "Theological Memory Distortion in the Jesus Tradition," 166: "Social Memory theorists use the term 'distortion' to mark the difference between memory of the past and past actuality."
[24] Barry Schwartz, "The Social Context of Commemoration: A Study in Collective Memory," *Social Forces* 61 (1982): 374.

on the adaptive capability of the present—an overemphasis that "undermines the notion of historical continuity."[25] In short, Schwartz' paradigm of memory construes the relationship between the past and the present in instances of remembrance as reciprocal.[26]

In this respect, the mobilization of memory in various media (oral testimonies, textual artifacts, monuments and tombs, rituals and festivals, music, iconography, etc.) represents the culmination of a complex, continuous negotiation between the past (including the actual past and subsequent representations of that past) as a constraint and the present (itself a product of the past) as a manipulator of the past.[27] But this mobilization of memories into durable forms does not mean that memories consequently "assume immobile form" (to borrow Kirk's language), even if they are physically a "*frozen moment* of the collective processes of establishing memory and identity."[28] This is not to deny, for example, that the textualization of the Gospel of Mark constituted an attempt to stabilize a particular understanding of Jesus or to minimize competing understandings.[29] The coalescing of memory into vehicular modes may

---

[25] Zerubavel, *Recovered Roots*, 5. Likewise, Tom Thatcher, "Preface: Keys, Frames, and the Problem of the Past," in Thatcher, *Memory and Identity in Ancient Judaism and Early Christianity*, 2: "Schwartz' work is characterized by a fierce commitment to the principle that the actual past and its subsequent commemorations are interfluential—interfluential to such an extent that one is never eclipsed by the other in any specific act of memory." Similarly, Rafael Rodríguez (*Structuring Early Christian Memory: Jesus in Tradition, Performance, and Text*, LNTS 407 [London: T&T Clark, 2010], 55; italics original) asserts: "In collective memory, neither the past nor the present precede the other; they are mutually affecting and dialectic. Our present is determinative for our image of the past (i.e., the past is made to reflect the present) *even as* our past is determinative for our image of the present (i.e., the present is shaped by and framed within the past)."

[26] Thus, in his work on the reception of Abraham Lincoln in the nineteenth and twentieth centuries (*Abraham Lincoln and the Forge of National Memory*), Schwartz demonstrates that continuity accompanies vicissitudes with respect to Lincoln's image across generations.

[27] Jeffrey K. Olick and Daniel Levy, "Collective Memory and Cultural Constraint: Holocaust Myth and Rationality in German Politics," *American Sociological Review* 62 (1997): 934; Zerubavel, *Recovered Roots*, 5; Fentress and Wickham, *Social Memory*, ix–40.

[28] Alan Kirk, "Memory Theory and Jesus Research," in *Handbook for the Study of the Historical Jesus*, ed. Tom Holmén and Stanley Porter (Leiden: Brill, 2011), 1:816; Hübenthal, "Social and Cultural Memory in Biblical Exegesis," 195 (italics original), respectively.

[29] On the textualization (and its significance) of the Gospels, see, e.g., Werner Kelber, *The Oral and Written Gospel: The Hermeneutics of Speaking and Writing in the Synoptic Tradition, Mark, Paul and Q* (Philadelphia: Fortress, 1983); Chris Keith, "Prolegomena on the Textualization of Mark's Gospel: Manuscript Culture, the Extended Situation, and the Emergence of the Written Gospel," in Thatcher, *Memory and Identity in Ancient Judaism and Early Christianity*, 161–86; Chris Keith, "Early Christian Book Culture and the Emergence of the First Written Gospel," in *Mark, Manuscripts, and Monotheism: Essays in Honor of Larry W. Hurtado*, ed. Chris Keith and Dieter T. Roth, LNTS 528 (London: T&T Clark, 2015), 22–39; Chris Keith, "The Competitive Textualization of the Jesus Tradition in John 20:30–31 and 21:24–25," *CBQ* 78 (2016): 321–37; Chris Keith, *The Gospel as Manuscript: An*

imply the presence of a social network hoping to maintain an enduring sense of identity in light of a shared, agreed-upon past.³⁰ Nevertheless, even relatively stabilized pasts undergo evolution precisely because they are the location of constant visitation, evaluation, and analysis, and thus, reconfiguration of a group's identity and ethos in the shadow of ever-shifting present demands. In this respect, the emergence of memory in media *perpetuates and further enables* a fluid reception history of memory across generations regardless of a social group's hope of maintenance.³¹ As we will see, the textualized memory of John's beheading in the Gospel of Mark perpetuated a stable and fluid reception history. Across the first three centuries of the Common Era, the basic impressions *that* John was beheaded and *that* John and Antipas were positive and negative figures, respectively, remained stable in "Christian" discourse. Simultaneously, however, the memory morphed from a tradition that exonerated Jesus as a victim of crucifixion and enhanced Jesus' prestige as a miracle worker to a tradition that embodied the inferiority of "Jews" to "Christians."

Applications of Social Memory in NT Scholarship

Although applications of social memory theory had appeared in German scholarship several years previously, Kirk and Thatcher formally introduced the theory to NT studies in their 2005 coedited volume, *Memory, Tradition, and Text*.³² Since the volume's publication, several studies have

---

Early History of the Jesus Tradition as Material Artifact (Oxford: Oxford University Press, 2020). See also Larry Hurtado, "Greco-Roman Textuality and the Gospel of Mark: A Critical Assessment of Werner Kelber's *The Oral and the Written Gospel*," *BBR* 7 (1997): 91–106.

30   Consider Schwartz' description of commemorative ritual: "As a standardized, repetitive, and symbolic activity that allows participants to define their relation to the past, commemorative ritual fixes in mind the events of the past, a process facilitated by the emotional assembling of the community itself" ("Where There's Smoke, There's Fire," 10). Cf. Sarah E. Rollens, "The Anachronism of 'Early Christian Communities,'" in *Theorizing "Religion" in Antiquity*, ed. Nickolas Roubekas, Studies in Ancient Religion and Culture (Sheffield: Equinox, 2019), 307–24, who is critical of the scholarly association between texts and specific early Christian "communities."

31   Egyptologist Jan Assmann argues that the materialization of tradition in the medium of writing—the transition of memory from living communication (communicative memory; *kommunikatives Gedächtnis*) to tradition (cultural memory; *kulturelles Gedächtnis*)—permits "the horizon of symbolically stored memory to grow far beyond the framework of knowledge functionalized as bonding memory. . . . In certain circumstances cultural memory liberates people from the constraints of bonding memory." See Jan Assmann, *Religion and Cultural Memory*, trans. Rodney Livingstone (Stanford: Stanford University Press, 2006), 21. On *kommunikatives Gedächtnis* and *kulturelles Gedächtnis* see idem, *Das kulturelle Gedächtnis. Schrift, Erinnerung und politische Identität in frühen Hochkulturen* (München: Beck, 1992), 48–56.

32   Alan Kirk and Tom Thatcher, eds., *Memory, Tradition, and Text: Uses of the Past in Early Christianity*, SemeiaSt 52 (Atlanta: Society of Biblical Literature, 2005); Jens Schröter, *Erinnerung an Jesu Worte: Studien zur Rezeption der Logienüberlieferung in Markus, Q und*

surfaced applying the theory's concepts. To provide one example, in 2006 Bockmuehl privileged "living memory" to understand the relationship between early Petrine and Pauline Christianity. He expanded to up to one hundred fifty years the threshold of living memory that Jan Assmann had previously estimated at forty to one hundred years.[33] Several other applications to various subjects could be cited.[34] More pertinent to my present purposes is the fact that the theory so far has found the most traction in Gospels research, principally historical Jesus studies, as is frequently observed.[35]

The fruits of the theory's materialization in Gospels research has led to the recognition that the Gospels are textual artifacts that have surfaced from commemorative activity. A prominent NT memory theorist, for example, has written:

> [M]emory analysis puts the proper complexion on the core datum of research, the gospel traditions. They are artifacts of memory; they have circulated along memorializing pathways; and by finding their way into the written medium they have navigated the major crisis of memory. The gospels, we might say, are the deep pools of early Christian memory.[36]

Thomas, WMANT 76 (Neukirchen-Vluyn: Neukirchener Verlag, 1997). Keith has written an overview of the emergence of social memory theory in NT studies. The sixth volume of *Early Christianity* divides this overview into two parts. See Chris Keith, "Social Memory Theory and Gospels Research: The First Decade (Part One)," *Early Christianity* 6 (2015): 354–76; Chris Keith, "Social Memory Theory and Gospels Research: The First Decade (Part Two)," *Early Christianity* 6 (2015): 517–42.

[33] Markus Bockmuehl, *Seeing the Word: Refocusing New Testament Study*, STI (Grand Rapids: Baker Academic, 2006), 169–70. Assmann (*Das kulturelle Gedächtnis*, 50–56) suggests a forty-year threshold for *kommunikatives Gedächtnis*. In other works, Assmann has suggested a three- to four-generation threshold. See Assmann, *Religion and Cultural Memory*, 30; Jan Assmann, "Communicative and Cultural Memory," in Erll and Nünning, *Cultural Memory Studies*, 111, 117.

[34] For references, see Keith, "Social Memory Theory (Part Two)," 518.

[35] Hübenthal, "Social and Cultural Memory in Biblical Exegesis," 176: "The only area in biblical research where social memory theory has gained reasonable currency is in historical Jesus research and even there it is treated highly critically and discussed extremely controversially." Keith, "Social Memory Theory (Part Two)," 518: "It is undeniable that social memory theory's most demonstrable inroads into New Testament scholarship reside in Jesus studies." For more recent similar comments, see, e.g., Sandra Hübenthal, "Reading the Gospel of Mark as Collective Memory," in *Social Memory and Social Identity in the Study of Early Judaism and Early Christianity*, ed. Samuel Byrskog, Raimo Hakola, and Jutta Jokiranta, NTOA/SUNT 116 (Göttingen: Vandenhoeck & Ruprecht, 2016), 69; Alan Kirk, *Memory and the Jesus Tradition*, The Reception of Jesus in the First Three Centuries (London: T&T Clark, 2018), 1.

[36] Kirk, "Memory Theory and Jesus Research," 1:842.

In a similar fashion, Keith considers "the written Gospels" to be instances of "Jesus memory."[37] In my estimation, this categorization of the Gospels as memory should be uncontroversial. This classification does not presume that the Gospels are instances of "historically accurate" replications of the past or eyewitness testimonies. Even if the Gospels did contain or largely consisted of autobiographical memories, this would not preclude their susceptibility to the vagaries of memory.[38] As my *Doktorvater* drilled into my head during my doctoral studies, access to eyewitness testimony does not gift historians with unmediated access to the actual past. Nor does the categorization of the Gospels as commemorative artifacts deny that the Jesus of history contributed to the formation of variegated perceptions of himself. Viewing the written narratives about Jesus as relics of processes of memory is not *a priori* to establish their "accuracy" or "inaccuracy."[39] What this categorization does achieve is forcing scholars to work out the historiographical implications of viewing the transmission of the Jesus tradition as an ebbing and flowing interplay between

[37] Keith, *Jesus' Literacy*, 61.

[38] See Richard Bauckham, *Jesus and the Eyewitnesses: The Gospels as Eyewitness Testimony*, 2nd ed. (Grand Rapids: Eerdmans, 2017), 6 (emphasis added), who argues that the Gospels "embody the testimony, *not of course without editing and interpretation*." Although Bauckham's insistence that the apparent eyewitness character of the Gospels does not preclude processes of interpretation, he has been the recipient of criticism for seemingly using the nature of eyewitness memory to claim that such testimony generally provides reliable access to the historical Jesus. See, e.g., Paul Foster, "Memory, Orality, and the Fourth Gospel: Three Dead-Ends in Historical Jesus Research," *JSHJ* 10 (2012): 191–227. Interestingly, a search of Bauckham's author index and bibliography reveals that the second edition of his work does not directly respond to Foster's criticisms leveled against the first edition.

[39] Keith, "Social Memory Theory (Part Two)," esp. 537–38. Other leading voices in the discourse likewise operate with a similar understanding of the theory. See, e.g., Jeffrey K. Olick, "Products, Processes, and Practices: A Non-Reificatory Approach to Collective Memory," *BTB* 36 (2006): 13; Rodríguez, *Structuring Early Christian Memory*, 41–80; Kirk, "Memory Theory and Jesus Research," 1:839; Hübenthal, "Social and Cultural Memory in Biblical Exegesis," 192. Nor does conceptualizing the Gospels as conduits of early memory about Jesus necessitate that we presume the Synoptic Gospels were *produced by* "Christian" mouthpieces. See Robyn Faith Walsh, *The Origins of Early Christian Literature: Contextualizing the New Testament within Greco-Roman Literary Culture* (Cambridge: Cambridge University Press, 2021), who offers a stimulating argument that the Synoptic Gospels were produced by elite "literate specialists" who might or might not have been professed Christ-followers. Walsh's new book arrived on my desk as my deadline for submitting this book arrived; unfortunately, therefore, I did not have the luxury of time to give it a thorough analysis in relationship to my project on social memory theory. Suffice it to say for now, however, that no matter what the present circumstances were that produced the Synoptic Gospels, Walsh's argument does not dismantle *that* the Jesus tradition was activated in a given present network. If Walsh is correct, it rather alters what many scholars have perceived to be the contours of the social frameworks that structured the production of the Synoptic Gospels. Our contention in chapter 3, moreover, that the Gospel of Mark critiques a client-ruler of Rome for his failure to measure up to elite ideals of manliness, seems to conform neatly with Walsh's configuration, at least theoretically.

the actual past, subsequent appropriations of the past, and the ever-shifting horizons of the present through which the transmission and textualization of the Jesus tradition took shape.

Accordingly, this new paradigm of the Jesus tradition has bred two chief historiographical consequences. The first consequence has been a methodological critique of the so-called criteria of authenticity with their indebtedness to form-critical conceptions of memory and tradition. Genuine glances at the Jesus of history, according to the form-critical paradigm, resided—if anywhere—behind several strata of interpreted material, material that reflected the *Sitz im Leben* of early Christian communities.[40] Hence the rise of criteria that historical Jesus scholars employed to sift and separate authentic from inauthentic Jesus material. Although the criteria have not been immune from attacks outside of memory discourse,[41] historical Jesus scholars who advocate for a "Jesus memory" approach have led the charge in the early twenty-first century in effecting what Bernier calls "the criteria approach's obituary."[42] Keith and Le Donne's coedited volume published in 2012, which dealt the final blow to the criteria, included contributing essays by Schröter, Rodríguez, and Allison, in addition to their own.[43] All five of these scholars have written monographs importing memory theory into the study of Christian Origins (and Keith has actually written three).[44] In essence, many of those who advance a memory paradigm reject the criteriological approach's notion of uncovering a pristine, unfiltered memory of the historical Jesus. Memory, as we have seen, is always localized in and shaped by subjective frameworks. To

---

[40] See Kirk, "Memory Theory and Jesus Research," 1:809, who summarizes the form-critical paradigm in this way: "The form critics equated memory with individual eyewitness recollection. While memory traces of this sort lay at the origins of the tradition, they were a residuum, largely inert with respect to developments in the tradition itself. The salient image was of so-called authentic memories of Jesus coming to be buried under multiple layers of 'tradition.'"

[41] See, e.g., Morna Hooker, "Christology and Methodology," *NTS* 17 (1971): 480–87; Morna Hooker, "On Using the Wrong Tool," *Theology* 75 (1972): 570–81.

[42] Jonathan Bernier, *The Quest for the Historical Jesus after the Demise of Authenticity*, LNTS 540 (London: T&T Clark, 2016), 1, n. 3.

[43] Chris Keith and Anthony Le Donne, eds., *Jesus, Criteria, and the Demise of Authenticity* (London: T&T Clark International, 2012). For other serious blows to the criteria, see, e.g., Rafael Rodríguez, "Authenticating Criteria: The Use and Misuse of a Critical Method," *JSHJ* 7 (2009): 152–67; Keith, *Jesus' Literacy*, 27–70; Dale C. Allison, "How to Marginalize the Traditional Criteria of Authenticity," in Holmén and Porter, *Handbook for the Study of the Historical Jesus*, 1:3–30.

[44] Schröter, *Erinnerung an Jesu Worte*; Anthony Le Donne, *The Historiographical Jesus: Memory, Typology, and the Son of David* (Waco, Tex.: Baylor University Press, 2009); Rodríguez, *Structuring Early Christian Memory*; Dale C. Allison, *Constructing Jesus: Memory, Imagination, and History* (Grand Rapids: Baker Academic, 2010); Keith, *Jesus' Literacy*; Chris Keith, *Jesus against the Scribal Elite: The Origins of the Conflict*, 2nd ed. (London: T&T Clark, 2020); Keith, *Gospel as Manuscript*.

search for a memory of Jesus external to localization or social shape, and thus purely immune of the present, is puzzling, to put it euphemistically.[45]

If the first consequence of the Jesus-memory approach was a methodological dismantling of the primary tool scholars utilized to uncover the "real" Jesus, then the second consequence was to rethink how historians could appropriately construct the historical Jesus moving forward. The memory approach's rejection of the criteria on the basis of viewing the Jesus tradition as social constructs has not led all theorists to campaign for a new "No Quest" period. Similar to Gadamer, who viewed subjectivity as the phenomenon that rendered both objectivity impossible and understanding possible,[46] some theorists have considered (at least implicitly) subjectivity both the problem of constructing the historical Jesus and its only solution.[47] The portrayals of Jesus in the Gospels are historical phenomena that, because they do exist, must be explained in terms of this dynamic interaction between the present and past. In this vein, Keith argues that any construction of Jesus must elucidate the various memories of him in light of the ever-shifting sociohistorical contexts that these memories continually shaped and in which they took shape.[48]

---

[45] Keith, *Jesus' Literacy*, 61, puts it more forwardly: "From the perspective of social memory theory, scholars in search of authentic Jesus traditions might as well be in search of unicorns, the lost city of Atlantis, and the pot of gold at the end of the rainbow. Not only are there no longer Jesus traditions that reflect solely the actual past, there never were." Cf. Le Donne, "Theological Memory Distortion in the Jesus Tradition."

[46] Gadamer, *Truth and Method*, 311–18.

[47] Keith, *Jesus' Literacy*, 62, 63–64: "The broader social memory of first-century Jews provided categories for their initial reception/remembering of Jesus. . . . [63–64] Whatever happened in Jesus' life and death, events to which we have no direct access but nevertheless happened, those historical realities set into motion interpretations/memories of him by those who encountered him." Put otherwise, the initial interpretations of Jesus in his social milieu were limited precisely because Jesus himself was located within a particular social matrix with its own symbolic universe that he invoked. Cf. also Le Donne, "Theological Memory Distortion in the Jesus Tradition," 167, who rightly qualifies the negative potential of subjectivity: "Distortion is, most commonly, a natural and benign function of memory selection . . . memory distorts the past to render it intelligible to the present. . . . Our memories demand a high degree of continuity in order to tie all of our shifting frames of meaning together. It is the integrity of this chain that determines its reliability." Le Donne continues on the next page: "It must be stated in no uncertain terms that *memory is distortion*. This is so regardless of any claims to veracity. If the criteria for veracity were defined by a given memory's *lack of distortion* all discussion about the past would be rendered futile" (p. 168, italics original).

[48] Keith, *Jesus' Literacy*, 61–68. Relatedly, Le Donne proposes identifying multiple commemorative trajectories in a bid to triangulate a mnemonic origin in the life of Jesus. See Le Donne, *Historiographical Jesus*, 86; Anthony Le Donne, "Memory, Commemoration and History in John 2:19–22: A Critique and Application of Social Memory," in *The Fourth Gospel in First-Century Media Culture*, ed. Anthony Le Donne and Tom Thatcher, LNTS 426 (London: T&T Clark, 2011), 186–204.

Social memory theory has not received an altogether warm welcome by NT scholars, however. One scholar refers to memory theory as one of three "dead-ends" in historical Jesus research.[49] Despite the shortcomings of this suggestion, this raises the question of the theory's utility outside of historical Jesus research.[50] What, then, does the theory have to offer?

Memory and Reception History

Since memory represents a complex interaction between the impact of the inherited past in the present and present social contexts that shape and activate recollection, social memory theory takes seriously the need to understand the reception of the past in the present. For my purposes, as I outlined in the introduction of this book, this involves shifting our attention away from uncovering a historical John the Baptist "behind" the Gospels to focusing attention on the reverberations of John's beheading in the first three centuries. By concentrating on the impact of John's beheading in the ever-shifting context of the present, we will see how the memory of John's violent death turned into a violent memory itself.

Furthermore, with its critical discourse acutely devoted to understanding the complex relationship between the past and the present, social memory theory is especially helpful for conceptualizing a reception historical investigation. Similar to social memory's import in Jesus studies discussed above, treating the Gospels as artifacts of memory reconfigures previous conceptualizations of reception history. For many scholars, reception is construed as an account of the impact, or aftereffects, of an originating text in various media (commentaries, homilies, art, etc.). For instance, Luz defines reception history as follows: "Reception history of the Bible is the history of the reception of biblical texts in periods subsequent to New Testament times."[51] Another scholar went so far as to regard *Wirkungsgeschichte* in terms of isolating the empirical effectiveness of a text in history.[52] Reception history, however, should not be simplistically conceptualized as the present receiving the past.[53]

---

[49] Foster, "Memory, Orality, and the Fourth Gospel."
[50] In his two-part overview of the first decade of social memory research in Gospels studies, Keith has issued a lengthy correction to many of Foster's claims that lead Foster to his conclusion. See Keith, "Social Memory Theory (Part One)"; Keith, "Social Memory Theory (Part Two)."
[51] Ulrich Luz, "The Contribution of Reception History to a Theology of the New Testament," in *The Nature of New Testament Theology: Essays in Honour of Robert Morgan*, ed. Christopher Rowland and Christopher Tuckett (Oxford: Blackwell, 2006), 123.
[52] Heikki Räisänen, "The Effective 'History' of the Bible: A Challenge to Biblical Scholarship?" *SJT* 45 (1992): 303–24.
[53] Jan Assmann, *Moses the Egyptian: The Memory of Egypt in Western Monotheism* (Cambridge, Mass.: Harvard University Press, 1997), 9. Like social memory theory's recognition that constructions of the past rely on—and are thus shaped by—the present, which

In view of the textualized Gospels as commemorative artifacts, the text-receiver paradigm of reception runs into two interrelated complications. First, the division between the Gospels (as originating texts) and reception (as receivers of such texts) is problematic. It is not merely the case that the written Gospels became major catalysts that enabled subsequent receptions in periods after their textualization, although this is certainly undeniable. The Gospels themselves, as commemorative texts, constitute the results of complex processes between the influences of the past and the always-evolving present. Put succinctly, the Gospel narratives form part of the reception history of precipitating stimuli *and* stimulate further reception.[54]

Procedurally, of course, this recognition does not change the order of our investigation: the Gospel of Mark remains our earliest extant source that recounts John's beheading; understanding this Gospel as commemorative artifact does not create new primary sources that would alter the objects of inquiry at our disposal. Recognizing the Gospels as artifacts of memory, however, is not to engage in scholarly pedantry. This recognition is important because the Gospels too are themselves the sites of commemorative contestation (as it pertains to John's beheading) in addition to stimulating further contestation. Thus, the heuristic framework for analyzing reception (that I will discuss below) applies to the Gospels as well as to the Gospels' early reception.

Second, because "historical representations are negotiated, selective, present-oriented, and relative . . . [and simultaneously] cannot be manipulated

---

is itself a product of the past, Gadamer's principle of *Wirkungsgeschichte* recognizes that the subject is always already impacted by the course of history by virtue of her own historicity. For Gadamer, "the central problem of hermeneutics" is the task of "historically effected consciousness" (*wirkungsgeschichtliches Bewußtsein*), that is, coming to an awareness of our own situation as beings already impacted by the course of history. See Gadamer, *Truth and Method*, 311–18 (esp. 312, 317–18). For the German text, see Hans-George Gadamer, *Wahrheit und Methode* (Tübingen: Mohr Siebeck, 1990), 305–12 (esp. 307, 312). Our situation as "already affected by history" "determines in advance both what seems to us worth inquiring about and what will appear as an object of investigation" (*Truth and Method*, 311). To deny this inherent subjectivity in the process of understanding in order to feign objectivity is tantamount to denying one's own historical existence (*Truth and Method*, 312). Or, to articulate the previous statement in Halbwachsian-type terms, denying that "the individual borrows from society everything that enables conceptualization of the past" (Keith, "Social Memory Theory [Part One]," 360) is tantamount to rejecting that one is—or has ever been—located within a social framework. In this sense, instances of remembrance embody *Wirkungsgeschichte* because they are always localized and impacted by the course of history. Cf. Assmann, *Religion and Cultural Memory*, 27, who notes the absence of "understanding without memory" and "existence without tradition." See further Olick, Vinitzky-Seroussi, and Levy, "Introduction," 44–45.

[54] To his credit, Luz, *Matthew in History: Interpretation, Influence, and Effects* (Minneapolis: Fortress, 1994), 23, recognizes that "biblical texts themselves are the result of a history of effects because they are not the ultimate point of departure . . . but products of human reception, human experiences, and human history."

at will,"[55] viewing reception history through the theoretical framework of social memory theory allows us to observe how social groups form and reinforce their identities. It permits us "to shift our focus from time to temporalities and thus to understand what categories people, groups, and cultures employ to make sense of their lives, their social, cultural, and political attachments, and the concomitant ideals that are validated."[56] In this sense, social memory theory reconfigures reception not as the commentary on a precipitating discourse, but as a fluid and dynamic process of identity formation. This interrelationship between memory and identity leads us to our heuristic framework for analyzing the reception of violence.

A Heuristic Framework for Studying Violence

In addition to reorienting scholars to focus on the reception of the past in the present, social memory theory also offers a beneficial framework for analyzing the reception of violent events. Four characteristics of commemorative activity are relevant in this regard: identity formation, interpretive keying, the violence of memory, and commemorative contestation. I do not regard these four features as an exegetical checklist wherein the interpreter plugs the primary data and awaits results. Rather, these features function as a heuristic analytical grid. They prime our imaginations so that we are sociologically informed, enabling us in turn to probe how violence communicates in its reception history—without stripping us of our agency in developing historical hypotheses. Before discussing these four commemorative features, a brief word on the key term "violence," however, is first in order.

Violence—Visible and Invisible

"Violence is a slippery concept—nonlinear, productive, destructive, and reproductive."[57] So opens the 2004 anthology of influential voices on the study of violence coedited by Scheper-Hughes and Bourgois. Their description is at once incredibly vague and acutely sensible. Any study on violence immediately runs into the problem of defining "violence" amidst all of its possible valences.[58] In

---

[55] Wulf Kansteiner, "Finding Meaning in Memory: A Methodological Critique of Collective Memory Studies," *HistTh* 41 (2002): 195.
[56] Olick, Vinitzky-Seroussi, and Levy, "Introduction," 37.
[57] Nancy Scheper-Hughes and Philippe Bourgois, "Introduction: Making Sense of Violence," in *Violence in War and Peace: An Anthology*, ed. Nancy Scheper-Hughes and Philippe Bourgois (Oxford: Blackwell, 2004), 1 (italics removed).
[58] What one social context considers a legitimate application of violence is subject to contestation in another, as John Kloppenborg ("The Representation of Violence in the Synoptic Parables," in *Mark and Matthew I: Comparative Readings: Understanding*

this study, I implement a bipartite metaphor: visible and invisible violence. Visible violence refers to those types of violent outbursts that, in general, are obvious, explicit, and often involve interpersonal bodily harm by one or more co-present human agents. Visible violence largely corresponds to what Žižek designates "subjective violence"[59] and is broad in scope: physical acts of injury, homicide, assassinations, rape, abuse, war, assault, execution, genocide, torture, police violence, riots, and bodily mutilation all would fall under this term.

Violence is not merely an instance of physical harm or injury to the body, however. It also exists in the social and cultural structures that frame everyday existence: poverty, rhetoric and ideology, overt and systemic racism, disease, hunger, gender disparity, and boundary demarcations and social hierarchies. Hence, theorists draw on a multiplicity of designations to conceptualize these different facets of violence, including Farmer's "structural violence,"[60] Bourdieu's "symbolic violence,"[61] Lawrence and Karim's "rhetorical violence,"[62]

---

the Earliest Gospels in Their First Century Settings, ed. Eve-Marie Becker and Anders Runesson, WUNT 271 [Tübingen: Mohr Siebeck, 2011], 323) observes. In contrast to the German Gewalt ("force"), the English term "violence" largely functions as a category of criminal designation—to ethically label something as evil, terrible, or horrific. According to Ari Z. Bryen (Violence in Roman Egypt: A Study in Legal Interpretation [Philadelphia: University of Pennsylvania Press, 2013], 54–55), ὕβρις ("violence") in Roman Egypt was "always understood to be prima facie wrong" and thus was often used to describe unjustifiable force against the human body or against one's dignity. But the term βία ("harm" or "damage") was the more appropriate term to categorize harm against a slave, since slaves were regarded as property (Bryen, Violence in Roman Egypt, 55; Kloppenborg, "Representation of Violence," 323). In contrast to the Greek ὕβρις, the Latin vis ("force" or "violence") did not necessarily carry a morally egregious connotation. In the Roman Empire, for example, a legitimate excuse for one's absence in a legal hearing was vis fluminis ("the force of a river"). See Jill Harries, "Violence, Victims, and the Legal Tradition in Late Antiquity," in Violence in Late Antiquity: Perceptions and Practices, ed. H. A. Drake (Aldershot: Ashgate, 2006), 88.

[59] Slavoj Žižek, Violence: Six Sideways Reflections (New York: Picador, 2008), 1.

[60] Paul Farmer, "On Suffering and Structural Violence: A View from Below," Daedalus 125 (1996): 261–83; Paul Farmer, Pathologies of Power: Health, Human Rights, and the New War on the Poor (Berkeley: University of California Press, 2003), esp. 29–50; Paul Farmer, "An Anthropology of Structural Violence," Current Anthropology 45 (2004): 305–25; Paul Farmer, "On Suffering and Structural Violence: A View from Below," Race/Ethnicity: Multidisciplinary Global Contexts 3 (2009): 11–28.

[61] Pierre Bourdieu and Loïc Wacquant, "Language, Gender, and Symbolic Violence," in An Invitation to Reflexive Sociology (Chicago: University of Chicago Press, 1992), esp. 167–74; Pierre Bourdieu, Masculine Domination, trans. Richard Nice (Cambridge: Polity, 2001).

[62] Bruce B. Lawrence and Aisha Karim, "General Introduction: Theorizing Violence in the Twenty-First Century," in On Violence: A Reader, ed. Bruce B. Lawrence and Aisha Karim (Durham, N.C.: Duke University Press, 2007), 11–12.

Oliver's "cultural racism,"[63] Scheper-Hughes' "everyday violence,"[64] Žižek's notions of "objective and systemic violence,"[65] and others.[66] For our discourse, invisible violence—so named because it is not always readily perceptible as "violence"—refers to those social pressures and cultural ingredients that nurture and enable visible forms of violence.

Thus, visible and invisible violence are not strictly dichotomous. They are inextricably intertwined, as the latter precedes the former. For example, Oliver cogently identifies "cultural racism" as a "societal practice" that contributes to the disproportionately high rates of violence among African-Americans in the United States.[67] He defines "cultural racism" in this way:

> "Cultural racism" . . . refer[s] to the systematic manner in which the White majority as a group has established its primary cultural institutions (e.g., education, mass media, and religion) to elevate and glorify European physical elements, achievement, and character while, at the same time, denigrating the physical elements, achievement, and character of non-White people. The primary distinction between institutional racism and cultural racism is that institutional racism has been implemented as a social practice that seeks to block or deny equal access to legitimate opportunities that facilitate survival, upward mobility, and racial equality in American society. In contrast, cultural racism functions as a social practice that is designed to diminish the cultural image and integrity of other groups, particularly African Americans.[68]

---

[63] William Oliver, "Cultural Racism and Structural Violence: Implications for African Americans," *Journal of Human Behavior in the Social Environment* 4 (2001): 1–26; idem, "Cultural Racism and Violence in African American Communities," in *Black Culture and Experience: Contemporary Issues*, ed. Venise T. Berry, Anita Fleming-Rife, and Ayo Dayo (New York: Peter Lang, 2015), 181–92.

[64] Nancy Scheper-Hughes, *Death without Weeping: The Violence of Everyday Life in Brazil* (Berkeley: University of California Press, 1992).

[65] Žižek, *Violence*, esp. 9–39.

[66] See, e.g., Mark S. Hamm, "Apocalyptic Violence: The Seduction of Terrorist Subcultures," *Theoretical Criminology* 8 (2004): 323–39.

[67] Oliver, "Cultural Racism and Violence," 185–89.

[68] Oliver, "Cultural Racism and Violence," 186. Oliver points to the glaring absence of African American representation in school-age social studies curricula as an example of cultural racism. He writes: "This is important because all societies and cultures use their history to celebrate their achievements and promote a positive personal and collective identity as a people. As such, the conspicuous absence of African Americans in history and social studies textbooks serves to reinforce and promote racial stereotypes while eroding the self-concept of African Americans" (p. 186). We might also point to the conspicuous omission of prominent Black Bostonian abolitionists—e.g., Lewis Hayden, William Cooper Nell, William Wells Brown, David Walker, Maria Stewart, and Eliza Ann Gardner—from the commemorative landscape of Boston's Emancipation Memorial and Public Garden as another example of cultural racism. Kevin M. Levin ("Black Bostonians Fought for Freedom from

Cultural racism is dangerous not only because it reinforces ideologies of African American racial inferiority and white supremacy among the white majority (whether explicitly or implicitly, intentionally or unintentionally), but also because it leaves African Americans "vulnerable to internalizing" this stratification.[69] As Oliver observes, such an eroded self-conceptualization "manifest[s]" as "overt and covert hostility toward other African Americans and, by implication, toward themselves."[70] In this way, the distance between racial inferiorization and visible violence is short. The ideological and systemic degradation of African Americans precipitates the creation and legitimization of, and indifference to, violence against African Americans, regardless of the racial identity of the perpetrator.[71] As Farmer once said in reference to extreme suffering in Haiti: "*Life choices are structured* by racism, sexism, political violence, and grinding poverty."[72]

In this light, adverse social and cultural matrixes crystallize into visible violence. These paradigms and organizing structures create the social, economic, and cultural conditions necessary for conflict to materialize in forms of visible harm, and importantly, often do not prevent their further perpetuation. Violence, therefore, "is not opposed to structure as something that exists external to structure; it is another form of structure, of processes, of practices."[73] This connection between visible and invisible violence is important for our focus on the memory of John's beheading.[74] For analytical purposes, I treat the violence of John's decapitation as an instance of visible violence. We will see, however, that as early "Christian" recipients

---

Slavery. Where Are the Statues That Tell Their Stories?" June 16, 2020, https://www.wbur.org/cognoscenti/2020/06/16/abraham-lincoln-statue-emancipation-memorial-kevin-m-levin/) observes this absence and rightly notes: "The absence of statues commemorating these men and women leaves visitors with the impression that African Americans contributed nothing to their own emancipation. Rather, these statues reinforce the myth that emancipation was a gift from white Americans."

[69] Oliver, "Cultural Racism and Violence," 186.
[70] Oliver, "Cultural Racism and Violence," 187.
[71] An obvious historical example of this short distance would be the coinciding of white supremacy with the lynching of African Americans during the lynching era (1880–1940). See James H. Cone, *The Cross and the Lynching Tree* (Maryknoll, N.Y.: Orbis Books, 2011), 1–29, for discussion.
[72] Paul Farmer, "On Suffering and Structural Violence," in Scheper-Hughes and Bourgois, *Violence in War and Peace*, 282 (italics added). See also Stephanie R. Montesanti and Wilfreda E. Thurston, "Mapping the Role of Structural and Interpersonal Violence in the Lives of Women: Implications for Public Health Interventions and Policy," *BMC Women's Health* 15, no. 100 (2015): 1–13, who show how structural and symbolic factors exacerbate the risk of gender-based violence against women.
[73] Lawrence and Karim, "Theorizing Violence," 7.
[74] Unless otherwise made explicit, visible types of violence will be in view throughout this study when I employ the unqualified term "violence."

press John's beheading into the service of organizing their identity, they also begin to redeploy his beheading in anti-Jewish directions. In this regard, the memory of John's beheading itself becomes *invisibly* violent. The dissemination and inscribing of ideology that inferiorizes Jews is invisibly violent because it can legitimize, lend approval to, and crystallize into practices of harm and injury against Jews in perpetuity. Anti-Jewishness—as a nurturer of violence—is a social pressure impregnated with dangerous potential.

Identity Formation

Some occurrences of violence pose something of a paradox: they defy "integration or dissolution" in terms of memory.[75] On the one hand, violence threatens our sense of continuity with our past, thereby calling into question conceptions of personhood, membership, and affiliation.[76] It renders identity dubious, under siege, in danger of termination. When violence bursts onto the scene we experience it precisely as such—a bursting, an eruption, a rupture of normalcy, an anomaly of everyday existence.[77] Kirk refers to such events as a

---

[75] Flora A. Keshgegian, "Finding a Place Past Night: Armenian Genocidal Memory in Diaspora," in *Religion, Violence, Memory, and Place*, ed. Oren Baruch Stier and J. Shawn Landres (Bloomington: Indiana University Press, 2006), 102.

[76] Amartya Sen (*Identity and Violence: The Illusion of Destiny* [London: Penguin, 2006], 19) observes that the anxiety one feels "about losing one's past and one's historical identity" reveals the "importance people tend to attach to a shared history and a sense of affiliation based on this history."

[77] Trauma theorists are quick to point out that traumatic effects of individual and cultural traumas—including instances of physical violence—vary depending on (1) one's relationship to the trauma, and (2) if the trauma is a simple or prolonged event. Susannah Radstone ("Trauma Studies: Contexts, Politics, Ethics," in *Other People's Pain: Narratives of Trauma and the Question of Ethics*, ed. Martin Modlinger and Philipp Sonntag, Cultural History and Literary Imagination 18 [Oxford: Peter Lang, 2011], 64) helpfully sets forth the notion of "secondary witness" to describe "those whose encounters with catastrophe or disaster take place at (at least) one remove." She includes interviewers, oral historians, readers of trauma fiction, and television audiences as examples of secondary witnesses. As such, she argues that these secondary witnesses are vulnerable to the same symptoms (even if in less concentrated levels of intensity) that are typically associated with the surviving victim of trauma. See also Renato Rosaldo, "Grief and a Headhunter's Rage," in Scheper-Hughes and Bourgois, *Violence in War and Peace*, 150 (italics removed): "The emotional force of a death . . . derives less from an abstract brute fact than from a particular intimate relation's permanent rupture." See also Judith Herman, Nancy Scheper-Hughes, and Philippe Bourgois, "Trauma and Recovery: The Aftermath of Violence—From Domestic Abuse to Political Terror," in Scheper-Hughes and Bourgois, *Violence in War and Peace*, 368–71. Cf. Wulf Kansteiner and Harald Weilnböck, "Against the Concept of Cultural Trauma (or How I Learned to Love the Suffering of Others without the Help of Psychotherapy)," in *A Companion to Cultural Memory Studies*, ed. Astrid Erll and Ansgar Nünning (Berlin: de Gruyter, 2010), 229–40, who are wary of the metaphor of "cultural trauma" insofar as it overlooks the concrete suffering of individuals who experience trauma.

"social disruption,"[78] a fracture between the past and the present that unsettles our sense of "equilibrium."[79] To be sure, the appearance of violence as anomalous is fundamentally illusory. As I indicated above regarding our notion of invisibility, violence "lives in the shapes that it appears to subvert."[80]

Nevertheless, the perception of violent events as glitches in the normal mechanisms of society renders violence an ostensibly unique phenomenon, one that threatens our return to normalcy. The assassination of U.S. President Kennedy in 1963 ruptured any sense of normalcy in communities across the country:

> The central preoccupation of the nation was with the details of what had happened and whether or not the president would live. University classes were interrupted and canceled, factory workers left their jobs and went home, stores closed their doors, and the everyday activities of the nation ground to a halt. Continuation of business as usual seemed to make little sense in view of the extraordinary events that were happening. Regular television programming was suspended and news coverage continuously reported on the events surrounding the assassination.[81]

The massacre at Wounded Knee in late December 1890 (when U.S. soldiers opened fire on nearly four hundred unarmed Lakota refugees) quelled (at least temporarily) the eschatological hopes of the Lakota who "had embraced the spirit dance in 1889 because it provided hope and renewal in the form of cleansing the earth of the whites and returning the spirits of deceased relatives and the buffalo."[82] The rupture between the past and the present that violence instigates also elicits uncertainty concerning the future. The 1941 attack on Pearl Harbor, for instance, occasioned "intense levels of fear that the attack was simply a forerunner of a planned invasion of California."[83] Certain violent events thrust individuals and collectives to the fringes of existence because they appear to destabilize continuity between the past, present, and future. Žižek, therefore, is right when he contends that prose, not poetry, seems impossible after Auschwitz. He reasons: "Poetry is always by definition, 'about' something that cannot be addressed directly, only alluded to."[84]

---

[78] Alan Kirk, "The Memory of Violence and the Death of Jesus in Q," in Kirk and Thatcher, *Memory, Tradition, and Text*, 191.
[79] Arthur Neal, *National Trauma and Collective Memory: Major Events in the American Century* (Armonk, N.Y.: Sharpe, 1998), 12. See also Žižek, *Violence*, 1–2.
[80] Lawrence and Karim, "Theorizing Violence," 7.
[81] Neal, *National Trauma*, 111.
[82] Michelene E. Pesantubbee, "Wounded Knee: Site of Resistance and Recovery," in Stier and Landres, *Religion, Violence, Memory, and Place*, 79.
[83] Neal, *National Trauma*, 4.
[84] Žižek, *Violence*, 5.

On the other hand, however, personhood, membership, and affiliation are forged through violent encounters and crystallized in narrations about the past. In this respect, the memory of violence becomes the locus of expressing identity. The 1994 Rwandan genocide remains a crucial matter to remember for all Rwandans, Hutu and Tutsi alike, and this is in part due to the fact that many Hutu and Tutsi are still coping with its aftereffects.[85] Buckley-Zistel observes: "The individual and the collective *raison d'être* of the nation and its people is built around the genocide."[86] Similarly, the Lakota "needed to incorporate the gravesite [at Wounded Knee] into their ceremonial cycle" in order to overcome the generations of despair and depression that the Wounded Knee massacre triggered.[87] Many Japanese soldiers who had committed heinous acts against civilians in occupied countries during WWII continue to struggle with "unwanted memories" that "can only be alleviated through achieving some degree of closure."[88] As a further example, in her ethnographic research on Hutu refugees in Tanzania—who had fled from Burundi as a result of the 1972 genocide—Malkki observes that the massacre "represented an end or a culmination in [their] mythico-history insofar as 'the past' that lived in Burundi stopped at the moment of flight."[89] Their "mythico-history" was thus divided into pre-massacre years and post-massacre years, and this not merely in a strict chronological sense, but also in "spatial, social, and symbolic" senses.[90]

As part of this process of forging identity via memory, violent pasts often become didactic or ethical frames for directing behavior. A survivor of the Rwandan genocide once stated: "We have to remember people who died in 1994. It is important to remember someone that you love, a relative, a friend. We have to commemorate it *in order to put a mechanism of prevention in place*, and to ask God to help us. For me, we cannot forget what happened."[91] In the decades

---

[85] Susanne Buckley-Zistel, "Between Pragmatism, Coercion and Fear: Chosen Amnesia after the Rwandan Genocide," in *Memory and Political Change*, ed. Aleida Assmann and Linda Shortt, PMMS (Basingstoke: Palgrave Macmillan, 2012), 78–79. In her earlier 2006 article, she observes that many victims of rape, who were purposefully raped by those aware of their own HIV positive status, continue to die as a result of the genocide. See Susanne Buckley-Zistel, "Remembering to Forget: Chosen Amnesia as a Strategy for Local Co-Existence in Post-Genocide Rwanda," *Africa: Journal of the International African Institute* 76 (2006): 139.

[86] Buckley-Zistel, "Remembering to Forget," 136; Buckley-Zistel, "Chosen Amnesia."

[87] Pesantubbee, "Wounded Knee," 79.

[88] Ridwan Nytagodien and Arthur Neal, "Collective Trauma, Apologies, and the Politics of Memory," *Journal of Human Rights* 3 (2004): 466.

[89] Liisa H. Malkki, *Purity and Exile: Violence, Memory, and National Cosmology among Hutu Refugees in Tanzania* (Chicago: University of Chicago Press, 1995), 58.

[90] Malkki, *Purity and Exile*, 58–59 (quotation, p. 59). Cf. Neal, *National Trauma*, 12: "Events that occurred in the personal lives of individuals prior to a trauma become mentally separated from the events that occurred after the trauma."

[91] Buckley-Zistel, "Chosen Amnesia," 78.

following WWII, Japan has repeatedly looked back to their actions in WWII "as a major referent for what to avoid in the future."[92] And the Lakota remember the gravesite at Wounded Knee as a source of motivation "to continue to struggle against cultural loss."[93] In the formation of commemorative traditions, we witness "the indelible infusion of constituent events and personae with categorical moral meanings."[94] Mnemonic communities often highlight the perceived vices or virtues of victims or perpetrators to exemplify marginal and ideal behavior. In the fourth century C.E., for example, Basil accentuated Antipas' oath that resulted in John the Baptist's death in order to forbid his readers from swearing oaths.[95] In this way, the past forces itself upon the present as an available symbol for the present, even as the present scans images of the inherited past to organize contemporary conditions and map conduct.

To reiterate, violence threatens to divest individuals and groups of their identities, but nevertheless often creates the impulse to combat such rupture. Violent events force themselves upon the present as phenomena that must be overcome in terms of memory. Social groups tend to commemorate violent catastrophes, solidifying them "into durable forms" with a view toward combatting "the danger of rupture."[96] Of course, traces of this rupture will never disappear fully:

> When traumatic injury is profound, as in the case of genocide or physical threat and torture, survivors are not able to put the pieces back together without retaining signs of breakage. There will always be scars. . . . [What] seems like "past" trauma shapes the present by its outstanding demands to be attended to and to have its losses and pain acknowledged. It manifests itself in current lives not simply as reminder and remainder but as present reality. The memories and presence of such trauma may exact a fierce loyalty around

---

[92] Neal, *National Trauma*, 28. See also Jay Winter, "Foreword: Rememberance as a Human Right," in Assmann and Shortt, *Memory and Political Change*, viii, who describes the Universal Declaration of Human Rights as "a normative statement of a standard against which to measure the behavior of the states in which we live." Similarly, Nytagodien and Neal, "Collective Trauma," 465.

[93] Pesantubbee, "Wounded Knee," 75.

[94] Kirk, "Memory of Violence," 200. For similar comments, see Neal, *National Trauma*, 17; Nytagodien and Neal, "Collective Trauma," 473–74; Alan Kirk, "Social and Cultural Memory," in Kirk and Thatcher, *Memory, Tradition, and Text*, 11–12; Buckley-Zistel, "Chosen Amnesia," 73; Wulf Kansteiner, "Genocide Memory, Digital Cultures, and the Aesthetization of Violence," *Memory Studies* 7 (2014): 407.

[95] Basil, *Letters*, 199.29.

[96] Kirk, "Social and Cultural Memory," 7. In multiple publications, Schwartz describes "commemoration" as a social activity whereby co-rememberers recognize happenings as particularly embedded with significance for groups, especially at the level of society (e.g., family, community). See, e.g., Schwartz, "Social Context of Commemoration," 377; Schwartz, *Abraham Lincoln*, 9–12. For similar comments, see Neal, *National Trauma*, 207.

which identity may constitute itself. In other words, the trauma, even though it is not fully articulated or even recognized as trauma, may become the guiding force of identity and meaning formation.[97]

The formation of identity, therefore, readily orbits around trauma: violent events seem to possess gravitational pull in the direction of memory. Wagner-Pacifici is surely correct when she suggests that events embedded in "conflict and contradiction" have an "intrinsic draw on us."[98]

Interpretive Keying

An important aspect of remembering violence involves what Schwartz designates interpretive "keying."[99] For Schwartz, crisis in the present represents the strongest incentive for social networks to invoke the past in a bid to understand the crisis.[100] His model of keying rests on the rudimentary—but solid—premise that perception is an act of identification, where one recognizes an object, event, or emotion by pairing it alongside a known symbol.[101] Thus, understanding keying involves considering how "participants in one primary event . . . interpret their experience by aligning it to another primary event."[102] He defines keying in this way:

> Keying transforms the meaning of activities understood in terms of one event by comparing them with activities understood in terms of another. Reactions to Woodrow Wilson's death in 1924, for example, assume new meaning when keyed to reactions to Lincoln's death in 1865. "Keying" is more than a new word for analogical thinking, more than a way individuals mentally organize their social experience; keying transforms memory into a cultural system because it matches publicly accessible (i.e., symbolic) models of the past (written narratives, pictorial images, statues, motion pictures, music, and songs) to the experiences of the present. . . . Keying is communicative movement—talk, writing, image- and music-making—that connects otherwise separate realms of history.[103]

[97] Keshgegian, "Finding a Place Past Night," 102.
[98] Robin Wagner-Pacifici, "Memories in the Making: The Shape of Things That Went," *Qualitative Sociology* 19 (1996): 306.
[99] Schwartz, *Abraham Lincoln*, 225–29.
[100] Similarly, Misztal, *Theories of Social Remembering*, 139: "Traumas, representing the extremities of human experience, are the occasions on which collective identities are most intensively engaged."
[101] Cf. Angela H. Gutchess and Maya Siegel, "Memory Specificity Across Cultures," in Assmann and Shortt, *Memory and Political Change*, 202, who note that the perception of the external world is influenced by culture in that people "reconcile [the external world] with existing knowledge and schemas."
[102] Schwartz, *Abraham Lincoln*, 226.
[103] Schwartz, *Abraham Lincoln*, 226.

For his part, Schwartz shows that Americans during the Great War summoned the image of Abraham Lincoln to articulate America's "role in the conflict as being on God's side against Satan."[104] The image of Lincoln paired to the war thus served to mobilize and moralize the war-time efforts.[105]

Outside of Schwartz' work, further examples that largely correspond to this notion of interpretive keying abound. Hung on the gallows in 1920 in Talbot County, Maryland, Isaiah Fountain "insisted that he be executed wearing a purple robe and crown, *to analogize his innocence* to that of Jesus Christ."[106] In memory terms, Fountain's keying of his social experience to the well-known symbols of Jesus' trial in John 19:1 is not mere analogy: it served to moralize himself alongside Jesus as a guiltless victim. At Auschwitz, commemorative images of women are keyed to the tropes of maternal and sexual suffering, creating a semantic context that understands the genocide as one that targeted even women and children.[107] As Jacobs argues, however, these frames also hold the ironic capacity to transform the remembered catastrophe in a negative way: to (1) reify the stereotype of a Jewish male as one who is absent and incapable of protecting his family and (2) promote voyeurism, and thus re-victimize the dead.[108] Further still, keying their prison conditions in Northern Ireland in the late 1970s to the conditions Jews experienced during the Holocaust allowed prisoners to express their humiliating experiences that eventually led to the so-called Dirty Protest (1978–1981): "It just reminded me of the Jews in the concentration camps because every man in the [visiting] room was bald and we were all very thin and frightened."[109] Interpretive keying, therefore, transforms the semantic and moral coloration of a phenomenon by filtering it through the lens of culturally charged scripts, tropes, or images from the

---

[104] Schwartz, *Abraham Lincoln*, 227.

[105] Moreover, at the outset of his monograph Schwartz observes that, in an attempt "to make sense of their grief," Bobby and Jackie Kennedy arrived at the Lincoln Memorial on the same day that U.S. President Kennedy was buried (*Abraham Lincoln*, ix). On the alignment of Kennedy and Lincoln, see also Neal, *National Trauma*, 32, 118.

[106] Sherrilyn A. Ifill, *On the Courthouse Lawn: Confronting the Legacy of Lynching in the Twenty-First Century* (Boston: Beacon, 2007), 15 (italics added).

[107] Janet Jacobs, "Gender and Collective Memory: Women and Representation at Auschwitz," *Memory Studies* 1 (2008): 211–25.

[108] Jacobs, "Gender and Collective Memory," 211–25.

[109] Begoña Aretxaga, "Dirty Protest: Symbolic Overdetermination and Gender in Northern Ireland Ethnic Violence," in Scheper-Hughes and Bourgois, *Violence in War and Peace*, 247 (brackets original). Social groups do not only comb the archival past to comprehend a violent present. They also look to the future. The meaning of violent events is thus constantly revisited in light of what continues to unfold. Writing in 2006, five years after the events of September 11, 2001, James E. Young ("The Stages of Memory at Ground Zero," in Stier and Landres, *Religion, Violence, Memory, and Place*, 214) argued that memorializing those events was no simple matter, since their meaning was still continuing to unfold, as they were when they first occurred.

archetypal past.[110] To put the matter succinctly, keying does not replicate the past; it comprehends the past by aligning it with a familiar symbol.

The Violence of Memory

As should be clear by now, selectivity characterizes individual and collective memory. Inherent to this idea of selectivity is the notion of forgetting. As A. Assmann and Shortt explain: "Every act of remembrance, whether individual or collective, necessarily involves selective, partial, or otherwise biased forms of forgetting."[111] It is here that we must abandon the presumption that remembering and forgetting form a strict dichotomy. The latter does not necessarily imply failure; the former does not always imply success. Rather, remembering presupposes forgetting because "it is impossible to see an object from every vantage-point."[112] Emphasizing one vantage point necessarily entails "forgetting" other possible perspectives.[113] Selectivity is an indispensable mechanism of memory. Without it the past remains an overwhelming mass of disjointed phenomena. Selectivity, then, serves as a scaffolding that renders the past intelligible in the present.

Although memory is necessarily selective, it is not inherently innocuous. Remembering is often dangerous. Remembering risks (re)creating invisible and visible forms of violence. One historian once opined: "If war is the continuation of politics by other means . . . violence is the continuation of conflict by means of physical force."[114] Building on this apodosis, we may formulate another thesis: if violence is the furtherance of conflict by means of physical harm, the memory of said harm reinscribes the precipitating conflict, which again structures instances of physical harm. The memory of violence, in other words, can inculcate ideology conducive to outbursts of violence:

---

[110] Kirk, "Memory of Violence," 193–94, 197; Le Donne, "Theological Memory Distortion in the Jesus Tradition," 172; James V. Wertsch, "Deep Memory and Narrative Templates: Conservative Forces in Collective Memory," in Assmann and Shortt, *Memory and Political Change*, 175.

[111] Aleida Assmann and Linda Shortt, "Memory and Political Change: Introduction," in Assmann and Shortt, *Memory and Political Change*, 5.

[112] Le Donne, "Theological Memory Distortion in the Jesus Tradition," 168.

[113] Not all instances of "forgetting" are made from the same cloth. Paul Connerton ("Seven Types of Forgetting," *Memory Studies* 1 [2008]: 59–71), for example, distinguishes between seven types of forgetting. Aleida Assmann ("From Collective Violence to a Common Future: Four Models for Dealing with a Traumatic Past," in Modlinger and Sonntag, *Other People's Pain*, 43–62) details four models of remembering/forgetting for navigating a violent past. And Paul Ricoeur ("Memory—Forgetting—History," in *Meaning and Representation in History*, ed. Jörn Rüsen [Oxford: Berghahn Books, 2006], 9–19) speaks of active and passive forgetting as representing two extremes along a continuum of forgetting.

[114] Bruce Lincoln, "Theses on Religion and Violence," *ISIM Review* 15 (2005): 12.

> When social groups constitute their identity in religious terms and experience themselves as a sacred collectivity (the faithful, the righteous, or God's chosen people, for instance), as a corollary they tend to construe their rivals in negative fashion (heretics, infidels, apostates, evil, bestial, demonic, satanic, etc.). Under such circumstances, the pursuit of self-interest—including vengeance for slights to one's pride (a.k.a. "honour")—can be experienced as a holy cause, in support of which any violence is justified.[115]

To reference Pennebaker again: "Powerful collective memories—whether real or concocted—can be at the root of wars, prejudice, nationalism, and cultural identities."[116]

In her research on the aftermath of the Rwandan genocide, Buckley-Zistel argues that Rwandans engage in what she terms "chosen amnesia."[117] Chosen amnesia is a deliberate refusal to remember certain aspects of the genocide, including the racial antagonisms between Hutu and Tutsi that fueled the massacres. To remember the causes of the genocide would have inevitably constructed the perpetrators and victims into antagonistic group identities. Consequently, chosen amnesia was viewed as (1) enabling peaceful coexistence between Hutu and Tutsi, and thus (2) a necessary deterrent of repeating the atrocity.[118] From this perspective, to remember certain aspects of the difficult past between Hutu and Tutsi was tantamount to recreating the antagonistic and invisible social structure that had sowed the seeds of visible violence.[119] Buckley-Zistel reveals a dark irony, however, when she contends that "chosen amnesia" fails to resolve social antagonisms. Such a strategy may inadvertently "lead to the very thing it is designed to prevent" if another dictatorship arises and aggravates these unresolved social antagonisms.[120] From this perspective, *not* to remember certain aspects of the genocide runs the risk of recreating violence.[121] In this light, A. Assmann's

---

[115] Lincoln, "Theses on Religion and Violence," 12.

[116] James W. Pennebaker, introduction to *Collective Memory of Political Events: Social Psychological Perspectives*, ed. James W. Pennebaker, Dario Paez, and Bernard Rimé (New York: Psychology Press, 1997), vii.

[117] Buckley-Zistel, "Chosen Amnesia." See also Buckley-Zistel, "Remembering to Forget."

[118] Buckley-Zistel, "Chosen Amnesia," 74–83.

[119] On the Rwandan genocide exemplifying antagonistic social relations, see Philip Gourevitch, "We Wish to Inform You That Tomorrow We Will Be Killed with Our Families: Stories from Rwanda," in Scheper-Hughes and Bourgois, *Violence in War and Peace*, 136–42 (esp. 140).

[120] Buckley-Zistel, "Chosen Amnesia," 85.

[121] Germany has faced similar difficulties in how to approach remembering WWII and the Shoah. After the Nuremberg Trials, Winston Churchill advocated forgetting, that is, not confronting Germany with the horrific memories of their past as a means of overcoming

claim that memories are "double edged" in that they have the capacity both to overcome and perpetuate violence is especially poignant.[122]

Bodily Mutilation and Commemorative Contestation

Human bodies signify. In the Greek and Roman worlds, for example, physiognomy was prevalent as a social and cultural strategy that interpreted the body's physicality, mechanisms, and dress as a means of identifying a person's inner character.[123] The prevalence of detailed physiognomic descriptions of figures in Greco-Roman histories and biographies makes the near-total absence of portrayals of Jesus' somatic physicality in the Gospels appear somewhat surprising.[124] The rhetorical and philosophical traction that physiognomic practices carried could have certainly helped the gospel writers negotiate Jesus' masculinity, messianic credentials, or relationship to the divine, especially since a "physiognomic consciousness" is evident in Josephus, Philo, and the Dead Sea Scrolls.[125] The body lends itself as a ready-to-use conduit of socially constructed meaning. Bodies function—or rather are made to function even as they lend themselves to function—as "expressions of the social world they

---

the war. See Aleida Assmann, "To Remember or to Forget: Which Way Out of a Shared History of Violence?" in Assmann and Shortt, *Memory and Political Change*, 58–59. In German eyes during the 1950s, forgetting the past represented "openness towards the future" (Assmann, "To Remember or to Forget," 59). Cf. Olick and Levy, "Collective Memory and Cultural Constraint," 928, n. 10. In later decades, however, the policy of forgetting from the 1950s "became negatively associated with denial and cover-up" (Assmann, "To Remember or to Forget," 61). Thus, remembering in the 1980s and 1990s became viewed "as a therapeutic tool to cleanse, to purge, to heal, to reconcile" (Assmann, "From Collective Violence," 47–54 [quotation, p. 50]). See further Olick, *In the House of the Hangman*.

[122] Assmann, "From Collective Violence," 59. Cf. Duncan Bell, "Introduction: Violence and Memory," *Millennium: Journal of International Studies* 38 (2009): 358: "Memory can bind people as well as driving them apart, catalyse and sustain the search for justice as well as motivating violence."

[123] "The underlying logic of the principles of physiognomy," as Callie Callon (*Reading Bodies: Physiognomy as a Strategy of Persuasion in Early Christian Discourse*, LNTS 597 [London: T&T Clark, 2019], 4) explains, "was predicated on the view that the body and soul were sympathetically related and intrinsically intertwined, and that each could act upon the other." Physiognomy as a social practice, of course, is not restricted to the ancient world. See, e.g., Martin Porter, *Windows of the Soul: The Art of Physiognomy in European Culture 1470–1780* (Oxford: Oxford University Press, 2005).

[124] On the Gospels as instances of ancient biography, see, e.g., Richard A. Burridge, *What Are the Gospels? A Comparison with Graeco-Roman Biography*, 3rd ed. (Waco, Tex.: Baylor University Press, 2018); Helen K. Bond, *The First Biography of Jesus: Genre and Meaning in Mark's Gospel* (Grand Rapids: Eerdmans, 2020). On the curious absence of physical descriptions of Jesus in the Gospels, see Joan E. Taylor, *What Did Jesus Look Like?* (London: T&T Clark, 2018), 1–14.

[125] See Taylor, *What Did Jesus Look Like?* 10–12, for references. On early Christian utility of the rhetorical power of physiognomy, see Callon, *Reading Bodies*.

inhabit," and thus as discursive channels of symbolic discourse.[126] As Douglas notes in her influential work, *Natural Symbols*, "the human body is the most readily available image" of a social structure.[127] To touch,[128] adorn,[129] modify,[130] or imprison[131] the body, therefore, configures gender identity, social affiliations, ideology, and social status specific to a sociocultural context.

Likewise, to mutilate or subject the body to physical forms of violence is to freight such violence with symbolic potential.[132] In Anglo-Norman England, Norman rulers utilized castration as a penalty for treason.[133] According to Van Eickels, masculinity constituted a prerequisite of political efficacy. Thus, to castrate a political enemy comprised "an appropriate form of royal revenge."[134] Further, the French revolutionaries who executed Louis XVI of France chose beheading as the mode of execution because of its fitting symbolism.[135] For a millennium, France's kings received the anointing of oil and the crown on their heads as the bodily enactment of their coronation. To decapitate the anointed

---

[126] Erica Reischer and Kathryn S. Koo, "The Body Beautiful: Symbolism and Agency in the Social World," *Annual Review of Anthropology* 33 (2004): 299. See also M. Andryael Tong, "'Given as a Sign': Circumcision and Bodily Discourse in Late Antique Judaism and Christianity" (PhD diss., Fordham University, 2019).

[127] Mary Douglas, *Natural Symbols: Explorations in Cosmology* (London: Barrie and Jenkins, 1973), 17.

[128] João De Pina-Cabral ("Tamed Violence: Genital Symbolism in Portuguese Popular Culture," *Man* 28 [1993]: 101–20) shows that, during festivals in Amarante, Portugal, teenage boys prod teenage girls (on the head or backside) with phallic-shaped cakes to publicly demarcate their personal gender identity.

[129] Although most Americans would recognize the (un)-adorned third finger on the left hand as an indicator of marital status, Reischer and Koo ("Body Beautiful," 300) argue that they likely would not possess the requisite cultural knowledge to recognize that white robes in India designate a woman's widowhood.

[130] As Asian facial features are frequently the object of pejorative stereotyping in American culture, Reischer and Koo ("Body Beautiful," 305) note that many Asian Americans actually surgically modify their eyes to communicate the qualities associated with a capitalistic work ethic (e.g., "attentiveness").

[131] Miranda Aldhouse-Green ("Chaining and Shaming: Images of Defeat, From Llyn Cerrig Bach to Sarmitzegetusa," *OJA* 23 [2004]: 319–40) argues that the utilization of the gang-chain publicly signifies the change in status and shame of the captive.

[132] See Kirk, "Memory of Violence," 192; Malkki, *Purity and Exile*, 94. The symbolism of somatic violence is observable in pop-cultural phenomena as well. Viv Burr, "'Oh Spike You're Covered in Sexy Wounds!' The Erotic Significance of Wounding and Torture in Buffy the Vampire Slayer," in *Sex, Violence, and the Body: The Erotics of Wounding*, ed. Viv Burr and Jeff Hearn (Basingstoke: Palgrave Macmillan, 2008), 137–56, has shown, for instance, that the cult classic television show *Buffy the Vampire Slayer* (starring Sarah Michelle Gellar) has several scenes of bodily torture throughout the series that are erotically charged.

[133] Klaus Van Eickels, "Gendered Violence: Castration and Blinding as Punishment for Treason in Normandy and Anglo-Norman England," *Gender History* 16 (2004): 588–602.

[134] Van Eickels, "Gendered Violence," 591.

[135] Connerton, *How Societies Remember*, 9–13.

head amounted to a "ritual revocation" of that coronation.[136] It expressed the people's intent to constitute a new social order moving forward—Connerton, therefore, notes: "Not simply the natural body of the king but also and above all his political body was killed."[137]

Regardless of a perpetrator's intention, moreover, the application of bodily violence is often experienced or perceived as the degradation of an individual's or group's humanity. Humiliating torture and disfigurement often infantilize their victims.[138] In the words of Scarry:

> Whatever pain achieves, it achieves in part through its unsharability, and it ensures this unsharability through its resistance to language. . . . Physical pain does not simply resist language but actively destroys it, bringing about an immediate reversion to a state anterior to language, to the sounds and cries a human being makes before language is learned.[139]

Furthermore, Malkki provides numerous graphic accounts of violent techniques used by Tutsi against Hutu in the 1972 Burundi genocide:

> The manners that the Tutsi employed—if, for example—yes, we are adults, well . . . for example: a pregnant woman (Hutu). There was a manner of cutting the stomach. Everything that was found in the interior was lifted out without cutting the cord. The cadaver of the mama, the cadaver of the baby, of the future, they rotted on the road. Not even burial. The mother was obliged to eat the finger of the baby. One cut the finger, and then one said to the mother: Eat! [. . .].[140]

She provides similarly disturbing accounts on the same page:

> The girls in secondary schools, they killed each other. The Tutsi girls were given bamboos. They were made to kill by pushing the bamboo from below [from the vagina] to the mouth. . . . For the pregnant women, the stomach was cut, and then the child who had been inside—one said to the mama: "Eat your child"—this embryo. One

---

[136] Connerton, *How Societies Remember*, 13. By contrast, Ilongot men of northern Luzon in the Philippines decapitate human heads in order to cast away the rage that is born of personal loss. See Rosaldo, "Grief and a Headhunter's Rage."

[137] Connerton, *How Societies Remember*, 9.

[138] See, e.g., Begoña Aretxaga, "Dirty Protest: Symbolic Overdetermination and Gender in Northern Ireland Ethnic Violence," *Ethos* 23 (1995): esp. 129; Aretxaga, "Dirty Protest" (2004), esp. 246.

[139] Elaine Scarry, "The Body in Pain: The Making and Unmaking of the World," in Scheper-Hughes and Bourgois, *Violence in War and Peace*, 366.

[140] Malkki, *Purity and Exile*, 91 (see 86–102 for her wider discussion).

had to do it. And then, other women and children, they were put inside a house—like two hundred—and then the house was burned.[141]

As Malkki persuasively indicates throughout her discussion, these methods of killing are not random acts of violence.[142] *How* people suffer is of utmost importance—violent atrocities of bodily mutilation are not void of meaning. The focus on specific body parts (e.g., vagina) and social relationships (e.g., mother-embryo) symbolically corresponds the procedures of killing to the sociopolitical intent "to destroy the procreative capability, the 'new life,' of the Hutu people."[143] Forcing women to consume their own children signified "a complete reversal of the 'progress of nature' in which the mother's body nurtures, forms, and brings into the world 'new life.'"[144] Similarly, Hutu viewed other methods of disfigurement—demolishing skulls, connecting the vagina/anus to the skull via bamboo, forcing fathers and daughters to drown together in incestuous positions—as stressing their powerlessness and dehumanization.[145] Especially with these accounts' emphasis on reproductive methods of torture, it is not surprising that the Hutu viewed the minority Tutsi as seeking "'to equalize the population, up until 50 percent.'"[146]

In commemorative activity, however, the symbolic frameworks of bodily violence are subject to contestation, "as those with competing claims over meaning try to inscribe their own version of reality onto individuals."[147] In this way, memory can become a process of negotiating the embodied resonances of

---

[141] Malkki, *Purity and Exile*, 91 (italics original).
[142] Malkki, *Purity and Exile*, 95–96, mentions that the Tutsi did not kill Hutu with bullets because that would have represented an honorable death.
[143] Malkki, *Purity and Exile*, 92.
[144] Malkki, *Purity and Exile*, 93.
[145] Malkki, *Purity and Exile*, 91–93.
[146] Malkki, *Purity and Exile*, 91.
[147] Doug Henry, "Violence and the Body: Somatic Expressions of Trauma and Vulnerability during War," *Medical Anthropology Quarterly* 20 (2006): 385. A social network's embrace of a narrative about its past implies the subordination of alternative or competing narrations. See Wertsch, "Deep Memory," 182. Lawrence and Karim, "Theorizing Violence," 10: "No representation of violence exists apart from its rhetorical opposite or sublimated counterpart." Consider, for example, the varying conceptualizations of Timothy McVeigh's intentions in the Oklahoma City bombing. Whereas McVeigh viewed himself as a patriot fulfilling his duty, American society has largely externalized his actions as one of an extremist, not a patriot. See Kenneth Foote, "On the Edge of Memory: Uneasy Legacies of Dissent, Terror, and Violence in the American Landscape," *Social Science Quarterly* 97 (2016): 115–22; Hamm, "Apocalyptic Violence." See also Assmann, "From Collective Violence," 54, who contends that "national memories" are generally "not dialogic but monologic," since they enhance identity and acclaim the collective self. See also Malkki, *Purity and Exile*, 55; Neal, *National Trauma*, 205–6. On the human body as a "site" of memory, see Misztal, *Theories of Social Remembering*, 141–45.

violence.[148] Hence, bringing a violent past to bear on the present often involves vilifying or casting as heroes the perpetrators or victims of a past atrocity. To return to Malkki's ethnographic research, the Hutu refugees framed their descriptions of bodily harm by underscoring the guilt of the perpetrators, thereby shifting "the dehumanizing gaze" to the Tutsi.[149] Marking perpetrators and victims into separate group identities, then, is implicit in this commemorative maneuver. In such instances, the body becomes a rhetorical instrument of transforming symbolic potentials, setting apart antagonistic groups from one another, or reaffirming the humanity of the degraded victims.[150] This is

---

[148] Cf. Neal, *National Trauma*, 17, who notes that remembering groups assign to a violent past "strong moralistic judgments in terms of right or wrong, good or bad, true or false."

[149] Malkki, *Purity and Exile*, 93.

[150] Cf. Jacobs, "Memorial at Srebrenica," whose study on gender representations at the memorial to genocide at Srebrenica (regarding the 1990s conflict in Bosnia-Herzegovina) makes the claim that the Serbian intent to destroy Bosnian culture, and thereby assert Serbian supremacy, motivated the sexual violence against Bosnian Muslim women (pp. 3–4). However, Jacobs observes that the commemorative narratives and texts at Srebrenica omit the trope of genocidal rape against Bosnian Muslim women. Instead, "the tropes of virtue and goodness" underscore gendered representation of women so that they are seen as "the grieving mother and wife" (p. 12). Accordingly, she argues that by forgetting about the genocidal rape, the commemorative site circumvented a detail of the past that would have presumably impeded the reconfiguration of patriarchal Muslim identity—which relied on the self-concept of women as virtuous and men as protectors—had it been remembered (p. 12). Even if one does not find Jacobs' interpretation of this particular site persuasive, her argument intersects with an important axiom regarding memory and identity: identity in the present is largely sustained by memory of the past that evaluates that past as somehow positive. A positive self-image of the past is often perceived as necessary for the self's continued existence. Thus, when confronted with a violent past that is humiliating, degrading, or positions the self (whether perpetrators or victims) in a negative light, two impulses are possible in terms of memory. First, the degradation is acknowledged but contested so as not to be debilitating, which we are presently discussing in the main text. Second, the event or the degrading aspects of it are repressed (whether actively or passively). Both impulses, however, are interrelated in that they are attempts at negotiating and overcoming trauma. On memory repression, see, e.g., Sigmund Freud, "An Autobiographical Study," in *The Freud Reader*, ed. Peter Gay (London: Vintage, 1989), 17, who observed the following regarding what his patients had forgotten in their lives: "Everything that had been forgotten had in some way or other been distressing; it had been either alarming or painful or shameful by the standards of the subject's personality. It was impossible not to conclude that that was precisely why it had been forgotten—that is, why it had not remained conscious." See also Misztal, *Theories of Social Remembering*, 141:

> Freud's focus on forgetting, or the selective omission of events, as an example of the reconstructive labour of memory, is in some respects similar to Halbwachs' emphasis on the normative nature of collective memory, seen as biased towards a positive image of the past. Because of the normative nature of collective memory aimed at defending group identity, a common response to a traumatic past is silence and inhibition. Studies suggest that forgetting and silence is a very frequent

also observable in how African Americans during the lynching era confronted the violent horrors of white supremacy, which served to call into question their very personhood: they turned to the blues to reassert "loudly and exuberantly their somebodiness, twisting and turning their sweaty bodies to the 'low down dirty blues.'"[151] As Henry contends: "Bodies do not simply express trauma; they are a place where identity and meaning can be actively reconfigured into socially and personally acceptable ways for understanding, coping, and creatively managing trauma."[152]

Rendering a violent past comprehensible, therefore, is hardly ever an apolitical or neutral social endeavor.[153] Like the contemporary accounts of violence we have discussed in this chapter, representations of bodily violence in the ancient world "do not simply reflect past realities."[154] They are fundamentally memory distortions, shaped by moral judgments that cast figures in negative or positive terms. As one leading specialist on violence in the ancient world argues, literary descriptions of "extreme forms of physical violence" often highlight the excessive violence attributed to emperors by ancient Roman historians.[155] These literary narratives are designed as "horror scenarios" that instill disgust in the reader and, accordingly, reflect "political disputes or the contemporary assessment of a political constellation."[156]

---

reaction as groups organize forgetting, reconstruction and positive distortion of the past in order to defend group values and their own image.

See also Juanjo Igartua and Dario Paez, "Art and Remembering Traumatic Collective Events: The Case of the Spanish Civil War," in Pennebaker, Paez, and Rimé, *Collective Memory of Political Events*, 80: "Halbwachs implicitly coincided with Freud in the fact that collective memory is biased toward forgetting that which is negative, and toward having a positive image of the past."

[151] Cone, *Cross and the Lynching Tree*, 14.
[152] Henry, "Violence and the Body," 391.
[153] Lawrence and Karim, "Theorizing Violence," 1: "Violence always has a context. Context shapes not just the actors or victims but also those who represent them. What is celebrated in one place may be mourned in another. Memory is never an equal balance, or a neutral lens, of human experience and history." See also K. Stephen Prince, "Remembering Robert Charles: Violence and Memory in Jim Crow New Orleans," *Journal of Southern History* 83 (2017): 297–328; K. Stephen Prince, *The Ballad of Robert Charles: Searching for the New Orleans Riot of 1900* (Chapel Hill: University of North Carolina Press, 2021).
[154] Walter Pohl, "Perceptions of Barbarian Violence," in Drake, *Violence in Late Antiquity*, 22.
[155] Martin Zimmermann, "Extreme Formen physischer Gewalt in der antiken Überlieferung," in *Extreme Formen von Gewalt in Bild und Text des Altertums*, ed. Martin Zimmermann, Münchner Studien zur Alten Welt (München: Herbert Utz Verlag, 2009), 155–92 (quotation, p. 155). Zimmermann distinguishes these "Formen extremer körperlicher Gewalt" ("extreme forms of physical violence") from "einfachen Gewaltszenen" ("scenes of simple violence") (p. 155).
[156] Zimmermann, "Extreme Formen physischer Gewalt," 155, 192.

Final Remarks

As we will see, underlying the tradition of John's beheading in its early reception history are the mechanisms of the social memory of violence that we have theorized in this chapter. At the heart of this commemorative history is the contestation of the symbolic potential of his violent beheading. Similar to the cultural power of Roman crucifixion in compelling early Christians to negotiate the degrading framework of Jesus' crucifixion when they remembered Jesus' death (e.g., Phil 2:5–11), those who remembered John's severed head show signs of the commemorative impulse to reconfigure the negative cultural script of beheading.

The early reception history of John's beheading shows that John's beheading is never replicated as such, but is actively constructed on the basis of the present. Early recipients *contest* the image of John's beheading by *keying* it to Jesus' crucifixion, thus constructing an interpretive framework where the innocence of both figures is mutually affecting and exonerating. Simultaneously, the degrading gaze of John's beheading shifts to ridicule Herod Antipas. As John's beheading is localized in the organization of "Jewish" and "Christian" *identity*, the morally deficient portrait of Antipas is *keyed* to contemporary Jews, thus generating a semantic context where Antipas' negative moral coloration is emblematic of Jewish identity. In this way, the memory of John's beheading becomes a *violent memory*, albeit invisibly. Did beheading in the ancient world, however, *really* constitute the sort of degrading violence that could force rememberers to negotiate its negative symbolism?

2
Cultures of Violence

Beheading in the Ancient World

> Human beings have often cut off one another's heads.
> They do not always cut off another's head.
> They often strenuously disapprove cutting off heads,
> yet someone somewhere is always cutting off someone else's
>   head for some reason.
> Why?[1]

> The deliberate separation of a head from
> its body is exclusively cultural.[2]

> [Arya Stark:] Could you bring back a man without a head?
> Not six times. Just once.
> [Thoros of Myr:] I don't think it works that way, child.[3]

Prior to our analysis of the commemorative contestation of John's decapitation, it is necessary to offer a cultural analysis of the ideology of beheading in the ancient world. Three observations prompt our exploration. First, social memory theory takes seriously that memories of violence from a previous present were constructed in the terms and symbols available to that present. To understand the communicative power of John's beheading, therefore, entails cultivating a level of familiarity with ancient discourses of a cut-off head. Second, interpreters have generally

---

[1] Regina Janes, *Losing Our Heads: Beheadings in Literature and Culture* (New York: New York University Press, 2005), 1.
[2] Janes, *Losing Our Heads*, 2. Cf. Werner Riess, introduction to *The Topography of Violence in the Greco-Roman World*, ed. Werner Riess and Garrett G. Fagan (Ann Arbor: University of Michigan Press, 2016), 1: "Violence is an intrinsic part of every human society and is always culturally defined."
[3] Alex Graves, "Kissed by Fire," *Game of Thrones* (HBO, April 28, 2013).

neglected bringing the ideological discourse of beheading to bear on understanding John's decapitation. Major monographs and gospel commentaries sparingly (if at all) appeal to ancient beheadings to elucidate his death.[4] This lacuna is especially palpable when compared to the deluge of scholarship that interprets the death of Jesus in light of our knowledge of ancient crucifixion.[5] In a field dominated by

[4] For examples of monographs in this regard, see Maurice Goguel, *Au seuil de l'Évangile: Jean-Baptiste*, BibH 40 (Paris: Payot, 1928), 51–56; Carl H. Kraeling, *John the Baptist* (New York: Scribner's Sons, 1951), 83–93; Jean Steinmann, *Saint John the Baptist and the Desert Tradition*, trans. Michael Boyes (London: Longmans, 1958), 101–9; Walter Wink, *John the Baptist in the Gospel Tradition*, SNTSMS 7 (Cambridge: Cambridge University Press, 1968), 8–13; Robert Webb, *John the Baptizer and Prophet: A Socio-Historical Study*, JSNTSup 62 (Sheffield: Sheffield Academic Press, 1991), 366–78; Daniel S. Dapaah, *The Relationship between John the Baptist and Jesus of Nazareth: A Critical Study* (Lanham, Md.: University Press of America, 2005); Joan E. Taylor, *The Immerser: John the Baptist within Second Temple Judaism* (Grand Rapids: Eerdmans, 1997), 213–59; Roland Schütz, *Johannes der Täufer*, ATANT 50 (Zürich: Stuttgart, 1967), 103–5. One exception of this omission is Michael Hartmann, *Der Tod Johannes des Täufers: Eine exegetische und rezeptionsgeschichtliche Studie auf dem Hintergrund narrativer, intertextueller und kulturanthropologischer Zugänge*, SBB 45 (Stuttgart: Verlag Katholisches Bibelwerk, 2001), 155, 159, 187–98. For examples of commentaries, see C. E. B. Cranfield, *The Gospel According to Saint Mark*, CGTC (Cambridge: Cambridge University Press, 1959), 206–13; D. E. Nineham, *Saint Mark* (Harmondsworth: Penguin, 1963), 171–76; Eduard Schweizer, *The Good News According to Mark* (Atlanta: John Knox, 1970), 131–35; William L. Lane, *The Gospel According to Mark*, NICNT (Grand Rapids: Eerdmans, 1974), 210–23; C. S. Mann, *Mark*, AB (New York: Doubleday, 1986), 293–98; Robert A. Guelich, *Mark 1–8:26*, WBC 34A (Dallas, Tex.: Word, 1989), 324–34; Morna D. Hooker, *The Gospel According to Saint Mark* (London: Black and Peabody, 1991), 157–62; Karl Kertelge, *Markusevangelium*, NEchtB (Würzburg: Echter Verlag, 1994), 64–67; Donald A. Hagner, *Matthew 14–28*, WBC 33B (Dallas, Tex.: Word, 1995), 409–13; Joachim Gnilka, *Das Evangelium nach Markus*, 5th ed., EKK (Neukirchen-Vluyn: Neukirchener Verlag, 1998), 1:243–53; Ben Witherington, *The Gospel of Mark: A Socio-Rhetorical Commentary* (Grand Rapids: Eerdmans, 2001), 212–16; R. T. France, *The Gospel of Mark*, NIGTC (Grand Rapids: Eerdmans, 2002), 251–59; Frances J. Maloney, *The Gospel of Mark: A Commentary* (Peabody, Mass.: Hendrickson, 2002), 125–28; Daniel J. Harrington, *The Gospel of Matthew*, SP (Collegeville, Minn.: Liturgical Press, 2007), 214–18; Robert H. Stein, *Mark*, BECNT (Grand Rapids: Baker Academic, 2008), 298–308; Craig A. Evans, *Matthew*, New Cambridge Bible Commentary (Cambridge: Cambridge University Press, 2012), 290–92. Even Malina and Rohrbaugh's social-scientific analysis of Mark 6:14–29 (Bruce J. Malina and Richard L. Rohrbaugh, *Social-Science Commentary on the Synoptic Gospels* [Minneapolis: Fortress, 1992], 216–17) does not once mention John's beheading, the postmortem manipulation of John's head, or the burial of John's headless body. Some commentators have considered (to varying extents) some facets of ancient beheadings. See, e.g., Erich Klostermann, *Das Markusevangelium*, HNT (Tübingen: Mohr Siebeck, 1971), 60–61; John R. Donahue and Daniel Harrington, *The Gospel of Mark*, SP (Collegeville, Minn.: Liturgical Press, 2002), 199–200; Adela Yarbro Collins, *Mark: A Commentary*, Hermeneia (Minneapolis: Fortress, 2007), 311–13. Collins cites Livy (*Ab urbe cond.* 39.43) at Mark 6:24–25 to claim that "the probable intent (or effect) of the pre-Markan story [is] to disparage the Herodian women" (p. 313).

[5] Hengel's comment from 1977—"There is still an urgent need for a comprehensive study of crucifixion and capital law in antiquity, including the Jewish world"—no longer

studies that emphasize the symbolic power of Roman crucifixion, parsing the cultural contours of ancient beheading is largely uncharted territory for NT scholars.

This characteristic oversight is quite unfortunate, moreover, because beheading was a well-known framework of meaning for those who lived in the Roman Empire. Jews who could read their cultural texts (or, more likely, listened as scribes read for them) were probably familiar with the traditions of severed heads and bodily mutilation that formed part of their heritage.[6] In the Roman Empire at large (and the Roman Republic before the imperial era), the severed head was a prevalent cultural trope and a (common) sight

---

rings true, at least not as an *urgent* need (Martin Hengel, *Crucifixion in the Ancient World and the Folly of the Message of the Cross* [Philadelphia: Fortress, 1977], xii). German and English works on crucifixion in antiquity, for example, by Kuhn, Chapman, Samuelsson, and Cook in 1982, 2008, 2011, and 2014, respectively, and the collaborative effort by Chapman and Schnabel in 2015 have largely answered Hengel's call. See Heinz-Wolfgang Kuhn, "Die Kreuzesstrafe während der frühen Kaiserzeit: Ihre Wirklichkeit und Wertung in der Umwelt des Urchristentums," *ANRW* 2.25.1:648–793; David W. Chapman, *Ancient Jewish and Christian Perceptions of Crucifixion*, WUNT 224 (Tübingen: Mohr Siebeck, 2008); Gunnar Samuelsson, *Crucifixion in Antiquity: An Inquiry into the Background and Significance of the New Testament Terminology of Crucifixion*, WUNT 310 (Tübingen: Mohr Siebeck, 2011); John Granger Cook, *Crucifixion in the Mediterranean World*, WUNT 327 (Tübingen: Mohr Siebeck, 2014); David W. Chapman and Eckhard J. Schnabel, *The Trial and Crucifixion of Jesus*, WUNT 344 (Tübingen: Mohr Siebeck, 2015). Accompanying these labors is a host of articles and essays dedicated to (Jesus') crucifixion in reference works and peer-reviewed journals. For reference essays, see, e.g., E. Brandenburger, "σταυρός," *NIDNTT* 1:391–405; Gerald G. O'Collins, "Crucifixion," *ABD* 1:1207–10; George Watson and Andrew Lintott, "Crucifixion," *OCD* 396; Michael O. Wise, "Crucifixion," in *The Eerdmans Dictionary of Early Judaism*, ed. John J. Collins and Daniel C. Harlow (Grand Rapids: Eerdmans, 2010), 500–501; J. Dennis, "Death of Jesus," *DJG*, 172–93. For peer-reviewed articles, see, e.g., John Granger Cook, "Envisioning Crucifixion: Light from Several Inscriptions and the Palatine Graffito," *NovT* 50 (2008): 262–85; John Granger Cook, "Crucifixion and Burial," *NTS* 57 (2011): 193–213; John Granger Cook, "Crucifixion as Spectacle in Roman Campania," *NovT* 54 (2012): 68–100; John Granger Cook, "Roman Crucifixions: From the Second Punic War to Constantine," *ZNW* 104 (2013): 1–32; Steven Muir, "Vivid Imagery in Galatians 3:1—Roman Rhetoric, Street Announcing, Graffiti, and Crucifixions," *BTB* 44 (2014): 76–86.

[6] See Gen 40:19; Judg 7:25; 1 Sam 5:4; 1 Sam 17:51, 54; 1 Kgdms 17:51, 54 LXX; 1 Sam 31:9; 1 Chr 10:9–10; 1 Chr 10:9–10 LXX (cf. 1 Kgdms 31:9 LXX); 2 Sam 4:1–12; 2 Kgdms 4:1–12 LXX; 2 Sam 20:10–22; 2 Kgdms 20:10–22 LXX; 2 Kgs 6:31 (similarly, 4 Kgdms 6:31 LXX); 2 Kgs 10:1–11; 4 Kgdms 10:1–11 LXX; Ps 151:7 LXX; Isa 9:13; Isa 9:13 LXX; see also 4Q163; Jdt 13–16; 1 Macc 7:39–50; 11:17; 2 Macc 15:28–36. Many Jewish texts retell these traditions. See, e.g., Josephus, *Ant.* 6.191–192 (cf. 1 Sam 17:54); *Ant.* 6.368–378 (cf.1 Sam 31:8–9); Philo, *Ios.* 96 (cf. Gen 40:19). Josephus also recasts two stories as beheadings that were not portrayed as beheadings in the HB or LXX: *Ant.* 6.193–204 (cf. 1 Sam 18:25; 1 Kgdms 18:25 LXX); *Ant.* 2.310 (Exod 10:28; Exod 10:28 LXX; Esth. Rab. 7:10 [cf. Esth 7:10]). Josephus in one instance recasts a beheading from the HB as a crucifixion (*Ant.* 2.73; cf. Gen 40:19). Further examples of beheading in Jewish literature abound. See Josephus, *War* 1.323–326 (*Ant.* 14.448–450); 1.342–343 (*Ant.* 14.464); 2.246; 6.360–362; *Ant.* 15.8–9; 17.273–277; 20.97–99 (cf. Acts 5:36); 20.117.

in war, public spectacles of violence, city sieges, and pre-burial/burial-denial enactments of public enemies.[7] Thus, the prevalence of the lines of discourse surrounding the severed head makes it more likely than not that early readers of John the Baptist's death understood his beheading along these lines of tradition that they inherited. In fact, as we will see in the next chapter, the Gospels dwell on the cultural contours of John's beheading, as if they *expect* readers to understand his death within this framework.

Third, the question remains whether cutting off a human head in the ancient world constituted the kind of degrading bodily mutilation that could be the locus of commemorative contestation, such as what we analyzed in the previous chapter. This question is legitimate to ask not only from a theoretical perspective, but also from a historical point of view, for historians frequently categorize beheading in the Greco-Roman world as simple, unaggravated, or an honorable form of execution. Berkowitz, for example, characterizes Roman decapitation as "its most honorable method [of execution]."[8] Another scholar refers to "death by decapitation" as "the least painful and degrading form of execution."[9] Similarly, Coleman differentiates between the "'aggravated' forms of capital punishment" (crucifixion, fire, and damnation to beasts) and "simple

---

[7] See *Iliad* 18.176–180; Herodotus, *Hist.* 7.238; Euphorion, *Pr. Frgmts.* 194; Polybius, *Hist.* 1.7.11–12; Livy, *Ab. urbe cond* 3.9.3; Ovid, *Metam.* 4.765–785; Dionysius of Halicarnassus, *Ant. rom.* 2.29; 3.58.4; 6.30.1–2; Velleius Paterculus, *Comp. Rom. Hist.* 2.119.1–5; 2.27.3; 2.70.2–3; Lucan, *Civ. W.* 2.160–173; Appian, *Bell. Civ.* 1.10.93; 3.26; Silius Italicus, *Pun.* 10.145–146; Dio Cassius, *Rom. hist.* 49.2–3; 56.21.5; Tacitus, *Hist.* 3.74; *Ann.* 14.64; Suetonius, *Nero* 49.4; Plutarch *Galb.* 27.2–4; *Ant.* 36. Plutarch refers to the Persian custom of using a knife (ξυρόν) to behead the condemned: "He turned back, and with one hand clutching Dareius by the hair, dragged him to the ground, and cut off (ἀπέτεμε) his head (τὸν τράχηλον) with the knife (τῷ ξυρῷ)" (Plutarch, *Art.* 29 [Perrin, LCL]). Perrin's rendering of τράχηλον as "head" in English is appropriate in that it conveys that this passage refers to a beheading. At first glance, "he cut his throat" may seem like the natural translation of τράχηλον (lit. "neck" or "throat") as the direct object of ἀποτέμνω (lit. "cut from" or "cut off"). However, three reasons make this option unlikely in this particular instance. First, the executioner clearly enters the chamber with the intent of beheading Dareius, as the context makes clear beforehand: ὁ δὲ δήμιος κληθεὶς ἧκε μὲν ξυρὸν ἔχων, ᾧ τὰς κεφαλὰς ἀποτέμνουσι τῶν κολαζομένων (*Art.* 29). Second, although Plutarch portrays the executioner initially refusing to behead Dareius, at the pressure of those outside the chamber the executioner concedes and fulfills his duty. The text and context do not convey that he slit Dareius' throat *instead of* beheading him. Third, the notion of slitting a throat is more frequently conveyed by other means, particularly in the usage of σφάζω and its cognates (see, e.g., Euripides, *Andr.* 410; *Cycl.* 399; *El.* 813). I am not aware of a single clear reference in Plutarch where τράχηλον is used to communicate a slit throat. Plutarch uses σφάζω and its cognates to communicate this idea. See Plutarch, *Dion.* 57.2; *Oth.* 2.3; *Vit. pud.* 4; *Amat. narr.* 3 (twice).

[8] Beth A. Berkowitz, *Execution and Invention: Death Penalty Discourse in Early Rabbinic and Christian Cultures* (Oxford: Oxford University Press, 2006), 162.

[9] Peter Garnsey, "Why Penalties Become Harsher: The Roman Case, Late Republic to Fourth Century Empire," *Natural Law Forum* 143 (1968): 147.

execution by decapitation."[10] Some NT scholars, moreover, have been quick to establish the extremeness of crucifixion by contrasting it with the simplicity of other forms of punishment.[11]

It is important to observe, however, that such claims that label beheading as the "most honorable" and "least degrading" form of execution are asserted, not in an absolute sense, but relatively. The degradation of beheading could be mitigated when it was performed quickly and discreetly "at the edge of town" to a citizen of status, especially as a contrast to the *summa supplicia* ("extreme punishments").[12] Rome often distributed punishment unequally between those of varying social ranks in order to maintain these distinctions even in death.[13] Executions in the Roman arena in the early Empire, for instance, upheld social stratifications by allocating types of punishment according to status.[14] Under such conditions, beheading could be construed (1) as a compressed form of dishonor, not void of dishonor altogether, (2) as an ideal manner of execution in relation to other methods, not as an ideal in itself, or (3) as a privilege of class status, not as an indicator of a virtuous death. Thus, although beheading *could* represent one's preferred manner of death on occasion—especially when confronted with what is perceived to be a more severe alternative—we are not

---

[10] Kathleen M. Coleman, "Fatal Charades: Roman Executions Staged as Mythological Enactments," *JRS* 80 (1990): 55.

[11] In reference to Mark 15:12–14, Lane (*Mark*, 556) comments: "Both the leaders of the people and the inflamed crowd demanded not simply capital punishment, but the most ignominious [sic] form of death, crucifixion." Cf. Craig A. Evans, *Mark 8:27–16:20*, WBC 34B (Nashville: Thomas Nelson, 2000), 484.

[12] Donald G. Kyle, *Spectacles of Death in Ancient Rome* (London: Routledge, 1998), 53. Similarly, Thomas Wiedemann, *Emperors and Gladiators* (London: Routledge, 1992), 69.

[13] Berkowitz, *Execution and Invention*, 153: "A criminal condemned to death in the Roman Empire might, among other penalties, end up either decapitated, exposed to wild beasts, crucified, burned alive, or condemned to be a gladiator, depending on his or her social status and on the nature of the crime." It is common to explain the variegated executions of Peter (crucifixion) and Paul (decapitation) by detailing the different forms of punishment imposed on Roman citizens versus non-citizens. See Valerio Marotta, "St. Paul's Death: Roman Citizenship and Summa Supplicia," in *The Last Years of Paul: Essays from the Tarragona Conference, June 2013*, ed. Armand Puig i Tàrrech and John M. G. Barclay, WUNT 352 (Tübingen: Mohr Siebeck, 2015), 247–69.

[14] J. C. Edmondson, "Dynamic Arenas: Gladiatorial Presentations in the City of Rome and the Construction of Roman Society during the Early Empire," in *Roman Theatre and Society*, ed. W. J. Slater (Ann Arbor: University of Michigan Press, 1996), 96–97: "To be condemned *ad gladium* (i.e., to decapitation by the sword) was less demeaning socially than to be crucified or burnt alive, which in turn were less demeaning punishments than to be condemned *ad bestias*. The normal result was death in all cases, but the niceties of social stratification had to be preserved even in death." Kyle (*Spectacles of Death*, 128) is thus convincing when he contends that the Epicurean concept of death as the great equalizer of individuals is not altogether true of all Roman thought.

dealing with a spectrum from dishonorable to honorable bodily injury, but with varying degrees of degradation.[15]

Although an important qualification, this relegation of beheading to the fringes of severity in relation to other corporeal punishments nevertheless fails to accentuate how and why the separation of a head from its body represented a degrading—and sometimes severely degrading—form of bodily mutilation. In this chapter, therefore, I seek to address this void by offering several points of nuance that highlight the degrading nature of ancient decapitations in the general context of John the Baptist. Three considerations in this regard are particularly important as they underscore elements of beheading vital for understanding the early reception of John's death: the inferiorization of the victim in relation to the perpetrator, the intersection of beheading and notions of life hereafter, and the public spectacle of the severed head.

Degradation of Beheading

As an initial remark, severing a head from its body was not necessarily a "quick" undertaking. The employment of swords, axes, or knives in the moment of detaching a head from the body did not by default imply a clean, "painless" cut with one swift stroke of the instrument. Epictetus mentions a certain Lateranus (whom Nero ordered to be beheaded) who had to offer his neck a second time because the first blow did not achieve its purpose: "For he stretched out his neck and received the blow, but, as it was a feeble one, he shrank back for an instant, and then stretched out his neck again" (Epictetus, *Diatr.* 1.1.19–20).[16] Further, in some circumstances beheading formed

---

[15] Although not an example of a Roman beheading, Plutarch's discussion of an unnamed Carian's decapitation is illustrative. According to Plutarch, *Art.* 14, the mother of Artaxerxes objects to the king regarding his command to have a certain Carian beheaded: "O, King, do not let this accursed Carian off so easily, but leave him to me, and he shall receive the fitting reward for his daring words" (Perrin, LCL). Upon the mother's appeal, the executioners instead rack the Carian on a wheel for a duration of ten days, gouge out his eyes, and then pour molten brass into his ears until he dies. The mother's comment does not reveal that beheading lacked severity, only that beheading in this particular circumstance was not a severe enough penalty.

[16] Oldfather, LCL. Judith's decapitation of Holofernes took more than one cut: "And she struck into his neck twice in her strength and took off his head from him" (Jdt 13:8 LXX). Archaeological evidence of decapitated inhumations in early and late Roman Britain correspond to the literary descriptions of beheadings varying between one or more strokes. For details, see Dorothy Watts, *Religion in Late Roman Britain: Forces of Change* (London: Routledge, 1998), 74–95; Katie Tucker, "'Whence This Severance of the Head?': The Osteology and Archaeology of Human Decapitation in Britain" (PhD thesis, University of Winchester, 2012), 109–33. Modern case studies likewise might suggest that severing a head from its body was not necessarily easy. See, e.g., Kamil Hakan Dogan, "Decapitation and Dismemberment of the Corpse: A Matricide Case," *Journal of Forensic Science* 55 (2010): 542–45, who reports seventy-one wounds to the head and back of a decapitated victim.

part of a complex series of ritualized violence, such as when it was combined with other forms of degrading harm: flogging,[17] crucifixion and/or impalement,[18] dragging,[19] and the dismemberment and mutilation of other parts of the body.[20] In these respects, beheading could conform to the ancient correspondence between a slow death and a shameful death.[21]

Perhaps not surprisingly, then, decapitation was not universally recognized as an "unaggravated" form of Roman execution. Following crucifixion and burning someone alive, Callistratus describes beheading as an extreme punishment (*Dig.* 48.19.28). Similarly, the *Pauli Sententiae* indicates crucifixion, burning, and beheading as the *summa supplicia* (*PS.* 5.17.2). Thus, O'Collins' description of decapitation as one of the "aggravated methods of execution" in Roman society is not without ancient precedent.[22] Further, even if some ancients carried out certain beheadings to minimize the humiliation that the victim faced, this did not preclude that others would perceive it through the filter of shame. According to m. Sanh. 7:3, decapitation was carried out thusly by the Jewish court:

> B. They would cut off his head with a sword,
> C. just as the government does.
> D. R. Judah says, "This is disgusting."

---

[17] See, e.g., Appian, *Hist. rom.* 3.9.5; Diodorus of Sicily, *Lib. Hist.* 36.4; 38.8; Dionysius of Halicarnassus, *Ant. Rom.* 3.58.4; 5.61.3; Livy, *Ab urbe cond.* 2.5; Plutarch, *Publ.* 6.99; Polybius, *Hist.* 1.7.12. In the Greek examples, the "scourging" appears as an aorist circumstantial participle and the "beheading" appears as an aorist (in)finite verb. Both actions are thus linked together as a coterminous event. I refrain from including *P. Oxy.* 22.2339 among these examples. It mentions that a judge was "about to behead" (μέλλοντες κεφαλίσαι) a certain Apollodotus (1.6). The judge then orders him to be scourged: καὶ ἐκέλευσεν αὐτὸν φλαγέλλας μαστιγωθῆναι (1.10–11). The two punishments are thus not combined. For a helpful transcription of the papyrus and for links to high resolution images, see http://www.papyri.info/hgv/25937.

[18] See, e.g., Gen 40:19; Philo, *Ios.* 96, 98; *Somn.* 2.213; Josephus, *Ant.* 6.374; 15.8–9; Herodotus, *Hist.* 8.21.3; Polybius, *Hist.* 8.21.3; cf. Dio Cassius, *Hist. rom.* 49.22.6; Plutarch, *Ant.* 36.

[19] See, e.g., Josephus, *War* 2.246.

[20] See, e.g., 2 Macc 15:30–33; Tacitus, *Hist.* 3.74.

[21] Martin Zimmermann ("Conclusion: Violence in Late Antiquity Reconsidered," in *Violence in Late Antiquity: Perceptions and Practices*, ed. H. A. Drake [Aldershot: Ashgate, 2006], 356, quoting Seneca, *Ira.* 1.6.4) claims that "[Seneca] took it for granted that the criminal should not die quickly but should suffer for a period commensurate to the gravity of his deed. The good lawmaker and statesmen should provide for a 'shameful and slow end' of those sentenced to death." Cf. Rhiannon Graybill, *Are We Not Men? Unstable Masculinity in the Hebrew Prophets* (Oxford: Oxford University Press, 2016), 3, who observes concerning Isa 20:1–5: "The complement to pain in Isaiah 20 is shame.... The abstract sign of shame depends upon the specific shaming of the prophet's body, through its exposure, its vulnerability, and its suffering."

[22] O'Collins, "Crucifixion," 1207. Cf. Tertullian, *Mart.* 4.9.

E. "But they put his head on a block and chop it off with an ax."
F. They said to him, "There is no form of death more disgusting than this one."[23]

Berkowitz appeals to m. Sanh. 7 to bolster her claim that the Jewish experience of Roman execution influenced rabbinic laws of execution.[24] She contends that the respective disputants "each wish to protect the criminal's body from indignity as best as possible."[25] However, what is important to underline for our purposes is that the Sages' proposal for the proper method of carrying out beheading is perceived by another (Rabbi Judah) as most disgraceful, and vice versa.

Rome, furthermore, could behead those who held a high social status in a bid to dishonor them. Emperor Claudius once sentenced a Roman tribune named Celer to beheading: "Celer he sent back to Hierosolyma in chains, and directed that he be handed over to the Judeans for torture and that, after he had been dragged around the city, in this way (οὕτω) his head be hacked off" (Josephus, *War* 2.246).[26] Mason observes the implication that the adverb οὕτω ("in this way") makes explicit: "This beheading, after torture and humiliation by foreigners, following the months-long journey back to Judea in anticipation, would be an extreme form of degradation for the tribune."[27] Antony's decision to behead Antigonus Mattathias emanated directly from the need to disgrace his memory:

> He [Antony] was the first Roman who decided to behead a king, since he believed that in no other way could he change the attitude of the Jews so that they would accept Herod, who had been appointed in his [Antigonus'] place. For not even under torture would they submit to proclaiming him king, so highly did they regard their former king. And so he thought that the disgrace (τὴν ἀτιμίαν) would somewhat dim their memory of him and would also lessen their hatred of Herod. (*Ant.* 15.9–10)[28]

Appian makes the following remark in his portrayal of the beheading of two Roman generals: "Sulla did not spare them because they were Romans, but

---

[23] Jacob Neusner, trans., *The Mishnah: A New Translation* (New Haven: Yale University Press, 1991).
[24] Berkowitz, *Execution and Invention*, 153–79.
[25] Berkowitz, *Execution and Invention*, 160.
[26] Josephus, *J.W.* 2.246 (Mason).
[27] Steve Mason, trans. and ed., *Flavius Josephus: Translation and Commentary*, vol. 1B: *Judean War 2* (Leiden: Brill, 2008), 199, n. 1545.
[28] Thackeray et al., LCL. Cf. Dio Cassius, *Hist. rom.* 49.22.6; Plutarch, *Ant.* 36. Cicero criticizes Verres (governor of Sicily) because "[Verres] had men of high rank and stainless character actually beheaded" (*Verr.* 4.64.144 [Greenwood, LCL]).

killed them both and sent their heads (τὰς κεφαλάς) to Lucretius at Praeneste to be displayed round the walls" (*Rom. Hist. Civ.* 1.10.93).[29]

Inferiority of the Victim and Superiority of the Perpetrator

The removal of the head from its body constituted a loss of identity, self-control, and virtue on the part of the victim; simultaneously, it represented an assertion of virtue, control, and enhanced esteem on the part of the perpetrator. The very physiology of the act positions the perpetrator as the possessor of power and victory, while stressing the victim's powerlessness. Insofar as "self-control" over one's body and "control" over others were hallmark characteristics of many elite ideals of masculinity in the Greco-Roman world, beheading was an integrally gendered phenomenon.[30] It could highlight the emasculation of the male victim—who now lacked somatic autonomy—and/or affirm the manliness of the victor—who now possessed control over the victim's head and body.[31] As Riess avers: "Whoever dominates another person or exerts violence against him or her is often physically and maybe also socially and economically superior and, thus, constructs the victim as weaker and inferior."[32] In this vein, honor and shame, vice and virtue, and power and powerlessness go hand in hand in the act of decapitation. To cast the "shadow" of inferiority on someone involves shining the "light" of superiority on someone else. This understanding of beheading is due in no small part to the symbolic importance of the human head. As the locus of recognition, one's head and one's identity are indelibly linked.[33] "[The head] symbolizes, like no other body-part, the person as a whole."[34] In this respect, the maiming of a person by separating their head from the rest of their body anonymizes the dead and acclaims the identity of the self.[35] It symbolizes the prestige of the victor at the expense of the loser.

[29] White, LCL. See also Velleius Paterculus, *Comp. Rom. Hist.* 2.27.3.
[30] On "(self-)control" as the chief virtue of many Greco-Roman conceptualizations of masculinity, see Colleen Conway, *Behold the Man: Jesus and Greco-Roman Masculinity* (Oxford: Oxford University Press, 2008), 15–34; Brittany E. Wilson, *Unmanly Men: Refigurations of Masculinity in Luke-Acts* (Oxford: Oxford University Press, 2015), 39–75; Susanna Asikainen, *Jesus and Other Men: Ideal Masculinities in the Synoptic Gospels*, BibInt 159 (Leiden: Brill, 2018), 19–45.
[31] See Rita Dolce, *"Losing One's Head" in the Ancient Near East: Interpretation and Meaning of Decapitation* (London: Routledge, 2018), 3, who observes that "a 'loss of self-control'" is "a meaning inherent from the outset in the condition of anyone who 'loses their head,' in either the metaphorical or the real sense."
[32] Riess, introduction to *Topography of Violence in the Greco-Roman World*, 3.
[33] Miranda Aldhouse-Green, "Chaining and Shaming: Images of Defeat, From Llyn Cerrig Bach to Sarmitzegetusa," *OJA* 23 (2004): 330.
[34] Hartmann, *Der Tod Johannes des Täufers*, 191 (translation mine).
[35] Virgil (*Aen.* 2.557–558) describes the separation of Priam's head from his body as that which anonymizes him: "He lies, a huge trunk upon the shore, a head severed from the neck, a corpse without a name (*sine nomine corpus*)!" (Fairclough, LCL).

This hierarchical positioning of the perpetrator over the beheaded victim is perceptible in several cases. Plutarch refers to a report that held a certain Fabius Fabulus as the one who beheaded Galba. Due to his inability to carry Galba's head by his hair (Galba was bald), he wraps it in his cloak. Fabius' companions urge him to publicly display his "deed of valour" (ἀνδραγαθίαν), or as I would translate it, his "*manly* virtue" (*Galb.* 27).[36] Fabius then proceeds to impale the head on a spear. To recontextualize Kloppenborg's phraseology: "Unseen honor is no honor at all."[37] Judith's heroics in cutting off Holofernes' head lead her to be blessed by the elders and every woman of Israel (Jdt 15:8–10, 12), afforded plunder (Jdt 15:11), celebrated in song (Jdt 16:1–17), and honored for the rest of her life (Jdt 16:21). "The all-controlling (παντοκράτωρ) Lord has set them aside by the hand of a woman (ἐν χειρὶ θηλείας)" (Jdt 16:5). Here, the virtue of the Lord is rendered visible by Judith's beheading of Holofernes. By contrast, the Assyrians react in horror at the sight of the general's headless body (Jdt 14:14–19; 15:1–3). According to Judith 14:18, the eunuch Bagoas exclaims, "One woman (μία γυνή) of the Hebrews has brought shame (αἰσχύνην) into the house of King Nebuchadnezzar, because (ὅτι) behold, Holofernes [is] on the ground and his head is not on him (ἡ κεφαλὴ οὐκ ἐστιν ἐπ' αὐτῷ)."

First Samuel 5:1–5 paints a picture of the superiority of YHWH to Dagon. After the Philistines capture the ark of God and place it in the house of Dagon, they awake on two occasions to witness Dagon fallen in a position of inferiority before the ark. On the second occasion, the text reads, "Dagon had fallen on his face to the ground before the ark of the Lord, and the head of Dagon and both his hands were lying cut off upon the threshold" (1 Sam 5:4 NRSV). Psalm 151 LXX juxtaposes David's beheading of the foreigner (i.e., Goliath) with removing "the disgrace" (ὄνειδος) from Israel.[38] Similarly, the Syriac text of the psalm reads, "But after I unsheathed his sword, I cut off his head; and I removed the shame from the sons of Israel."[39] Josephus' account of the death of Jebosthos (*Ant.* 7.46–52) mentions that the two Benjamites killed and beheaded Jebosthos to elevate their social status and procure security:

> [They] reckoned that if they killed Jebosthos they would receive great gifts (δωρεῶν) from David and that their deed would bring them a military command (στρατηγίας) or some other mark of confidence (τινος ἄλλης πίστεως) from him. . . . They made their

---

[36] LSJ, s.v. "ἀνδραγαθία" defines the noun as "manly virtue." "Deed of valour" is the translation of Perrin, LCL.
[37] John S. Kloppenborg, *Christ's Associations: Connecting and Belonging in the Ancient City* (New Haven: Yale University Press, 2019), 44.
[38] BDAG, s.v. "ὄνειδος," offers the following definition for the term ὄνειδος: "loss of standing connected with disparaging speech."
[39] Ps 151B:2 (5ApocSyrPs 1b) (Charlesworth, *OTP* 2:615).

way into the particular room where Saul's son lay asleep, and killed him. Then they cut off his head and, travelling a whole night and day with the thought of fleeing from those whom they had wronged to one who would accept their deed as a kindness and offer them security (ἀσφάλειαν), they came to Hebron. Here they showed the head of Jebosthos to David and presented themselves as his well-wishers, who had removed his enemy and rival for the kingdom. (*Ant.* 7.47–49)[40]

Seneca refers to the boast of Volesus: "Only recently Volesus, governor of Asia under the deified Augustus, beheaded three hundred persons in one day, and as he strutted among the corpses with the proud air of one who had done some glorious deed worth beholding, he cried out in Greek, 'What a kingly act!'" (*Ira.* 2.5.5).[41] When Perseus utilizes Medusa's severed head to defeat Andromeda (the sea serpent), as Malamud says, Ovid makes it clear that "Perseus, new owner of the head, has assumed the Gorgon's petrifying power."[42] The owner of the severed head has procured power by divesting the victim of control. Or, as Voisin puts it in reference to Roman head-hunting, "to cut off the head of an enemy is to appropriate an other's energy that adds to and reinforces one's own superiority."[43]

As a final example, the tombstone of Insus son of Vodullus similarly exhibits triumphalism at the expense of the defeated. The stone, unearthed in Lancaster, England, in 2005 by the University of Manchester Archeological Unit, measures between two and three meters in height, nearly one meter in width, and weighs nearly fifteen hundred pounds.[44] It depicts a Roman horseman holding both a sword and a barbarian's decapitated head in his right hand. Beneath the victor's right foot kneels the barbarian's headless corpse. The inscription written beneath the depiction commemorates Insus by using triumphant terminology:

DIS MANIBVS INSVS VODVLLI [. . .] CIVE TREVER EQVES ALAE AVG [.] VICTORIS CVRATOR DOMITIA [. . .]

To the shades of the dead. Insus son of Vodullus, citizen of the Treveri, cavalryman of the *ala Augusta*, troop of Victor, *curator*, his heir had this set up.[45]

---

[40] Marcus, LCL.
[41] Basore, LCL.
[42] Martha Malamud, "Pompey's Head and Cato's Snakes," *CP* 98 (2003): 31.
[43] Jean-Louis Voisin, "Les Romains, chasseurs de têtes," in *Du châtiment dans la cité. Supplices corporels et peine de mort dans le monde antique*, Table ronde de Rome (9–11 novembre 1982) (Rome: École Française de Rome, 1984), 274 (translation mine).
[44] Stephen Bull, *Triumphant Rider: The Lancaster Roman Cavalry Tombstone* (Lancaster: Lancashire Museums, 2007).
[45] Inscription and translation provided by Bull, *Triumphant Rider*, 10.

68   A Dangerous Parting

Bull captures how the postures of the two figures casts them in a superior-inferior relationship: "Apart from the decapitated condition, the fallen barbarian['s] ... position of abasement, crumpled, small, and partially naked is deliberate. The beard and long hair of his decapitated head ... show his barbarism and uncivilized status. His abject defeat is further emphasised by the foot of Insus which appears to rest on the small of his back."[46] This commemorative artifact, therefore, can be construed according to what Aldhouse-Green (in reference to Trajan's Column and the Bridgeness slab from the Antonine Wall) calls "the triumph of *romanitas*" and the "'grammar' of defeat."[47]

Beheading, Burial, and Life in the Hereafter

The beheading of a corpse and the postmortem manipulation of a severed head could ridicule the dead not only in the protracted moments surrounding death and burial, but also in life in the hereafter. I use the term "hereafter" broadly to encompass variegated ideologies of death in Greek, Roman, Jewish, and Christian frameworks, including notions of an afterlife in a realm of the dead (e.g., the underworld), a resuscitated existence on earth of a recently deceased person, and an eschatological embodied resurrection of the dead. Of course, space does not permit a comprehensive analysis of such discursive frameworks.[48] Instead, for present purposes, we will focus on their ideological intersection with the specter of mutilated and dismembered bodies.

The social requisite of properly disposing the dead in the ancient world is a well-known truism.[49] "All societies use culturally appropriate rituals of

---

[46] Bull, *Triumphant Rider*, 18.

[47] Aldhouse-Green, "Chaining and Shaming," 328–30.

[48] In addition to the studies cited in this discussion, see, e.g., Alan F. Segal, *Life after Death: A History of the Afterlife in Western Religion* (New York: Doubleday, 2004); Jan Assmann, *Death and Salvation in Ancient Egypt*, trans. David Lorton (Ithaca, N.Y.: Cornell University Press, 2005); Alexander Achilles Fischer, *Tod und Jenseits im Alten Orient und Alten Testament* (Neukirchen-Vluyn: Neukirchener Verlag, 2005); Nicola Laneri, ed., *Performing Death: Social Analyses of Funerary Traditions in the Ancient Near East and Mediterranean* (Chicago: Oriental Institute of the University of Chicago, 2007). For primary data on the range of Roman beliefs concerning the afterlife, see especially Valerie M. Hope, *Death in Ancient Rome: A Sourcebook* (London: Routledge, 2007), 211–47.

[49] Homer, *Il.* 22.337–343, indicates that Hector begged Achilles to return his body home for proper disposal instead of letting the dogs devour it. The Levitical code allowed Israelite priests—who were otherwise instructed not to have contact with a corpse—to bury their close family (Lev 21:1–9; cf. 21:10–15). The Twelve Tables' injunction on burning or burying bodies within the city limits, the tombs and monuments on the peripheries that visitors first saw when visiting Rome, the elaborate funeral procession for the death of noblemen, and the popularity of burial clubs for those with modest means—all of these features attest to the weight ancient Romans placed on properly caring for the dead. See Keith Hopkins, *Death and Renewal*, Sociological Studies in Roman History 2 (Cambridge: Cambridge University Press, 1983), 201–55; Kyle, *Spectacles of Death*, 13. See also Matt 8:21–22; Luke 9:59–60. In addition to ancient Greece, Rome, and Israel, the importance of

separation or rites of passage to come to terms with the emotional intensity of killing and death, to lay the dead to rest, and . . . to restore the social fabric and let the living move on."[50] Accordingly, it is by observing death that we can illuminate individual and group anxieties about life. As Metcalf and Huntington explain: "Life becomes transparent against the background of death, and fundamental social and cultural issues are revealed."[51] One such social and cultural issue that mortuary rituals reveal in the Greek and Roman worlds in particular is that many believed they could influence their social and cultural position in the afterlife.[52] For example, with respect to Petronius, *Sat.* 71, one historian has observed that the prearrangements of "Trimalchio for his funeral and the care of his grave reveal a common Roman perception that people could influence their status and care after death."[53]

Significantly, therefore, when the living did not bury the dead, they prevented the dead from possessing a favorable transition into the afterlife.[54] After his death, the spirit of Patroclus visited Achilles as the latter slept, beseeching Achilles to bury him in speed so that he may "pass within the gates of Hades" (*Il.* 23.65–74)[55] Patroclus was thus unable to join the other dead on the other side of the river until he had been buried. Similarly, Virgil recounts that the ferryman Charon is not able to transport the unburied dead across the banks of the waters "until their bones have found a resting place" (*Aen.* 6.327–328).[56]

---

coming to terms with death is similarly palpable in ancient Mesopotamia, Egypt, Anatolia, and Syria. See Robert Garland, *The Greek Way of Death* (London: Duckworth, 1985), 1–37; Hiroshi Obayashi, ed., *Death and Afterlife: Perspectives of World Religions*, Contributions to the Study of Religion 33 (New York: Greenwood Press, 1992); Byron R. McCane, *Roll Back the Stone: Death and Burial in the World of Jesus* (Harrisburg, Penn.: Trinity Press International, 2003); John J. Collins et al., "Death, the Afterlife, and Other Last Things," in *Religions of the Ancient World: A Guide*, ed. Sarah Iles Johnston (Cambridge, Mass.: Belknap Press, 2004), 470–95.

[50] Kyle, *Spectacles of Death*, 1–2.

[51] Peter Metcalf and Richard Huntington, *Celebrations of Death: The Anthropology of Mortuary Ritual*, 2nd ed. (Cambridge: Cambridge University Press, 1991), 2. Douglas J. Davies, *A Brief History of Death* (Oxford: Blackwell, 2005), 1: "The history of death is a history of self-reflection. Who are we?"

[52] Cf. William J. Murnane ("Taking It with You: The Problem of Death and Afterlife in Ancient Egypt," in Obayashi, *Death and Afterlife*, 35) observes that the ancient Egyptian pharaohs had endowments established "to pay the mortuary priests who provided for the eternal well-being of the deceased's spirit."

[53] Kyle, *Spectacles of Death*, 141. On p. 128 of the same study, Kyle writes: "Ancient cemeteries show that the kingdom of the dead was not an egalitarian realm."

[54] J. M. C. Toynbee, *Death and Burial in the Roman World* (Baltimore: Johns Hopkins University Press, 1971), 43: "To leave a corpse unburied had unpleasant repercussions on the fate of the departed soul."

[55] Murray, LCL.

[56] Fairclough, LCL.

70   A Dangerous Parting

But a favorable transition into the afterlife was also prevented when the integrity of the body necessary for proper burial was violated, as in cases of corpse abuse, mutilation, and dissolution.[57] "Treatment of corpses remained one of the means by which men could hurt, humiliate, or honour one another, express contempt or respect."[58] Hence, as the Trojans and Greeks struggled for the possession of Patroclus' corpse, Iris arrived from Olympus imploring Achilles to protect Patroclus' dead body. Iris stressed Hector's eagerness "to cut the head from the tender neck and fix it on the stakes of the wall" and Achilles' consequent "reproach, if [Patroclus] comes to us a corpse mutilated in any way" (*Il.* 18.176–180).[59] In his *Satires* (3.254–267), Juvenal describes a man whose body was crushed by a wagon-full of rocks. No trace of remaining limbs or bones were found. Accordingly, Juvenal writes that the man "is already a newcomer sitting on the bank, shuddering at the hideous ferryman. The wretched man has no hopes of a bark across the muddy torrent, because he doesn't have a coin in his mouth to offer" (*Sat.* 3.264–267).[60]

In such contexts where properly burying an intact cadaver was a vital social obligation and a factor in the favorable transition of the deceased to an afterlife mode of existence, beheading, as a method of violating the integrity of the human body, could be perceived as interrupting normal mortuary practices surrounding the deceased and tarnishing the social well-being of the victim past the point of death.[61] Consider the description of Sulla's proscriptions in the aftermath of the Battle at the Colline Gate in Rome (82 B.C.E.) in Lucan's *De Bello Civili*:

> When the heads, dissolving in corruption and effaced by lapse
> of time, had lost all distinctive features, their wretched parents
> gathered the relics they recognized and stealthily removed them.
> I remember how I myself, seeking to place on the funeral fire

---

[57] Jean-Pierre Vernant, "La belle mort et le cadavre outragé," in *La mort, les morts dans les sociétés anciennes*, ed. Gherardo Gnoli and Jean-Pierre Vernant (Paris: Éditions de la Maison des sciences de l'homme, 1990), 67: "The purpose of funerary practices is revealed with the most clearness precisely where they are failing, and chiefly where they are ritually denied, in the procedures of insulting the enemy's cadaver" (translation mine).

[58] Robert Parker, *Miasma: Pollution and Purification in Early Greek Religion* (Oxford: Clarendon Press, 1983), 46. Herodotus (*Hist.* 7.238) writes about Xerxes' treatment of the dead body of Leonidas: "Having thus spoken, Xerxes passed over the place where the dead lay; and hearing that Leonidas had been king and general of the Lacedaemonians, he bade cut off his head and impale it. It is plain to me by this especial proof among many others, that while Leonidas lived king Xerxes was more incensed against him than against all others; else had he never dealt so outrageously with his dead body; for the Persians are of all men known to me the most wont to honour valiant warriors" (Godley, LCL).

[59] Murray, LCL.

[60] Braund, LCL.

[61] Similarly, Aldhouse-Green, "Chaining and Shaming," 330.

denied them the shapeless features of my murdered brother, scrutinised all the corpses slain by Sulla's peace: round all the headless bodies I went, seeking for a neck to fit the severed head. (*Civ. W.* 2.166–173)[62]

This text connects the quest to *reunite* the severed head and headless body with the intent to *properly* dispose of the dead. The separation of the head from its body, and its concomitant consequences (diachronic defacement and an anonymized neck), represented an obstacle to such intentions.[63] Hinard, moreover, cogently associates the loss of recognition of a decapitated person during Sulla's proscriptions with the loss of recognition and status in the realm of the dead.[64]

The anxiety for the reunion of the bodiless head and headless body in burial is also apparent in Tacitus' description of the burials of Piso and Titus Vinius (69 C.E.):

He [Otho] was then carried through the heaps of dead bodies, while the forum still reeked with blood, first to the Capitol and then to the Palatine; after that he allowed the bodies to be given up for burial and burning. Piso was laid to rest by his wife Verania and his brother Scribonianus, Titus Vinius by his daughter Crispina, after they had discovered and redeemed their heads, which the assassins had kept for profit. (*Hist.* 1.47)[65]

The apprehension at the possibility of corpse abuse by decapitation, furthermore, sometimes prompted individuals to make arrangements before their deaths so that they were not buried mutilated.[66] Perhaps the most well-known example of this anxiety is Nero, who "made his companions promise, first and above all else, that no one was to have his head, but to arrange somehow that he be buried unmutilated" (Suetonius, *Nero* 49).[67] Thus, beheading was not always a method "of execution" in the ancient world. The ancients frequently

---

[62] Duff, LCL. See Elaine Fantham, ed., *Lucan. De Bello Civili. Book II.* (Cambridge: Cambridge University Press, 1992), 111: "An individual survivor, not the poet, is reporting."
[63] As Mark Thorne ("*Memoria Redux*: Memory in Lucan," in *Brill's Companion to Lucan*, ed. Paolo Asso [Leiden: Brill, 2011], 372) puts it, the severed head undercuts "attempts to memorialize the dead."
[64] François Hinard, "La male mort. Exécutions et statut du corps au moment de la première proscription," in *Du châtiment dans la cité*, 308–9.
[65] Moore, LCL. For further evidence that demonstrates the importance of reuniting a head with its body for burial, see Tacitus, *Hist.* 1.41, 49; Suetonius, *Galb.* 20; Plutarch, *Galb.* 28.
[66] See Hope, *Death in Ancient Rome*, 42–43.
[67] As quoted in Hope, *Death in Ancient Rome*, 43.

beheaded those who had already died.⁶⁸ They could leave dismembered heads/bodies unburied, often as food for birds and wild animals, or similarly throw the heads/bodies in a sea or river as food for fish.⁶⁹

Some social constructions of life in the hereafter involved the idea that the dead replicated in the afterlife their physical wounds and honor/shame from their moment of death. Many Romans and Greeks thought that the soul retained "the marks and mood of the moment of death."⁷⁰ In his discussion of the Greeks' views of life in Hades, Garland vividly describes fallen warriors

---

⁶⁸ See, e.g., Herodotus, *Hist.* 7.238; Velleius Paterculus, *Comp. Rom. Hist.* 2.119.1–5; Tacitus, *Ann.* 14.64; Josephus, *Ant.* 9.125–131; 14.448–450, 464; *War* 1.323–326, 342–343. An example from the HB is the explicit beheading of Saul's corpse in 1 Sam 31:1–13 (cf. Josephus, *Ant.* 6.368–378). The corresponding passage in 1 Chr 10:1–14 (1 Chr 10:1–14 LXX) implicitly makes this suggestion. First Chronicles 10:10 does make it clear that Saul did indeed lose his head (the Philistines display it in their temple). But the verbal expression וישאו ("and they took") in relationship to the direct object ראשו ("his head") in 1 Chr 10:9 does not readily translate into "they took *off* his head." Admittedly, נשא ("to take") appears in a <verb + direct object> relationship with ראש ("head") in Gen 40:19 to describe the beheading of Pharaoh's chief baker: "In three days Pharaoh will take up your head from upon you." In the context of Gen 40:19, however, the notion of separation—that is, taking the head up and off the chief baker—is supplied by the prepositional phrase מעליך ("from upon you") (cf. Gen 40:13, where the chief cupbearer's head is "lifted up" in the sense that he is restored to office). Thus, the imagery of a beheading disappears from Gen 40:19 without the presence of מעליך ("from upon you"). Comparably, 4Q163 (4Qpap pIsaᶜ) frgs. 4–6 col. I 6 has the preposition מן ("from") prefixed to ישראל ("Israel") to convey the idea of separation, that is, cutting off a head *from* Israel: "And YHWH has cut off from Israel (מישראל) head and tail" (trans. Florentino Garcia Martínez and Eibert Tigchelaar, in *The Dead Sea Scrolls: Study Edition*, vol. 1 [Leiden: Brill, 1997]). In this respect, since the clause in 1 Chr 10:9 lacks the idea of separation, it is best to conclude that 1 Chr 10:9 does not portray the moment of Saul's beheading. In attempting to infer when Saul lost his head in this account, therefore, one option is to suppose the Chronicler expects the reader to "fill in the gaps" of the narrative by assuming the Philistines first beheaded Saul before "they took his head" to the temple. A second option is also to "fill in the gaps" and suppose that Saul managed to behead himself when he "fell on his own sword" (1 Chr 10:4). In this light, it is interesting to notice that the Babylonian Talmud contains a tradition that draws a parallel between Saul falling "on his own sword" and being punished in his "neck" (b. Sotah 10a). No Jewish interpretive tradition to my knowledge, however, explicitly claims that Saul lost his head the moment he hit his neck on the sword. It seems best, therefore, to treat 1 Chr 10:1–14 as implying that the Philistines beheaded Saul's corpse before "taking" it. See further, Ralph W. Klein, *1 Chronicles*, Hermeneia (Minneapolis: Fortress, 2006), 287: "The Chronicler has reworded his *Vorlage* in 1 Sam 31:9. . . . The rest of the Chronicler's account, in any case, presupposes that Saul's head had been cut off and no further attention is given to the stripping of the king." By contrast, 1 Kgdms 31:1–13 LXX does not portray Saul losing his head at all. In this text, the Philistines take and fasten Saul's body (σῶμα) to the wall of Beth Shan (31:10).

⁶⁹ See, e.g., Gen 40:19; 2 Macc 15:30–33; Appian, *Samn. Hist.* 3.9.3; Tacitus, *Hist.* 3.74. On birds preventing burial by consuming the human body, see Suetonius, *Aug.* 13.2: "For instance, to one man who begged humbly for burial, [Octavian] is said to have replied: 'The birds will soon settle that question'" (Rolfe, LCL).

⁷⁰ Kyle, *Spectacles of Death*, 129.

as "eternally blood-bespattered."[71] The dead who converse with Odysseus in Hades are preoccupied with "the memory of their life or the shame they experienced in the manner of their death."[72] This idea that a physically injured body could affect the victim in the afterlife finds expression in a late second- or early third-century C.E. anonymous text from Egypt. One scholar describes the papyrus as offering "the grisliest description of the underworld to come down to us from antiquity."[73] The text mentions the visitor in the underworld at the Shores of Ugliness beholding the corpses of those beheaded:

> So swiftly he came to that toilsome land, the Shores of Ugliness. There, sitting on a rock, when he had bound a reed with corpse's hair, he took bait and feeding the hook sent it down to the deepest depths. Yet when he drew forth the swimming hair, since he could then catch nothing at all. . . . For stretched around there lay a vast plain, full of corpses of dreadful doom, beheaded (πελεκιζομένων) or crucified. Above the ground stood pitiable bodies, their throats but lately cut. Others, again, impaled, hung like the trophies of a cruel destiny. The Furies, crowned with wreaths, were laughing at the miserable manner of the corpses' death. There was an abominable stench of gore.[74]

Two brief observations about this narration are in order. First, the dead bear a recognizable form of existence: the marks of mutilation they received in the moments of their deaths are perceptible. Something about their appearance made the manner of their death not only perceptible to the visitor but also distinguishable from other types of mutilated corpses.[75] Those that were beheaded in death retained such a mutilated existence beyond death. Second, the text notes that the corpses were the subject of continued mockery because of the manner of their death. Those that were beheaded in death retained the shame associated with beheading beyond death.[76]

---

[71] Garland, *Greek Way of Death*, 74. Similarly, Alan E. Bernstein (*The Formation of Hell: Death and Retribution in the Ancient and Early Christian Worlds* [London: UCL Press, 1993], 30) observes that, while in Hades Odysseus saw those slain in battle who were still clothed in their bloodstained armor (Homer, *Od.* 11.41).

[72] Bernstein, *Formation of Hell*, 23–33 (quotation, p. 26).

[73] Garland, *Greek Way of Death*, 76.

[74] Trans. Denys L. Page, in *Select Papyri*, vol. 3: *Poetry*, LCL 360 (Cambridge, Mass.: Harvard University Press, 1941), 421.

[75] Cf. Bernstein, *Formation of Hell*, 27, who notes that, in Odysseus' journey to the underworld, the dead do not have flesh or bone because the funeral pyre consumed them. Nevertheless, they do have a soul and an image that makes them recognizable.

[76] As another example of the dead maintaining the wounds from their death, consider Virgil's portrayal of Aeneas in the region of the underworld known as the Fields of Mourning (*Aen.* 6.440–476). The Trojan sees (1) Eriphyle "pointing to the wounds her cruel son had dealt" (*Aen.* 6.445–446) and (2) Dido "with wound still fresh" (*Aen.* 6.450) (Fairclough, LCL).

While the mutilated dead frequently replicated their dismembered figure in their afterlife abode of existence, the resumption of life in the self-same body on earth was, for a beheaded person, impossible. Of course, the ostensible resuscitation or revivification of a recently deceased corpse was not unknown in the ancient world, especially in Jewish tradition. The prophets Elijah and Elisha were both said to have brought the dead back to life (1 Kgs 17:17–24; 2 Kgs 4:18–37). Jesus too held a reputation as a miracle-worker, which occasionally included reviving those thought to be dead (Mark 5:21–24, 35–43; Luke 7:11–17; John 11:1–44). But these accounts involve the resuscitation of a corpse with a fully intact body. Elisha's method of reviving the Shunammite's son, for example, included lying on the child's cadaver and touching the child's "mouth," "eyes," and "hands" with his own "mouth," "eyes," and "hands;" as the child is revived, his "flesh" warms, he "sneezes" seven times, and his "eyes" open (2 Kgs 4:34–35). The child, in other words, had a face; and if he had a face, we can safely assume the text leads us to envision that he had a head (unless we are to envisage an absurd image of Elisha reviving a face sans cranial substructure). It is not unreasonable to suggest that a severed head posed a more daunting problem to resuscitation in antiquity than death by illness or disease, for the latter did not necessarily involve the fragmentation or obliteration of the apex of the body. How could the restoration of bodily functions—breathing, seeing, eating, sneezing, walking, maintaining a vital temperature—possibly occur in cases of decapitation? How could reanimation occur when the severed head faced prolonged public exposure, decomposition, or digestion by wild animals, birds, and fish? How could vitality return to a headless corpse when the severed head was unconnected from its body's burial, stolen for profit, or otherwise transported a vast geographic distance away from its cadaver (for public display, proof of death, or as a trophy)?

The problem that beheading presented to the prospect of revivification finds indirect corroboration in early Jewish discussions of the eschatological resurrection of the dead. For some Jews, bodily mutilation posed a serious dilemma to the idea of an embodied resurrection, especially if the resurrection body had a measure of continuity with the self-same deceased body. This dilemma is perceptible as an underlying substructure in texts that frame the hope of bodily resurrection so that it overcomes the problem of a body that suffered physical violence or decomposition.[77] In the lengthy account of the martyrdom of the seven brothers with their mother in 2 Maccabees 7:1–42, the brothers undergo horrid forms of torture and death, including dismemberment, frying in a pan of fire, and scalping. After the first two brothers meet their fate, the third brother sticks out his tongue, sets forth his

---

[77] For a cogent analysis of the nature of human embodiment and resurrection in the following (and other) early Jewish texts, see especially C. D. Elledge, *Resurrection of the Dead in Early Judaism: 200 BCE–CE 200* (Oxford: Oxford University Press, 2017), 20–31.

hands, and exclaims: "I got these from Heaven . . . and from him I hope *to get them back again*" (2 Macc 7:11 NRSV, italics added). A similar account of martyrdom under Antiochus IV Epiphanes in 2 Maccabees 14:37–46 portrays Razis—gruesomely injured after failed attempts to fall on his sword and throw himself down a wall—taking his entrails in his hands and heaving them at the nearby crowd while "calling upon the Lord of life and spirit *to give them back to him again*" (2 Macc 14:46 NRSV, italics added). Both martyrs position the hope for resurrection as the solution to the problem of bodily corrosion.

Daniel's prophecy of resurrection claims that the physical remains of "those who sleep *in the dust of the earth* shall awake, some to everlasting life, and some to shame and everlasting contempt" (Dan 12:2 NRSV, italics added). As Elledge reasonably suggests, what sleeps in the dust of the earth includes "the body of the deceased wise teachers who have fallen 'by the edge of the sword or (were) burned or captured or plundered' in the preceding stages of the vision (11:33)."[78] The Similitudes of 1 Enoch promise resurrection to "those who have been *destroyed in the desert*, those who have been *devoured by wild beasts*, and those who have been *eaten by the fish of the sea*" (1 En. 61:5).[79] The *Messianic Apocalypse* (4Q521) describes the resurrection as a time when the Lord "will heal *the critically wounded*" (frg. 2 col. II 12).[80] Thus, although a mutilated body posed a problem to the notion of a bodily resurrection, it did not represent an insurmountable one: successful resurrection required a powerful act of God. Jews could overcome the dilemma of a disintegrated body by appealing to the power of the divine creator in reassembling constituent parts—bones, tendons, and flesh—and restoring the breath of life in an act of recreation (Ezek 37:1–14).[81]

[78] Elledge, *Resurrection of the Dead*, 23.
[79] E. Isaac, *OTP* 1:42.
[80] Michael O. Wise, Martin Abegg, Jr., and Edward Cook, trans., *The Dead Sea Scrolls: A New Translation* (New York: HarperCollins, 1996).
[81] "Originally," Ezek 37:1–10 did not portray a literal resurrection of individuals. As Ezek 37:11–14 makes clear, God explains the vision of dry bones to the prophet as a metaphor of the collective restoration of the nation of Israel. See especially Karin Schöpflin, "The Revivification of the Dry Bones: Ezekiel 37:1–14," in *The Human Body in Death and Resurrection: Deuterocanonical and Cognate Literature Yearbook 2009*, ed. Tobias Nicklas, Friedrich V. Reiterer, and Joseph Verheyden (Berlin: de Gruyter, 2009), 67–85. Nevertheless, Ezek 37 formed the basis of subsequent conceptualizations of a literal, embodied resurrection of individuals, such as in *Pseudo-Ezekiel* (4Q385). On *Pseudo-Ezekiel* reinterpreting Ezek 37:1–14 as a description of the future bodily resurrection, see Schöpflin, 80–83; Mladen Popović, "Bones, Bodies and Resurrection in the Dead Sea Scrolls," in Nicklas, Reiterer, and Verheyden, *Human Body in Death and Resurrection*, 230–36; Daniel W. Hayter, "'How Are the Dead Raised?' The Bodily Nature of Resurrection in Second Temple Jewish Texts," in *The Body in Biblical, Christian, and Jewish Texts*, ed. Joan E. Taylor, LSTS 85 (London: T&T Clark, 2014), 133–34. On appealing to the divine power of creation to substantiate the claim of bodily resurrection, see Elledge, *Resurrection of the Dead*, 78–82.

Christian discourse on the resurrection of the dead similarly envisions bodily resurrection in creative ways that circumvent the efficacy of bodily fragmentation and decomposition.[82] In a passage that evokes Ezekiel 37 and explicitly appeals to the power of God as creator over the resurrection of the dead, the *Apocalypse of Peter* refers to God commanding "the wild beasts and the fowls . . . to restore all the flesh that they have devoured" (Apoc. Pet. 4).[83] Similarly, an apocryphal quotation in Tertullian's *The Resurrection of the Flesh* reads, "And I will command the fish of the sea, and they shall vomit up the bones that were consumed, and I will bring joint to joint and bone to bone" (*Res.* 32.1).[84] One is also reminded of the martyrdom accounts of Justin and Paul (both from the second century C.E.). Although both stories do not definitively elucidate whether their resurrection is embodied or disembodied, they do conceptualize each character's beheading as a particular problem for the hope of a resurrection:

> The prefect turned to Justin: "If you are scourged and beheaded (ἀποκεφαλισθῇς), do you believe that you will ascend to heaven (μέλλεις ἀναβαίνειν εἰς τὸν οὐρανόν)?" "I have confidence from my perseverance," said Justin, "if I endure. Indeed, I know that for those who lead a just life there awaits the divine gift even to the consummation." The prefect Rusticus said: "You think, then, that you will ascend (ἀναβήσῃ)?" "I do not think," said Justin, "but I am fully convinced of it." The prefect Rusticus said: "If you do not obey, you will be punished." Justin said: "We are confident that if we suffer the penalty we shall be saved (σωθῆναι)." The prefect Rusticus passed judgement: "Those who have refused to sacrifice to the gods are to be scourged and executed in accordance with the laws." (*Acts Justin* A.5)[85]

> When Paul was brought to him in accordance with the edict, he stood by his sentence, saying, "Decapitate (τραχηλοκοπήσατε) this man, lest he should take on strange ideas as his own." And Paul said, "Caesar, it is not for a short time that I live for my king. Know that even if you cut off my head (τραχηλοκοπήσῃς), I will do this: I will appear to you after I have been raised (ἐγερθείς) again, so that you

---

[82] On the conundrum of the bodily resurrection of the mutilated dead in early Christian theology, see, e.g., Dale C. Allison, *Night Comes: Death, Imagination, and the Last Things* (Grand Rapids: Eerdmans, 2016), 19–44; Candida R. Moss, *Divine Bodies: Resurrecting Perfection in the New Testament and Early Christianity* (New Haven: Yale University Press, 2019).

[83] Trans. J. K. Elliott, in *The Apocryphal New Testament: A Collection of Apocryphal Christian Literature in an English Translation Based on M. R. James* (Oxford: Clarendon, 1993).

[84] Trans. Richard Bauckham, in *The Fate of the Dead: Studies on the Jewish and Christian Apocalypses*, NovTSup 93 (Leiden: Brill, 1998), 273.

[85] Trans. Herbert Musurillo, in *The Acts of the Christian Martyrs* (Oxford: Oxford University Press, 1972), 46–47.

may know that I did not die but am alive in my king Jesus Christ, who judges the entire world." (*Mart. Paul* 4)[86]

In the former text, the prefect, Rusticus, poses a question that presumes that beheading ran up against Justin's hope for resurrection. The fact that Rusticus poses this question twice reinforces this dilemma. Justin's belief in God's power, however, instils him with confidence that the beheading would not necessarily work in this regard.[87] In the latter text, Paul's address to Caesar—that he will appear to Nero *even after* Paul's head is severed—simultaneously acknowledges and combats the presumption that the severed head would thwart his resurrection and ensure separation from Caesar. Converged in both the *Acts of Justin and His Companions* and the *Martyrdom of Paul*, therefore, are competing ideologies regarding the ultimate power of beheading. The efficacy of beheading in preventing the possibility of resurrection supplies the logical traction on which the characters' debates pivot. In this respect, Kyle's claim that Christian conceptualizations of resurrection fueled Romans in their abuse of Christian corpses seems quite reasonable.[88]

The Public Spectacle of Beheading

The broadcasting of a severed head is a ubiquitous theme in ancient literature and visual artifacts. Many texts highlight the public display, and thus visibility, of the beheading proper.[89] Other texts stress the presentation, and thus seen manipulation, of a previously severed head.[90] Publicly detached heads can

---

[86] Trans. David L. Eastman, in *The Ancient Martyrdom Accounts of Peter and Paul* (Atlanta: SBL Press, 2015), 132–33.
[87] The author of Revelation similarly sees "the souls of those beheaded" (τὰς ψυχὰς τῶν πεπελεκισμένων) alive and with Christ: "They lived (ἔζησαν) and reigned with the Christ for a thousand years" (Rev 20:4).
[88] Kyle, *Spectacles of Death*, 243.
[89] See, e.g., Livy, *Ab urbe cond.* 2.5; Dionysius of Halicarnassus, *Ant. rom.* 2.29; 6.30.1–2; Polybius, *Hist.* 1.7.11–12; Josephus, *Ant.* 6.191–192; *War* 2.246; 6.360–362. See also Dionysius of Halicarnassus, *Ant. rom.* 3.58.4. The prepositional phrase ἐν τῷ φανερῷ in this text either modifies the adverbial participle αἰκισθέντες ("having been scourged") or the finite verb ἀπεκόπησαν ("they beheaded"). This ambiguity does not suggest that a private beheading took place after a public scourging. Rather, even though the aorist participle conveys that the scourging occurred before the beheading, the two actions are presented as a single complex by virtue of their grammatical linkage. As a result, ἐν τῷ φανερῷ is best seen here as modifying both actions. Therefore, Cary's LCL translation ("scourged and beheaded in public") is apropos.
[90] Hector was eager to behead Patroclus' corpse "and fix it on the stakes of the wall" (Homer, *Il.* 18.177 [Murray, LCL]). Telesinus' head was placed on a spear and paraded around the walls of Praeneste (Velleius Paterculus, *Comp. Rom. Hist.* 2.27.3). According to Josephus, David presented six hundred heads to King Saul (*Ant.* 6.203–204). The Philistines "fastened [Saul's] head in the temple of Dagon" (1 Chr 10:10). So also, 1 Chr 10:10 LXX; cf. 1 Kgdms 31:9 LXX. Jehu had the heads of Ahab's seventy sons displayed "before

communicate, and effectively so, even though they can no longer control their faculties.[91] The highly publicized spectacle of a broken, beheaded person could render visible the degradation of the beheaded in the ways that we have discussed in this chapter. If, as Kloppenborg states (albeit in a different context), "unseen honor is no honor at all,"[92] then perhaps dishonor that is not seen is likewise no dishonor.

Additionally, a leading historian on violence in antiquity classifies Rome's public displays of violence as a "category of rhetoric" that "could generate the strongest emotional response" and "have the deepest impact."[93] "[Violence] was an important basis for [Rome's] existence, pertaining as it did not only to victoriousness over external enemies but also to the internal order of the state."[94] Under this construal, the spectacle of a severed head was a preventative and deterrent mechanism aimed at safeguarding sociopolitical stability.[95] Such spectacles conveyed a strong message to the beholder(s): the same dehumanized fate awaits those who emulate the victim.[96] By beheading or displaying the severed

the gate" (πρὸ τῆς πύλης) in two heaps (Josephus, *Ant.* 9.127). Nicanor's head was transported to Jerusalem and there displayed: "they stretched out [the head and hand] among Jerusalem" (ἐξέτειναν παρὰ τῇ Ιερουσαλημ) (1 Macc 11:47). According to 2 Macc 15:28-36, Nicanor's head was sent to Jerusalem (15:30-31), its tongue cut out (15:33), and exhibited on the citadel: "He fastened (ἐξέδησεν) Nicanor's head from the citadel, manifest for all (ἐπίδηλον πᾶσιν) and an apparent (φανερόν) sign (σημεῖον) of the Lord's help" (15:35). The NRSV translation of 2 Macc 15:35b ("a clear and conspicuous sign to every one of the help of the Lord") understands both ἐπίδηλον and φανερόν as modifying σημεῖον, whereas my translation suggests an adverbial understanding of the first adjective and an attributive understanding of the second adjective. Whichever option one prefers in unraveling the text's grammatical ambivalence, neither translation hinders the clear emphasis on the visibility of Nicanor's displayed head.

[91] In Celtic tradition, however, the severed head could speak and sing. See Watts, *Religion in Late Roman Britain*, 79-80. Ovid's portrayal of the beheading of Emathion has Emathion's severed head uttering curses on the altar: "Chromis struck off his head with his sword: the head fell straight on the altar, and there the still half-conscious tongue kept up its execrations and the life was breathed out in the midst of the altar-fires" (*Metam.* 5.103-106 [Miller, LCL]).

[92] Kloppenborg, *Christ's Associations*, 44.

[93] Zimmermann, "Violence Reconsidered," 345. Cf. Malamud, "Pompey's Head and Cato's Snakes," 33: "The point of decapitation as a weapon of terror is that it is at once terrifyingly concrete and powerfully metaphorical."

[94] Zimmermann, "Violence Reconsidered," 347.

[95] See Coleman, "Fatal Charades," 48, who distinguishes between prevention and deterrence in the Roman penal system. For Coleman, prevention concerns eliminating the culprit's behavior and deterrence concerns inhibiting potential culprits.

[96] Cf. Kyle, *Spectacles of Death*, 7: "Some [anthropologists and sociologists] suggest that all social order is ultimately based on violence. To reinforce the social order violence must be performed or proclaimed in public, and public violence tends to become ritualized into games, sports, and even spectacles of death." On violence as a spatially charged phenomenon, see Josiah Osgood, "The Topography of Roman Assassination, 133 BCE-222 CE," in Riess and Fagan, *Topography of Violence*, 209-27; Werner Riess, "Where to Kill in Classical

heads of those viewed as criminals and revolutionaries, Rome sought to prevent culprits from repeating offenses, to quell current insurgencies, dissuade future revolutionaries, and thus to assert social order and control.[97]

Beheading as a mechanism of social control, furthermore, was often applied to the leader of a group, rather than the group in its entirety. For example, Polybius (*Hist.* 11.27–30) recounts Scipio summoning an assembly in the marketplace where he addresses a multitude of mutineers. Toward the end of his speech, Scipio metaphorically differentiates between the leaders and the rest of the mutineers by comparing the latter to the sea and the former to the violent winds that fall upon the sea (11.29.9–13). The sea appears to share the same harmful character as the winds when the wind stirs it (11.29.10). Accordingly, Scipio determines to punish the leaders of the revolt and grant amnesty to the rest: without the wind's influence, the sea's power is tamed. Polybius mentions the perceptible fear on the insurgents' countenance as the leaders of the revolt were punished in their sight: "The multitude of mutineers were so thoroughly cowed by fear of the surrounding force and the terror that looked them in the face, that while some of their leaders were being scourged and others beheaded, none of them changed his countenance or uttered a word, but all remained dumbfounded, smitten with astonishment and dread" (Polybius, *Hist.* 11.30.2–3).[98] After the leaders were punished, the remaining mutineers "took their oath to the tribunes that they would obey the orders of their officers and be guilty of no disloyalty to Rome. Scipio then by successfully nipping in the bud what might have proved a great danger restored his forces to their original discipline" (*Hist.* 11.30.4–5).[99]

Final Remarks

As our preceding discussion has shown, in the ancient world, the severed head represented an ignominious type of somatic violence that could inferiorize the victim (while enhancing the prestige of the perpetrator), interrupt proper burial, thereby impacting the victim in the afterlife, prevent the revivification of a recently deceased corpse, and relatedly pose a problem to the idea of an embodied resurrection in the eschaton. The fragmentation of the integrity of the body at the neck was symbolically freighted with the potential to

---

Athens: Assassinations, Executions, and the Athenian Public Space," in Riess and Fagan, *Topography of Violence*, 77–112; Fagan, "Urban Violence: Street, Forum, Bath, Circus, and Theater."

[97] On beheading as an instrument of ensuring sociopolitical stability, see, e.g., Josephus, *Ant.* 20.117; Polybius, *Hist.* 1.7.12; Dionysius of Halicarnassus, *Ant. rom.* 2.29; Livy, *Ab urbe cond.* 2.5; 4.10. Cf. Josephus, *Ant.* 17.273–277; 20.97–99.

[98] Paton, LCL.

[99] Paton, LCL. Similarly, Livy, *Ab urbe cond.* 28.29: "Such was the end and outcome of the mutiny of the soldiers which began at Sucro" (Moore, LCL).

diminish the cadaver's personhood and recognizability in death and beyond death—into life in the hereafter. The spectacle of cutting off a head, and/or the showcasing of a previously severed head, rendered these symbolic potentials visible. Honor and shame were publicly apportioned in this way and sometimes further served as a controlling mechanism to quell or prevent rebellions and insurgencies.

In commemorative activity, however, these scripts of beheading are subject to contestation. While the sight of the severed head could invoke the superiority of the perpetrator, this established hierarchy does not necessitate that those who witness a beheading, or perpetuate a memory thereof, agree that the performer and casualty truly stand in superior and inferior positions to one another, respectively. Tradents could employ a number of strategies to negotiate these cultural fault lines. One could reconfigure the reputation of the victim by emphasizing their heroic courage, self-sacrificial service for others, or refusal to compromise their convictions when confronted with severe death.[100] Or relatedly, one could transfer the degrading gaze to the perpetrator by underscoring the virtue or innocence of the sufferer, and thus characterize the actions of the performer as unjust.[101]

Permutations of such strategies are discernable in some of the accounts of beheading we have referenced in this chapter.[102] We noted above, for example, that Volesus, the proconsul of Asia in the early first century of the Common Era, reportedly beheaded three hundred people in a single day. According to Seneca, Volesus saw this as a "glorious deed worth beholding" and thus proudly exclaimed, "'What a kingly act!'" as he "strutted among the corpses" (*Ira.* 2.5.5)[103] Although Seneca attributes the cultural content of beheading (as an act that publicly organizes the perpetrator into holding a dominant and prestigious power dynamic over the victim) to Volesus' actions, he carefully negotiates this script. The philosopher frames his portrayal of Volesus by first

---

[100] See Jan Willem van Henten and Friedrich Avemarie, *Martyrdom and Noble Death: Selected Texts from Graeco-Roman, Jewish and Christian Antiquity* (London: Routledge, 2002); Elizabeth A. Castelli, *Martyrdom and Memory: Early Christian Culture Making* (New York: Columbia University Press, 2004), 33–68.

[101] Conversely, Kyle, *Spectacles of Death*, 13: "The condemnation of persons to the arena to face death in ways tantamount to torture and corpse abuse raised concerns about justification, purification, and avoidance of contamination or religious pollution. It was not difficult, but it was necessary that the Roman community somehow assured itself that the killing was acceptable and even positive and therapeutic—that the victims were justly executed criminals, traitors, prisoners of war, paid volunteers, or dangerous heretics."

[102] In addition to the example of Volesus, see also Josephus, *Ant.* 7.50–52, where David insists that the beheaded victim, Jebosthos, was "a righteous man" (ἄνδρα δίκαιον), and characterizes the deed of those who cut off his head as that of "evil-doing men" (κακούργοις ἀνδράσι).

[103] Basore, LCL.

distinguishing between those who epitomize anger and those who exemplify brutality. For Seneca, those who exude the latter are those who take pleasure in the mangling and killing of people "from whom they have neither received injury nor think even themselves that they have received one." Anger develops into cruelty and brutality when it disregards mercy and forgets "every conception of the human bond" (*Ira.* 2.5.3).[104]

Seneca then proceeds to identify Hannibal (who supposedly exclaimed at the scene of a trench full of human blood, "'O beauteous sight!'" [*O formosum spectaculum*]) and Volesus ("'What a kingly act!'" [*O rem regiam*]) as prototypes of brutality. In social memory terms, Seneca *keys* Volesus (first century C.E.) to Hannibal, and Hannibal (third century B.C.E.) to Volesus, by aligning these two figures—who are from separate epochs of history—as archetypes of brutal men who rejoice in the undue spilling of human blood. The upshot of this alignment is that the characterization of their respective actions each acts one upon the other: their excessive cruelty is thus mutually reinforced. Accordingly, Seneca makes explicit his moral verdict on Volesus' actions: "This was not anger, but an evil still greater and incurable" (*Ira.* 2.5.4–5).[105] Rather than these beheadings exhibiting Volesus' enhanced reputation, Seneca contests this line of discourse by refracting it through a cultural framework of brutality.

A comparable reconfiguration occurs in reference to the death of Cicero in Plutarch's biographical account of Antony:

> After Cicero had been butchered, Antony ordered his head to be cut off, and that right hand with which Cicero had written the speeches against him. When they were brought to him, he gazed upon them exultantly, laughing aloud for joy many times; then, when he was sated, he ordered them to be placed on the rostra in the forum, just as though he were putting insult upon the dead, and not rather making a display of his own insolence in good fortune and abuse of power. (*Ant.* 20)[106]

Similar to Seneca's attribution of the ideological substance of beheading to Volesus' actions, Plutarch here marks the postmortem bodily mutilation of Cicero as that which signifies Antony's victory over the one who had previously "written speeches against him." Plutarch's mentioning of Cicero's writings against Antony is perhaps not without further significance. In the second *Philippic*, Cicero levelled a sharp response to Antony, who had criticized Cicero for his "inappropriate jocularity."[107] As one classicist has made clear,

---

[104] Basore, LCL.
[105] Basore, LCL.
[106] Perrin, LCL.
[107] Mary Beard, *Laughter in Ancient Rome: On Joking, Tickling, and Cracking Up* (Berkeley: University of California Press, 2014), 101–2 (quotation, p. 101). See Cicero, *Phil.* 2.39–40.

"one of Cicero's trademarks, for better or worse, was his capacity to get people laughing—or his sometimes irritating inability to refrain from doing so."[108] Thus, since the two figures shared a tumultuous history that involved a dispute over laughter,[109] for Antony's response to be laughter at the sight of Cicero's severed head and appendage perhaps further accentuates his victory, or at the least the joy he took in it (Antony had the last laugh, so to speak). Regardless, similar to Seneca's negotiation of Volesus' ostensible prestige, Plutarch counterbalances Antony's supposed victory by altering its framework. Antony's public display of Cicero's severed parts in the forum to insult Cicero (and interrupt honorable burial) is refracted through the lenses of "insolence" and the "abuse of power."[110]

More examples could certainly be discussed, but these suffice to demonstrate that beheading constituted a highly symbolic form of localized communication that could compel tradents to contest its potential to degrade a victim along different lines of cultural discourse. In this chapter, we have emphasized three such lines in particular that could highlight the degradation of a beheaded person: power, (proper) burial and life in the hereafter, and the public spectacle of violence. As we will see, the degradation of John the Baptist's beheading is reconfigured along these axes in its early commemorative history.

---

[108] Beard, *Laughter in Ancient Rome*, 101. A page earlier in her discussion, Beard describes Cicero as "the most infamous funster, punster, and jokester of classical antiquity."

[109] In Plutarch's biography of Cicero, Plutarch makes explicit that the hands of Cicero that Antony ordered to be cut off were the hands that had written the "Philippics" (*Cic.* 48.4).

[110] Under this construal, we might suggest, rather colloquially, that Cicero managed to reap one more laugh: Antony may have had the last laugh, but the joke was on him.

3

Contesting Violence

John's Beheading and Degradation in the Gospel of Mark

> If John's beheading is a castration,
> it is Herod's phallus on the platter, not John's.[1]

Beheading in the ancient world signaled degradation along three cultural fault lines: the power of the perpetrator over the victim, the corpse abuse of separating a head from its body's burial, and the public spectacle of the severed head. The earliest written memory of John the Baptist's death (Mark 6:14–29)[2] acknowledges the ignominious potential his particular manner of death carried. However, Mark contests the common cultural assumption and refracts that framework's degrading gaze away from the victim of violence in three ways. First, Mark keys John's beheading to Jesus' crucifixion, thereby mapping the two figures' virtue onto one another (and, likewise, their opponents' vice onto one another). Second, Mark reconfigures Herod Antipas' masculinity and efficacious rule. Third, Mark contextualizes John's beheading so that it serves to enhance Jesus' reputation as a prestigious healer and to exhibit

---

[1] Nicole Wilkinson Duran, "Return of the Disembodied or How John the Baptist Lost His Head," in *Reading Communities Reading Scripture: Essays in Honor of Daniel Patte*, ed. Gary A. Phillips and Nicole Wilkinson Duran (Harrisburg, Penn.: Trinity Press International, 2002), 287.

[2] The Gospels of Mark and Matthew contain the earliest traditions that narrate the beheading of John the Baptist (Mark 6:14–29; Matt 14:1–12). The Gospel of Luke briefly mentions that John was arrested and beheaded by Herod Antipas (Luke 3:19–20; 9:7–9). Josephus (*Ant.* 18.116–119) also narrates John's death, but makes no mention of decapitation as the method of John's execution. My primary focus is on Mark because the commemorative maneuvers therein overlap to an extent with Matthew. Avoiding considerable repetition will allow us to devote more attention in the next chapter to understanding how later recipients in the second and third centuries capitalize on the impact of the commemorative maneuvers first established in the Gospel of Mark.

Antipas' paranoia. Collectively, in Mark's memory of John's beheading, the violence of John's death functions as an essential component to establish a distance between the moral configurations of John the Baptist, on the one hand, and the Herodian court, on the other hand. For the reader's easy reference, I have provided an English translation of Mark 6:14–29 below:

> ¹⁴ And the king, Herod, heard [of it], for [Jesus'] name became known and "they" were saying: "John the Baptist has been revived from the dead and for this reason powers are at work in [Jesus]." ¹⁵ But others were saying: "He is Elijah." Still others were saying: "[He is] a prophet like one of the prophets." ¹⁶ But when Herod heard [of it], he kept saying,: "He whom I beheaded, John, this one has been revived." ¹⁷ For Herod himself sent and took control of John and bound him in prison because of Herodias, the wife of Philip, his brother, because [Herod] married her. ¹⁸ For John had been saying to Herod: "It is not lawful for you to have the wife of your brother." ¹⁹ Now, Herodias held a grudge against him and wanted to kill him, but she was not able to, ²⁰ for Herod feared John, knowing him to be a righteous and holy man; and he kept protecting him. When [Herod] heard him, he was greatly perplexed, and kept listening to him gladly. ²¹ But an opportune day arrived when Herod on his birthday hosted a banquet for his great ones, chiliarchs, and first ones of Galilee. ²² When his daughter Herodias entered and danced, she pleased Herod and those reclining [with him]. The king said to the girl: "Ask me [for] whatever you want, and I will give [it] to you." ²³ And he swore to her: "Whatever you request of me I will give to you up to half of my kingdom." ²⁴ Having exited, she said to her mother: "What shall I request?" And she said: "The head of John the Baptist." ²⁵ She entered immediately with haste to the king and requested: "I want—at once—you to give me on a platter the head of John the Baptist." ²⁶ Although the king was deeply grieved, because of the oaths and those reclining he did not want to refuse her. ²⁷ Immediately the king sent and ordered an executioner to bring his head. [The executioner] went and beheaded him in the prison, ²⁸ brought his head on a platter, and gave it to the girl. And the girl gave it to her mother. ²⁹ When his disciples heard [of it], they came and took his body, and placed it in a tomb.

The Degradation of John's Beheading

Two features of the Markan portrayal of John's death are important to underscore at the outset for our purposes. The first feature is the structural relationship of the episode to its wider narrative context. This feature involves two sub-elements. (1) John's death constitutes the interior of an intercalation between Jesus sending the twelve with power to confront (ritually) impure spirits and demons (6:6b/7–13) and the twelve's return (6:30).³ Fowler once referred to the intercalation here as "especially puzzling" in comparison to the other six intercalations in the Gospel of Mark (3:20–35; 5:21–43; 11:12–25; 14:1–11; 14:53–72; 15:6–32).⁴ This literary framing device—where John's beheading slithers into the middle of another tradition—causes the interpreter to pause and consider how John's decapitation (the interior component) relates to Jesus' authority as a healer (the exterior frame). The introduction of the tradition of John's death points in this direction as well: it subsumes John's death under the theme of Jesus' reputation as one who possesses powers (6:14). (2) Mark's sequence involves a retrospection, introduced by the explanatory conjunction γάρ ("for") in 6:17. This temporal "flashback" raises the question of how Mark integrates John's beheading into the wider narrative context of Mark's Gospel. Both sub-elements play an integral role in how Mark reconfigures the shame of John's beheading, and we will return to them later in this chapter.

The second feature of the Markan portrayal is that it dwells on the cultural lines of beheading that could emphasize the degradation of the victim. Mark focuses on the public transportation of John's severed "head" (κεφαλή) from person to person, so that the reader's gaze is fixated on John's dismembered condition:

> Mark 6:24: "Having went out, she said to her mother: 'What shall I ask for?' And she [her mother] said: 'The head (κεφαλήν) of John the Baptist.'"
>
> Mark 6:25: "I wish that at once you would give to me on a platter (ἐπὶ πίνακι) the head (τὴν κεφαλήν) of John the Baptist."⁵
>
> Mark 6:27a: "And immediately, the king sent and ordered an executioner to bring (ἐνέγκαι) his head (κεφαλήν)."⁶
>
> Mark 6:27b: "Having departed, he [the executioner] beheaded (ἀπεκεφάλισεν) him in the prison."⁷

---

³ On intercalation in the Gospel of Mark, see, e.g., Tom Shepherd, "The Narrative Function of Markan Intercalation," *NTS* 41 (1995): 522–40; Robert Fowler, *Let the Reader Understand: Reader-Response Criticism and the Gospel of Mark* (Harrisburg, Penn.: Trinity Press International, 2001), 142–44. On pneumatic impurity, see Matthew Thiessen, *Jesus and the Forces of Death: The Gospels' Portrayal of Ritual Impurity within First-Century Judaism* (Grand Rapids: Baker Academic, 2020), 123–48.
⁴ Fowler, *Let the Reader Understand*, 143.
⁵ Cf. Matt 14:8—the girl asks for the "head" (κεφαλήν) of John the Baptist "on a platter" (ἐπὶ πίνακι).
⁶ Cf. Matt 14:9—Herod orders John's head "to be given" (δοθῆναι).
⁷ Cf. Matt 14:10—Herod sends orders for John to be beheaded (ἀποκεφαλίζω) in prison.

> Mark 6:28a: The executioner (or Herod) "brought (ἤνεγκεν) his head (τὴν κεφαλὴν) on a platter (ἐπὶ πίνακι)."[8]
>
> Mark 6:28b: The executioner (or Herod) "gave (ἔδωκεν) it [the head] (αὐτήν) to the girl."[9]
>
> Mark 6:28c: The girl "gave (ἔδωκεν) it [the head] (αὐτὴν) to her mother."[10]

Significantly, however, the account proceeds by juxtaposing the manipulation of John's severed head vis-à-vis his headless body. His "head" (κεφαλή) and "body" (πτῶμα) are *separated* at burial:

> Mark 6:29: "His [presumably John's] disciples came and took his body (τὸ πτῶμα) and placed it (αὐτό) in a tomb."[11]

This differentiation (and its cultural significance) between the respective fates of John's head (κεφαλή/αὐτή) and body (πτῶμα/αὐτό) escapes the purview of many biblical interpreters.[12] Malina and Rohrbaugh, for instance, overlook this differentiation: their analysis on John's death fails to comment *in toto* on 6:27–29.[13] Many scholars who devote attention to the depiction of John's burial in 6:29 focus on discursive matters, such as the precise geographic location where John's body was likely buried—Samaria-Sebaste and Machaerus are popular destinations in this regard.[14] Other scholars, alternatively, tend

---

[8] Cf. Matt 14:11—John's "head" (κεφαλή) "was brought" (ἠνέχθη) "on a platter" (ἐπὶ πίνακι).

[9] Cf. Matt 14:11—John's head "was given" (ἐδόθη) to the girl.

[10] Cf. Matt 14:11—The girl then "brings" (ἤνεγκεν) "it [the head]" (αὐτῆς) to her mother.

[11] Cf. Matt 14:12—"His [presumably John's] disciples came, took the body (τὸ πτῶμα) and buried it [the body] (αὐτό)."

[12] Cf. Craig A. Evans, *Jesus and the Ossuaries: What Jewish Burial Practices Reveal about the Beginning of Christianity* (Waco, Tex.: Baylor University Press, 2003), 13–14; Edmondo Lupieri, "John the Baptist in New Testament Traditions and History," *ANRW* 2.26.1:436, n. 17. For examples of medieval poets who wrote about the different fates of John's head and body, see Greti Dinkova-Bruun, "The Beheading of John the Baptist in Medieval Poetic Discourse," in *Decapitation and Sacrifice: Saint John's Head in Interdisciplinary Perspectives: Text, Object, Medium*, ed. Barbara Baert and Sophia Rochmes (Leuven: Peeters, 2017), esp. 45–46.

[13] Bruce J. Malina and Richard L. Rohrbaugh, *Social-Science Commentary on the Synoptic Gospels* (Minneapolis: Fortress, 1992), 216–17. Similarly, C. E. B. Cranfield, *The Gospel According to Saint Mark*, CGTC (Cambridge: Cambridge University Press, 1959), 204–13; Karl Kertelge, *Markusevangelium*, NEchtB (Würzburg: Echter Verlag, 1994), 64–67.

[14] Erich Klostermann, *Das Markusevangelium*, HNT (Tübingen: Mohr Siebeck, 1971), 61; C. S. Mann, *Mark*, AB (New York: Doubleday, 1986), 298: "Whatever later tradition may suggest, it is to be presumed that the body was buried near Machaerus (assuming this to be the place of execution)." Another discursive matter in commentary on Mark 6:29 is the origins of the tradition of John's beheading. Ben Witherington (*The Gospel of Mark: A Socio-Rhetorical Commentary* [Grand Rapids: Eerdmans, 2001], 216) utilizes 6:29 to speculate

to make the problematic assertion that John's burial stresses that he was honored in death. Along this line, Donahue and Harrington's claim is typical: "Since *proper* burial was a sign of honor and of divine favor John is honored in death."[15] Another interpreter even refers to the burial of John at Mark 6:29 as "ein tröstlicher Abschluß" ("a comforting conclusion").[16]

Such readings, however, neglect understanding 6:29 in light of 6:24–28. In other words, they fail to notice or parse the significance of the separation of John's head from its body. Hartmann rightly observes that "der Sieg über Johannes und seine Entehrung" ("the victory over John and his defamation") are demonstrated by means of the display of John's head on the platter.[17] But when Hartmann immediately proceeds to say, "Wo das Haupt danach verbleibt, sagt der Text nicht" ("Where the head remains thereafter, the text does not say"), he misses the sharp contrast the text draws between the fates of John's head (κεφαλή, 6:24–28) and body (πτῶμα, 6:29).[18] From this perspective, the text *does* indicate, albeit by subtraction, where the head remains: *not* with the body.[19]

If Mark were interested in providing the precise geographic locality of the severed head, we can probably assume that he would have specified

---

that the tradition of John's death originates within the circle of John's disciples, since John's disciples apparently continued to exist even after the Baptist's demise (cf. Acts 19:1–12). For an argument that Mark 6:14–29 originates in John the Baptist circles, see Joseph Thomas, *Le Mouvement Baptiste en Palestine et Syrie* (Gembloux: J. Duculot, 1935), 110–11. Knut Backhaus (*Die "Jüngerkreise" des Täufers Johannes: Eine Studie zu den religionsgeschichtlichen Ursprüngen des Christentums*, Paderborner Theologische Studien 19 [Paderborn: Schöningh, 1991], 169) argues that Mark 6:14–29 shows no serious interest in John's disciples. Further, some scholars make the important observation that Mark 6:29 foreshadows Mark 15:43–46. See, e.g., D. E. Nineham, *Saint Mark* (Harmondsworth: Penguin, 1963), 176; Josef Ernst, *Das Evangelium nach Markus* (Regensburg: Verlag Friedrich Pustet, 1981), 185; Joachim Gnilka, *Das Evangelium nach Markus*, 5th ed., EKK (Neukirchen-Vluyn: Neukirchener Verlag, 1998), 251; Frances J. Maloney, *The Gospel of Mark: A Commentary* (Peabody, Mass.: Hendrickson, 2002), 127; Robert H. Stein, *Mark*, BECNT (Grand Rapids: Baker Academic, 2008), 307.

[15] John R. Donahue and Daniel Harrington, *The Gospel of Mark*, SP (Collegeville, Minn.: Liturgical Press, 2002), 200 (italics added). Similarly, Ernst Lohmeyer, *Das Evangelium des Markus* (Göttingen: Vandenhoeck & Ruprecht, 1967), 121; Ernst, *Evangelium nach Markus*, 185; Rudolf Pesch, *Das Markusevangelium* (Freiburg: Herder, 1984), 343.

[16] Rudolf Schnackenburg, *Das Evangelium nach Markus* (Düsseldorf: Patmos-Verlag, 1966), 156. Adela Yarbro Collins (*Mark: A Commentary*, Hermeneia [Minneapolis: Fortress, 2007], 314) is more sober and refers to the burial as "an act of piety" on the part of John's disciples.

[17] Michael Hartmann, *Der Tod Johannes des Täufers: Eine exegetische und rezeptionsgeschichtliche Studie auf dem Hintergrund narrativer, intertextueller und kulturanthropologischer Zugänge*, SBB 45 (Stuttgart: Verlag Katholisches Bibelwerk, 2001), 198.

[18] Hartmann, *Tod Johannes des Täufers*, 198.

[19] The same observation can be made of Matt 14:11–12. See John Nolland, *The Gospel of Matthew*, NIGTC (Grand Rapids: Eerdmans, 2005), 585, who merely asks the question, "Are we to think of John's body as buried headless?"

accordingly.[20] Instead, the emphasis of Mark's portrayal seems to be on the fact *that* John's head and body were separated in burial, as both fragments were transported away from one another—one on a platter; the other with John's disciples. As we saw in the previous chapter, the separation of a head from its body constituted a type of somatic violence that degraded the victim by interrupting *proper* burial (inhibiting the victim's reincorporation in an afterlife mode of existence) and preventing the possibility of being bodily *revived* to resume life on earth. Again, to overcome a violent death that involved the fragmentation or decomposition of the body required a creative act of power by God in the eschatological resurrection of the dead. That early readers might understand John's beheading in light of its intersection with notions of death and life in the hereafter, moreover, is reinforced by the fact that the Markan account not only ends the tradition with a spotlight on corpse abuse, but also begins the story by portraying Herod Antipas contemplating (1) the fact that John was beheaded, alongside (2) speculation that John had been revived (Mark 6:14, 16).[21] We will return to this point of intersection later in this chapter.

Further, the public parade of John's severed head (6:27–28) renders visible Herodias' victory and power over John the Baptist, who had previously criticized her marriage to Herod Antipas (6:18–19). Antipas had married Herodias, the wife of his brother, while his brother was still alive. In doing so, Herod divorced his wife, the daughter of the Nabatean king Aretas IV, whose kingdom bordered Herod's jurisdiction of Perea on the east side of the Jordan. This divorce would eventually lead Aretas to go to war and defeat Herod's army (Josephus, *Ant.* 18.109–115).[22] As Mark portrays the matter, John does not rebuke Herod for divorcing his wife (it was lawful for a man to divorce his wife [Deut 24:1–4]), but for marrying his brother's wife, which was deemed "impurity" by the Torah (Lev 20:21; cf. Lev 18:16).[23] As Taylor puts it: "Illicit bodily

[20] That John's head remained on a platter in contrast to its headless body gave rise in the medieval period to a cult of relics surrounding John's severed head. See Barbara Baert, *Caput Johannis in Disco (Essay on a Man's Head)*, trans. Irene Schaudies, Visualizing the Middle Ages 8 (Leiden: Brill, 2012), 22–44.

[21] Similarly, Ezra P. Gould, *The Gospel According to St. Mark*, ICC (Edinburgh: T&T Clark, 1896), 110: "Herod dwells upon the thought, that this prophet who has now risen from the dead was beheaded by himself. Hence the relative clause, which contains the statement of the beheading, is placed first and ἐγώ is expressed."

[22] Josephus indicates that many Jews interpreted Antipas' defeat by Aretas as divine recompense for Antipas' execution of John the Baptist (*Ant.* 18.116, 119).

[23] Joan E. Taylor, *The Immerser: John the Baptist within Second Temple Judaism* (Grand Rapids: Eerdmans, 1997), 239. Conversely, as Taylor notes on the same page: "In the case of a *dead* brother who was childless, a man was obligated to marry his widowed sister-in-law (Deut. 25:5–10)" (italics added). Josephus claims that Antipas (after "falling in love with Herodias") married Herodias while his half-brother, "Herod," was still alive (*Ant.* 18.110 [Feldman, LCL]). Technically, Mark's account does not explicitly specify whether his brother was still alive when Antipas married Herodias, but that seems to

connections between people resulted in a corresponding bodily impurity."²⁴ Assuming that John the Baptist did indeed emerge on the public scene around the fifteenth year of the reign of Tiberius (c. 27–29 C.E.) (Luke 3:1–3), Antipas had already been the subject of controversy regarding Torah-observance when he forcibly relocated some Galileans to the newly built capital city, Tiberias. In 18–19 C.E., Antipas constructed Tiberias (to honor the emperor) over the site of demolished tombs on the western shore of the Sea of Galilee. Many Jews thus viewed the establishment of Tiberias as contrary to the law because it brought settlers into contact with corpse impurity (Josephus, *Ant.* 18.36–38).²⁵

Numerous scholars have rightly observed that the Herodian court would likely perceive John's criticism as endangering the internal stability of the Galilean and Perean political landscape.²⁶ Especially since John attracted large crowds, was associated with the wilderness, and conducted his prophetic activity of repentance and ritual immersion in and around the Jordan River (Mark 1:4–5, 9), his rebuke of their marriage could lead to the "incitement of

---

be the underlying logic that makes sense of the passage. Rivka Nir, *The First Christian Believer: In Search of John the Baptist*, New Testament Monographs 38 (Sheffield: Sheffield Phoenix, 2019), 246–51, however, argues that John's rebuke of Herod's marriage reflects *distinctively* Christian ideas of divorce and remarriage rather than mainstream Jewish ones. I do not find her argument persuasive. For a response to her arguments, see Nathan L. Shedd, review of *The First Christian Believer: In Search of John the Baptist*, by Rivka Nir, *RBL*, 2020, http://www.sblcentral.org. See also Origen, *Comm. Matt.* 10.21: "On the one hand, some suppose that Herod married Herodias (the wife of the brother) after Philip died and left behind a daughter, although the law permits marriage [only] in the case of childlessness. On the other hand, having not found any clear indication Philip had died, we consider Herod's transgression to be greater still because he took away the brother's wife while he was even alive." Origen here makes a reference to others who apparently claim that Herod's marriage to Herodias violated Deut 25:5–6 LXX, which permits a man to marry his brother's wife insofar as the brother had died and had not produced a child with his wife. Origen uses this reference to exacerbate the severity of Herod's "transgression." Herod married his brother's wife not only despite the fact that Philip *had* produced a child with Herodias, but also despite the apparent fact that Philip had not yet *died*. Caesarius of Arles (*Serm.* 218) similarly claims that John the Baptist repudiated Herod for taking "the wife of a man who was still living" (Mueller, FC). So also Jerome, *Comm. Matt.* 14.3–4.

²⁴ Taylor, *Immerser*, 239.

²⁵ Antipas minted coins to commemorate the founding of Tiberias. One side of the coins refers to Antipas as "tetrarch" and contains an image of a reed plant or palm branch (Matt 11:7//Luke 7:24). The opposite side of the coins displays a wreath and includes the name "Tiberius." See further Seán Freyne, *The Jesus Movement and Its Expansion: Meaning and Mission* (Grand Rapids: Eerdmans, 2014), 61.

²⁶ See, e.g., Robert Webb, *John the Baptizer and Prophet: A Socio-Historical Study*, JSNTSup 62 (Sheffield: Sheffield Academic Press), 1991, 373–77; E. P. Sanders, *The Historical Figure of Jesus* (London: Penguin, 1993), 92–94; Taylor, *Immerser*, 213–41; Joel Marcus, *John the Baptist in History and Theology* (Columbia: University of South Carolina Press, 2018), 98–112.

those in Perea and Galilee to revolt against [Antipas]."²⁷ In other words, John's critique, and especially because it was *his* critique, posed a threat to the stability of the realm. From this vantage point, Herodias plotted to behead John to ensure sociopolitical equilibrium.

In this vein, the account's apparent "dependence" on the Esther tradition is all the more striking insofar as it accentuates Herodias' triumph over John.²⁸ As is well known among scholars, Antipas' promise of "up to half his kingdom" to Herodias' daughter in Mark 6:22-23 linguistically parallels the promise King Xerxes made to Esther:

> Mark 6:22: εἶπεν ὁ βασιλεὺς τῷ κορασίῳ, αἴτησόν με ὅ ἐὰν θέλῃς, καὶ δώσω σοι. ("And the king said to the little girl: 'Ask me whatever you want, and I will give [it] to you.'")
>
> Mark 6:23: ὅ τι ἐάν αἰτήσῃς δώσω σοι **ἕως ἡμίσους τῆς βασιλείας μου**. ("Whatever you ask I will give to you **up to half my kingdom**.")
>
> Esther 5:3 LXX: καὶ εἶπεν ὁ βασιλεύς Τί θέλεις, Εσθηρ, καὶ τί σού ἐστιν τὸ ἀξίωμα; **ἕως τοῦ ἡμίσους τῆς βασιλείας μου** καὶ ἔσται σοι. ("And the king said: 'What do you want, Esther? What is your request? **Up to half of my kingdom** and it will be [given] to you.'")
>
> Esther 5:6 LXX: εἶπεν ὁ βασιλεὺς πρὸς Εσθηρ Τί ἐστιν, βασίλισσα Εσθηρ; καὶ ἔσται σοι ὅσα ἀξιοῖς. ("And the king said to Esther: 'What is it, queen Esther? Whatever you request will be [given] to you.'")

---

²⁷ Taylor, *Immerser*, 240. Josephus (*Ant.* 18.116-119) does not indicate that John criticized Antipas' marriage to Herodias. However, he does underscore that Antipas put John to death preemptively because he feared that John's sway over the crowds might lead to political insurrection (*Ant.* 18.118). Conversely, Matt 14:5 claims that Antipas wanted to kill John the Baptist, but "feared the crowd because they regarded [John] as a prophet." By contrast still, Mark 6:19 portrays Herodias as the one who wants to kill John and that Antipas feared John and wanted to protect him. On the wilderness and the Jordan River as cultural symbols of the exodus and conquest, which could inflame revolutionary ideology, see Webb, *Baptizer and Prophet*, 360-66. See also Josephus, *Ant.* 20.97-99. On the rebuke of socioeconomic conditions closely tied to the idea of repentance from sin in Jewish tradition, see James G. Crossley, *Jesus and the Chaos of History: Redirecting the Life of the Historical Jesus*, Biblical Refigurations (Oxford: Oxford University Press, 2015), 96-111.

²⁸ For a helpful survey of the overlap between the Esther tradition and John's beheading, see Roger Aus, *Water into Wine and the Beheading of John the Baptist: Early Jewish-Christian Interpretation of Esther 1 in John 2.1-11 and Mark 6.17-29*, BJS 150 (Atlanta: Scholars Press, 1988), 41-74. Aus analyzes ten "affinities" between the portrayal of John's beheading in Mark 6:14-29 and an array of early Jewish tradition regarding Esther (pp. 41-66). His study attests to the complex tradition-history of Esther, including contradictory characterizations of chief figures at times. The dating of the transmission history of the Jewish midrashim and targumim on Esther, however, is difficult to pinpoint, and so, the direction of influence between these traditions and John's beheading is not always certain. See Crossley, *Jesus and the Chaos of History*, 149: "Passages cited by Aus are centuries later than the Gospel passages which in itself is a problem."

Esther 7:2 LXX: εἶπεν δὲ ὁ βασιλεὺς . . . Τί ἐστιν, Εσθηρ βασίλισσα, καὶ τί τὸ αἴτημά σου καὶ τί τὸ ἀξίωμά σου; καὶ ἔστω σοι **ἕως τοῦ ἡμίσους τῆς βασιλείας μου**. ("And the king said . . . 'What is it, queen Esther? What is your ask and what is your request? Let it be [given] to you **up to half my kingdom**.'")

In addition to Mark 6:22–23 referencing the book of Esther (5:3, 6; 7:2) in this capacity, other points of connection persist. The "girl" (κοράσιον) who dances in front of the "king" (βασιλεύς) and his guests is said to "please" (ἀρέσκω) Antipas (Mark 6:22).[29] The same terminology is found in Esther. According to Esther 2:9 LXX, "the girl (κοράσιον) pleased (ἤρεσεν) him [the king] and found favor before him."[30] The motif of "pleasing" is stressed throughout the MT of Esther 2 (2:4, 9, 14, 15, 17).[31] According to Aus' count, the substantive "king" refers to Ahasuerus (Xerxes) 136 times in the Hebrew and 157 times in the LXX.[32]

In the Esther tradition, moreover, Mordecai entreats Esther to speak to the king on behalf of the Jews ("to deliver us from death," Esth 4:8 LXX), even as Esther fears "entering" (εἰσέρχομαι) the inner court of the king (Esth 4:11 LXX). According to Mark, Herodias' daughter "enters" (εἰσέρχομαι) Herod's banquet hall (6:22), "goes out" (ἐξέρχομαι) to consult with her mother (6:24), and—after her mother entreats her to ask for John's head—"enters" (εἰσέρχομαι) the banquet again to make the request known (6:25). To whatever extent Mark maps John's beheading onto the Esther

---

[29] The characterization of Antipas as a "king" in Mark (6:14, 22, 25, 26, 27) is curious because Antipas never in fact held the title "king." He was rather a "tetrarch." His attempt to garner the title "king" ultimately led to his exile. Josephus and the Gospel of Luke do not designate Antipas a "tetrarch" (Luke 3:19; 9:7; Acts 13:1; Josephus, *Ant.* 17.188; 18.241–256; *War* 2.178–183). Interestingly, Matthew begins the story of John's death by referring to Antipas as a "tetrarch" (14:1), but then at 14:9 refers to Herod Antipas as ὁ βασιλεύς ("the king"). Mark Goodacre (*The Synoptic Problem: A Way Through the Maze* [London: T&T Clark International, 2001], 73) categorizes this feature of Matt 14:9 as an example of "editorial fatigue." Moreover, Collins (*Mark*, 303) observes that the title "tetrarch" is applied to Antipas by two inscriptions (Cos and Delos). Similarly, Casey (*Jesus of Nazareth*, 338–44) observes that Antipas minted coins with his title "tetrarch" on the reverse side and with a reed plant on the front side. In addition to the Cos and Delos inscriptions, Morton Jensen (*Herod Antipas in Galilee: The Literary and Archaeological Sources on the Reign of Herod Antipas and its Socio-Economic Impact on Galilee* [Tübingen: Mohr Siebeck, 2006], 203–14) notes a recently identified coin of Antipas (dated to 4 C.E.) that reads "Tetrarch, Herod" on the front. Some scholars suggest that Mark's utilization of the term "king" derives from "local custom." See, e.g., Cranfield, *Saint Mark*, 206. Joel Marcus (*Mark 1–8: A New Translation with Introduction and Commentary*, AB 27 [New York: Doubleday, 2000], 398–99 [quotation, p. 398]) recognizes that the "title 'king' is technically inaccurate" but attributes its usage to Markan irony. Aus, *Water into Wine*, 41, attributes its usage to Mark's dependence on the Esther tradition.

[30] See also Esth LXX: 1:21; 2:4; 5:13.
[31] Aus, *Water into Wine*, 54.
[32] Aus, *Water into Wine*, 41.

tradition, according to this configuration, Herodias and her daughter ostensibly occupy the parts played by Mordecai and Esther, respectively, in acting to quash a perceived threat.[33]

The public parade of John's head on a platter and the separation of his head from his body at burial freighted John's death with symbolic potential.[34] This postmortem manipulation of John's head can be understood as casting the Herodian family and John in a superior-inferior relationship—John's head and body are controlled and his identity divested by Antipas and the Herodian women. Yet, while Mark includes narrative elements that could invoke the degradation of the beheaded victim, as we will see, he remembers John's beheading in such a way that its symbolic potential does not reflect poorly on John the Baptist. Mark restrains the potentially degrading symbolism of John's bodily mutilation by bringing it into tension with other elements that contest the degrading framework.

Keying John's Beheading to Jesus' Crucifixion

In the Gospel of Mark, the beheading of John the Baptist and the crucifixion are closely tied together. This pairing is perceptible in particular by the repetition of terminology across the accounts of their arrests and deaths. Just as John the Baptist is "handed over" (παραδοθῆναι, 1:14), "grasped" (ἐκράτησεν, 6:17), and "bound" (ἔδησεν, 6:17), so also Jesus is "handed over" (παραδίδωμι, 3:19; 9:31; 10:33 [twice]; 14:10–11, 18, 21, 41–42, 44; 15:1, 10, 15; cf. 13:9, 11–12), "grasped" (κρατέω, 14:44, 46; cf. 12:12; 14:1, 49), and "bound" (δέω, 15:1). Just as Antipas initially listens to John the Baptist "gladly" (ἡδέως, 6:20) but later demands John's beheading in the midst of social pressure (6:26–27), so also a crowd initially listens to Jesus "gladly" (ἡδέως, 12:37) in Jerusalem but later demands Jesus' crucifixion after the chief priests stir them up (15:11, 13–14). Following their deaths, the bodies of John and Jesus (πτῶμα, 6:29; 15:45) are "placed" (τίθημι, 6:29; 15:46, 47; 16:6) "in a tomb" (ἐν μνημείῳ, 6:29; 15:46).

---

[33] For this reason, we might speculate (1) that Mark has taken over a tradition sympathetic to the Herodian court—one that positioned Herodias as the heroine who saved her people from an internal threat; or (2) that Mark has created the affinity with the Esther tradition to mock the Herodian court as mere posers of a heroic past.

[34] Commenting on Mark 6:14–29, Hartmann (*Tod Johannes des Täufers*, 195) rightly observes that the public display of John's head is highly symbolic: "Erst im öffentlichen Raum zeigt sich auch die eigentliche symbolische Tiefendimension der Enthauptung.... Die Demonstration bzw. Präsentation des Hauptes stellt dann den sichtbaren Sieg über den Gegner dar" ("The actual symbolic depth dimension of the beheading only becomes evident in the public space.... The demonstration or presentation of the head then presents the visible triumph over the opponent" [translation mine]). Importantly, however, the idea that the postmortem public display of a severed head is freighted with symbolism does not necessarily mean that private beheadings are always less emblematic. As we will see in the next chapter, Origen freights the secrecy (i.e., privacy) of the moment of John's beheading in prison with symbolic potential. Thus, it is important to observe that, although John's head is publicly displayed, his beheading proper occurs in prison.

In addition to the linguistic parallels, we can also point to the implicit identification of John the Baptist as Elijah *redivivus*, whose suffering antedates the suffering of the son of man (9:11–13).³⁵ Interpreters have long noticed these linguistic parallels as well as John's association with Elijah. The presence of these features has led to a widespread recognition: John's beheading in the Gospel of Mark serves to forerun or anticipate Jesus' death.³⁶

---

³⁵ In reference to Mark 9:1–13, Brian C. Dennert (*John the Baptist and the Jewish Setting of Matthew*, WUNT 403 [Tübingen: Mohr Siebeck, 2015], 40–41) writes: "The disciples do not seem to have recognized John as Elijah, as their question points to a belief that Elijah has not yet come. While Jesus does not explicitly name John as Elijah, the description that 'they did to him whatever they wanted' (9:13) combined with the allusions in the death of John and use of Mal 3:1 to introduce John identifies him as the 'Elijah to come.' The passage thus defends the Elijanic identity of John, using the suffering of the Son of Man to substantiate a suffering Elijah." Strictly speaking, Mal 3:1 does not specify that the "messenger" is Elijah (cf. Mal 4:5–6). However, Mark's (1) insinuation that John the Baptist is the messenger of Mal 3:1 (1:2–4), (2) alignment of Jesus with the one who "is coming after" John (1:7, 9; cf. Mal 4:5–6; see also 3 Kgdms 19:20 LXX—ἀκολουθήσω ὀπίσω σου), (3) close approximation of the clothing worn by John and Elijah (1:6; cf. 2 Kgs 1:8), and (4) idea that Elijah has already come "first" (9:9–13; cf. Mal 4:5–6) make it clear, albeit indirectly, that the Markan John the Baptist embodies the messenger of Mal 3:1 and Elijah of Mal 4:5–6. See Ernst Lohmeyer, *Johannes der Täufer* (Göttingen: Vandenhoeck & Ruprecht, 1932), 34, who attributes "das Fehlen einer offenen Identifizierung des Täufers mit Elija" ("the lack of an open identification of the Baptist with Elijah") in 9:9–13 to Mark's narrative technique of indirectness. The alignment of John and Elijah *across* the Synoptics is not monolithic. Walter Wink, *John the Baptist in the Gospel Tradition*, SNTSMS 7 (Cambridge: Cambridge University Press, 1968), 43: "Luke divests John of the role of Elijah *redivivus* which Mark had suggested and Matthew had developed." So also Catherine M. Murphy, *John the Baptist: Prophet of Purity for a New Age* (Collegeville, Minn.: Liturgical Press, 2003), 41–83; Mark Goodacre, "Mark, Elijah, the Baptist and Matthew: The Success of the First Intertextual Reading of Mark," in *Biblical Interpretation in Early Christian Gospels*, vol. 2: *Matthew*, ed. Tom Hatina, LNTS 310 (London: T&T Clark, 2008), 73–84. Cf. Webb, *Baptizer and Prophet*, 62–65, who argues that Luke (like Mark and Matthew) does portray John as Elijah *redivivus*. The Fourth Gospel has John outright deny his Elijanic identity (John 1:21).

³⁶ A. E. J. Rawlinson, *St Mark* (London: Methuen, 1925), 83; Willi Marxsen, *Mark the Evangelist: Studies on the Redaction History of the Gospel*, trans. Roy A. Harrisville (Nashville: Abingdon, 1969), 30–53; Walter Wink, *John the Baptist in the Gospel Tradition*, SNTSMS 7 (Cambridge: Cambridge University Press, 1968), 16–17; Morna D. Hooker, *The Gospel According to Saint Mark* (London: Black and Peabody, 1991), 158–59; Josef Ernst, *Johannes der Täufer: Interpretation, Geschichte, Wirkungsgeschichte*, BZNW 53 (Berlin: de Gruyter, 1989), 28–29; Webb, *Baptizer and Prophet*, 53–54; R. T. France, *The Gospel of Mark*, NIGTC (Grand Rapids: Eerdmans, 2002), 257; Mark McVann, "The 'Passion' of John the Baptist and Jesus before Pilate: Mark's Warnings about Kings and Governors," *BTB* 38 (2008): 153. The Gospel of Matthew similarly aligns the deaths of John and Jesus, making the former's beheading foreshadow the latter's crucifixion. See Janice C. Anderson, *Matthew's Narrative Web: Over, and Over, and Over Again*, JSNTSup 91 (Sheffield: JSOT Press, 1994), 89–90; William D. Davies and Dale C. Allison, *A Critical and Exegetical Commentary on the Gospel According to Saint Matthew*, ICC (London: T&T Clark, 1988), 2:476. See also Hippolytus (third century C.E.), who intimates that Jesus would preach in Hades since Jesus' forerunner, John, also preached in Hades when Antipas executed him (*Antichr.* 45). In the same century, Origen also indicates that John the Baptist died and descended into the underworld as Jesus' precursor in order to proclaim the coming of Jesus (*Hom. Luc.* 4.5).

A historical-critical approach to this recognition would identify such literary foreshadowing as an indication of the account's legendary character and proceed to hypothesize the geneaological development of the convergence of John's and Jesus' deaths.[37] A social memory approach, however, is not so much helpful in tracing the prehistory of a tradition and charting its sources as it is in illuminating the sociological and cultural impact of the alignment of John's beheading to Jesus' crucifixion.[38] Mark 6:14–29 reflects the chief characteristics of the commemorative maneuver that memory theorists label "keying." The pericope analogically keys John's beheading to Jesus' crucifixion, but this alignment does not serve as a mere comparison of the two figures' deaths. Rather, their convergence transforms the memory of John's beheading into a "cultural system," as John's beheading is integrated into an emerging cultural script (Jesus' crucifixion).[39]

The goal of interpretive keying is not to retrieve or duplicate an event, but to comprehend, to "unlock" the past by associating it with an intelligible framework of reference.[40] From this perspective, keying the beheading to the crucifixion does not imitate the "actual past," nor does it simply function literarily to foreshadow Jesus' demise. It also fuses the cultural substance of John's beheading to resemble that of Jesus' crucifixion. As it pertains to the degradation of the victim that narrating a beheading can invoke, the upshot of this keying is that both figures are mutually exonerated as victims of ignominious, gruesome deaths (innocent by association); and both deaths offer a moral indictment of their opponents who had them unjustly executed (guilty by association).[41]

Keying John's beheading to the crucifixion maps the innocence of Jesus onto that of John, and vice versa. In their death narratives, both figures are portrayed as innocent but nevertheless put to death as political leaders navigate social pressure. Mark claims that Herod is cognizant of the fact that John "was a righteous and holy man" (6:20).[42] Although Antipas sought to protect

---

[37] See Martin Dibelius, *Die urchristliche Überlieferung von Johannes dem Täufer* (Göttingen: Vandenhoeck & Ruprecht, 1911), 78–80; John P. Meier, *A Marginal Jew: Rethinking the Historical Jesus*, vol. 2: *Mentor, Message, and Miracles*, ABRL (New York: Doubleday, 1994), 2:171–76; Gerd Theissen, *The Gospels in Context: Social and Political History in the Synoptic Tradition* (Minneapolis: Fortress, 1991), 81–96.

[38] Similarly, Sandra Hübenthal, "Gospel of Mark," in *The Reception of Jesus in the First Three Centuries*, ed. Chris Keith et al. (London: T&T Clark, 2020), 1:59–60.

[39] Barry Schwartz, *Abraham Lincoln and the Forge of National Memory* (Chicago: University of Chicago Press, 2000), 226.

[40] Hübenthal, "Gospel of Mark," 60.

[41] See Nathan L. Shedd, "John the Baptist," in the online *T&T Clark Jesus Library*, forthcoming.

[42] See Stein, *Mark*, 304, who writes in reference to 6:20: "The turmoil in Herod's mind makes his action all the more damnable."

John, "he did not wish" (οὐκ ἠθέλησεν) to reject the girl's wish for John's head because of his oaths and dinner guests, and so he has John beheaded (6:26–27). Similarly, Mark claims that Pilate was cognizant of the fact that the chief priests had "handed him [Jesus] over because of envy" (15:10). Pilate even asks the crowd after they insist for Jesus to be crucified, "Why? What evil (κακόν) has he done?" (15:14). Although he tries apparently to protect Jesus by presenting the crowd with an opportunity to release "the king of the Jews" (15:9), Pilate "wishes" (βουλόμενος) to satisfy the crowd; and so he has Jesus flogged and handed over to be crucified (15:15), in accordance with the crowd's "wish" (θέλετε, 15:9, 12).[43] With Mark's alignment of John's innocence to Jesus' innocence, the reader is guided to pass a moral judgment on their deaths: John is evaluated as unjustly executed insofar as Jesus is unjustly executed; accordingly, Jesus is exonerated insofar as John is exonerated. Keying renders their exonerations as mutually contingent and affecting in this way.

Simultaneous to aligning the innocence of Jesus and John is an association between the opponents of Jesus and those who act to put John to death. As we have already seen, Antipas is made to reflect Pilate. Herodias, however, is made to reflect the chief priests and scribes. Herodias wanted "to kill" (ἀποκτεῖναι) John—after John criticizes Antipas' marriage to her (6:18)—only to have her plot delimited by Antipas, who "feared" (φοβέομαι) John (6:19–20). The chief priests and scribes similarly seek to arrest and/or kill Jesus (after he criticizes them), but their strategies are regulated by fear:

> Mark 11:18: "And the chief priests and scribes heard it and they kept seeking how they might destroy him [Jesus]; for they were afraid (ἐφοβοῦντο) of him, because the crowd was amazed at his teaching."

> Mark 12:12: "And they [the chief priests, scribes, and elders—see 11:27] kept seeking to arrest him, but they were afraid (ἐφοβήθησαν) of the crowd, for they knew that he spoke this parable against them. And they left him and departed."

---

[43] Thus, in response to Helen Bond's argument (*Pontius Pilate in History and Interpretation*, SNTSMS 100 [Cambridge: Cambridge University Press, 1998], 112) that "nothing in Pilate's previous behaviour has given any hint that the governor does regard Jesus as innocent," it must be emphasized that the Markan Pilate does not explicitly indicate that Jesus was truly guilty of the charges brought against him. Mark portrays Pilate bending to the will of the crowd, not acknowledging the credibility of their claims against Jesus. On Mark's presentation of Pilate as a weak ruler see Susan Miller, *Women in Mark's Gospel*, JSNTSup 259 (London: T&T Clark International, 2004), 83. Cf. Bond, *Pontius Pilate*, 105–19, who argues that, although Mark does not portray Pilate as a weak ruler, he is still implicated in the death of Jesus. So also Susanna Asikainen, *Jesus and Other Men: Ideal Masculinities in the Synoptic Gospels*, BibInt 159 (Leiden: Brill, 2018), 70–71.

Mark 14:1: "And the chief priests and the scribes kept seeking how in cunning they might arrest and kill (ἀποκτείνωσιν) him; for they were saying, 'Not during the festival, or else there may be a riot among the people.'"[44]

Mark also keys Herodias to Judas Iscariot. Just as Herodias manages to initiate John's beheading on an "opportune" (εὐκαίρου, 6:21) day,[45] Judas kept seeking an "opportune time" (εὐκαίρως) to hand Jesus over (14:11). Thus, although interpretive keying consistently aligns John to Jesus and creates a distance between their moral coloration and that of their opponents, the specific interpretive frame of reference for the Herodian court fluctuates.[46]

The metamorphosis of John's beheading into a cultural schematic—one that exonerates John and Jesus as victims of violent deaths and offers a moral indictment of their opponents—also particularizes Jesus' royal personality relative to "king" Antipas.[47] Of the twelve occurrences of the substantive "king" (βασιλεύς) in Mark, eleven refer either to Antipas or Jesus, five in reference to Antipas in the present passage (6:14, 22, 25, 26, 27) and

---

[44] See also Mark 14:55 where the chief priests and Sanhedrin "kept seeking" (ἐζήτουν) testimony in order to put Jesus to death.

[45] Mark draws attention to this element of the story in 6:21 by means of a genitive absolute construction: γενομένης ἡμέρας εὐκαίρου ("when an opportune day came about").

[46] This fluctuation is further apparent by analyzing how the repetition of the verb θέλω ("I want") in reference to the Herodian court in Mark 6:14–29 meshes with the "will" of other characters in the Gospel of Mark. The (in)appropriate orientation of one's "will" is a prominent theme in Mark, especially in the context of the three passion predictions (8:27–33; 9:30–32; 10:32–34) and the passion narrative (14:1–15:47). See, e.g., the "will" of the Herodian women consists of "wanting" (θέλω) to kill John (6:19), to place his head on a platter (6:25). Antipas does *not* "want" (θέλω, 6:26) to deny the girl's request for John's head because he made a public oath in front of his banquet guests to give to the girl whatever she "wants" (θέλω, 6:22, 26). The "will" of the Herodian court accords with others whose "will" (θέλω) is construed negatively in Mark's text (e.g., 12:38–40; 15:9, 11, 12–13; cf. 9:34–35; 10:35–44). We can also observe Pilate's "will" that is described in 15:15 using a near synonymn of θέλω: "Pilate, wanting (βουλόμενος) to satisfy the crowd, released for them Barabbas and handed over Jesus, after flogging him, to be crucified." See BDAG, s.v. "βούλομαι." The "will" of the Herodian court, moreover, diverges from other characters whose "will" is evaluated positively in Mark's text (e.g., 1:40–41; 3:35; 10:51; 14:36). Although the utility of the term "social outcast" is questionable, Miller's contrast (*Women in Mark's Gospel*, 84) captures the gist of the matter: "Unlike the Herodians, those who suffer diseases and live as social outcasts express desires which are compatible with the will of God.... The desires of Herodias, her daughter and Herod bring torment and death to others." On the repetition of θέλω cognates in Mark's Gospel, see Abraham Smith, "Tyranny Exposed: Mark's Typological Characterization of Herod Antipas (Mark 6:14–29)," *BibInt* 14 (2006): esp. 281–86.

[47] Geoffrey D. Miller, "An Intercalation Revisited: Christology, Discipleship, and Dramatic Irony in Mark 6.6b–30," *JSNT* 35 (2012): 182: "Mark's reference to Herod as a king should immediately grab the reader's attention; the title is inaccurate, for Herod was merely a 'tetrarch' (τετράρχης) [sic]."

six occurences in reference to Jesus in the passion narrative (15:2, 9, 12, 18, 26, 32). No other figure is characterized as such in Mark's narrative.[48] The distribution of this term, therefore, facilitates a contrast between the two "kings."[49]

Whereas Antipas orders the beheading of John the Baptist (6:22–27), Jesus voluntarily lays down his life for the benefit of many (10:45).[50] While Antipas "sends" (ἀποστέλλω) lackeys to arrest John (6:17) and an executioner to behead John (6:27), Jesus—in the passage that forms the exterior frame in which the account of John's death is intercalated (6:6b-13, 30)—"sends" (ἀποστέλλω) the twelve disciples to proclaim repentance, to exorcise demons, and to heal the sick.[51] Whereas Jesus, in the ensuing passage (6:31–44), feeds a crowd of five thousand men with five loaves and two fish, Antipas plates a severed head (ripe with corpse impurity) on a serving platter at his birthday banquet (6:28).[52] In respect to these points of difference, the interconnection between John's death and Jesus' death serves to sharpen Jesus' royal stature.

The association of John with Elijah adds another cultural frame of reference to the keying of John's and Jesus' deaths. In his 1968 classic redaction-critical analysis of John-the-Baptist tradition, Wink averred that the suffering of the Baptist in Mark 6:17–29 is not explained until the descent from the transfiguration in 9:9–13.[53] Jesus' connection therein between John and Elijah (9:13) implies that "John's suffering as Elijah-incognito prepares the way for the fate of Jesus."[54] Wink is not wrong that the descent from the transfiguration (9:9–13) explicitly frames the death of John the Baptist in terms of the suffering of Elijah *redivivus*. In this

---

[48] The occurrence of βασιλεύς in Mark 13:9 is generic and does not specify the identities of those who receive this title.

[49] R. Alan Culpepper, "Mark 6:17–29 in Its Narrative Context: Kingdoms in Conflict," in *Mark as Story: Retrospect and Prospect*, ed. Kelly R. Iverson and Christopher W. Skinner, SBLRBS 65 (Atlanta: Society of Biblical Literature, 2011), 154.

[50] Culpepper, "Mark 6:17–29 in Its Narrative Context," 163.

[51] Similarly, Stein, *Mark*, 302.

[52] For a contrast between Herod's and Jesus' masculinity in their roles as dinner hosts (6:14–29; 6:32–44), see Peter-Ben Smit, *Masculinity and the Bible: Surveys, Models, and Perspectives* (Leiden: Brill, 2017), 62, who argues that Herod's "loss of self-control is precisely what initiates his downfall as a credible and masculine ruler." On Herod's lack of self-control, see further below.

[53] Wink, *John the Baptist in the Gospel Tradition*, 13.

[54] Wink, *John the Baptist in the Gospel Tradition*, 17. So also Hooker, *Mark*, 158–59; William L. Lane, *The Gospel According to Mark*, NICNT (Grand Rapids: Eerdmans, 1974), 215, 223; Webb, *Baptizer and Prophet*, 53–54; Christos Karakolis, "Narrative Funktion und christologische Bedeutung der markinischen Erzählung vom Tod Johannes des Täufers (Mk 6:14–29)," *NovT* 52 (2010): 135–55. Cf. Taylor, *Immerser*, 281–88, who suggests that 9:11–13 is only intelligible if read as an independent unit, one that configures John/Elijah as the "son of man" in 9:12.

way, the speculation regarding whether Jesus is Elijah (6:15; 8:27) is clarified once and for all.[55] Prior to the transfiguration, however, the Gospel of Mark has already linked (1) John with Elijah *and* (2) Jesus with Elijah (and Elijah's successor, Elisha).

For example, the Gospel's description of John's clothing attire—camel's hair and a leather belt around the waist (1:6)—is surely a nod to the hairy man Elijah himself, who sported a similar garb (4 Kgdms 1:8 LXX).[56] Like Elijah, Jesus is served by wild animals and angels in the wilderness (1:13; cf. 1 Kgs 17:2-6; 19:4-9). Both Elijah and Jesus issue calls for followers (1 Kgs 19:19-21; Mark 1:16-20); at the same time, Elisha and Jesus are both said to come "after" (ὀπίσω) Elijah and John, respectively (1 Kgs 19:19-21; Mark 1:7, 9).[57] Jesus reanimating a dead child in 5:21-24, 35-43 recalls Elijah and Elisha, who also revived the dead (1 Kgs 17:17-24; 2 Kgs 4:18-37).[58] Thus, by the time Mark recounts John's beheading in 6:17-29, which is introduced in 6:15 by the report of speculation that Jesus might be Elijah, an alert reader—one who is aware of these Elijanic resonances—might filter John's conflict with the Herodian court through the framework of Elijah's conflict with King Ahab and Queen Jezebel (1 Kgs 17-19).[59] After all, Elijah rebuked King Ahab for violating the law by worshiping Baal (1 Kgs 18:17-19; cf. Exod 20:3; 34:14; Deut 5:7; 6:13-14), a violation explicitly connected to Ahab's marriage to Jezebel (1 Kgs 16:29-33); Jezebel plotted Elijah's demise (1 Kgs 19:2). The thematic resemblance with John's beheading is hard to ignore.[60] As Hübenthal notes: "The story of [Elijah/Elisha] and their signs is clearly and vividly recalled in Mark's Gospel" although "this mainly goes without direct quotations or unambiguous allusions; references are more associative and occur on a structural level."[61] At a bare minimum, Mark enabled a reception

---

[55] Similarly, Hübenthal, "Gospel of Mark," 67: "The assessment of [the configuration of Jesus in the terms of Elijah/Elisha] by the character Jesus himself . . . is negative: Even though the feeding story in 6:30-44 might have evoked connections with Jesus, the linking of Elijah with John the Baptist (9:13) finally puts this idea to rest."
[56] Marcus, *John the Baptist in History and Theology*, 49-54.
[57] For discussion, see Marcus, *John the Baptist in History and Theology*, 88-89.
[58] For further connections between Elijah/Elisha and John/Jesus, see Hübenthal, "Gospel of Mark," 66-67.
[59] So also Culpepper, "Mark 6:17-29 in Its Narrative Context," 149.
[60] First Kings 21:25: "Indeed, there was no one like Ahab, who sold himself to do what was evil in the sight of the Lord, urged on by his wife Jezebel" (NRSV). On the similarities and differences between 1 Kgs 17-19 and Mark 6:14-29, see Silvia Pellegrini, *Elija—Wegbereiter des Gottessohnes: Eine textsemiotische Untersuchung im Markusevangelium*, Herders Biblische Studien 26 (Freiburg: Herder, 2000), 280-81; David M. Hoffeditz and Gary E. Yates, "Femme Fatale Redux: Intertextual Connection to the Elijah/Jezebel Narratives in Mark 6:14-29," *BBR* 15 (2005): 199-221. See also 2 Kgs 6:31, where the prophet Elisha faces the threat of beheading from the king of Israel.
[61] Hübenthal, "Gospel of Mark," 67 (italics removed).

history of reading the tradition of John's death against this Elijanic backdrop (assuming Markan priority, at least).[62]

In light of this discussion, the script of John's severed head highlighting the degradation of the Baptist while enhancing the heroic prestige of Herodias is turned on its head. Although Herodias' influence over the "girl" (who "pleases" the "king" Antipas) in her bid to quell the threat of the Baptist resembles Mordecai's influence over Esther (a "girl" who likewise "pleases" a "king") in his bid to thwart the deadly threat of Haman, this resemblance is counterbalanced by the commemorative impact of keying John's beheading to Jesus' crucifixion. Mark refracts the image of the Herodian court by aligning them with an alternative cultural schematic: the opposition to Jesus and Elijah. Thus, rather than filling the role of Mordecai, Herodias more closely resembles the chief priests, scribes, Judas Iscariot, and Jezebel. In this respect, Herodias' affinity with the Mordecai-Esther tradition serves to sharpen the reader's aversion to her: she poses as the masculine hero Mordecai but really stands in a cultural line of opposition to God's prophets. Duran is right: "The reader who knows and loves Esther and Judith hates Herodias, the more so for her resemblance to them."[63] Antipas' alignment to Pilate and King Ahab, moreover, underscores the innocence of John/Jesus and Antipas' disregard for the law. Simultaneously, keying sets up an antithesis between two kingly figures—Antipas and Jesus—and situates the conduct of the latter positively and the former negatively. The application of this cultural framework to the death of John the Baptist, therefore, positions John as unjustly executed and the Herodian court as those responsible for putting an innocent person to death. In this way, Jesus' unjust crucifixion vindicates John as a victim of beheading even as John's beheading functions to exonerate Jesus as a victim of crucifixion and to enhance his prestige as king.

John's Beheading in the Gospels of Matthew and Luke

Outside the Gospel of Mark, the Gospels of Matthew and Luke are the only extant texts from the first century that mention the beheading of John the Baptist (Matt 14:1–12; Luke 9:7–9; cf. Luke 3:19–20).[64] Allison once

---

[62] For example, in his *Commentary on Matthew*, Jerome claims that John the Baptist rebuked Herod and Herodias "with the same authority with which Elijah had rebuked Ahab and Jezebel" (*Comm. Matt.* 14.3–4 [Scheck, FC]).

[63] Nicole Duran, "Having Men for Dinner: Deadly Banquets and Biblical Women," *BTB* 35 (2005): 123. See also Crossley, *Jesus and the Chaos of History*, 152, 154: "Esther's sexuality is constructed positively while Salome's is construed negatively. . . . Both [Esther and Salome-Herodias] use their culturally constructed power to please but one uses it to save life, the other(s) to kill."

[64] Josephus mentions John's death, but not the beheading of John (see *Ant.* 18.116–119). The Gospel of John does not mention John's death, let alone his beheading. But, see Augustine, *Tract. Ev. Jo.* 14.5.3, where he claims that Jesus' crucifixion and John's beheading exemplified the saying in John 3:30 ("He must increase, but I must decrease"). So also Augustine, *Serm.* 307.1.

observed that "fewer" scholars "have spoken of Matthew" in the same way that many—following Martin Kähler's famous description in the nineteenth century—have evaluated the Gospel of Mark: "as a passion narrative with an extended introduction."[65] Despite Matthew's passion narrative occupying "a proportionately smaller amount of space," he contends that Matthew's "entire narrative leans forward, so to speak, to its end, so that the reader of Matt. 1–25 is never far from thinking of the ensuing chapters, 26–28."[66] As part of this overall narrative effect, John's beheading "leans forward" to Jesus' crucifixion in Matthew's narration.[67] Just as John is "grasped" (κρατέω, Matt 14:3) and "bound" (δέω, Matt 14:3), so also Jesus is "grasped" (κρατέω, Matt 21:46; 26:4, 48, 50, 55, 57) and "bound" (δέω, Matt 27:2). John's "disciples" (μαθητής, Matt 14:12) bury John; Joseph of Arimathea was "discipled" (μαθητεύω, Matt 27:57) by Jesus and placed Jesus' corpse in a tomb (Matt 27:57–61).[68] Thus, like Mark's portrayal, Matthew keys John's beheading to Jesus' crucifixion. Consequently, Matthew also employs a cultural schematic in which John and Jesus are mutually vindicated as victims of hostile opposition.

Matthew's account follows Mark 6:14–29 in its general outline but heavily abbreviates the tradition.[69] As part of this truncation, however, Matthew establishes Antipas as the primary antagonist among the characters in the Herodian court. It is Antipas, not Herodias, who "wants" (θέλω) "to kill" (ἀποκτείνω) John the Baptist (Matt 14:5; cf. Mark 6:19). However, he is not able to kill John: he "fears" (φοβέω) the "crowd" (ὄχλος) "because they held him as a prophet" (προφήτης) (Matt 14:5). Matthew thus amalgamates the Markan characterization of Antipas (who "fears" [φοβέω] John, Mark 6:20) and Herodias (who "wants" [θέλω] "to kill" [ἀποκτείνω] John but could not do so, Mark 6:19) into the Matthean Antipas.[70] As such, the Matthean

---

[65] Dale C. Allison, *Studies in Matthew: Interpretation Past and Present* (Grand Rapids: Baker Academic, 2005), 217.

[66] Allison, *Studies in Matthew*, 217.

[67] Gary Yamasaki, *John the Baptist in Life and Death: Audience-Oriented Criticism of Matthew's Narrative*, JSNTSup 167 (Sheffield: Sheffield Academic Press, 1998), 132: "In [the] account of John's execution, the narratee is prompted to see this depiction of John's fate as a precursor of Jesus' fate."

[68] For further possible thematic links between John's death and Jesus' death in Matthew, see, e.g., Allison, *Studies in Matthew*, 225–26; Dennert, *John the Baptist*, 238–54; David L. Turner, *Matthew*, BECNT (Grand Rapids: Baker Academic, 2008), 365: "Antipas's reluctance to behead John may anticipate Pilate's reluctance to crucify Jesus (14:9; 27:18–24)."

[69] Nolland, *Gospel of Matthew*, 581; Daniel J. Harrington, *The Gospel of Matthew*, SP (Collegeville, Minn.: Liturgical Press, 2007), 216–17; Craig A. Evans, *Matthew*, New Cambridge Bible Commentary (Cambridge: Cambridge University Press, 2012), 291; Dennert, *John the Baptist*, 244.

[70] At first glance, Matthew appears to alter the type and object of the "fear" that governs Mark's Antipas. Mark's Antipas seems to fear John out of a sense of reverence as he listens gladly to the prophet and protects him (6:20). Matthew's Antipas fears the reputation of

Antipas, not Herodias, is keyed to the chief priests and Pharisees who sought to take hold of Jesus, but "feared" (φοβέω) the "crowds" (ὄχλος) "because they held him as a prophet" (προφήτης) (Matt 21:46).[71] Thus, one scholar observes: "Matthew has inserted the behavior of the Jewish leaders into the portrayal of Herod, linking these groups together."[72] The point of connection is significant because, as we will see in the next chapter, Justin Martyr and Origen collectively will redeploy the Herodian court's (especially Antipas') ethical conduct so that it is keyed not merely to particular first-century Jewish leaders, but also to contemporary "Jews."

By portraying Antipas as the chief protagonist, Matthew shows some restraint in configuring a John-Elijah/Herodias-Jezebel framework around John's beheading.[73] Nevertheless, Matthew does establish John as a prophet, even as Elijah *redivivus*. In fact, the Gospel of Matthew is the most explicit of the Synoptic Gospels in identifying John as Elijah.[74] The Matthean parallel (Matt 17:9–13) to Jesus' descent from the transfiguration in Mark 9:9–13 explicitly links John the Baptist to Elijah, whose suffering precedes that of the "son of man": "Then the disciples understood that he [Jesus] spoke to them concerning John the Baptist" (Matt 17:13).[75] Prior to the account of John's beheading, furthermore, the Matthean Jesus identifies John as a prophet (11:9), the greatest human (11:11), and Elijah (11:15: "If you are willing to accept [it], he [John] is Elijah who is to come."). In conjunction with the note that the crowd thought of John as a prophet (Matt 14:5) in the account of

---

John among the populace as a prophet (and, therefore, what killing such a person could instigate). This contrast could be two sides of the same coin, however. Mark's Antipas fears John in view of his reputation as a "righteous and holy man" (6:20). Protecting John could thus be seen as a measure to prevent a potential uprising springing from his death. Matthew, then, makes this explicit by asserting that Antipas feared John's reputation among the crowd. The key difference between the accounts is that Mark attributes the desire to kill John—but the inability to do so—to Herodias and Matthew attributes this to Antipas.

[71] See also Matt 27:15–23 where the "crowd(s)" (ὄχλος, 27:15–23) "want" (θέλω, 27:15, 17, 21) Barabbas released, but Jesus crucified. Cf. Matt 21:23–27.

[72] Dennert, *John the Baptist*, 247.

[73] Similarly, Dennert, *John the Baptist*, 244–45. Dennert's ensuing claim that Matthew's account thereby "paints Herod in a more negative light" (*John the Baptist*, 245), however, is an oversimplification. As we will see, the Markan Herod's positive appraisal of John and desire to protect him from Herodias heightens Herod's loss of masculinity—he is ultimately unable to control the Herodian women. On the softening of the Elijah-Jezebel connection in the Matthean account, see Harrington, *Gospel of Matthew*, 214–18.

[74] In this respect, the reduction of the Elijah-Jezebel framework in Matt 14:1–12 is, as Dennert, *John the Baptist*, 244, remarks, "somewhat surprising." This surprise is compounded in light of Matt 17:12–13 where John and Elijah are associated together in connection with John's death.

[75] Richard J. Erickson, "The Jailing of John and the Baptism of Jesus: Luke 3:19–21," *JETS* 36 (1993): 457: "Matthew improves on Mark by actually interpreting Elijah as John the Baptist (Matt 17:13)."

John's decapitation, therefore, Matthew situates Antipas negatively as one who is hostile to God's prophets.[76]

Luke, similar to Mark and Matthew, recounts that speculation surrounded the identities of John and Jesus (Mark 6:14–16//Matt 14:1–2//Luke 9:7–9), but departs from Mark and Matthew by not narrating John's beheading (Mark 6:17–29//Matt 14:3–12), only mentioning that Antipas had John beheaded (Luke 9:9).[77] Like Mark, Luke structures the speculation regarding John/Jesus as the interior of an intercalation between the sending out of the twelve disciples and their return (Luke 9:1–6, 10). According to Luke 9:9—"Herod said: 'John I myself beheaded; but who is this about whom I am hearing such things?'"—Antipas differentiates Jesus from John on the basis of the method with which Herod had John executed. This remark, however, does not negate that this saying connects John's death to Jesus' death in two ways. First, Herod's rhetorical question "foreshadows Jesus' question and Peter's confession, which Jesus interprets through the suffering of the Messiah (9:18–22)."[78] Second, the differentiation between the two figures allows the narrator to add a final remark to Luke 9:9: "And he [Herod] was seeking to see him [Jesus]." Thus, Luke 9:9 prepares the narrative for Jesus' future interaction with Herod.[79] Herod "will reappear in connection with the plot against Jesus and in connection with Jesus' death (13:31–33; 23:7–11; Acts 4:27)."[80]

Luke, interestingly, has a "mixed" portrayal of John and Elijah. In the infancy narrative, Luke associates John the Baptist with the "spirit and power of Elijah" (Luke 1:17). Luke also affiliates Jesus with Elijah (e.g., raising of the widow's son—Luke 7:7–17 [cf. 1 Kgs 17:17–24]; fire from heaven—9:51–56 [cf. 2 Kgs 1:10–14]).[81] Yet Luke also distances John from an Elijanic identity. Luke omits certain traditions in which Mark and Matthew make a connection

---

[76] Matthew heightens this cultural construct. Rather than structuring John's beheading as the interior of an intercalation between the sending and return of the twelve disciples (as does Mark and Luke), he inserts the account directly after the episode of Jesus' visit to his hometown, which is framed as a rejection of the prophets (Matt 13:53–58). On the rejection of the prophets in Matthew, see Matt 5:12; 17:12–13; 23:29–37. Herod's desire to kill John in Matt 14:5 connects him with his father, Herod the Great, who similarly sought to kill Jesus in Jesus' infancy (Matt 2:1–18).

[77] Earlier in his Gospel, however, Luke had linked Antipas' arrest of John with the latter's rebuke of Antipas (Luke 3:19–20; cf. Mark 6:17–18; Matt 14:3–4).

[78] François Bovon, *Luke: A Commentary on the Gospel of Luke 1:1–9:50*, Hermeneia (Minneapolis: Fortress, 2002), 349.

[79] I. Howard Marshall, *The Gospel of Luke: A Commentary on the Greek Text*, NIGTC (Exeter: Paternoster, 1978), 355; Joel B. Green, *The Gospel of Luke*, NICNT (Grand Rapids: Eerdmans, 1997), 362.

[80] Green, *Gospel of Luke*, 360–61.

[81] See further, Goodacre, "Mark, Elijah, the Baptist and Matthew," 83; James A. Kelhoffer, *The Diet of John the Baptist: "Locusts and Wild Honey" in Synoptic and Patristic Interpretation*, WUNT 176 (Tübingen: Mohr Siebeck, 2005), 129–32.

between John and Elijah. The note on John's clothing (Mark 1:6//Matt 3:4) that parallels the appearance of Elijah in 4 Kingdoms 1:8 LXX has no Lukan counterpart. Nor does Luke recount the descent from the transfiguration where Mark 9:9–13 implies John is Elijah, and Matthew 17:9–13 makes this identification explicit. In this light, the absence of a Lukan counterpart to Mark 6:17–29, which as we have seen has a measure of resemblance to the Elijah-Ahab-Jezebel conflict, may reflect a redactional impulse to moderate Elijanic associations with John.[82]

Despite John's distance from an Elijanic identity in Luke, Luke's John "was a prophet without equal."[83] According to Luke 1:76, John the Baptist "will be called a prophet of the Most High." The characterization of John as a prophet continues as John receives his prophetic call in Luke 3:2: "During the high-priesthood of Annas and Caiaphas, the word of God came upon John the son of Zechariah in the wilderness." Given his evaluation of John, then, it is not surprising that Luke's antipathies reside with Antipas in the episode of John's imprisonment: "And Herod the tetrarch, having been rebuked by him [John] concerning Herodias, the wife of his brother, and concerning all the evil things which he did, Herod also added this to them all: he locked up John in prison" (Luke 3:19–20).[84] Finally, Herod's question in Luke 9:9 ("John I myself beheaded; but who is this about whom I am hearing such things?") "leads the reader to class Herod as yet another character who 'hears but does not understand' (8.10)."[85]

---

[82] Likewise, the Gospel of John's distancing of John from Elijah (John 1:21) may also explain the absence of a Johannine counterpart to Mark 6:17–29//Matt 14:3–12. For alternative theories on this Lukan and Johannine omission, see Marcus, *John the Baptist in History and Theology*, 213–14, n. 1. See also Regina Janes, "Why the Daughter of Herodias Must Dance (Mark 6.14–29)," *JSNT* 28 (2006): 456: "Luke's motive for deleting the story seems to be its misogyny." For a study that argues that Luke portrays John as Elijah, see Jaroslav Rindos, *He of Whom It Is Written: John the Baptist and Elijah in Luke*, ÖBS 38 (Frankfurt am Main: Lang, 2010). For a rebuttal of Rindos, see Clare K. Rothschild, review of *He of Whom It Is Written: John the Baptist and Elijah in Luke*, by Jaroslav Rindos, *RBL*, 2012, http://www.bookreviews.org: "[Rindos] never considers the possibility that attributing *only* Elijah's spirit and power to John *denies* him Elijah's identity, as does Luke's omission of (1) John's clothing, (2) John's diet, (3) Jesus' statement that John was the Elijah who was to come (Mark 9:11–13||Matt 17:10)" (italics original). Rothschild's rebuttal is reminiscent of Origen's interpretation of Luke 1:17: "Luke does not say, 'in the soul of Elijah,' but, 'in the spirit and power of Elijah.' Power and spirit dwelt in Elijah as in all the prophets and, with regard to his humanity, in the Lord and Savior as well" (*Hom. Luc.* 4.5 [Lienhard, FC]).

[83] Brent Kinman, "Luke's Exoneration of John the Baptist," *JTS* 44 (1993): 595. See also Erickson, "Jailing of John," 455–66.

[84] See Erickson, "Jailing of John," 455: "Luke's sympathies clearly lie with John the Baptist in John's encounter with Herod Antipas (Luke 3:19–20)."

[85] John A. Darr, *Herod the Fox: Audience Criticism and Lukan Characterization*, JSNTSup 163 (Sheffield: Sheffield Academic Press, 1998), 164.

These elements of Matthew and Luke, therefore, despite their different emphases, nevertheless share the common thread of contesting the degrading potential John faces as a victim of beheading. Both drive a sharp divide between John the Baptist, constructed positively as God's prophet, and Herod Antipas, constructed negatively as one who puts God's prophet to death. As we will see in the final chapter, this divide takes some dangerous turns in its reception history in the second and third centuries.

Negotiating Herod Antipas' Masculinity

As we have seen, Mark contests the ignominious capacity of John the Baptist's beheading by keying John to the sympathetic protagonist Jesus and thus also associating John's opponents with Jesus' opposition. In this respect, the beheading and postmortem public display of John's severed head do not so much exhibit Herodias' superiority and triumph over John as they showcase her resemblance to those who opposed, or those whose actions resulted in the death of, God's innocent agents. At this juncture, we will explore how Mark contests the degrading framework of John's decapitation in a further way: by negotiating Herod Antipas' masculine reign. Rather than highlighting the shame of his death, John's beheading projects a damning shadow over Antipas' royal efficacy.

Some readers, however, may be suspicious of such an argument. A long line of interpreters has understood one or more of the Herodian women as primarily at fault in Mark's portrayal, and for compelling reasons.[86] Three explanations in

---

[86] Janes, "Why the Daughter of Herodias Must Dance," 449: "The episode lays the blame principally on Herodias, who sought John's death and told her daughter what to ask." Prior to Janes, Janice Capel Anderson, "Feminist Criticism: The Dancing Daughter," in *Mark and Method: New Approaches in Biblical Studies*, ed. Janice Capel Anderson and Stephen D. Moore (Minneapolis: Fortress, 1992), 120, asserted that "more extended comments and inside views of Herod seem designed to win sympathy for Herod . . . [but Herodias is presented] unsympathetically as a woman with a grudge." See also Collins, *Mark*, 313; Crossley, *Jesus and the Chaos of History*, esp. 148, 153–54, 158. For an earlier version of his argument, see Crossley, "History from the Margins: The Death of John the Baptist," in *Writing History, Constructing Religion*, ed. James G. Crossley and Christian Karner (Aldershot: Ashgate, 2005), 147–61. This line of argumentation departs from other interpreters who claim that Mark casts a negative shadow primarily over Herod Antipas. Murphy, *John the Baptist*, 127, for example, writes that "the story leaves one angry with Herod, who has elevated pleasure, indiscretion, and his own honor above the righteousness of [John]." Donahue and Harrington, *Gospel of Mark*, 199, claim that "the ultimate blame falls on Herod." See also Jennifer A. Glancy, "Unveiling Masculinity: The Construction of Gender in Mark 6:17–29," *BibInt* 2 (1994): 34–50, who all but exonerates the Herodian women from blame while highlighting how scholars have underappreciated Antipas' responsibility. To be clear, Glancy does not suggest that Mark approves of the Herodian women's actions in the story, only that "Herodias herself is not represented as a monster, nor is there any hint that the desire of mother and daughter grows out of their sexuality" (p. 42). The only "hint of a grotesque

particular are frequently forwarded. First, the synoptic shift from designating Herodias as the one who "wanted to kill him [John]" in Mark 6:19 to the description of Herod Antipas as the one who "wanted to kill him [John]" in Matt 14:5 suggests that Matthew "paints Herod in a more negative light" than Mark.[87] After all, the Markan Antipas harbored a positive inclination toward John, as Antipas "listened to him [John] gladly" and "protected" John (6:20). Or, as Augustine asserted in the early fifth century: "Herod loved John."[88] Second, the perceived dangerousness of female sexual seduction diminishes Antipas' responsibility for John's death. According to Crossley, for example, "in first-century Palestine there was an established association between evil and seductive female sexuality."[89] He appeals to a number of relevant texts to illustrate this claim, including Proverbs 7:25–26, where wrongdoing takes on the persona of a seductive woman: "Do not let your hearts turn aside to her ways; do not stray into her paths; for many are those she has laid low, and numerous are her victims" (NRSV).[90] Wisdom was also associated with the luring sexuality of a woman, as in 11Q5 col. XXI 11–18.[91] These synonymously gendered personifications of evil and wisdom form what Crossley terms a "dangerous ambiguity."[92] Accordingly, he reasons, "And Antipas was indeed lured and in the context of the construction of dangerous ambiguity Mark 6.17–29 is relieving Antipas of some of the blame in that it was hardly his fault he was attracted to the 'young girl.'"[93]

Third, Mark "all but exonerates Antipas for the death of John" in that "Antipas is trapped by an *honorable* motive: that of keeping his oath in front of witnesses."[94] This reasoning makes a great deal of sense. According to Numbers

---

edge to female subjectivity and desire" that Glancy detects is Mark 6:24–25 where the daughter makes the additional requirement of John's head *on a platter* (p. 50). Thus Miller, *Women in Mark's Gospel*, 78–79, who argues that Glancy "ignores the cruelty of the women" is not altogether accurate. One might argue that Glancy downplays the women's cruelty, but she does not ignore it.

[87] Dennert, *John the Baptist*, 245.

[88] Augustine, *Serm.* 308.1 (trans. Edmund Hill, in *Sermons* [306–340A], ed. John E. Rotelle, The Works of Saint Augustine: A Translation for the 21st Century 3/9 [Hyde Park, N.Y.: New City Press, 1994]).

[89] Crossley, *Jesus and the Chaos of History*, 151.

[90] Crossley, *Jesus and the Chaos of History*, 151–52.

[91] Crossley, *Jesus and the Chaos of History*, 152.

[92] Crossley, *Jesus and the Chaos of History*, 152–53. Page 152: "Wisdom may be construed as sexually appealing but this is also, of course, how the female personification of evil is constructed and, in Proverbs, the language to describe both is clearly overlapping and it is potentially difficult to distinguish between the two (Prov. 7.11–12; 8.1–3)."

[93] Crossley, *Jesus and the Chaos of History*, 152–53.

[94] Taylor, *Immerser*, 245 (italics added). See also Miller, *Women in Mark's Gospel*, 83: "There is an implication that Herod's company of guests are more likely to think badly of Herod for breaking his oath than for his murder of John." Crossley, *Jesus and the Chaos of History*, 154: "The background of binding oaths and vows would have provided Mark

30:3 LXX (MT: Num 30:2), "whoever vows a vow to the Lord or swears an oath (ὀμνύω) or determines with determination about his soul shall not profane his word; *all* things that come out of his mouth, he shall do."[95] Even the Roman emperor Gaius Caligula is not exempt from the cultural requisite of keeping his word to Agrippa (Josephus, *Ant.* 18.289–304).[96] Thus, when Antipas "swears an oath" (ὀμνύω) to the daughter (6:23) and fulfills it (6:27–28), there is apparently no indication that Antipas' oath-*keeping* was foolish or that his prioritization of his own honor was dishonorable.

In view of these arguments, Mark's evaluation of Herod is rather apologetic, especially compared to his depiction of Herodias. Or so it seems. Here we will argue that Mark negotiates this potentially sympathetic composition of Antipas so that Antipas' credibility as a masculine and just ruler are put on dubious display. Significantly, John's severed head serves as an essential component of this configuration. As a preliminary remark, however, we must acknowledge that Mark does indeed place blame on the Herodian women for their role in John's death in 6:17–29. Unquestionably, Mark depicts Herodias as the one who held the grudge against John and wanted to kill him (6:19). Further, despite her mother expressing only the desire for John's head (6:24), the daughter supplies the "macabre addition," namely the requirement of John's head "on a platter."[97] And, as we have already seen, the Herodian women are constructed as a negative contrast to the Mordecai-Esther dynamic in the Esther tradition.[98]

Antipas' Loss of Masculinity

Conway has demonstrated that the "specter of lost manliness, of a slide into effeminacy, was frequently raised before the eyes of the literate male audience."[99] In this sense, to be truly a "man" (*vir*; ἀνήρ) in the Greco-Roman world was proven not so much by one's biological sex, but on one's

---

6.17–29 with further reasons to maintain Antipas' innocence and blame Salome-Herodias because Antipas, obviously, must do the honourable thing and keep his word."

[95] I have italicized "all" to reflect the grammatical emphasis on the all-encompassing nature of the construction πάντα ὅσα ἐάν (lit. "all things, as many things as").

[96] Crossley, *Jesus and the Chaos of History*, 154–55. See also Deut 23:21–23; Eccl 5:5; Sir 23:11; cf. Mark 14:71.

[97] Asikainen, *Jesus and Other Men*, 63. Notice too that Mark draws attention to this additional element by fronting the prepositional phrase ἐπὶ πίνακι ("on a platter") before the accusative construction in 6:25: θέλω ἵνα ἐξαυτῆς δῷς μοι ἐπὶ πίνακι τὴν κεφαλὴν Ἰωάννου τοῦ βαπτιστοῦ ("I wish that, immediately, you would give me, on a platter, the head of John the Baptist"). See also Miller, *Women in Mark's Gospel*, 79: "The girl, therefore, is responsible for the associations of John's death with a cannibalistic meal."

[98] See also Miller, *Women in Mark's Gospel*, 81: "The account of Herodias and her daughter offers an evil counterpart to the faithful women we see elsewhere in the Gospel (5.21–43; 7.24–30; 14.3–9)."

[99] Conway, *Behold the Man*, 15–34 (quotation, p. 17).

lived-out "virtue" (*virtus*; ἀνδρεία), and thus "manliness."[100] For a man to maintain his reputation as such, his "manliness" or "virtue" needed to be performed.[101] Accordingly, Conway asserts that "acting like a man required one to assume the active role in private sexual practice as well as one's public life. At the same time, such a role also required the careful display of control and restraint, both with respect to one's passions—sexual and otherwise—and in terms of treatment of the other."[102] Another scholar of masculinity elucidates the connection between self-control and power, and reaches a similar conclusion:

> In the Greco-Roman world, masculinity and power go hand in hand, with a manly man exercising power over others in terms of sexual, paternal, political, and military power, and exercising power—or self-control—over himself in terms of controlling his own body and emotions. In brief, to be a man in the ancient world meant to wield power over others and power over oneself.[103]

Thus, *mastery* of the self (i.e., "self-control" [αὐτοκράτωρ])—pertaining as it did to moderation in one's sexual behavior, emotions, luxury, and control over others—comprised a chief virtue of ideal masculinity in this cultural context.[104]

From this perspective, it is striking to observe that Mark constructs the account of John's decapitation in such a way to showcase Antipas' sudden and swift loss of masculinity. That the account takes on gendered nuances

---

[100] See Conway, *Behold the Man*, 22–23.

[101] Asikainen, *Jesus and Other Men*, 30: "The quintessential masculine virtue was ἀνδρεία or *virtus*. Both the Greek word ἀνδρεία and the Latin word *virtus* derive from the gender-specific terms for 'man' (ἀνήρ and *vir*, respectively), and they can thus be translated as 'manliness' or 'manly behavior.' Both words characterize the ideal behavior of a man." On gender performativity in critical discourse, see, e.g., Judith Butler, *Gender Trouble: Feminism and the Subversion of Identity* (New York: Routledge, 1990).

[102] Conway, *Behold the Man*, 22.

[103] Wilson, *Unmanly Men*, 59.

[104] See Conway, *Behold the Man*, 15–34; Wilson, *Unmanly Men*, 39–75 (esp. 64–75); Asikainen, *Jesus and Other Men*, 19–45 (esp. 29–35). Undoubtedly, competing versions of what constituted the truly masculine man existed in this cultural climate, as Asikainen, *Jesus and Other Men*, 19–45, has shown. The present contention that Antipas does not exemplify the ideal man does not stand or fall on envisioning one construction of "hegemonic" masculinity in the ancient world (with "self-control" as its hallmark characteristic). Rather, the point is that "self-control" is demonstrably present as an, or *the*, chief ingredient in many constructions of the ideal man. In turn, this enables us to interpret how some first-century readers would have gauged Antipas' credibility as a masculine ruler. On "hegemonic masculinity" in critical discourse, see Tim Carrigan, Bob (R. W.) Connell, and John Lee, "Toward a New Sociology of Masculinity," *Theory and Society* 14 (1985): 551–604; R. W. Connell, *Masculinities*, 2nd ed. (Berkeley: University of California Press, 2005), 76–81; R. W. Connell and James W. Messerschmidt, "Hegemonic Masculinity: Rethinking the Concept," *Gender and Society* 19 (2005): 829–59.

is perceptible linguistically by the observation that Antipas identifies John according to the gender-specific term, "man" (ἄνδρα, 6:20), and thematically by noticing that Antipas "took control over" (ἐκράτησεν, 6:17) the Baptist, imprisoning him. To head off Herodias' grudge against the Baptist, moreover, Antipas exercises his political power to protect John (6:20), succeeding for a time. On the occasion of his birthday banquet, however, Antipas' political efficacy in this regard is undone at the neck of John the Baptist.[105] Herod ostensibly exercises his political power as he "commands" John's head to be cut off (6:27). In actuality, Antipas is shown to be in no control at all, as Herodias gains power over the Baptist's fate when Antipas swears an oath to give to the girl whatever she wants (6:22–23). Unbeknownst to Antipas (the girl "exits" the banquet hall to consult her mother, Herodias), it is Herodias who recommends that the girl ask for John's head (6:24). The swiftness (εὐθύς, "immediately," 6:27) with which Antipas commands for John's decapitation, furthermore, is not characteristic of his political power, but is dictated by the urgency of the daughter's request (εὐθὺς μετὰ σπουδῆς, "immediately with haste," 6:25). "Instead of controlling the women of his family, Herod is manipulated by them."[106]

Antipas' ignorance of the forces that control him behind the scenes is exemplified in how Mark frames the public parade of John's severed head. Mark devotes considerable attention to exhibiting the careful request *and* delivery of John's head:

> Request (outside the banquet hall): *Herodias* tells the *girl* to ask for John's head (6:24)
>
> Request (inside the banquet hall): The *girl* asks *Herod* for John's head on a platter (6:25)
>
> Request (inside the banquet hall): *Herod* commands John to be beheaded (6:27a)
>
> Execution (in prison): The *executioner* beheads John in prison (6:27b)
>
> Delivery (inside the banquet hall): The *executioner* brings the head on a platter (6:28)
>
> Delivery (inside the banquet hall): *Herod/executioner* gives the head to the *girl* (6:28)
>
> Delivery (outside the banquet hall): The *girl* gives the head to *Herodias* (6:28)

---

[105] Mark sets up the sharp contrast between Antipas exercising control over John the Baptist (6:17–20) and Antipas' swift loss of masculinity in this regard (6:21–29) grammatically by means of a genitive absolute construction in the Greek of 6:21 ("But an opportune day arose" [Καὶ γενομένης ἡμέρας εὐκαίρου]).

[106] Asikainen, *Jesus and Other Men*, 66.

Not only does Mark portray Antipas as unaware of Herodias' manipulation in effecting John's death, he also never indicates that Antipas became cognizant that Herodias ended up with John's severed head. Antipas only has contact with the executioner and the girl, whereas the girl only has contact with Antipas and Herodias. At the textual level, therefore, Herodias and Antipas never come into direct contact regarding the request for, nor the transportation of, John's head. The head is transported between the other characters; the spatial separation between Antipas (inside the banquet hall) and Herodias (outside the banquet hall) is not breached.[107]

In this way, the textualized public display of John's lonesome head accentuates Antipas' loss of control. Rather than Herodias' triumph exhibiting John's emasculation, her triumph—exemplified in the carefully framed parade of John's detached head—renders Antipas' loss of control (and his ignorance of this loss) gruesomely visible for readers to witness. Mark counterbalances the prestige of Herodias' victory and the potential emasculation of John by bringing these cultural fault lines into tension with the framework of Antipas' severed masculinity. In this light, Antipas' apologetic stance toward John in Mark 6:20 does not serve to relieve Antipas of responsibility for John's death, but to *sharpen* Antipas' loss of control as he is ultimately inefficacious in protecting John.[108]

Further, although some or many first-century readers might not blame Antipas for falling prey to the eroticism of the dancing κοράσιον ("[young] girl") (in accordance with the established first-century ideology of the dangerousness of female sexual seduction), Mark does not encourage this reading.

---

[107] Readers will inevitably fill in the narrative gaps on the tersely recounted delivery of John's head (6:28). Since (1) the girl demands John's head *at this very moment* (and Herod obliges), (2) the transportation of the severed head invertedly mirrors the request for John's head (in terms of character interaction), and (3) the head is delivered on a serving dish, the text thereby guides readers to assume (1) that the banquet scene is still in play and thus (2) when the girl delivers the head to Herodias, she once again exits the banquet hall to do so (6:28). Ultimately, Mark does not indicate that Herodias ever enters the banquet hall, nor that Herod exits it. Readers, then, are not prompted to cross these structural boundaries to imagine that the girl delivers the head to Herodias within Herod's gaze. See also Justin Martyr, at *Dial.* 49.4, who seems to construe the banquet scene as still in play as he describes Herod as commanding John's head "to be brought *in*" (ἐνεχθῆναι).

[108] Marcus, *Mark 1–8*, 398 (italics added and removed): "Throughout the passage, moreover, we see that this supposed 'king' is not even in control of himself, much less of his subjects; he is rather *overmastered* by his emotions which swing wildly from superstitious dread (6:14, 16) to awe, fascination, and confusion (6:20), to a sexual arousal that seems to border on insanity (6:22–23) to extreme depression (6:26). . . . Herod is merely one who appears to rule (cf. 10:42), whereas actually his strings are pulled by others." Similarly, Miller, *Women in Mark's Gospel*, 83: "Herod is presented as a man who is torn apart by conflicting desires, and is depicted as the antithesis of a true ruler because others manipulate his emotions."

Instead he frames the tradition so that it takes on incestuous overtones.[109] In some early manuscripts, including Codices Sinaiticus (א) and Vaticanus (B), the girl whose dance apparently arouses[110] Antipas and his dinner guests is described as "his" (αὐτοῦ) daughter, i.e., Antipas' daughter (6:22).[111] But caution is in order here. As Stiebert explains,

> anthropological literature acknowledges incest taboos as universal, or near-universal among human societies (with any exceptions having dubious legitimacy).... What precisely constitutes incest is, however, variously understood. Incest, therefore, is a cultural concept and what is incestuous (and illegal) in one society may be a close-kin marriage (and legal) in another.[112]

The specific prohibition of a father from having sexual relations with his daughter is conspicuously absent in the rather detailed incest prohibitions lists of Leviticus 18 and 20. This absence contrasts sharply, for instance, from Hittite law that expressly forbids men from incestuous relations with their daughters.[113] One possible explanation for this omission in the Levitical Code is that the father's lordship over his daughter extended to the sexual arena as well. Another explanation is that such a prohibition is so self-

---

[109] Some scholars appeal to the dancing daughter to doubt the "historicity" of the tradition's portrayal. See, e.g., Morton Scott Enslin, "John and Jesus," *ZNW* 66 (1975): 13: "That a royal princess should dance in such a gathering is hardly likely." Cf. Charles H. Scobie, *John the Baptist* (London: SCM, 1964), 180: "But when we remember the moral standards of the Herodian family, we can believe anything." Marcus, *Mark 1–8*, 396, sees several inaccuracies in the Markan pericope, but argues that the feature of the dancing girl "is not one of them." Like Scobie, he appeals to the moral depravity of the Herodian lineage to substantiate his claim. See further Gould, *Gospel According to St. Mark*, 113.

[110] Marcus (*Mark 1–8*, 396) observes that the verb ἤρεσεν ("pleased") (Mark 6:22) often has sexual connotations in the Septuagint (e.g., LXX: Gen 19:8; Job 31:10). See also Crossley, *Jesus and the Chaos of History*, 153. Ambrose (*Concerning Virgins* 3.6.27) thinks that the girl exposed her nakedness. Cf. Hartmann, *Der Tod Johannes des Täufers*, 162–68, 177–78, who argues that the daughter's dance and the verb ἤρεσεν do not have erotic overtones. For Hartmann, the banquet scene reflects the benevolent response of a superior (Herod) to his inferior (the girl) who paid him homage. Hence, he describes the motif of Herod's wish as the "freundliche Zuwendung" ("friendly devotion") of the powerful (p. 177). See also Nolland, *Gospel of Matthew*, 582, who notes that "dancing need not be erotic to give delight and to stir gratitude." Crossley does not interact with Hartmann, whose argument could potentially bolster Crossley's overarching assessment of Herod's guilt in that it eliminates the idea of sexual passion motivating Herod's promise. Even if Hartmann is correct, the elimination of this feature of the story does not detract from the other ways we show in this chapter that Mark negotiates Antipas' political credibility.

[111] Uncials that also reflect this reading include D, L, and Δ. The ninth-century minuscule 565 also follows this reading.

[112] Johanna Stiebert, *Fathers and Daughters in the Hebrew Bible* (Oxford: Oxford University Press, 2013), 102–3.

[113] Stiebert, *Fathers and Daughters*, 106.

evident that there is no need to commit it to writing. One is reminded of Plato, *Leg.* 8.838b, where such incest is prevented by means of an "unwritten law" (νόμος ἄγραφος).[114]

Regardless, the injunction in Leviticus 18:6 against sexual relations with "any flesh of his relative" (כל שאר בשרו) may constitute an umbrella prohibition that, by implication, extends to the father-daughter relationship (Lev 18:6).[115] Similarly, Leviticus 18:17 prohibits a man from sexual intimacy with "a woman and her daughter" (אשה ובתה), which may be understood as referring to daughters and stepdaughters.[116] Some early manuscripts at Mark 6:22, including Codices Alexandrinus (A) and Ephraemi Rescriptus (C), alternatively read that the dancing girl was "her" (αὐτῆς) daughter, i.e., Herodias' daughter.[117] So, whether a first-century reading of 6:22 constituted αὐτοῦ ("his") or αὐτῆς ("her"), the possibility remains that this tradition could generate suspicions of incestuous lust motivating Antipas' actions.

For those readers in the Greco-Roman world whose ideology of incest was not necessarily informed by Torah, Mark's specification of kinship between Antipas and the daughter (whether by blood or through marriage) would likely at least raise the question of permissable sexual encounters between men and women. Classical Greek authors frequently spew invectives against intercourse with daughters. Euripides characterizes such sex as barbaric:

> That is the way all barbarians are: father (πατήρ) lies with daughter (θυγατρί), son with mother, and sister with brother, nearest kin murder each other, and no law prevents any of this. Do not introduce such customs into our city. For it is also not right for one man to hold the reins of two women. Rather, everyone who wants to live decently is content to look to a single mate for his bed. (*Andr.* 173–180)[118]

Consider also Xenophon's *Cyropaedia*: "Neither does a father (πατήρ) fall in love with (ἐρᾷ) his daughter (θυγατρός), but somebody else does; for fear of God and the law of the land are sufficient to prevent such love (ἔρωτα)."[119] In Plato, sexual union between a man and his daughter receives a series of vitriolic vituperations:

---

[114] Similarly, Xenophon, *Mem.* 4.4.19–23.
[115] HALOT, s.v. "בְּשָׂר" renders שְׁאֵר בְּשָׂרוֹ as "his close relative."
[116] See Stiebert, *Fathers and Daughters*, 107.
[117] Uncials that also reflect this reading include W and Θ. The "family thirteen" manuscripts, several minuscules, and the eleventh-century lectionary 253 also follow this reading.
[118] Kovacs, LCL.
[119] Xenophon, *Cyr.* 5.1.10 (Miller, LCL). BDAG, s.v. "ἐράω" lists *Cyr.* 5.1.10 as conveying "sexual attraction." LSJ, s.v. "ἔραμαι" describes the verb as "of the sexual passion." The cognate noun ἔρως is likewise defined as "love, mostly of the sexual passion" (LSJ, s.v. "ἔρως").

> Whenever any man has a brother or sister who is beautiful. So too in the case of a son or daughter, the same unwritten law is most effective in guarding men from sleeping with them, either openly or secretly, or wishing to have any connexion with them,—nay, most men never so much as feel any desire (ἐπιθυμία) for such connexion. . . . [T]hese acts are by no means holy (μηδαμῶς ὅσια), but hated of God (θεομισῆ) and most shamefully shameful (αἰσχρῶν αἴσχιστα). (*Leg.* 8.838b–c)[120]

Plato excludes sexual intercourse with a daughter for men even after the men are no longer of the age to procreate:

> When the women and men cease to be of the age to have children, we shall leave the men free, I think, to have intercourse with whoever they wish, except with a daughter, a mother or the daughter's children or the mother's mothers; and the women likewise except with a son, a father and their sons and fathers. (*Resp.* 5.461b–c)[121]

The first-century C.E. Stoic philosopher, Musonius Rufus, in some of his lectures, discusses how men should treat their wives and daughters. His twelfth lecture (entitled "On Sexual Indulgence") argues that those men who indulge in sex outside of marriage do so out of a lack of self-control.[122] Again, if we are to understand the girl's dance and/or the pleasure Antipas took in it as erotically charged, the fact that Mark further describes the girl as his (step)daughter enables the impression that incestuous lust led Antipas to swear a nearly unqualified oath, and thus place his control over the Baptist in a vulnerable position. In this vein, some or many first-century readers likely would blame Antipas on account of not exercising proper control over his sexuality.[123]

Beheading a Righteous Man

Oath ideology similarly does not necessarily relieve Antipas from blame in that he made the honorable choice in keeping his oath by having John beheaded. Despite the binding quality of oaths and vows, at least some ancients could apprehend certain circumstances that render (1) breaking an oath permissible, or (2) breaking or keeping an oath a choice between two evils, particularly when fulfilling an oath or vow conflicts with another moral imperative. Cicero argues that some promises should not be kept, such as when Neptune "offered

---

[120] Bury, LCL.
[121] Emlyn-Jones and Preddy, LCL.
[122] See Beryl Rawson, *Children and Childhood in Roman Italy* (Oxford: Oxford University Press, 2003), 208. Other examples of primary data that criticize sexual relations with daughters abound (e.g., Virgil, *Aen.* 6.623; Sextus Empiricus, *Pyr.* 3.246).
[123] See also Malina and Rohrbaugh, *Social-Science Commentary*, 216: "In non-elite eyes, honorable males would not allow a female family member to perform such a display; their failure to prevent her from doing so pegs them as shameless."

[Theseus] three wishes" and Theseus proceeded to wish "for the death of his [Theseus'] son Hippolytus." Likewise when Agamemnon swore to sacrifice "the most beautiful creature born that year within his realm" and proceeded to do so; according to Cicero, "he [Agamemnon] ought to have broken his vow rather than commit so horrible a crime" (*Off.* 3.25).[124] For Cicero, therefore, it seems that breaking an oath was preferable to killing and child sacrifice.

Josephus specifies that Jephthah's sacrifice of his daughter as a burnt offering (see Judg 11:29–40) was "neither sanctioned by the law (νόμιμον) nor well-pleasing to God (θεῷ κεχαρισμένην); for he had not by reflection probed what might befall or in what aspect the deed would appear to them that heard of it" (*Ant.* 5.266).[125] For Josephus, Jephthah's fulfillment of his vow conflicts with Torah.[126] Josephus' note about Jephthah's lack of forethought suggests that (1) the consquences involved in fulfilling a vow should be taken into consideration before proceeding to satisfy it; and that (2) the reputation one might acquire from oathkeeping should be contemplated beforehand. According to the Mishnah, moreover, Rabbi Eliezer avered (m. Ned. 9:1) that a vow could be discharged if it conflicted with the imperative to honor one's mother or father (Exod 20:12; Deut 5:16). In a similar context, m. B. Bat. 8:5 indicates that oaths made in contradiction to Torah are not valid.

Swearing an oath at all could also cast a negative shadow over the oath-swearer. The Matthean Jesus' comment on swearing is an obvious example that comes to mind:

> Again, you have heard that it was said to those of ancient times, "You shall not swear falsely, but carry out the vows you have made to the Lord." But I say to you, Do not swear at all.... Let your word be "Yes, Yes" or "No, No"; anything more than this comes from the evil one. (Matt 5:33–34, 37 NRSV)

According to Josephus, the Essenes view swearing at all worse than perjury: "Any word of theirs has more force than an oath; swearing (τὸ ὀμνύειν) they avoid, regarding it as worse than perjury (τῆς ἐπιορκίας), for they say that one who is not believed without an appeal to God stands condemned already

---

[124] Miller, LCL.

[125] Thackeray et al., LCL. In his account of Jephthah's daughter, moreover, Josephus (*Ant.* 5.263–266) omits Judg 11:29 ("Then the spirit of the Lord came upon Jephthah" [NRSV]). Accordingly, Tal Ilan ("Flavius Josephus and Biblical Women," in *The Bible and Women*, vol. 3.1: *Early Jewish Writings*, ed. Eileen Schuller and Marie-Theres Wacker [Atlanta: SBL Press, 2017], 176) writes: "Because being equipped with divine power should have made Jephthah's vow superfluous, this could be the reason why Josephus skips over the verse. In so doing Jephthah loses in the eyes of Josephus the favor or grace of God."

[126] Josephus fails to cite how the sacrifice is not sanctioned by Torah, but it is possible that the Torah's moral imperatives against child sacrifice (Lev 18:21; 20:2; Deut 12:31; 18:10) inform his comments.

(ἤδη)" (*War* 2.135).¹²⁷ While the Essenes view swearing worse than swearing falsely, Philo considers swearing worse than even "to swear truly" (εὐορκεῖν):

> To swear not at all is the best course and most profitable to life, well suited to a rational nature which has been taught to speak the truth so well on each occasion that its words are regarded as oaths; to swear truly (εὐορκεῖν) is only, as people say, a "second-best voyage," for the mere fact of his swearing (ἤδη γὰρ ὅ γε ὀμνύς) casts suspicion on the trustworthiness of a man. (*Decal*. 17.84)¹²⁸

Although Philo recognizes that fulfilling a vow is the second-best course of action, swearing an oath at all nevertheless casts a suspicious gaze on the one who swears. Swearing too much could also cast a negative shadow over the oath-swearer. According to Sir 23:11, a "much-swearing man" (ἀνὴρ πολύορκος) is viewed as filled with "lawlessness" (ἀνομίας).¹²⁹ And Philo says that "[the habit of] much-swearing" (ἡ πολυορκία) casts suspicion on one's credibility (*Spec*. 2.8). According to the Mishnah, one should not be "profuse in [making] vows" (m. Demai 2:3).¹³⁰

Even though Mark does not explicitly denounce Antipas for keeping an oath already sworn, he still casts Antipas' oath according to a negative framework. The Markan tradition clearly stresses the Baptist's virtue. Mark characterizes John as one concerned with fidelity to Torah (6:22).¹³¹ And Antipas recognizes that John is a "righteous (δίκαιον) and holy man" (6:20). This element itself is likely enough to enable some readers to question Antipas' political integrity. As Plutarch quotes Brutus as saying, "Base and unjust men who put to death the good and just (δικαίους ἄνδρας, lit. "righteous men") [are] unfit to rule."¹³²

But we might further suggest that since Antipas' decision to fulfill his oath is structured by the social pressure to keep one's word *alongside* the social reality of John's virtue, some first-century readers might rebuke Antipas for keeping his oath rather than breaking it to save John's life.

---

¹²⁷ Thackeray, LCL.
¹²⁸ Colson, LCL.
¹²⁹ Sirach 23:11 continues, "If he disregards [the oath], he sins doubly." In contradistinction to the Essenes and Philo, then, Sir 23:11 seems to indicate disregarding one's oath as worse than swearing an oath in the first place. Nevertheless, swearing itself is still characterized negatively even if fulfilling an oath is the best course of action once already sworn. Cf. Eccl 5:5 (MT: Eccl 5:4): "It is better that you should not vow (לֹא־תִדֹּר) than that you should vow and not fulfill it" (NRSV).
¹³⁰ Trans. Jacob Neusner, in *The Mishnah: A New Translation* (New Haven: Yale University Press, 1991).
¹³¹ See Lev 18:16; 20:21; cf. Deut 25:5–10. See Marcus, *John the Baptist in History and Theology*, 58–59.
¹³² Plutarch, *Brut*. 52 (Perrin, LCL).

Although commenting on the Matthean account centuries later, Origen's remarks are heuristically illustrative in this respect: "And the prophet was beheaded because of oaths, in relation to which the right thing to do was to break the oaths rather than keep them. For the accusation of rashness when making an oath and of breaking an oath because of rashness, and the accusation of putting a prophet to death to keep an oath are not the same" (*Comm. Matt.* 10.22).[133] Augustine, as a further example, views it as the lesser of two evils for Antipas to break his oath than shed the Baptist's blood (*Serm.* 308.1–2).[134]

As we have already seen, moreover, Antipas' entrance into the oath is prompted by promiscuous sexual passion toward his (step)daughter. Not only does Mark frame Antipas' offer so that it is prompted by promiscuous sexual passion, the content of his oath—the immoderate "*half* of [his] kingdom" (ἡμίσους τῆς βασιλείας μου) (6:23)—further underlines his lack of self-control and moderation. This uncontrol is all the more apparent to those readers aware that Antipas was not really a king, but a tetrarch, and thus did not possess the requisite political power to accomplish his oath if the girl had chosen to activate the full weight of his offer. Beyond this, it is perhaps not insignificant that Mark portrays Antipas as making *multiple* oaths to the daughter:

> 6:22: "The king said to the girl, 'Ask me for whatever you wish, and I will give it to you.'"
>
> 6:23: "And he swore to her, 'Whatever you ask me, I will give you, up to half my kingdom.'"

Mark 6:26 indicates that Antipas did not wish to reject the daughter's wishes out of regard for his "oaths" (ὅρκους). As Duran succinctly puts it, Herod "talks too much."[135] So, whether Mark expects readers to blame Antipas for keeping his oath or not, he still construes the precipitating conditions that gave rise to Antipas entering into an oath, the content of the oath, and perhaps even the amount of oaths sworn as excessive.[136] In these regards,

---

[133] Heine, OECT.

[134] Bede (Thomas C. Oden and Christopher A. Hall, eds., *Mark*, ACCS 2 [Downers Grove: InterVarsity Press, 1998], 85–86) insinuates, by appealing to 1 Sam 25:2–39, that Herod should have broken his oath: "There is an urgent necessity for us to break our oath, rather than turn to another more serious crime in order to avoid breaking our oath. David swore by the Lord to kill Nabal, a stupid and wicked man, and to destroy all his possessions. But at the first entreaty of the prudent woman Abigail, he quickly took back his threats, put back his sword into its scabbard, and did not feel that he had contracted any guilt by thus breaking his oath in this way."

[135] Duran, "Return of the Disembodied," 284.

[136] To be clear, Mark does not directly classify Antipas as a "much-swearing" man, but his narration of Antipas making multiple oaths may nevertheless evoke such an association.

Asikainen's judgement is correct: "Herod [Antipas] does not exemplify the ideal of masculine self-control."[137]

Bearing in mind our preceding discussion, it is reasonable to conclude that the Markan tradition's recognition of John's masculinity—"a righteous and holy man (ἄνδρα)" (6:20)—and Antipas' ensuing bid to protect John heighten Antipas' loss of manly virtue. The scholarly strategy of locating the blame for John's death primarily on the Herodian women at the expense of—or even relative to—Herod Antipas, is not unreasonable, in my estimation, insofar as this strategy does not preclude a construct of an emasculated Antipas. The tradition paints both Antipas and the Herodian women with a negative brush: "The truth is that the threads of guilt here are tangled."[138]

Ridiculing Antipas and Enhancing Jesus' Prestige as Healer

So far, we have analyzed two ways that Mark contests the violence of John's death. Instead of highlighting the prestige of the perpetrators—the Herodian court—and the degradation of the victim—John the Baptist—John's beheading is refracted through the lenses of Jesus' crucifixion and Antipas' loss of masculinity. Here I will argue a third way that Mark contests the degradation of John's decapitation: John's beheading serves to enhance Jesus' prestige as a healer of bodily impurity and, simultaneously, to ridicule Antipas' paranoia that a beheaded man is once again alive.

My argument here requires some explanation, for it runs up against how scholars have typically understood (1) the relationship between Antipas' comment in Mark 6:16 that John has been raised from the dead and the populace's speculation in Mark 6:14 that Jesus is the revived and empowered John the Baptist; and (2) the relationship between the narrative of John's beheading in Mark 6:17–29 and the speculation of Jesus' identity in Mark 6:14–16 (which introduces and frames the narrative of John's beheading). In her classic commentary on the Gospel of Mark, Hooker writes:

---

[137] Asikainen, *Jesus and Other Men*, 65. See also Smith, "Tyranny Exposed," 271, who identifies a ruler's "display of excess" as a stock feature of ancient tyrant-types. Antipas' excessiveness could also be perceived from the observation that he held a luxurious banquet, inviting his "great ones," "rulers of a thousand," and "the first ones of Galilee" (6:21). Smith, "Tyranny Exposed," 278: "Mark's depiction of Antipas' dinner party (to which Herod Antipas invites Romans among his guests) in juxtaposition to the languishing imprisonment of a prophet elsewhere described as a wilderness ascetic thus marks Antipas' sumptuary excess." See further Hartmann, *Tod Johannes des Täufers*, 187–89, who (citing Seneca, *Controversiae* 9.2.4; *Ep.* 83.25; Valerius Maximus, *Memorable Doings and Sayings*, 9.2.2; Plutarch, *Crass.* 33.4) argues that the ancient literary motif of bringing a head to a feast functions to demonstrate the excessive cruelty of the one responsible (directly or indirectly) for the executed person's death.

[138] Duran, "Return of the Disembodied," 290.

> Between the account of the sending out of the Twelve and that of their return, Mark inserts an account of Herod's reaction to the rumours about Jesus, together with the story of his beheading of John the Baptist. There seems no logical connection between the two themes, but the somewhat artificial insertion provides an interlude for the disciples to complete their mission.[139]

The apparent disconnect between the rumors of Jesus' identity in 6:14–16—whether he might be John the Baptist *redivivus*, Elijah *redivivus*, or another one of the prophets—and the ensuing retrospection on John's beheading in 6:17–29 has continued to confound scholars. A steady current of scholarship, however, has argued that 6:17–29 functions to clarify that Jesus was not the revived John the Baptist (6:14, 16) and thus did not derive his powers from his connection to the Baptist.[140]

One interpreter, for example, has written: "Is Jesus John raised from the dead? Is Jesus the returned John? That question—which no one thinks any longer to ask—Mark is intent on making sure we never ask again."[141] Witherington advocates for this understanding as well: "What prompts this story is that, as we are told in v. 14, some thought Jesus was John the Baptizer redivivus. . . . This story then clarifies matters for the Markan audience by distinguishing between the two men, while at the same time foreshadowing the sort of violent end that Jesus would also come to."[142] Later in his analysis, Witherington is more emphatic: "The point is that people with their own speculations were not coming up with the notion that Jesus was Messiah or Lord, and in a biography this story about the Baptist is crucial, *for it clears up once and for all that Jesus is not John.*"[143]

In my estimation, Kraemer sets forth the most substantial case for this position, for she takes seriously the cultural ideology of beheading that informs this interpretation. She summarizes her understanding as follows:

> In my view, these narratives respond to early Christian anxieties and contestations about the relationship between Jesus and John: they are fashioned to refute not simply the suggestion that John the Baptist has been resurrected but more precisely the possibility that Jesus is John raised from the dead by telling a narrative in which the body of John is desecrated in a manner that makes it impossible to

---

[139] Hooker, *Saint Mark*, 158.
[140] According to the Gospel of John, John the Baptist is said to have performed no signs (John 10:41). Cf. Luke 1:17.
[141] Janes, "Why the Daughter of Herodias Must Dance," 446–47.
[142] Witherington, *Gospel of Mark*, 212.
[143] Witherington, *Gospel of Mark*, 214 (italics added).

resurrect it, at least physically, by severing the head from the body, and by leaving the head with Herodias while burying the corpse.[144]

She defends this claim with an important observation: Antipas' evaluation of the Baptist's identity in 6:16 can be read as a question ("Has John, whom I beheaded, been raised?") and not necessarily an indicative statement ("John, whom I beheaded, has been raised."). In fact, she insists, this is "exactly" how Luke 9:9 ("I beheaded John: who is this one about whom I hear such things?") understands Antipas' response to the rumors: "The author of Luke thus implies that Antipas thinks that Jesus cannot be John, because Antipas had previously beheaded him."[145] Hence, she reasons that "further implicit in Antipas's objection is precisely the notion that something about beheading John makes it impossible for him to be resurrected in the body of Jesus."[146] For Kraemer, therefore, Mark 6:17–29 "is constructed to provide a compelling answer to the question not of why John was *executed* but of why John was *executed by decapitation*, or why, following his execution by some other means, his head was then severed from his body."[147]

This interpretive option has much that seems to work in its favor. That Mark constructs a narrative that carefully details the separation of John's head from its body's entombment raises the issue of the interconnection between death, burial, and bodily violence. As we observed in the previous chapter, the separation of a head from its body's burial constituted a type of corpse abuse that impacted the victim into the afterlife, including nullifying the possibility of a revived life on earth for a recently deceased person. For Kraemer to assert that this idea subverts the possibility of John's revivification in the person of Jesus (6:14, 16) makes a great deal of sense, especially since Luke's Antipas in Luke 9:9 clearly differentiates between Jesus and John on the basis of the latter's beheading.

This interpretation also follows the vast history of interpreters who have observed that Antipas' speculation in 6:16 regurgitates in a nutshell the populace's speculation in 6:14—that the source of Jesus' powers derives from the fact that he is the revived John the Baptist:

---

[144] Ross S. Kraemer, "Implicating Herodias and Her Daughter in the Death of John the Baptizer: A (Christian) Theological Strategy?" *JBL* 125 (2006): 341. Similarly, Lupieri, "John the Baptist," 436, n. 17.

[145] Kraemer, "Implicating Herodias," 342.

[146] Kraemer, "Implicating Herodias," 342.

[147] Kraemer, "Implicating Herodias," 342 (italics original). See also Pellegrini, *Elija*, 284, 287 (quotation, p. 287), who argues that since John is "enthauptet und begraben" ("beheaded and entombed"), the story of 6:17–29 dispels the hypotheses entertained in 6:14 and 6:16. Following Pellegrini, Dennert, *John the Baptist*, 37, likewise asserts that John's death "shows that Jesus cannot be the resurrected John."

Mark 6:14: "And King Herod heard [of it], for his [Jesus'] name had become known. And some were saying that John the Baptist has been raised from the dead and because of this powers are at work in him [Jesus]."

Mark 6:16: "But when Herod heard [of it], he was saying: 'He whom I beheaded, John, this one has been raised.'"

Aus, for instance, has written, "In contrast to others, who consider Jesus to be Elijah or a prophet of old, Herod Antipas believes he is the resurrected John, whom he has beheaded."[148] He continues this line of thought in a footnote that reads, "To this extent, Herod's view in 6:16 agrees with the opinion of 'some' in v. 14."[149] As a further example, Culpepper likewise sees an essential connection between the opinions of the populace and Antipas: "Verses 14–16 report and explain Herod's identification of Jesus as John, 'who had been raised.'"[150] He then attempts to explain Antipas' underlying logic in connecting the presence of powers in Jesus and the reality of John's revivification in the person of Jesus.[151] Seeing this connection between 6:14 and 6:16 goes back nearly two millenia to the earliest "interpreter" of the Gospel of Mark—the Gospel of Matthew. At 14:2 Matthew condenses Mark 6:14, 16 into a singular utterance by Herod Antipas: "This one [Jesus] is John the Baptist. He has been raised from the dead and because of this powers are at work in him [Jesus]."[152]

The view that the violence of John's death functions to dispel the idea that the source of Jesus' healing powers derives from his identity as the revived John the Baptist, however, suffers from certain shortcomings. First, readers of

---

[148] Aus, *Water into Wine*, 70.

[149] Aus, *Water into Wine*, 70, n. 182.

[150] Culpepper, "Mark 6:17–29 in Its Narrative Context," 153. For other interpreters who draw an equivalent line between 6:14 and 6:16, see, e.g., Stein, *Mark*, 302; Bas M. F. van Iersel, *Mark: A Reader-Response Commentary*, trans. W. H. Bisscheroux, JSNTSup 164 (Sheffield: Sheffield Academic Press, 1998), 219–20. See also Evans, *Jesus and the Ossuaries*, 14: "Herod's declaration that Jesus must be John, whom he beheaded, attests to the despot's fearful respect of the power he sensed was at work in Jesus, a power that not only must be from beyond the confines of the mortal realm, but a power not limited by the conventions of death, burial, and resurrection."

[151] Culpepper, "Mark 6:17–29 in Its Narrative Context," 153.

[152] Many Markan manuscripts perhaps inadvertently conflate 6:14 and 6:16 by writing the singular verb ἔλεγεν ("He [Antipas] was saying") at 6:14 rather than the plural ἔλεγον ("They were saying"). As Bruce M. Metzger (*A Textual Commentary on the Greek New Testament*, 2nd ed. [Stuttgart: Deutsche Bibelgesellschaft, 1994], 76) suggests: "Copyists altered [the plural ἔλεγον] to ἔλεγεν in agreement with ἤκουσεν, not observing that after the words καὶ ἤκουσεν ὁ βασιλεὺς Ἡρῴδης the sentence is suspended, in order to introduce parenthetically three specimens of the opinions held about Jesus . . . and is taken up again at ver. 16, ἀκούσας δὲ ὁ Ἡρῴδης." As such, Metzger is probably right that the plural ἔλεγον represents an earlier reading than the singular ἔλεγεν.

Mark's Gospel are already aware of the fact that Jesus is not John the Baptist. After a scant five-verse indication of John's immersive activity and preaching in 1:4–8, readers encounter simultaneously Jesus and John at the River Jordan (1:9–11). The former is baptized by the latter (1:9). Moreover, as Jesus ascends from the water, the voice from heaven makes Jesus' identity plain for the reader: "You are my beloved son (ὁ υἱός μου ὁ ἀγαπητός), in you I am well pleased" (1:11). Informed by the prologue, readers who arrive at 6:14–16 hardly take seriously the hypothesis that Jesus was John raised from the dead.[153] Scholars like Witherington (quoted above) who adamantly claim that John's beheading (Mark 6:17–29) conclusively clarifies for readers that Jesus is not John (Mark 6:14, 16) do not account for the fact that this conclusion was definitively reached at the very opening of Mark's Gospel.

Second, under this interpretation's construal, translating Herod's comment in Mark 6:16 as a question rather than a declarative statement does not necessarily render the semantic forces of Mark 6:16 and Luke 9:9 in precisely the same manner:

> Mark 6:16 (as a declarative statement): "Having heard, Herod was saying: 'The one whom I beheaded, John, this one has been raised!'"

> Mark 6:16 (as a question): "Having heard, Herod was saying: 'The one whom I beheaded, John, has this one been raised?'"

> Luke 9:9: "Herod said: 'John I myself beheaded. But who is this about whom I hear such things?'"

For Luke's Herod, Kraemer is correct to assert that the beheading of John renders the Baptist's association with Jesus as an impossibility. According to Luke 9:7, Herod heard that some thought that Jesus was John the Baptist raised from the dead. Herod's response in Luke 9:9 departs from this idea by clearly differentiating Jesus from John *on the basis of* John's mutilated body.[154] The same, however, cannot be said of Mark 6:16. Rather, as one medievalist puts

---

[153] Similarly, Maloney, *Gospel of Mark*, 126: "The reader ... knows that all suggestions miss the point, but the question 'Who is Jesus?' continues to be raised by the characters in the story." So also Miller, "Intercalation Revisited," 181–82.

[154] I therefore disagree with Nathanael Vette and Will Robinson's criticism of Kraemer: "The comment of Antipas in Luke 9:7 [sic], 'John I beheaded etc.' (Ἰωάννην ἐγὼ ἀπεκεφάλισα) is best seen as expressing skepticism towards resurrection, not the resurrection of a beheaded person *per se*" ("Was John the Baptist Raised from the Dead? The Origins of Mark 6:14–29," *Biblical Annals* 9 [2019]: 337, n. 5). Their critique falters on their ignorance of the ideology of beheading, which they acknowledge two sentences previously in the same footnote: "We are not aware of tradition stipulating that beheaded persons could not be resurrected." See the previous chapter where we identified traditions that are evidence of this stipulation.

it, "John's decapitation is introduced through Herod's confusion as *not having worked*."[155] If Herod can genuinely consider the possibility that John has been revived *in view of his knowledge that John was beheaded* (Mark 6:16: "The one whom I beheaded, John, has this one been raised?"), then proceeding to recount the narrative of John's beheading (6:17-29) hardly clarifies matters. To put the problem interrogatively: How does narrating a beheading dispel rumors that Jesus is John when the fact of John's beheading does not prevent Herod from aligning these two figures in the first place?

One possible way to make this line of argumentation hold currency requires us to understand Herod's question in Mark 6:16 as a question suspicious of the rumors in 6:14 that Jesus is John and not as a genuine question that doubts the efficacy of John's beheading in preventing revivification. As a suspicious question (in effect, "The one whom I beheaded, John, has [not] been revived, [has he]?"), Antipas' query allows Mark in 6:17-29 to *reinforce* the ludicrousness of the rumor that Jesus is John (Mark 6:14) by giving the reader access to knowledge that Antipas possesses: John was harmed in a way that made this impossible—his head and body are currently divided and in the possession of separate parties (the girl [to Antipas' knowledge at least] and the disciples, respectively).[156] In this respect, Mark 6:16 and Luke 9:9 accord well with one another instead of possessing incongruent semantic forces. Under this configuration, moreover, Antipas' comment in 6:16 does not regurgitate the rumor in 6:14 that Jesus is John, but serves to cast doubt on this equivalence—doubt that is then substantiated by the narrative of John's decapitation in 6:17-29. Thus, I can agree with the conclusion that the account of John's beheading serves to distinguish between Jesus and John (6:14), but not with how scholars usually arrive at this conclusion.

Be that as it may, there is another compelling way to understand Herod's comment in 6:16. Herod Antipas' remark in Mark 6:16 ("He whom I beheaded, John, this one has been raised") is not a comment wherein Antipas (1) considers the possibility that Jesus *is* the revived and empowered John the Baptist (like the populace supposes in 6:14) or (2) directly addresses the rumors in 6:14 that Jesus is John, but rather *a fixation on Jesus' capacity as a healer to revive the beheaded John the Baptist*. In other words, Jesus implicitly occupies the unexpressed direct agency of the passive verb ἐγείρω ("to raise/revive") in

---

[155] Nicola Masciandaro, "*Non potest hoc corpus decollari*: Beheading and the Impossible," in *Heads Will Roll: Decapitation in the Medieval and Early Modern Imagination*, ed. Lariss Tracy and Jeff Massey, MRAT 7 (Leiden: Brill, 2012), 20 (italics original).

[156] How Mark construes Herod's remark in 6:16 is grammatically ambiguous. Mark does not clearly indicate if Herod's comment is a declarative statement, genuine question, or suspicious question. Mark certainly could have disambiguated the matter and marked this as a suspicious question by inserting and fronting a negative μή ("not") particle. Such a maneuver would implicitly deliver a negative answer to Herod's question of John's revivification.

6:16: "He whom I beheaded, John, this one has been raised [by Jesus]."[157] Thus, ἠγέρθη ("[John] was revived") in 6:16 is not a divine passive, but a passive construction expressed in view of the spread of Jesus' fame as an active healer (6:6b–13, 14).

My interpretation is compelling for several reasons. First, Herod's comment in 6:16 need not be construed as rearticulating the rumors the populace holds in 6:14:

> Mark 6:14: "And King Herod heard [of it], for his [Jesus'] name had become known. And some were saying that John the Baptist has been raised from the dead and because of this powers are at work in him [Jesus]."

> Mark 6:16: "But when Herod heard [of it], he was saying: 'He whom I beheaded, John, this one has been raised.'"

Mark portrays the populace (the "some") as trying to identify the source of Jesus' powers. Combined with the additional rumors recounted in 6:15 that Jesus might *be* Elijah or one of the prophets, the populace's suggestion that John has been raised is seen by the majority of scholars as a statement that views Jesus as John the Baptist *redivivus*. Yet Mark 6:16 can equally plausibly be read not as a rearticulation of this view, but as a remark that shifts the focus from identifying the source of Jesus' powers to Antipas' preoccupation with contemplating how Jesus has exercised those powers. After all, Antipas' comment in 6:16 is set apart grammatically from the rumors in 6:14–15 by a participial construction, whereas the rumors in 6:14–15 are listed smoothly by a series of finite verbs:

> 6:14: ἔλεγον ("[some] were saying")
>
> 6:15a: ἄλλοι δὲ ἔλεγον ("but others were saying")
>
> 6:15b: ἄλλοι δὲ ἔλεγον ("but others were saying")
>
> 6:16: ἀκούσας δὲ Ἡρῴδης ἔλεγεν ("But when Herod heard, he was saying")

Moreover, the rumors recounted in 6:14–15 are parenthetical to Antipas hearing of Jesus' fame (6:14a, 16).[158] Further still, Antipas' remark does not repeat the causal construction from 6:14—καὶ διὰ τοῦτο ἐνεργοῦσιν αἱ δυνάμεις ἐν

---

[157] Consequently, Herod indirectly dispels the rumor that Jesus is John (6:14). His admission that Jesus revived John from the dead presumes that they are in fact two separate people.

[158] Metzger, *Textual Commentary on the Greek New Testament*, 76.

αὐτῷ ("and for this reason powers are at work in him")—that specifically raises the issue of the cradle of Jesus' authority and power.

Rather, Herod's comment is short and ambiguous. He only contemplates that John has been revived. He neither explicitly asserts that Jesus is the revived John nor that Jesus revived John from the dead. The problem is that the former understanding has been reinscripted through the centuries, starting with the Gospel of Matthew in Matthew 14:2 ("This one [Jesus] is John the Baptist. He has been raised from the dead and because of this powers are at work in him [Jesus]."), as aforementioned.[159] To be sure, if a scholar offers a new interpretation of a passage that has never been forwarded—such as what I am doing here to my knowledge—the history of interpretation can alert us to the possibility that this new configuration is unjustifiable. However, it is also true that an entire trajectory of interpretation across time and space can obscure legitimate alternative interpretations. In this vein, Matthew 14:2's disambiguation of Mark 6:16 might be seen as conditioning subsequent interpreters down to the present to read Herod's remark in Mark 6:16 as a rehash of the populace's speculation in 6:14. Once an ambiguous saying has been rendered unambiguous and subsequently reinscribed, it is difficult for readers to lend credence to—let alone distinguish—alternative potentials, such as the possibility that Herod here considers that Jesus has reanimated John from death.

Second, that Herod considers the possibility that Jesus employed his power to revive John does not run roughshod over our emphasis throughout this book that Mark recounts the mutilation of John's body in a way that decreed its revivification visibly impossible. Instead, the narrative of John's beheading retrospectively serves to reveal a hint of mockery behind Mark's portrayal of Herod in that Herod incredulously considers that John has overcome a type of death designed not to be overcome; or it at least compounds Antipas' paranoia at the prospect that John is once again alive.[160] From this latter line of thought,

---

[159] Even those interpreters who try to conceptualize the revivification of John as more or less a colloquialism for Jesus being a new John—or as possessing the same spirit as John (just as Elijah's spirit rested on Elisha, 2 Kgs 2:1-15)—nevertheless still make an essential connection between 6:14 and 6:16. See, e.g., Stein, *Mark*, 301-2 (quotation, p. 302): "Herod's explanation in 6:16 is the same as one of the suggestions in 6:14—'John, whom I beheaded, this one has been raised.'" See also Collins, *Mark*, 304. I do not, moreover, find these idiomatic interpretations convincing because, again, Mark guides readers to understand John's demise and the rumor of his revivification in light of their intersection with ideologies of violence, death, and burial.

[160] We might speculate—but it remains speculation—that Antipas can consider the possibility of John's revivification not only because of Jesus' reputation as a healer, but also because he fears that John's head and body were somehow ultimately reunited in burial. Mark certainly does not make such an observation. But the last Herod saw of it in Mark's portrayal, John's head was in the possession of the girl. He is not definitively aware, unlike readers of 6:17-29, that the head and body remained separated, with the former in the possession of Herodias and the latter buried. In the medieval period, Jacobus de Voragine

we can plausibily imagine that Antipas is paranoid because he is acutely aware of how he abused John's corpse and interrupted proper burial (6:24–29).[161] At the same time as emphasizing Antipas' paranoia, the cultural ideology of beheading accentuates the impressive prestige Antipas attributes to Jesus' healing capacities. The reputation of Jesus that reaches Antipas' ears is such that it causes Antipas to entertain the unimaginable: that Jesus has raised a beheaded man from the dead.

That the mutilation of John's body in 6:17–29 functions to enhance Jesus' reputation as a healer and ridicule Antipas' paranoia remains an interpretive possibility no matter whether we translate 6:16 as a declarative statement, genuine question, or even a suspicious question. As a declarative statement ("He whom I beheaded, John, this one has been revived."), Herod's remark asserts as possible that Jesus revived John from the dead—an affirmation that 6:17–29 underlines as

compiled a tradition in the *Legenda aurea* that portrays Herodias as burying John's head separate from his body as a safeguard "because she feared that the prophet would return to life if his head was buried with his body" (see Jacobus de Voragine, *The Golden Legend: Readings on the Saints*, trans. William Granger Ryan [Princeton: Princeton University Press, 2012], 523). I am not aware, however, of any tradition in antiquity that links reuniting a severed head and its body in burial with restoring hope in the resumption of life on earth for a beheaded victim. Scholarship on decapitated inhumation in Roman Britain has fluctuated between interpreting decapitated burials as hindering or aiding the dead's entry into the underworld. For discussion and citations, see Dorothy Watts, *Religion in Late Roman Britain: Forces of Change* (London: Routledge, 1998), 74–95. In Jewish ideology, overcoming bodily mutilation within the confines of death required a creative act of God in the eschatological resurrection of the dead. Whether a reunited head and body in burial would make revivification possible in ancient ideology or not, that John's head and body are separated in burial still enables readers to cast a ridiculing gaze toward Antipas' paranoia, for we are aware as readers that the head and body remain a distance apart, which secures beyond doubt that Jesus has not revived John.

[161] Alan E. Bernstein (*The Formation of Hell: Death and Retribution in the Ancient and Early Christian Worlds* [London: UCL Press, 1993], 84–106) demonstrates that many Greeks and Romans believed the barriers between the living and the realm(s) of the dead to be "porous." The unburied dead can visit the living in order to (1) haunt or punish the living for neglect of burial, (2) implore the living to bury them, (3) request the living to correct an imperfect burial, and (4) demand vengeance on those who murdered them. Accordingly, Bernstein comments, "The dead were neither as fully dead nor as fully alive as the living might wish. . . . Death itself was no absolute boundary. . . . The spirit knows what happens to the corpse" (p. 98). Denying full or partial burial ran the risk of not securing safe separation from the dead. As Bernstein says, "Burial worked in two ways. It provided access to the underworld for the dead, but also, in principle at least, it safely isolated them from human habitation" (p. 93). Although Mark does not portray John the Baptist as a "ghost" who returns to the realm of the living to haunt Antipas for his improper burial, the cultural anxiety of recompense for an improper burial was a social factor that could conceivably explain Antipas' fixation on John's revivification. Mark, unfortunately, does not provide further detail. But the portrayal of Antipas preoccupied with the idea of John's reanimation after John had suffered corpse abuse certainly activates the reader's imagination to construe Antipas as paranoid for his maltreatment of the Baptist.

ludicruous due to the detailed nature of John's mutilation. As a genuine question ("He whom I beheaded, John, has this one [indeed] been revived?"), Herod's comment at least promotes the possibility that Jesus has raised John—a possibility that 6:17–29 dispels but nevertheless stresses that Jesus' reputation was such that it generated Antipas' paranoia. As a suspicious question ("He whom I beheaded, John, this one has [not] been revived, [has he]?"), Herod's remark is not categorically different from these other two nuances. Its divergence is a matter of estimating Herod's doubt regarding the efficacy of beheading in preventing John's revivification to a different degree. Rather than supposing that Antipas doubts that John's bodily mutilation prevented his bodily reanimation, this option affirms—with only a slight hint of doubt—that the violence applied to John's body thwarted his resuscitation. Nevertheless, the portrayal of Antipas as even entertaining this question attests to the impressive reputation of Jesus' miraculous activity that had reached Antipas' ears. He is, we might suggest, attempting to assure himself that John is safely beheaded and that Jesus cannot possibly have reanimated this perceived threat.[162]

Third, John's beheading bolstering Jesus' reputation as a healer makes sense of Mark's narrative context. In his recent study, *Jesus and the Forces of Death*, Thiessen cogently argues that the Gospel of Mark portrays Jesus—as the possessor of the "holy spirit" (πνεύματι ἁγίῳ, 1:8)—unleashing a "holy contagion" against the sources of ritual uncleanness (discharges of blood, *lepra*, unclean spirits/demons, and corpses), healing and restoring to ritual purity (holiness) those in a state of uncleanness (Mark 1:23–28; 1:40–45; 5:1–21; 5:21–24, 35–43; 5:25–34).[163] As we stated at the outset of this chapter, the story of John's beheading sits "on the margin of the narration" as an interior of an intercalation, between Jesus giving his disciples power over "unclean spirits" (6:7) and their return.[164] This structural mechanism raises the question of how John's beheading intersects with the theme of Jesus' healing reputation. While scholars typically treat Mark 6:14–16 as concerned with navigating the source of Jesus' power, it is equally plausible that 6:16 shifts the focus to Jesus'

---

[162] In reference to the parallel saying in Matt 14:2, John Chrysostom suggests that Herod is so fraught with horror that he is attempting to remind himself that he had John beheaded (*Hom. Matt.* 24.4). Chrysostom is right to notice that Antipas is portrayed as paranoid, but does not connect this paranoia with the notion that Jesus is functioning as the agent who revives John from the dead, especially since Matthew's conflation of Mark 6:14 and 6:16 at Matt 14:2 eradicates this as an interpretive possibility.

[163] Thiessen, *Jesus and the Forces of Death*. Thiessen is right to distinguish between moral impurity and ritual impurity in the Levitical code and first-century Jewish ideology. Ritual impurity is a state of existence that everyone would naturally find themselves in from time to time (through contact with a corpse, sexual intercourse, etc.), and is not moral wrongdoing per se.

[164] Maurice Goguel, *Au seuil de l'Évangile: Jean-Baptiste*, BibH 40 (Paris: Payot, 1928), 52 (translation mine).

employment of that power. In the previous chapter of this Gospel, Mark has just portrayed Jesus as reviving a dead girl—and thus overcoming the power of corpse impurity—using the same verb (ἐγείρω) to describe the revivification there (5:41) as he does here in reference to John (6:16). Mark also uses the same noun (κοράσιον) to designate the dead girl there (5:41) as he does in reference to the dancing girl in this episode (6:22, 28 [twice]).[165]

The theme of ritual (im)purity continues in the account of John's death. John's rebuke of Herod's marriage to Herodias evokes the issue of bodily purity. To quote Taylor again: "Illicit bodily connections between people resulted in a corresponding bodily impurity."[166] John is then explicitly identified as a "righteous and holy (ἅγιον) man" (6:20). But the retraction of John's ritual holiness is textually visualized as John's severed head is publicly paraded: John is now a fragmented corpse, potent with bodily contagion. The public transportation of John's severed head from a prison to a banquet on a platter thus transforms the serving dish and banquet hall from an instrument and space that foster communion to an instrument that spreads corpse impurity and a space marked by ritual contagion.

With these contextual clues in place, when Herod becomes aware of Jesus' growing fame—fame that is inextricably intertwined with his activity as a healer of ritual impurity—it reasonably follows that Herod wonders whether Jesus has once again overcome the power of ritual impurity, and somehow restored the bodily integrity and ritual purity of the Baptist. As this matter pertains to the contestation of the degradation of John as a victim of beheading, this understanding alters the negative framework of John's decapitation. By framing the tradition of John's mutilated and impure state of existence (6:17–29) in reference to Antipas' consideration that Jesus has revived John the Baptist (6:16), Mark deploys John's beheading so that it enhances the impressive prestige of Jesus' miraculous activity and mocks the Herodian king. Jesus' reputation grew to the extent that it even had Antipas contemplating the ridiculous: the return to an unbroken bodily life on earth for a broken, a beheaded, man.

Final Remarks

In this chapter, we have argued that Mark contests the degrading framework of John's decapitation in three ways. He keys John's beheading to another instance of gruesome bodily injury—Jesus' crucifixion—thereby establishing

---

[165] Both stories, moreover, form part of a structural intercalation. John's beheading constitutes the interior of an intercalation, whereas the raising of Jairus' daughter comprises the exterior frame of an intercalation (5:21–24, 35–43).

[166] Taylor, *Immerser*, 239.

a symbolic system that (1) configures the two prophets as innocent victims and (2) casts their opponents as perpetrators who unjustly put the righteous to death. He positions the public display of John's severed head so that it accentuates Antipas' loss of masculinity. And finally, he frames the account of John's beheading in reference to Antipas' preoccupation with the possibility of John's resumption to a whole life on earth. In doing so, the symbolic potential of John's degradation beyond death is refracted to enhance Jesus' reputation as a healer of bodily impurity, while mocking the so-called king for his paranoia at the prospect of a beheaded man returning to life. As a consequence, Mark perpetuates Antipas' historical reputation of disregarding purity regulations (Josephus, *Ant.* 18.36–38), since Antipas contributes to the spread of corpse impurity by serving it on a platter.

With these maneuvers, Mark acknowledges but reconfigures the negative potential that remembering bodily violence risks invoking for the victim. This commemorative text thus functions as the locus of mastering and redistributing shame. However, the constructive process of overcoming the violence of John's beheading risks creating invisible violence. The dangerousness of remembering John's bodily violence is noticeable when the reception history of such violence is brought into view. Subsequent handlers of the tradition of John's beheading disseminate a culture of invisible violence as they localize the negative characterization of the Herodian court in their present social frameworks. The dangerous impact of this process of localization is most clearly observable in Justin Martyr's *Dialogue with Trypho* and Origen's *Commentary on Matthew*. As we will see in the next chapter, both recipients contest the degradation of John's beheading, but dangerously so, by making the moral coloration of the Herodian court emblematic of contemporary Jews.

4

The Violence of Memory

Christian Identity via Anti-Jewish Polemic

Severed heads are manifestations of a given present social and cultural location. As the memory of John's beheading is localized in early "Jewish" and "Christian" disputes in the second and third centuries, John's decapitated head begins to reflect the contours of Christian anti-Jewish polemic. In this respect, John's beheading becomes invisibly violent in its early reception history. Similar to the Gospel of Mark's commemorative contestation of the potentially degrading death of the Immerser, subsequent handlers of the tradition negotiate the degrading image of John's severed head, but in socioculturally specific ways that move the tradition in anti-Jewish directions.[1] Here, I will examine two

[1] I employ the term "anti-Jewish" to describe the construction or perpetuation of cultural systems that construe Jews/Judaism according to a framework of negative stereotypes, compressed moral schematics, or ideological patterns that inferiorize Jews/Judaism in relation to Christians/Christianity. I utilize the term "anti-Jewish" instead of "anti-Semitic" to shed, inasmuch as possible, anachronistic overtones that the latter expression tends to elicit in a post-Holocaust world. Adele Reinhartz (review of *Judaism: The Genealogy of a Modern Notion*, by Daniel Boyarin, *Reading Religion*, 2018, http://www.readingreligion.org) will remind historians that while "some degree of anachronism is inherent to the study of the past," some anachronisms are more acceptable than others. Although "anti-Semitism" is employed in a variety of ways (including as a synonym of "anti-Judaism"), in general its usage communicates "racist discrimination against Jews for the simple reason that they are Jews," a racial polemic particularly associated with the rise of Nazi Germany (Anders Gerdmar, *Roots of Theological Anti-Semitism: German Biblical Interpretation and the Jews, from Herder and Semler to Kittel and Bultmann*, Studies in Jewish History and Culture 20 [Leiden: Brill, 2009], 5–8 [quotation, p. 7]). See also Frederick Schweitzer, "Persecution of Diaspora Jews: History of Jewish Persecution and Expulsion," in *Encyclopedia of the Jewish Diaspora: Origins, Experiences, and Culture*, ed. M. Avrum Ehrlich (Santa Barbara, Calif. ABC-CLIO), 95: "Anti-Semitism may be defined basically as fear and hatred of the Jews." On the various nuances of "anti-Semitism," see Ritchie Robertson, "Varieties of Anti-Semitism," in Ehrlich, *Encyclopedia of the Jewish Diaspora*, 103–7, who mentions theological, economic, racial, and nationalist

prominent examples of this phenomenon: Justin Martyr's *Dialogue with Trypho* (second century) and Origen's *Commentary on Matthew* (third century).

Contesting John's Beheading: Justin Martyr's *Dialogue with Trypho*

Composed in the middle of the second century (c. 160 C.E.), Justin Martyr's *Dialogue with Trypho* rehearses a debate (spread out over two days) between a Christian philosopher (Justin himself) and a Jew named Trypho.[2] Trypho identifies himself—or rather, Justin portrays Trypho as self-identifying—as a Hebrew refugee of the recent war (*Dial.* 1.3), a reference to the Bar Kokhba Revolt (c. 132–135 C.E.). According to Eusebius (*Hist. eccl.* 4.18.6), the debate occurred in the city of Ephesus. These two pieces of evidence together suggest a setting for the purported conversation in Ephesus around the end of the revolt (c. 135 C.E.).

Written decades later (*Dial.* 120.6 refers to the *First Apology* [c. 153 C.E.]), Justin's account of the dialogue raises a number of critical issues that occupy scholarly attention. These issues include the question of the "historicity" of the episode, to what extent the conversation reflects paradigmatic interactions between Jews and Christians in the second century, and relatedly, how cognizant Justin seems to be of Jewish ideologies in his portrayal.[3] Two features of the literary context of Justin's *Dialogue with Trypho*, however, are significant for our present discussion: the sustained differentiation between the first and second person in Justin's and Trypho's

---

anti-Semitisms. See also Mark H. Gelber, "Literary Anti-Semitism," in Ehrlich, *Encyclopedia of the Jewish Diaspora*, 107, who defines "literary anti-Semitism" as "the potential or capacity of a text to encourage or positively evaluate anti-Semitic attitudes or behaviors in accordance, generally, with the delineation of such attitudes and behaviors by social scientists and historians." On the use of anti-Semitism as a synonym for anti-Jewishness, see John T. Pawlikowski, "Anti-Judaism," in *A Dictionary of Jewish-Christian Relations*, ed. Edward Kessler and Neil Wenborn (Cambridge: Cambridge University Press, 2005), 19.

[2] At *Dial.* 120.6 (cf. *2 Apol.* 15.1) Justin identifies himself as of the Samaritan people. Throughout the debate he aligns himself with τὰ ἔθνη ("the gentiles") in distinction from "you" (Jews), as we will see.

[3] Helpful introductions to Justin's life and works include, e.g., L. W. Barnard, *Justin Martyr: His Life and Thought* (Cambridge: Cambridge University Press, 1966); E. Glenn Hinson, "Justin Martyr," *ER* 7:5043–45; Paul Parvis, "Justin Martyr," *ExpTim* 120 (2008): 53–61; Denis Minns and Paul Parvis, eds., *Justin, Philosopher and Martyr: Apologies*, OECT (Oxford: Oxford University Press, 2009), 32–70; Denis Minns, "Justin Martyr," in *The Cambridge History of Philosophy in Late Antiquity*, ed. Lloyd P. Gerson (Cambridge: Cambridge University Press, 2010), 258–69; David E. Nyström, *The Apology of Justin Martyr: Literary Strategies and the Defence of Christianity*, WUNT 462 (Tübingen: Mohr Siebeck, 2018), 1–18. See also the various contributing essays in Sara Parvis and Paul Foster, eds., *Justin Martyr and His Worlds* (Minneapolis: Fortress, 2007). For an excellent review of previous scholarship on Justin's *Apologies* and the *Dialogue with Trypho*, see Michael Slusser, "Justin Scholarship: Trends and Trajectories," in Parvis and Foster, *Justin Martyr and His Worlds*, 13–21. For a review focused on Justin's *Apologies*, see Nyström, *Apology of Justin Martyr*, 8–10.

The Violence of Memory 131

discourse; and the coming of Elijah before the Christ. As we will see, both features stand at the heart of how Justin refracts John's beheading in anti-Jewish directions, and thus how John's beheading is localized and implicated in Christian anti-Jewish polemic.[4]

"We/Us" (Christians) and "You" (Jews)

The setting of the present dialogue between Justin and Trypho in the aftermath of the failed Bar Kokhba revolt is significant for Justin's argumentation. The Jews faced horrific post-revolt consequences, including banishment from Jerusalem and the land of Judea.[5] Hence, Trypho is introduced as a Jewish refugee currently residing in Greece (*Dial.* 1.3). According to Justin, during the recent war, Bar Kokhba "ordered that *only* the Christians should be subjected to dreadful torments, unless they renounced and blasphemed Jesus Christ" (*1 Apol.* 31).[6] In view of this recent political history and its enduring effects in the present, Justin appeals to the collective memory of the Jews' past to frame and legitimize the afflictions confronting Jews in their present social situation. For Justin, the purpose of the custom of circumcision—passed on from Abraham—was to distinguish Jews from pagans and Christians, so that *only* Jews would suffer the aforementioned present afflictions (*Dial.* 16). Furthermore, as Fredriksen and Irshai observe, the Jews' exile from "homeland and Temple" derives from their misapprehension of Scripture and "their enduring national character"—epitomized by their murder of the prophets and Jesus and perpetuated by their continued rejection of Jesus as the Christ.[7] Justin tells Trypho that "The above-mentioned tribulations were justly imposed upon you, for you have murdered the just one, and his prophets before him; now you spurn those who hope in him, and in him who sent him, namely, almighty God" (*Dial.* 16).[8] In saying this, Justin keys the past to the present, drawing a close connection between contemporary Jews and the ethical

---

[4] In this chapter, I employ the Greek text of Justin Martyr's work provided by the following critical edition: Edgar J. Goodspeed, *Die ältesten Apologeten* (Göttingen: Vandenhoeck & Ruprecht, 1914). For a critical edition of Justin's *Dialogue with Trypho* with a French translation, see Philippe Bobichon, *Justin Martyr, Dialogue avec Tryphon: Édition critique, traduction, commentaire*, 2 vols. (Fribourg: Academic Press, 2003). For a history of the manuscript and print traditions of Justin's works, see Minns and Parvis, *Justin*, 3–31.

[5] For a discussion of the political, religious, and socioeconomic upheavals in Judea in the aftermath of the revolt, see Menahem Mor, *The Second Jewish Revolt: The Bar Kokhba War, 132–136 CE*, BRLJ 50 (Leiden: Brill, 2016), 468–85.

[6] Falls, FC (italics added).

[7] Paula Fredriksen and Oded Irshai, "Christian Anti-Judaism: Polemics and Policies," in *The Cambridge History of Judaism*, vol. 4: *The Late Roman-Rabbinic Period*, ed. Steven T. Katz (Cambridge: Cambridge University Press, 2006), 982.

[8] Falls, FC (italics added).

configuration of Jewish behavior from selectively emphasized episodes in Jewish history.⁹

Built into this keying is Justin's strongly unequal differentiation between Jews (that is, Jews whose identity did not revolve around the claim that Jesus was the messiah) and Christians. Bobichon is right to assess the configuration between Christians and Jews in the *Dialogue with Trypho* in this way: "The image of the Jews is linked to that of Christians through an unambiguous and definitive antithetical relationship: Justin constantly opposes one and the other on the intellectual, moral, and religious plane, without taking into account any particularity that might mitigate his purpose."¹⁰ This antithetical relationship in the discourse is achieved across the threshold of the first and second person. In large measure, both Justin (the self-portrayed Christian) and Trypho (the portrayed Jew) employ (1) the first-person plural to self-define themselves (and those who belong to their in-group) and (2) the second-person plural to distance themselves from one another (and the larger group whom the other represents).¹¹

For Justin, the first and second person serve as a chief threshold through which he launches his anti-Jewish polemic. From his perspective, "you" (plural) consists of non-Christian Jews (like Trypho) who "are the sources of evil prejudice" against Christ and Christ-followers (*Dial.* 17.1),¹² killed/crucified the Christ (14.8; 16.4; 17.1; 32.2; 133.6),¹³ killed or caused God's prophets to suffer (16.4; 39.1; 112.5; 120.5),¹⁴ regard "Christians" (Χριστιανῶν) as advocates of a "godless heresy" (17.1), do not understand the Scriptures and/or prophets (29.2; 120.5),¹⁵ are unwise and foolish children (32.5), have uncircumcised hearts (16.1), have no memory of worshipping God (46.6), are without prophetic gifts (82.1), "sacrifice your own children to the demons" (19.6; 133.1),¹⁶ and do not repent (133.6). "Justin . . . aligns his differentiation between those who understand the Jewish scriptures and those who do not

---

⁹ It must be emphasized that the ethical configuration of Jewish history that Justin portrays is precisely that: *Justin's* portrayal (not objective history).

¹⁰ Bobichon, *Justin Martyr*, 90–91 (translation mine).

¹¹ Justin's employment of the second-person plural does not derive merely from the presence of Trypho's companions in the conversation. It would indeed be odd for Justin to accuse *only* Trypho and his companions of crucifying Jesus, considering Jesus died approximately one hundred years prior to this apparent dialogue. It is preferable to view Trypho as (for Justin) typical of a broader collectivity because Justin tends to incorporate Trypho (and Trypho's companions presumably) into a collective frame of reference, as we will see.

¹² Cf. *Dial.* 133.6.

¹³ See also *Dial.* 72.3 where Justin is explicit in his specification that "(the) Jews" (Ιουδαῖοι) determined to crucify the Christ. Cf. *Dial.* 40.4 ("the elders of your people [τοῦ λαοῦ ὑμῶν] and the priests laid hands on him and put him to death").

¹⁴ Cf. *1 Apol.* 49.1–5.

¹⁵ Cf. *1 Apol.* 31.5.

¹⁶ Similarly, in *Dial.* 46.6 Justin claims that Isaiah rebuked you (ὑμᾶς) for sacrificing "your (ὑμῶν) children to idols" (cf. Isa 57:5).

The Violence of Memory 133

with a distinction between Jews and non-Jews, as if these two types of contrasts were complementary."[17]

Justin repeatedly draws on Jewish Scripture and tradition to key disobedient Israel there spoken of to "you" (plural) who reject Jesus as the Christ.[18] Justin relates the suffering of "you" Jews after the Bar Kokhba Revolt to the disobedient Israelites in Leviticus 26:40–41 whom God "will destroy in the land of their enemies" (*Dial.* 16.1).[19] Again, Justin claims the Jews' suffering derives from their treatment of their prophets and the Christ. Justin contrasts the "you" (plural) who killed Christ and the prophets and who curse Jesus-followers "in your (ὑμῶν) synagogues" with "us" (ἡμῶν) on whom "you (plural) do not have (ἔχετε) authority to lay hands" (*Dial.* 16.4). Justin brings the past to bear upon the present—and maps the present onto the past—in his appropriation of Isaiah 29:14 LXX in *Dial.* 32.5:

> And all these things which I was saying in digression I am speaking to you (ὑμᾶς), so that you may be persuaded at length by that which has been spoken against you (ὑμῶν) by God, namely, that you are (ἐστε) foolish children: "Therefore, behold, I will proceed to remove this people (λαόν), and I will remove them, and I will take away the wisdom of their wise ones and hide the understanding of their understanding ones." Will you stop (παύσησθε) deceiving both yourselves (ἑαυτούς) and those who hear you (ὑμῶν), and [instead] learn from us (ἡμῶν) who were made wise from the grace of the Christ?

Justin thus identifies the Jewish "people" (λαός) God speaks against in Isaiah 29:14 LXX as "you" (plural) and contrasts this "you" with "us," whose identity revolves around Christ. In a similar vein, Justin classifies "you" (plural) who hate "us" as those Israelites who, according to Elijah in 1 Kings 19:10, killed God's prophets and altars (*Dial.* 39.1). Justin identifies the gentiles of Malachi 1:11 as "us" who "bring to him sacrifices—the bread of the eucharist and the cup of the eucharist" (*Dial.* 41.3)—and draws on Malachi 1:10–12 to contrast "us" with "you" who profane God's name (*Dial.* 41.2–3).[20]

---

[17] Susan Wendel, *Scriptural Interpretation and Community Self-Definition in Luke-Acts and the Writings of Justin Martyr*, NovTSup 139 (Leiden: Brill, 2011), 184.

[18] By contrast, Justin identifies "us" who "have been led to God through this crucified Christ" as "the true spiritual Israelite and descendant of Judah, Jacob, Isaac, and Abraham" (*Dial.* 11.5).

[19] See also Judith M. Lieu, *Christian Identity in the Jewish and Graeco-Roman World* (Oxford: Oxford University Press, 2004), 82.

[20] That Justin's usage of the second-person plural is capable of enveloping more than the co-present interlocutors is perceptible when we consider matters from Trypho's perspective. Unlike Justin, Trypho has only one interlocutor present in the conversation, namely, Justin. Yet, Trypho will communicate to Justin in the second-person plural as well. Similar to Justin's use of the second-person plural, Trypho's use of the second-person plural is not due to the

Thus, "we/us" in Justin's direct speech largely refers to gentile Christians whose identity revolves around a specific version of Christology,[21] and who may be regarded as the true Israelite and Judahite (*Dial.* 11.5; 123.6–9; 125.5; 135.3). As Wendel maintains:

> Justin attempts to claim Israel's identity and inheritance for Gentile Christ-believers. The corollary of this assertion appears to be a

---

presence of Trypho's companions. Trypho does not address them in his dialogue with Justin. The companions are clearly not Christ-followers (see *Dial.* 8–9). Trypho associates "you" with those whose identity revolves around the Christ. Speaking directly to Justin alone at 10.4, Trypho says: "If, therefore, you have (ἔχεις) a defense on these points and can show on what place you hope (ἐλπίζετε), even though you do not observe the law, this we will very gladly hear (ἀκούσαιμεν) from you (σου)." Trypho's seamless shift between the singular verb ἔχεις, the plural verb ἐλπίζετε, and back to the singular pronoun σου indicates his perception that Justin's ideology is representative of a larger group. Moreover, the usage of the first-person plural verb ἀκούσαιμεν in opposition to the singular σου intimates that Trypho does not see himself (and Jews like him) as belonging to this other group. This distinction is all the more perceptible when we observe that Trypho identifies Justin (and Justin-like Christians) in this pericope as not observant of the law. This identification is significant because elsewhere in the dialogue, Trypho is an advocate for observing the law (8.3–4; 10.1; cf. 47.1). At 32.1, Trypho similarly views Justin as representative of a larger group when he responds to Justin: "Oh person (ἄνθρωπε), these and such scriptures compel us to wait for the glorious and great one who, as Son of Man, receives the eternal Kingdom from the ancient of days. But this so-called Christ of yours (ὑμέτερος) has come without honor and without glory." According to 77.1, Trypho urges Justin to show that Isa 7:14 refers to Justin's Christ: "Carry on for us, then, so that we may see how you demonstrate (ἀποδεικνύεις) that [passage] speaks of this Christ of yours (ὑμέτερον)." With Trypho's fluctuation between the second-person singular and plural, both 32.1 and 77.1 show that Trypho locates Justin's individual thoughts within a wider network. The wider network, moreover, is identified by a certain recognition of the Christ, one that departs from Trypho's own social network.

[21] In addition to the ensuing discussion, two recognitions undergird this definition of Justin's use of "we/us" as "largely" gentile Christians who hold a specific Christology. First, Justin indicates his awareness of some contemporary Jews who are "leaving the way of error" and becoming disciples of Christ (39.2). According to 47.3, Justin remains open to receiving Jews into the ranks of "us" as long as they do not compel gentile Christians to be circumcised or to keep the Sabbath. And, in the closing chapter, Justin prays that Trypho and Trypho's companions would believe "like us" (ἡμῖν ὅμοια) that "ours is the Christ of God" (*Dial.* 142.3). Thus, Wendel, *Scriptural Interpretation*, 184, is right that "even though Justin recognizes that some Jews believe in Jesus, he frequently contrasts non-Jewish Christ-believers with Jews, as if these two designations served as fitting labels for insiders and outsiders to the Christ-believing community, respectively." Second, Justin distinguishes "us" who are "the disciples of the true and pure teaching of Jesus Christ" from those who "confess themselves to be Christians (Χριστιανούς)—and confess the crucified Jesus as both Lord and Christ—and do not teach his doctrines, but the [doctrines] of the spirits of error" (*Dial* 35.2). Thus, for Justin, "we/us" is not a shorthand inclusive of all Christians (whether Jewish or gentile). Rather, it consists predominantly (but not exclusively) of gentile Christians and excludes those "Christians" whom Justin regards as teachers of error. This is important because, as I discuss below, Justin will closely align non-Christian Jews with erroneous Christians, implicitly polemicizing with the latter by associating them with the former.

denunciation of the Jewish nation. According to Justin, ethnic Israel rightfully incurred punishment in the destruction of the temple in 70 C.E. and after the Bar Kokhba revolt (*Dial.* 16.1–4, 25.5, 108.3; *1 Apol.* 47–49); their culpability, especially in killing Christ, led to their ultimate disinheritance.[22]

Justin asserts that God "is well pleased toward the gentiles (τὰ ἔθνη) also, and receives the sacrifices from us (παρ' ἡμῶν) more glady than from you (παρ' ὑμῶν)" (*Dial.* 29.1). "We rejoice (χαίρομεν) even though we die, because we believe God will raise us (ἡμᾶς) up through his Christ and make [us] incorruptible, unfeeling, and immortal" (46.7). The prophetic gifts "formerly among your (ὑμῶν) people" "were transferred to us (ἡμᾶς)" (82.1). Because of their inability to interpret Scripture correctly, Justin denies Jews of their ownership of Scripture and reclaims it: "Do you recognize (ἐπιγινώσκεις) them, Trypho? They are contained in your (ὑμετέροις) Scriptures, or rather not in yours (ὑμετέροις) but in ours (ἡμετέροις). For we (ἡμεῖς) trust in them, but you (ὑμεῖς), although you read [them], you do not understand (νοεῖτε) the mind in them" (*Dial.* 29.2).[23] The Scriptures and the prophets are two categories of reference that Justin can register positively even if he subsumes them under the label of "you" (Jews).[24]

As we will soon see, Justin keys John's beheading to this post-revolt context by activating it across the threshold of his first and second person discourse. In doing so, John's severed head serves as cultural frame of reference from the archival past to frame and legitimize the post-revolt affliction of non-Christian Jews. As the past of John's death bears upon the present, John's beheading is made to reflect and orient a socioculturally specific present.

Internal Christian Polemic via Anti-Jewishness: The Matter of Elijah

Justin's anti-Jewish polemic is not merely targeted at Jews, however. His discourse takes the form of a dialogue with a Jew named Trypho, but the function

---

[22] Susan Wendel, "Interpreting the Descent of the Spirit: A Comparison of Justin's Dialogue with Trypho and Luke-Acts," in Parvis and Foster, *Justin Martyr and His Worlds*, 95. Similarly, Frédéric Manns, "Justin's Dialogue with Trypho," in *The Beginnings of Christianity*, ed. Jack Pastor and Menachem Mor (Jerusalem: Yad Ben-Zvi Press, 2005), 365–75; Bruce Chilton, "Justin and Israelite Prophecy," in Parvis and Foster, *Justin Martyr and His Worlds*, 82–84. See also Tessa Rajak, *The Jewish Dialogue with Greece and Rome: Studies in Cultural and Social Interaction*, AGJU 48 (Leiden: Brill, 2001), 514, who claims that the dialogue's "militant supersessionism undoubtedly contributed to the construction of the fence between Judaism and Christianity."

[23] In this passage in particular, moreover, Justin's seamless shift from the second-person singular ἐπιγινώσκεις in addressing Trypho to the second-person plural shows that he views Trypho as representative of a larger group identity, one that departs from Justin's.

[24] See further *Dial.* 8.1–2; 26.1; 48.4; 82.1; 112.3; 120.5.

of his inferiorization of Jewish interpretation of Scripture and ethical behavior can also combat Christian rivals.[25] As Boyarin puts it:

> Justin is a writer fighting, as it were, on two fronts, against heresy and against Judaism. Arguably in his writing as well, these two battles are deeply implicated in one another. Justin is obsessed with the question of those who call themselves Christians and are not (*Dialogue* 35:80). This work of self-definition is carried out through a contrast with something called *Ioudaismos*.[26]

Likewise, more recent scholarship on Justin's *Dialogue with Trypho* has departed from the traditional understanding of the work merely "as an extended argument for the superiority of 'Christianity' over against 'Judaism.'"[27] In his 2018 monograph, den Dulk suggests that "virtually every topic in the *Dialogue* . . . is immediately pertinent to the contest between Justin's kind of Christianity and those of his demiurgical rivals."[28] Justin's rhetorical maneuver of casting Jewish ideology in an inferior light is intimately interwoven with his aim of asserting the superiority of his version of Christology over competing versions.[29]

The term "'Jew' [functions] as a negative code-word within purely Christian internal debate. . . . [T]o call an opponent a 'Jew' was to call him in the most profound and definitive way possible an un-Christian, indeed, an anti-Christian."[30] As the matter pertains to Justin's commemorative reception of John's beheading, Justin will make the Christology of Justin's Christian rivals resemble Jewish ideology regarding the messiah, rendering their Christology inferior by association with what Justin regards as incorrect thought. The intersection of this Christological rivalry with Jewish thought centers on Justin's construction of ideology regarding Elijah:

> Καὶ ὁ Τρύφων· Ἐμοὶ μὲν δοκοῦσιν, εἶπεν, οἱ λέγοντες ἄνθρωπον γεγονέναι αὐτόν, καὶ κατ' ἐκλογὴν κεχρῖσθαι, καὶ Χριστὸν γεγονέναι, πιθανώτερον ὑμῶν λέγειν τῶν ταῦτα ἅπερ φῂς λεγόντων. καὶ γὰρ

---

[25] See David Nirenberg, *Anti-Judaism: The Western Tradition* (New York: W. W. Norton, 2013), 97–106.

[26] Daniel Boyarin, *Border Lines: The Partition of Judaeo-Christianity* (Philadelphia: University of Pennsylvania Press, 2004), 38.

[27] Matthijs den Dulk, *Between Jews and Heretics: Refiguring Justin Martyr's Dialogue with Trypho* (London: Routledge, 2018), 2.

[28] Dulk, *Between Jews and Heretics*, 5.

[29] That Justin's rhetoric is not merely aimed at "Judaism" (so to speak) raises a potential objection to my argument that, in the hands of Justin, John's death perpetuates anti-Jewishness: Should the *Dialogue with Trypho* be regarded as anti-Jewish if the "real" recipients of Justin's rhetoric are Christians, not Jews? The answer is a resounding yes. Whether they are the envisioned recipients of Justin's polemics or not, Justin makes denigrating the Jews a vital component of his argumentation.

[30] Fredriksen and Irshai, "Christian Anti-Judaism," 984.

πάντες ἡμεῖς τὸν Χριστὸν ἄνθρωπον ἐξ ἀνθρώπων προσδοκῶμεν γενήσεσθαι, καὶ τὸν Ἠλίαν χρῖσαι αὐτὸν ἐλθόντα. Ἐὰν δὲ οὗτος φαίνηται ὢν ὁ Χριστός, ἄνθρωπον μὲν ἐξ ἀνθρώπων γενόμενον ἐκ παντὸς ἐπίστασθαι δεῖ· ἐκ δὲ τοῦ μηδὲ Ἠλίαν ἐληλυθέναι, οὐδὲ τοῦτον ἀποφαίνομαι εἶναι. (*Dial.* 49.1)

And Trypho said: "Those who are saying he was a person, was anointed according to choice, and became Christ seem to speak more credibly than you (plural) who are saying these things which you (singular) are expressing. For, all of us also are expecting the Christ to be a person of persons, and Elijah to anoint him, having come. But if this one appears to be the Christ, it is necessary to understand [him] to be a person of persons in everything. But, from the [fact that] Elijah has not yet come, I am not declaring this one to be [the Christ]." (*Dial.* 49.1)

From this passage that precedes Justin's reference to John's beheading, we can observe that Justin's Trypho understands that Justin's Christology is not idiosyncratic, but indicative of a larger group of thought. Hence Trypho portrays Justin (or rather, Justin portrays Trypho as portraying Justin) as singularly expressing (φής) what "you" (plural) claim (ὑμῶν . . . τῶν . . . λεγόντων). According to the previous chapter of the dialogue, Trypho describes Justin's Christology in the following way:

Τὸ γὰρ λέγειν σε προϋπάρχειν Θεὸν ὄντα πρὸ αἰώνων τοῦτον τὸν Χριστόν, εἶτα καὶ γεννηθῆναι ἄνθρωπον γενόμενον ὑπομεῖναι, καὶ ὅτι οὐκ ἄνθρωπος ἐξ ἀνθρώπου, οὐ μόνον παράδοξον δοκεῖ μοι εἶναι, ἀλλὰ καὶ μωρόν. (*Dial.* 48.1)

For you to say that this Christ preexisted, being God before the ages, and then endured to be begotten and become a person, and [was] not a person from a person not only seems to me to be paradoxical, but also foolish. (*Dial.* 48.1)

Justin's threefold belief that the Christ "preexisted" as God, then was begotten and became a person, and was not "a person from a person" thus departs from those Christians to whom Trypho alludes using the third person in *Dial.* 49.1 (quoted above). Whereas Justin and Justin-like Christians hold to the preexistence of the Christ as God, these other Christians hold what we will call an adoptionistic Christology: they believe "he is a person," "was anointed" (κεχρῖσθαι), and thus "became Christ."

In *Dial.* 49.1 Justin portrays Trypho as specifying that he [Trypho] finds this adoptionistic Christology more persuasive than Justin's viewpoint because it aligns well with Jewish opinion ("all of us") that the Christ will be "a person of persons" and anointed (χρῖσαι) by Elijah.³¹ For Justin's Trypho, Christ's anointing by Elijah is bound up in and suggestive of his thoroughly human origin—not his preexistence. The messiah's anointing precludes the possibility of preexistence.³² Since Justin, however, held that Jesus already preexisted as the Christ, the idea of Elijah coming *and* anointing someone to be the Christ represented a challenge to Justin's Christology. The anointing directly opposed his belief in the Christ's preexistence. This unit, therefore, hints at three groups in Justin's construction: Jews who believe the messiah will be anointed, adoptionistic Christians who believe that Jesus was anointed (who resemble the Jews), and Justin-like Christians who argue that the notion of preexistence precludes the idea of adoption/anointing.

Trypho's argument in *Dial.* 49.1 continues. He entertains the notion of Jesus' identity as the Christ by means of a third-class conditional statement. The protasis ("If this one appears to be the Christ") assumes the reality of the premise for the sake of argument. The apodosis consists of two clauses, introduced by the correlative conjunctions μέν ("on the one hand") and δέ ("but, on the other hand"): (1) "on the one hand, it is necessary to understand [him] to be a person of persons in everything," but (2) "on the other hand, from the [fact that] Elijah has not yet come, I am not declaring this one to be [the Christ]." According to Trypho, Elijah has not yet come; consequently, Jesus cannot be the Christ, even from an adoptionistic vantage point.³³

Trypho's objection to Jesus' messianic identity rests on his expectation that Elijah would precede and anoint the messiah, but has yet to do so.³⁴ Thus, it is

---

³¹ The πάντες ἡμεῖς ("all of us") is not inclusive of Justin, since Trypho has already indicated in *Dial.* 48.1 that Justin does not believe Jesus is "a person of persons" (ἄνθρωπον ἐξ ἀνθρώπων). Justin himself states as much in *Dial.* 54.2: οὐκ ἔστιν ὁ Χριστὸς ἄνθρωπος ἐξ ἀνθρώπων ("The Christ is not a person of persons").

³² This line of reasoning is confirmed by Trypho's rhetoric elsewhere in the dialogue. According to *Dial.* 87.1–2, Trypho appeals to the spirit *empowering* the messiah in Isa 11:1–3 to question Justin's belief in the preexistence of the messiah. See Wendel, "Interpreting the Descent," 97: "Trypho wonders why Jesus would need the powers of the Spirit to fulfill this messianic mission if he was in fact preexistent." Jesus' preexistence as the Christ, in other words, is at odds with the expectation that the Christ would be anointed with the spirit. Justin's rebuttal in *Dial.* 87.3–88.2 carefully avoids describing the descent of the spirit upon Jesus as a messianic anointing. Wendel ("Interpreting the Descent," 98) explains that the descent serves a different purpose in Justin's reasoning: "Rather than presenting the descent of the Spirit upon Jesus as a messianic anointing by John, a Jewish prophet and type of Elijah, Justin asserts that the Spirit-baptism of Jesus had the effect of removing the Spirit from Jews and their prophets. In this way, the Spirit-baptism of Jesus represents a transfer of the very presence and powers of God from the Jewish people to Jesus." See further Wendel, *Scriptural Interpretation*, 268–71.

³³ Similarly, Oskar Skarsaune, *The Proof from Prophecy: A Study in Justin Martyr's Proof-Text Tradition: Text-Type, Provenance, Theological Profile* (Leiden: Brill, 1987), 195.

³⁴ The centrality of Elijah to the contention between Trypho and Justin is apparent also from the observation that the matter of Elijah arguably stimulates the entire dialogue.

not the case that Trypho believes Elijah will precede the coming of the Christ and Justin does not. The first part of Justin's response (*Dial.* 49.2) to Trypho's objection (49.1) will illuminate this point:

> Κἀγὼ πάλιν ἐπυθόμην αὐτοῦ· Οὐχὶ Ἠλίαν φησὶν ὁ λόγος διὰ Ζαχαρίου ἐλεύσεσθαι πρὸ τῆς ἡμέρας τῆς μεγάλης καὶ φοβερᾶς τοῦ Κυρίου; Κἀκεῖνος ἀπεκρίνατο· Μάλιστα. Ἐὰν οὖν ὁ λόγος ἀναγκάζῃ ὁμολογεῖν, ὅτι δύο παρουσίαι τοῦ Χριστοῦ προεφητεύοντο γενησόμεναι, μία μὲν ἐν ᾗ παθητὸς καὶ ἄτιμος καὶ ἀειδὴς φανήσεται ἡ δὲ ἑτέρα, ἐν ᾗ καὶ ἔνδοξος καὶ κριτὴς ἁπάντων ἐλεύσεται, ὡς καὶ ἐν πολλοῖς τοῖς προλελεγμένοις ἀποδέδεικται, οὐχὶ τῆς φοβερᾶς καὶ μεγάλης ἡμέρας τοῦτ' ἔστι τῆς δευτέρας παρουσίας αὐτοῦ πρόοδον γενήσεσθαι τὸν Ἠλίαν νοήσομεν τὸν λόγον τοῦ Θεοῦ κεκηρυχέναι; Μάλιστα, ἀπεκρίνατο. (*Dial.* 49.2)

> And I again inquired of him: "Does not the word through Zechariah say Elijah is to come before the great and terrible day of the Lord?" And he answered: "Certainly." "If, then, the word compels [you] to confess that two advents of the Christ to occur were being prophesied—one in which [the Christ] will appear in suffering, without honor, and without beauty, but the other in which [the Christ] will come in glory and [as] judge of all (as has been shown by the many things that have been foretold)—[then] shall we not suppose [that] the word of God to have proclaimed [that] Elijah is to be forerunner of the terrible and great day, that is, of his second advent?" "Certainly," he replied. (*Dial.* 49.2)

With one exception, Justin does not introduce any new ideas into his argument, but reiterates notions he and Trypho hold in common at this juncture in the debate. Trypho has already conceded to Justin's claims that the prophets foretold two advents of the Christ—the first characterized by suffering, shame, and dishonor, the second by glory and honor (*Dial.* 36.1; 39.7).[35] And, as we

---

In the opening chapter, Trypho introduces himself to Justin as "a Hebrew of the circumcision, having fled from the recent war" (*Dial.* 1.3). Trypho, in turn, inquires as to Justin's philosophy (*Dial.* 1.6). After a lengthy autobiographical account detailing his philosophical background (*Dial.* 2-7), Justin finally reveals in chapter 8 that he is a Christian philosopher (*Dial.* 8.1-2). This revelation sparks both Justin's and Trypho's attempts to convince the other of the truth of their viewpoints (*Dial.* 8.2-4). Significantly, Trypho's objection to Justin's position centers on Elijah: "But if Christ has become, and exists somewhere, he is unknown, nor does he yet know of himself, or have any power until Elijah comes to anoint him and make him manifest to all. But you, having received an empty report, fashion some Christ for yourselves, and for his sake you are being destroyed without purpose" (*Dial.* 8.4). As in *Dial.* 49.1, in *Dial.* 8.4 Trypho links his rejection of the actuality of the Christ's advent to the apparent fact that Elijah has not yet come to anoint and empower him.

[35] At first sight, Justin's inference introduced by the conditional particle ἐάν and inferential conjunction οὖν appears to be logically fallacious. How does Trypho's acknowledgement

have seen, Trypho indicates in *Dial.* 49.1 (cf. 8.4) his belief that Elijah will forerun the Christ. The new supposition Justin builds toward is the assimilation of these elements.[36] That Elijah will come as a forerunner more specifically of the *second* advent of the Christ (the day of the Lord), although perhaps not a radically novel idea at this point in the debate, is a new supposition Justin makes that Trypho is quick to affirm ("Certainly" is his response [*Dial.* 49.2]).[37] Both Justin and Justin's Trypho believe Elijah will be the forerunner of the messiah's second advent.

Ideology regarding Elijah, therefore, is fundamental to Justin's and Trypho's respective Christologies and a key source of their disagreement concerning Jesus' status as the Christ. For both, Elijah will come before the messiah's second coming. For Trypho, Elijah has not yet come ahead of the first coming to anoint the Christ. As a consequence, the Christ has not arrived. Trypho thus calls into question Justin's claim that Jesus is the Christ. In *Dial.* 49.1 Trypho issues his argument that the *anointing* of the Christ by Elijah is more compatible with those Christians who hold an *adoptionistic* Christology (i.e., that Jesus was "anointed" and "became" the Christ). To contest the adoptionistic Christology of his Christian rivals, Justin stages his argument as if he is combating with a Jewish mode of thinking—hence, Justin constructs his Jewish interlocutor as aligning himself/Jews with Justin's Christian rivals.

As we will see, in *Dial.* 49.3–5 Justin's strategy is to harness John's beheading to claim that Elijah *has* already come ahead of the Christ's first advent but *without* also affirming that Elijah anointed the Christ. An acknowledgement of John the Baptist as Elijah, then, becomes an integral piece of Justin's larger aim of demonstrating the superiority of his position—that the Christ was not anointed (adopted) by Elijah. In effect, Justin utilizes Jewish ideology as a negative foil to establish the hegemony of his proto-orthodox Christology among competing Christian versions. The degradation of John's beheading, albeit contested, is a small but integral component of this complex configuration.

Dialogue with Trypho 49.3–5: Contesting John's Beheading

Καὶ ὁ ἡμέτερος οὖν Κύριος, ἔφην, τοῦτο αὐτὸ ἐν τοῖς διδάγμασιν αὐτοῦ παρέδωκε γενησόμενον, εἰπὼν καὶ Ἠλίαν ἐλεύσεσθαι· καὶ

---

of Elijah to forerun the day of the Lord mean that he has agreed to the idea of two advents of the Christ? The answer is that it does not. Instead of building on the previous sentence, Justin appears to be drawing on their wider discussion in which Trypho has already conceded to Justin that the prophets speak of two advents of the Christ (*Dial.* 36.1; 39.7).

[36] Grammatically, the culmination of Justin's thought in this regard is apparent in that this new supposition constitutes the apodosis of a lengthy conditional construction, whereas the already agreed-upon elements are relegated to the protasis.

[37] Justin expects Trypho to affirm this new supposition, as the negative particle οὐχί at the beginning of the apodosis insinuates.

ἡμεῖς τοῦτο ἐπιστάμεθα γενησόμενον, ὅταν μέλλῃ ἐν δόξῃ ἐξ οὐρανῶν παραγίνεσθαι ὁ ἡμέτερος Κύριος Ἰησοῦς Χριστός, οὗ καὶ τῆς πρώτης φανερώσεως κῆρυξ προῆλθε τὸ ἐν Ἠλίᾳ γενόμενον Πνεῦμα τοῦ Θεοῦ, ἐν Ἰωάννῃ τῷ γενομένῳ ἐν τῷ γένει ὑμῶν προφήτῃ, μεθ᾽ ὃν οὐδεὶς ἕτερος λοιπὸς παρ᾽ ὑμῖν ἐφάνη προφήτης· ὅστις ἐπὶ τὸν Ἰορδάνην ποταμὸν καθεζόμενος ἐβόα· Ἐγὼ μὲν ὑμᾶς βαπτίζω ἐν ὕδατι εἰς μετάνοιαν· ἥξει δὲ ὁ ἰσχυρότερός μου, οὗ οὐκ εἰμὶ ἱκανὸς τὰ ὑποδήματα βαστάσαι· αὐτὸς ὑμᾶς βαπτίσει ἐν Πνεύματι ἁγίῳ καὶ πυρί. οὗ τὸ πτύον αὐτοῦ ἐν τῇ χειρὶ αὐτοῦ, καὶ διακαθαριεῖ τὴν ἅλωνα αὐτοῦ, καὶ τὸν σῖτον συνάξει εἰς τὴν ἀποθήκην, τὸ δὲ ἄχυρον κατακαύσει πυρὶ ἀσβέστῳ. Καὶ τοῦτον αὐτὸν τὸν προφήτην συνεκεκλείκει ὁ βασιλεὺς ὑμῶν Ἡρώδης εἰς φυλακήν, καὶ γενεσίων ἡμέρας τελουμένης, ὀρχουμένης τῆς ἐξαδέλφης αὐτοῦ τοῦ Ἡρώδου εὐαρέστως αὐτῷ, εἶπεν αὐτῇ αἰτήσασθαι ὃ ἐὰν βούληται. Καὶ ἡ μήτηρ τῆς παιδὸς ὑπέβαλεν αὐτῇ αἰτήσασθαι τὴν κεφαλὴν Ἰωάννου τοῦ ἐν τῇ φυλακῇ· καὶ αἰτησάσης, ἔπεμψε, καὶ ἐπὶ πίνακι ἐνεχθῆναι τὴν κεφαλὴν Ἰωάννου ἐκέλευσε. διὸ καὶ ὁ ἡμέτερος Χριστὸς εἰρήκει ἐπὶ γῆς τότε τοῖς λέγουσι πρὸ τοῦ Χριστοῦ Ἠλίαν δεῖν ἐλθεῖν· Ἠλίας μὲν ἐλεύσεται καὶ ἀποκαταστήσει πάντα· λέγω δὲ ὑμῖν ὅτι Ἠλίας ἤδη ἦλθε, καὶ οὐκ ἐπέγνωσαν αὐτόν, ἀλλ᾽ ἐποίησαν αὐτῷ ὅσα ἠθέλησαν. καὶ γέγραπται ὅτι τότε συνῆκαν οἱ μαθηταὶ ὅτι περὶ Ἰωάννου τοῦ Βαπτιστοῦ εἶπεν αὐτοῖς. (*Dial.* 49.3–5)

Therefore, in his teachings he handed on, our Lord was also saying this same thing would occur, when he said Elijah is also to come. And we understand this is to occur whenever our Lord Jesus Christ is about to appear in glory from the heavens, whose first manifestation a herald—the spirit of God which was in Elijah—preceded in [the person of] John who was a prophet among your (plural) people, after whom no other remaining prophet has appeared with you (plural). He, while sitting by the Jordan River, was crying out: "On the one hand, I baptized you (plural) in water for repentance; on the other hand, the one stronger than me will come, whose sandals I am not sufficient to carry. He will baptize you (plural) in the holy spirit and fire. Concerning him, his winnowing shovel [is] in his hand. He will clean out his threshing floor. He will gather the grain into the barn, but the chaff he will burn up in unquenchable fire." And this same prophet your (plural) king Herod had shut up in prison. As the birthday celebrations were finishing [and] the niece of Herod himself was dancing suitably for him, he said to her to ask for whatever she wishes. And the mother of the girl was instigating her to ask for the head of John who was in the prison. And after she asked, he sent and commanded for the head of John to be brought in on a platter. Therefore, our Christ had also said on earth at that time to those who were saying it was necessary for Elijah to come first: "On the one hand, Elijah will come and restore all things. On the other hand, I say to you that Elijah already came and you did not recognize him, rather they did to him as many things as they wished." And it is written: "Then the disciples understood that he spoke to them concerning John the Baptist." (*Dial.* 49.3–5)

We will break down our analysis of Justin contesting the degrading potential of John as a victim of beheading by reading this passage on three intersecting levels. On one level, Justin implicitly acknowledges the degrading character of John the Baptist's beheading. Throughout the *Dialogue with Trypho*, Justin claims the prophets spoke of two advents of the Christ. In stark contrast to the second of these,[38] the first advent is described as inglorious, dishonorable, and full of suffering.[39] Before Trypho concedes this distinction (*Dial.* 36.1; 39.7), he utilizes the violent death of Jesus—the crucifixion—to argue that "this so-called Christ of yours was dishonorable and inglorious" (32.1), thereby questioning Jesus' identity as the Christ. Trypho's underlying logic is that, since the Christ's coming is to be full of honor and glory, Jesus' crucifixion *ipso facto* discounts him from a claim to this identity. Justin also readily acknowledges Jesus' suffering and crucifixion as contemptible, but as a reflection of the shameful nature of his first advent and, therefore, an indicator of his messianic status (32.1–2; 40.1–5; 49.7–8; 110.2). Just as Justin posits two advents of the Christ, he also expects Elijah to forerun the Christ at each advent (49.3). As a corollary, Elijah's first advent mirrors the degradation of the messiah's first advent (49.7). The identification in *Dial.* 49.3 and 49.5 of John the Baptist as the Elijah of the first advent, therefore, implicitly signals this characterization.[40]

The violent treatment of John's person that culminates in the public display of his severed head facilitates John's connection to Elijah. At *Dial.* 49.4 Justin's reference to John's death is truncated, at least in comparison to the parallel references in the Gospels of Mark and Matthew. Absent in Justin's articulation are the following elements: (1) the speculation surrounding Jesus' identity,[41] (2) Herod's or Herodias' motivation for seeking John's death,[42] (3) the identity of the guests invited to Herod's birthday banquet,[43] (4) the conflict in Herod

---

[38] E.g., *Dial.* 14.8; 31.1; 32.1–2; 35.8; 45.4; 54.1; 69.7; 110.2; 120.4.
[39] E.g., *Dial.* 14.8; 31.1; 32.1–2; 36.1; 52.1; 121.3.
[40] Similar to *Dial.* 49.3, *Dial.* 88.2 refers to John the Baptist as the "herald" (κῆρυξ) of the Christ's advent and "forerunner" (προϊών) of "the way of baptism." See also *Dial.* 51.3 (cf. Matt 11:12–15//Luke 16:16) where John is identified as the Elijah to come.
[41] Mark 6:14–16//Matt 14:1–2; cf. Luke 9:7–9.
[42] Mark 6:17–20//Matt 14:3–5; cf. Luke 3:19–20; Josephus, *Ant.* 18.116–119.
[43] Mark 6:21; cf. Matt 14:6. Although *Dial.* 49.4 does not specify the identities of the guests presumably present at Herod's birthday celebration, the preposition prefixed to the infinitive ἐνεχθῆναι ("to be brought in") suggests that the presentation of John's head occurred in the midst of the celebrations, open to the gaze of those present.

because of his oaths and invited guests,[44] and (5) the tradition that certain disciples arrived and buried John's headless body.[45] Instead, Justin largely dwells on the violent treatment of John's person. The inferential conjunction διό ("therefore") that begins *Dial.* 49.5, then, makes it clear that Justin bases (at least in part) the identification of John the Baptist as the Elijah of the first advent in Matthew 17:10–13 on John's beheading. The public presentation of John's severed head enables Justin to make this connection.

On a second level, however, Justin refracts the degradation of John's beheading. Just as Jesus' crucifixion is a signpost of the Christ's inglorious first coming in Justin's reckoning, so also John's beheading is a reflection of the ignominy of Elijah's first forerunning. Put otherwise, rather than the shame of John's beheading and Jesus' crucifixion *ipso facto* discounting them from their respective identities (Elijah and Christ), Justin harnesses the degrading script of their violent deaths to reinforce their contested identities. Justin will go even further in *Dial.* 49.7–8 to argue that the first advent of Elijah and Christ only held the *appearance* of ignominy; the "concealed" reality is that God's power was at work in the first advent.

Additionally, Justin contests John's beheading in such a way that its negative potential is brought into tension with other elements. Specifically, Justin pits a rhetorical distance between John the Baptist and Herod by rendering them as positive and negative figures, respectively. In *Dial.* 49.3, he introduces John by describing him as "a prophet among your (plural) people" (ἐν τῷ γένει ὑμῶν προφήτῃ), inculcated with God's Spirit (49.3). Justin holds the Jewish prophets in high esteem.[46] They are "holy" (82.1; 120.5[47]), "blessed" (48.4; 112.3), and will inherit—alongside Christians—the kingdom of God (26.1; 120.5). And Justin implies in 8.1–2 that his "affection for the prophets" was a factor that compelled him to become a Christian philosopher.

In distinction from the Baptist, therefore, in *Dial.* 49.4 Justin depicts Herod as rejecting and killing God's *prophet*. The text draws particular attention to

[44] Mark 6:26//Matt 14:9.
[45] Mark 6:29//Matt 14:12.
[46] To be sure, Justin is also aware of "false prophets" alongside the "holy prophets" in Israel's history (see, e.g., *Dial.* 82.1). He does not categorize John the Baptist, however, as a false prophet. Rather, he seems to count John among the holy prophets since the Baptist was instilled with "God's Spirit which was also in Elijah" (49.3). Elsewhere in the *Dialogue with Trypho*, Justin regards Elijah as one of God's empowered prophets (87.4) and not a false prophet (69.1).
[47] The adjective ἁγίοις in the prepositional phrase σὺν τοῖς ἁγίοις πατριάρχαις καὶ προφήταις ("with the holy patriarchs and prophets") modifies "the prophets" and not merely the "the patriarchs." This is evident from the observation that the article τοῖς governs both nouns (cf. *Dial.* 26.1 where each noun is governed by its own article: μετὰ τῶν πατριαρχῶν καὶ τῶν προφητῶν). Regardless, the prophets are paired in this text with Israel's patriarchs who will partake in God's "eternal kingdom."

this phenomenon by fronting the adjectival construction τοῦτον αὐτὸν τὸν προφήτην in the independent clause "this same prophet (τοῦτον αὐτὸν τὸν προφήτην) your King Herod had shut up in prison." In his employment of αὐτός ("this *same* prophet"), moreover, Justin brings his characterization of John the Baptist as God's spirit-endowed prophet in *Dial.* 49.3 to bear upon the sequence of actions Herod takes against the Baptist in *Dial.* 49.4. In so doing, John's status as prophet reverberates throughout the passage and constructs Herod as the one who had God's prophet imprisoned and beheaded. Further, whereas Mark 6:25 and Matthew 14:8 portray the daughter as urging the grisly supplement of John's head "on a platter" (ἐπὶ πίνακι), *Dial.* 49.4 depicts Herod as commanding this addition. The Herodian women here merely ask for John's head. Clearly, therefore, Justin creates a divide in his characterizations of the prophet John and Herod.

On a third level, Justin's contestation moves in anti-Jewish directions. He weaponizes the divide between John the Baptist and Herod by integrating it into his anti-Jewish polemic. As we observed above, Justin advances his anti-Jewish rhetoric across the threshold of "you" and "us." It is not without significance, then, that after referring to Jesus as "our Lord" (ὁ ἡμέτερος κύριος) in *Dial.* 49.3, Justin designates Herod in *Dial.* 49.4 as the *Jews'* King: "*Your* (ὑμῶν) king Herod had this same prophet [John] shut up in prison."[48] From a social memory perspective, Justin keys Herod's treatment of the Immerser to the cultural

---

[48] The exact referent of "King Herod" in *Dial.* 49.4 is not immediately clear. The royal appellation could reflect Justin's dependence on Markan tradition, since the Gospel of Mark characterizes Antipas as "King" (Mark 6:14–29; see also Matt 14:9). But establishing such dependence on the basis of a shared designation is tenuous; an overlap does not necessarily indicate direct influence. Further, Justin's narration of the story of John's head on a platter (*Dial.* 49.4) is truncated in comparison to Mark and Matthew, making it difficult to ascertain his knowledge of the Markan and Matthean versions of the tradition. See Harold W. Hoehner, *Herod Antipas* (Grand Rapids: Zondervan, 1980), 123, who notes that in *Dial.* 49.4 "only twelve words out of fifty-six … have verbal correspondence with Matthew and Mark. All twelve words appear in both synoptic accounts." The royal designation could also reflect Justin's impression that Herod the Great (Antipas' father) reigned during the death of John the Baptist. After all, Justin does not specify that this "King Herod" in *Dial.* 49.4 was "Antipas." According to Josephus, Herod the Great did hold the title "King of the Jews" (*Ant.* 14.381–385), whereas Antipas did not. As Frank E. Dicken ("Herod as Jesus' Executioner: Possibilities in Lukan Reception and *Wirkungsgeschichte*," in *Characters and Characterization in Luke-Acts*, ed. Frank E. Dicken and Julia A. Snyder, LNTS 548 [London: T&T Clark, 2016], 203–5) suggests, Justin may anachronistically indicate at *Dial.* 52.3 that Herod the Great was ruling when Jesus was crucified. However, elsewhere Justin shows an awareness that King Herod (the Great) who had slaughtered the innocents (*Dial.* 77–78; cf. Matt 2:16–18) was a different "King Herod" than the one to whom Pilate sent Jesus (cf. Luke 23:6–12) prior to the latter's crucifixion (*Dial.* 103.3–4). If Justin thought that John the Baptist died during the same Herodian reign as Jesus, then it might be preferable to conclude that "King Herod" in *Dial.* 49.4 refers to Herod Antipas, the ruler of Galilee during Jesus' death. Regardless of the precise referent, however, the important point at the moment

system of Jewish history that Justin selectively construes as marked by dubious ethical behavior. By closely aligning Herod with "you (Jews)," he incorporates Herod into the vast network of actions characterstic of disobedient Israel. The imprisonment and ensuing death of John the Baptist in this regard becomes yet another example of the Jews putting their own prophets to death (actions that, for Justin, derive from their inability or unwillingness to interpret Scripture correctly). Justin refracts the degrading gaze of John's death to implicate Herod and the Jews, making the latter bear the moral coloration of the former. This alignment is especially conspicuous because the Herodian dynasty's Jewish background was highly suspect from the first century onwards.[49] And Justin demonstrates an awareness of this suspicion (*Dial.* 52.3). The overall effect of this keying maneuver in Justin's rhetoric is that John's beheading is localized to the post-revolt conditions antagonizing contemporary Jewish refugees; John's death thereby serves to explain and legitimize these conditions.[50] Justin perpetuates the dangerous cultural motif of the Jews as killers of God's prophets who, therefore, incur traumatic consequences for such killings.

Justin also aligns John's beheadings to a key component of his competitive social context: the matter of Elijah. Justin appeals to Matthew 17:10–13 in *Dial.* 49.5 to establish that, contrary to Trypho's viewpoint, Elijah *has* come. Indeed, the pronoun ἡμέτερος ("our") qualifying the noun Χριστός ("Christ") makes it clear that Justin aligns his ideology to that of Jesus (and Jesus' disciples, Matt 17:13). Simultaneously, Justin elevates his position over that of Trypho and the Jews by distancing their Elijanic ideology from Jesus'. A brief analysis of his appeal to Matt 17:10, 12 in *Dial.* 49.5 will clarify this claim:

A. Matt 17:10, 12: τί οὖν οἱ γραμματεῖς λέγουσιν ὅτι Ἠλίαν δεῖ ἐλθεῖν πρῶτον; . . . [12] λέγω δὲ ὑμῖν ὅτι Ἠλίας ἤδη ἦλθεν

"Why, then, are the scribes saying that it is necessary for Elijah to come first? . . . [12] But I say to you that Elijah already came."

B. *Dial.* 49.5: διὸ καὶ ὁ ἡμέτερος Χριστὸς εἰρήκει ἐπὶ γῆς τότε τοῖς λέγουσι πρὸ τοῦ Χριστοῦ Ἠλίαν δεῖν ἐλθεῖν. . . . λέγω δὲ ὑμῖν ὅτι Ἠλίας ἤδη ἦλθε.

---

is *that* Justin keys "Herod" to the cultural system of the death of the prophets and to the upheavals confronting Jews in the latter half of the second century of the Common Era.

[49] See Josephus, *War* 1.123; *Ant.* 14.9; Eusebius, *Hist. eccl.* 1.6. On this issue, see, e.g., Hoehner, *Antipas*, 5–6, n. 2. See also Joel Marcus, *John the Baptist in History and Theology* (Columbia: University of South Carolina Press, 2018), 103–5.

[50] A similar commemorative phenomenon is observable in Josephus' account of the death of John the Baptist (*Ant.* 18.116–19). Josephus twice conveys that some Jews conceptualized the defeat of Antipas' armies in his military conflict with Aretas as divine vengeance for Antipas' execution of the Baptist.

> "Therefore our Christ had also said on earth at that time to those who were saying it was necessary for Elijah to come first.... But I say to you that Elijah already came."

Whereas in Matthew 17:10 those who speak of the necessity of Elijah coming first are expressly classified as "the scribes" (οἱ γραμματεῖς), *Dial.* 49.5 anonymizes this specification. This anonymizing, however, allows the Matthean Jesus' claim that "Elijah already came" (Ἠλίας ἤδη ἦλθε[ν]) to speak more smoothly to Justin's present social framework—itself comprising Jews (like Trypho) whose denial of Jesus' identity as the Christ is based on their claim that "Elijah has *not* yet come" (μηδὲ Ἠλίαν ἐληλυθέναι) (*Dial.* 49.1).

At this juncture one might expect Justin to claim that Elijah not only came but also anointed Jesus with the spirit of God. "That would be a perfect answer to Trypho's challenge in *Dial.* 8:3 and 49:1."[51] For Justin, however, admitting that John anointed Jesus would support the adoptionistic Christology of his Christian opponents—whose Christology Justin constructs (via Trypho) as closer to Jewish ideology than his own, as we discussed above. To assert that Elijah anointed Jesus, then, would not be the "perfect" answer to Trypho's quarrel, but would hinder Justin's Christology that is configured around the notion that Jesus preexisted as the Christ. So he stops short of making this contention. Instead, his strategy is to acknowledge the coming of Elijah but ignore the anointing. Justin will not overlook the descent of the spirit on Jesus altogether, however. Later in his argument, as Skarsaune rightly observes, Justin contends that Jesus' reception of the spirit at his baptism signified not the empowering of Jesus, but the removal of the spirit among the Jews:

> The elaborate exposition about Elijah's spirit being transferred to John (*Dial.* 49:3–8), and the Jewish kings being anointed by the spirit present in the prophets—runs out into nearly nothing in *Dial.* 52–54. There is no question of John anointing Jesus; on the contrary, what happens is that Jesus does something to John: He makes him stop prophesying and baptizing (*Dial.* 51:2; 52:3f)! . . . Just as Jesus made John cease prophesying and baptizing, so he puts an end to the distribution of the gifts of the Spirit among the Jews.[52]

Overall, therefore, the direct link between John and the prophet Elijah in *Dial.* 49.3–5, established on John's decapitation (*Dial.* 49.4), does not merely reconfigure the degradation John's severed head to reinforce John's identity

---

[51] Skarsaune, *Proof from Prophecy*, 196.
[52] Skarsaune, *Proof from Prophecy*, 196, 197. Similarly, Tertullian claims that John the Baptist possessed the spirit of God until the instant that Jesus was baptized. See Edmondo Lupieri, "John the Gnostic: The Figure of the Baptist in Origen and Heterodox Gnosticism," *StPatr* 19 (1989): 324.

as the inglorious Elijah of the messiah's first advent. It also weaves his death into the intricate tapestry of Justin's rhetorical aim of asserting the superiority of his ideology over his competitors' Christological ideology. Justin presses John's death into the present horizon of attacking the validity of his staged Jewish opponents' ideology as part of his larger project of undermining the adoptionistic Christology of his implicit Christian opponents. Establishing the beheaded John as Elijah is a necessary preliminary step for Justin to make in this regard. If he can affirm, against Trypho, that Elijah has already forerun the messiah (with John's beheading being the definitive signal of this forerunning) without also *anointing* the messiah, then he can cast doubt on Christian conceptualizations of Christology that held Jesus had been anointed or adopted as the Christ. Thus, not only is John's beheading localized in the aftermath of the failed second Jewish revolt to legitimize the affliction of second-century Jews, but it is also pressed into the service of local internal Christian dispute. Even as cultural images of the past force themselves upon the present as ready-to-use symbols to frame the present, the past is always remade in the image of the present because the past can only be verbalized in the context of the present.

Contesting John's Beheading: Origen's *Commentary on Matthew*

Origen (c. 186–255 C.E.) left Alexandria and took up residence in Caesarea Maritima in 232 C.E.[53] "This was to be his only real home for the rest of his life."[54] By the end of the second century—and continuing through the third century—Caesarea had a thriving Jewish presence and was a major center of rabbinic study.[55] Heine thinks it is probable that Origen had "contact and conversations" with Jews there, including Rabbi Hoshaya, who had established a rabbinic school in the city two years prior to Origen's arrival.[56] "In Caesarea Origen was forced to think theologically about the relationship between Jews and Christians in ways that he had not had to do in Alexandria."[57] While Origen's anti-Jewish polemics are perhaps not as obviously abusive as other early

---

[53] For helpful studies and introductions on Origen's life and works, see, e.g., Pierre Nautin, *Origène: sa vie et son oeuvre* (Paris: Beauchesne, 1977); Joseph W. Trigg, *Origen*, ECF (London: Routledge, 1998), 1–66; John A. McGuckin, ed., *The Westminster Handbook to Origen* (Louisville: Westminster John Knox, 2004), 1–44; Henning Graf Reventlow, *History of Biblical Interpretation*, vol. 1: *From the Old Testament to Origen*, trans. Leo G. Perdue, RBS 50 (Atlanta: Society of Biblical Literature, 2009), 174–99; Ronald E. Heine, "Origen," in *The Routledge Companion to Early Christian Thought*, ed. D. Jeffrey Bingham (London: Routledge, 2010), 188–203.
[54] Trigg, *Origen*, 36.
[55] Ronald E. Heine, *Origen: Scholarship in the Service of the Church* (Oxford: Oxford University Press, 2010), 147.
[56] Heine, *Origen*, 148.
[57] Heine, *Origen*, 174. See Trigg, *Origen*, 11, who claims that the Jewish presence in Alexandria during Origen's time was apparently small. Cf. Peter W. Martens, *Origen and*

church fathers' (e.g., Melito of Sardis, Tertullian, John Chrysostom), his assessment of Jews and Judaism as inferior to Christians and Christianity "proved all the more dangerous for the future, in that it is so thoroughly argued, on a broad textual basis."[58]

In the remainder of this chapter, we will analyze one such textual basis on which Origen advances anti-Jewish ideology: the account of John's beheading (Matt 14:1–12) in what is perhaps Origen's final exegetical work in Caesarea, the *Commentary on Matthew* (c. 244–249 C.E.).[59] The passage in question "rumbles with the undertones of the debate between the Church and the Synagogue."[60] Similar to his predecessors, Origen's discourse in *Comm. Matt.* 10.21–22 (Matt 14:3–12) fixates on cultural elements of John's beheading that hold the capacity to invoke the humiliation of a severed victim. The postmortem public display of John's severed head during Herod's birthday dinner (Matt 14:11) situates the head as an object of disdain.[61] The separation of his head and body renders him perpetually "dead, divided, and not unbroken" (*Comm. Matt.* 10.22; cf. Matt 14:10–12).[62]

However, Origen's allegorical interpretation of the tradition reallocates the degrading inflection of John's fragmented body to underscore the Herodian court's maltreatment of prophecy. This reallocation takes on anti-Jewish characteristics as Origen localizes John's beheading in his present social framework by keying the Herodian court's violent treatment of John's body to contemporary Jewish rejection of Christ, the prophets, and prophecy.[63] He infuses contemporary Jews with the moral character of the Herodian court insofar as their refusal to adhere to "true" Christian teaching mimics the court's regard for prophets and prophecy. Consequently, Origen reinscribes the Jews as kill-

---

Scripture: The Contours of the Exegetical Life, OECS (Oxford: Oxford University Press, 2012), 135.

[58] Joseph S. O'Leary, "Judaism," in *The Westminster Handbook to Origen*, ed. John A. McGuckin (Louisville: Westminster John Knox, 2004), 135. See also Joseph S. O'Leary, "The Recuperation of Judaism," in *Origeniana Sexta*, ed. Gilles Dorival and Alain le Boulluec, BETL 118 (Leuven: Leuven University Press, 1995), 373, where he claims that Christianity's absorption, in Origen's thought, of all facets of Jewish identity "had a more enduring negative effect than the ill-considered vituperations of a Chrysostom."

[59] For an argument claiming that Origen wrote the *Commentary on Matthew* after *Contra Celsum*, see Ronald E. Heine, introduction to *The Commentary of Origen on the Gospel of St Matthew*, OECT (Oxford: Oxford University Press, 2018), 24–28.

[60] Heine, *Origen*, 227.

[61] *Comm. Matt.* 10.22: καταφρονεῖται δὲ προφητεία ἐπὶ πίνακι ἀντὶ ὄψος προσαγομένη ("[The people] despise prophecy which is brought on a platter instead of prepared food").

[62] I describe the division of John's head and body as a perpetual state in order to bring out the sense of the present tense verb ἔχουσιν in Origen's statement: "They have (ἔχουσιν) it [the prophetic word, i.e., John] dead, divided, and not unbroken."

[63] Cf. Jerome, *Comm. Matt.* 14.13: "After the head of the prophet was cut off by the Jews and by the king of the Jews, prophesying among them lost its tongue and voice" (Scheck, FC).

ers of God's prophets. Yet, at the same time, Origen will retain and harness the degrading gaze of somatic violence on the victim in that John's beheaded body, juxtaposed to Jesus' crucified body, becomes a cultural symbol that etches the inferiority of Jewish teaching next to Christian teaching. While Justin Martyr locates the absence of prophecy among Jews to the moment of Jesus' immersion, John's beheading frames Origen's understanding of the Jews' current status as a collective without possession of true prophecy and teaching.

John the Prophetic Word among the Jews

In this passage, John—particularly his head—functions as a symbol of the presence or the vitality of prophecy among the Jews.[64] Collectively, the adjective προφητικός ("prophetic") and its cognates (the nouns προφήτης ["prophet"] and προφητεία ["prophecy"]; the verb προφητεύω ["I prophesy"]) occur in reference to—or in close association with—John no fewer than fifteen times in *Comm. Matt.* 10.21–22:

> 1. "Just as 'the law and the prophets (οἱ προφῆται) [were] until John,' after whom the prophetic (προφητική) gift ceased from among the Jews" (*Comm. Matt.* 10.21)
>
> 2. "Because the last of the prophets (τῶν προφητῶν) was executed lawlessly by Herod" (*Comm. Matt.* 10.21)
>
> 3. "The binding and the locking up of the prophetic (τὸν προφητικόν) word/reasoning" (*Comm. Matt.* 10.21)
>
> 4. "Therefore, John, adorned with prophetic (προφητικῇ) boldness" (*Comm. Matt.* 10.22)
>
> 5. "Herod seized, bound, and put away John in prison, not daring to kill entirely the prophetic (προφητικόν) word/reasoning" (*Comm. Matt.* 10.22)
>
> 6. "[Her] seemingly graceful movements . . . are the reason there is no longer a prophetic (προφητικήν) head/source among the people" (*Comm. Matt.* 10.22)
>
> 7. "Concerning him [John] the savior says: 'But why did you go out? To see a prophet (προφήτην)? Indeed, I say to you—and more than a prophet (προφήτου)'" (*Comm. Matt.* 10.22)
>
> 8. "But we must give thanks to God because, although the prophetic (προφητική) gift was removed from the people" (*Comm. Matt.* 10.22)
>
> 9. "But [the people] despise prophecy (προφητεία) which is brought on a platter instead of prepared food" (*Comm. Matt.* 10.22)
>
> 10. "And the prophet (ὁ προφήτης) is beheaded because of oaths" (*Comm. Matt.* 10.22)

---

[64] Similarly, Lupieri, "John the Gnostic," 325.

> 11. "For the accusation of recklessness of making oaths, of breaking oaths because of recklessness, and the accusation of prophetic (προφητικῆς) execution in order to keep oaths are not the same" (*Comm. Matt.* 10.22)
>
> 12. "And not for this reason only is he [John] beheaded, but also because of those reclining who wanted the prophet (τὸν προφήτην) to be executed rather than to live" (*Comm. Matt.* 10.22)
>
> 13. "Having locked up the prophetic (τὸν προφητικόν) word/reasoning in prison" (*Comm. Matt.* 10.22)

This enumeration increases from fifteen to twenty if we include the five occurrences where, although not applying the terms directly to John himself, Origen is relating John to Jesus, the prophets, or prophecies, more generally:

> 14. "But the Jews do not have the head/source of prophecy (τῆς προφητείας) because they deny the head/summation of all prophecy (προφητείας), Christ Jesus" (*Comm. Matt.* 10.22)
>
> 15. "Not in openness do the present Jewish people deny the prophecies (τὰς προφητείας), but implicitly and in secret they deny them and are convicted by not believing them" (*Comm. Matt.* 10.22)
>
> 16. "'In the same way if they had believed the prophets (τοῖς προφήταις), they would have accepted the one being prophesied (τὸν προφητευόμενον)'" (*Comm. Matt.* 10.22)

The inventory continues to grow if we count the instances where the terms function as the grammatical antecedents of pronouns, as with τὰς προφητείας ("the prophecies") in numeral fifteen above ("in secret they deny them [αὐτάς] and are convicted by not believing them [αὐταῖς]").[65]

As a prophet, John is "a herald of the truth" who criticizes Herod's marriage to Herodias on account of its contrariness to the law (*Comm. Matt.* 10.21). At *Comm. Matt.* 10.22, Origen carefully describes John with a series of four participial clauses that underscore this criticism stems from his prophetic identity:

> Therefore, John—adorned (κεκοσμημένος) in prophetic boldness, not terrified (καταπληττόμενος) of Herod's royal position, nor passing over in silence (παρασιωπῶν) so great a transgression (as if out of awe of death), full (πληρωθείς) of God's will—was reasoning (ἔλεγε) to Herod: "It is not lawful for you to have her, for it is not lawful for you to have your brother's wife." (*Comm. Matt.* 10.22)

---

[65] I exclude one occurrence from this entire inventory: the appearance of the term προφητεία at the end of *Comm. Matt.* 10.22. Here Origen uses the term to introduce a "prophecy" (see John 19:36; Exod 12:46; Ps 33:21) he understands as referring particularly to Jesus and emphatically *not* John.

Origen reinforces his understanding of John as "the prophetic reasoning" (τὸν προφητικὸν λόγον) who "was reasoning" (ἔλεγε) to Herod as such.

The Herodian Court's Treatment of Prophecy

Origen's methodical characterization of John as prophet serves to underscore the gravity of the violent treatment the Herodian court takes against his body. The symbolism of John's head as the source of prophecy accentuates the court's character as the imprisoners, killers, and despisers of prophets and prophetic teaching, whose actions result in the absence of prophecy among the Jews. It underscores that the Herodian court's actions are motivated by something other than, indeed contrary to, "prophetic reasoning": "lawless reasoning" or "wretched teaching." And, finally, Origen reconfigures John's beheading into a self-inflicted symbolic beheading of Herod and the Jews—a decapitation that results in a tangible shift in their political power to authorize executions. Such a shift Origen casts as divine prudence in ensuring the spread of pedagogy regarding the Christ.

After indicating that Herod imprisoned John the Baptist because of the latter's rebuke of Herod's marriage to Herodias (his brother Philip's wife), Origen says:

> Ὁ μὲν Ἡρώδης, κρατήσας τὸν Ἰωάννην, δήσας ἀπέθετο ἐν τῇ φυλακῇ, μὴ τολμῶν πάντη ἀποκτεῖναι τὸν προφητικὸν λόγον καὶ ἀνελεῖν ἀπὸ τοῦ λαοῦ. Ἡ δὲ τοῦ βασιλέως τῆς Τραχωνίτιδος γυνή, πονηρά τις οὖσα δόξα καὶ μοχθηρὰ διδασκαλία, θυγατέρα ἐγέννησεν ὁμώνυμον, ἧς τὰ δοκοῦντα εὔρυθμα κινήματα ἀρέσαντα τῷ Ἡρώδῃ τὰ γενέσεως ἀγαπῶντι πράγματα, αἴτια γεγένηται τοῦ μηκέτι εἶναι ἐν τῷ λαῷ κεφαλὴν προφητικήν. (*Comm. Matt.* 10.22)

> On the one hand, Herod, having grasped and bound John, put [him] away in prison, because he did not dare kill the prophetic word/reasoning entirely and remove it from the people. On the other hand, the wife—who is evil glory and a wretched teaching—of the king of Trachonitis gave birth to a daughter who had the same name, whose seemingly graceful movements—which pleased Herod who loves the matters of birth—are the reason why a prophetic head/source is no longer among the people. (*Comm. Matt.* 10.22)

Origen allegorizes Herodias as a "wretched teaching" (μοχθηρὰ διδασκαλία) before indicating that her daughter "had the same name."[66] This detail,

---

[66] According to Matt 14:6, however, the daughter's name is not provided; she is merely called "the daughter of Herodias" (ἡ θυγάτηρ τῆς Ἡρῳδιάδος). Here, Origen appears to be harnessing Markan tradition that claims the daughter's name was Herodias (Mark 6:22). Because they literally share the same name, the symbolism Origen draws from this is shared between the mother and daughter. Origen is clearly aware of the Gospel of Mark (see, e.g., *Comm. Matt.* 10.20).

moreover, is not a random piece of biographical data. By claiming that Herodias and her daughter share the same name, Origen is making a not too clandestine assertion that the daughter is also a "wretched teaching." The idea is that "wretched teaching" wields power over the Jews. For Origen, the daughter's "movements" (an allusion to her dance in Matt 14:6) are the cause of the prophet's decapitation and thus the absence of prophecy. He refers to her dancing as "seemingly graceful." The implication is that her graceful dance was only ostensibly so. His assessment is more direct two sentences later: "The dance of Herodias was contrary to holy dancing" (*Comm. Matt.* 10.22). Birthday celebrations are the occasions when those who dance are ruled by "lawless reasoning" (παρανόμου . . . λόγου); "their motions" seek to satisfy "that [lawless] reasoning" (ἐκείνῳ τῷ λογῷ) (*Comm. Matt.* 10.22).[67] Origen's initial depiction of the daughter's movements as "seemingly graceful" constitutes an ironic moral indictment of the daughter.

Similar to his symbolic construal of the "wretched" Herodian women is Origen's interpretation of the dinner guests at Herod's birthday celebration. After detailing that John was beheaded because of the oaths Herod made to the dancing daughter, Origen claims the guests wanted John to be executed: "And not for this reason only is he [John] beheaded but also because of those reclining, who want the prophet to be executed rather than to live. And those who celebrate his birthday recline and stand by with the wretched reasoning which was ruling the Jews" (*Comm. Matt.* 10.22).[68] Origen presents the Herodian women and the dinner guests in a united front against the Baptist. Just as Herodias (and her daughter) is a symbol of "wretched teaching" (μοχθηρὰ διδασκαλία) and birthdays are the occasions "when lawless reasoning rules" (παρανόμου βασιλεύοντος λόγου) those—like the daughter—who dance, so also the guests participate in the festivities "with the wretched reasoning that rules (λόγῳ μοχθηρῷ βασιλεύοντι) the Jews."

Herod too is configured as actively opposed to prophetic reasoning in his violent management of the Baptist. Origen interprets Herod's imprisonment of John as a "symbol (σύμβολον) of the binding and locking up of prophetic reasoning (λόγον τὸν προφητικόν)" (*Comm. Matt.* 10.21). Herod's lack of "boldness" (which Origen stresses by fronting it in its clause) by murdering John secretly in prison directly contrasts with John who was "adorned in

---

[67] Origen does not object to all dancing. For Origen, the logion, "We piped for you and you did not dance" (see Matt 11:17//Luke 7:32), supports the categorical existence of "holy dancing." See *Comm. Matt.* 10.22.

[68] Whereas Mark 6:26 and Matt 14:9 do not explicitly identify the inner motivations of the dinner guests—only that Herod did not want to break his oath "because of those reclining"—Origen seems to presume that Herod's reasoning was elicited by the dinner guests making their opinions known on the matter.

prophetic boldness" (προφητικῇ παρρησίᾳ κεκοσμημένος) while criticizing Herod (*Comm. Matt.* 10.22).[69]

In addition to situating the imprisonment and beheading of John the Baptist as the moment when the presence of "the prophetic gift" (ἡ προφητικὴ χάρις) was removed from the "the Jews" (Ἰουδαίων),[70] Origen localizes John's beheading as a temporal marker that frames a particular modification of Herod's political power in the first century:

> Ἔχει δὲ οὕτως ἡ τοῦ Ματθαίου λέξις· Ὁ γὰρ Ἡρῴδης κρατήσας τὸν Ἰωάννην, ἔδησεν αὐτὸν ἐν τῇ φυλακῇ. Εἰς ταῦτ᾿ οὖν δοκεῖ μοι ὅτι, ὥσπερ ὁ νόμος καὶ οἱ προφῆται μέχρι Ἰωάννου μεθ᾿ ὃν ἔληξεν ἡ προφητικὴ ἀπὸ Ἰουδαίων χάρις, οὕτως ἡ τῶν βασιλευσάντων ἐν τῷ λαῷ ἐξουσία μέχρι τοῦ ἀναιρεῖν τοὺς νομιζομένους ἀξίους θανάτου αὐτοῖς ὑπάρχουσα ἕως Ἰωάννου ἦν, καὶ ἀναιρεθέντος τοῦ τελευταίου τῶν προφητῶν παρανόμως ὑπὸ τοῦ Ἡρῴδου ἀφῃρέθη ὁ Ἰουδαίων βασιλεὺς τῆς τοῦ ἀναιρεῖν ἐξουσίας. . . . Τάχα δὲ καὶ ἀφῃρέθησαν τὴν ἐξουσίαν ταύτην Ἰουδαῖοι, τῆς θείας παρασχούσης προνοίας τῇ τοῦ Χριστοῦ διδασκαλίᾳ ἐν τῷ λαῷ νομήν, ἵνα, κἂν κωλύηται ὑπὸ Ἰουδαίων αὕτη, ἀλλὰ μὴ μέχρι ἀναιρέσεως τῶν πιστευόντων χωρῇ, δοκούσης κατὰ νόμον γίγνεσθαι. (*Comm. Matt.* 10.21)

> Now, the word of Matthew has it thusly: "For Herod, having grasped John, bound him in the prison." Therefore, in reference to these things, it seems to me that just as "the law and the prophets [were] until John," after whom the prophetic gift ceased from the Jews, in this way the authority (up to the execution of those thought to them worthy of death) of those ruling among the people was existing until John. When the last of the prophets was executed lawlessly by Herod, the king of the Jews was cut off of the authority to execute. . . . Perhaps the Jews also were cut off of this authority because divine foresight allowed the teaching of the Christ spreading among the

---

[69] This is the only occurrence of the verb φονεύω ("I murder") in *Comm. Matt.* 10.21–22. Thus, Origen here departs from his preference to use the verbs ἀποκεφαλίζω ("I behead"), ἀφαιρέω ("I cut off"), or ἀναιρέω ("I execute/take away") in referring to John's execution/decapitation (the verbs ἀποκτείνω ["I kill"] and ἀποτέμνω ["I behead"] are used only once each). Coupled with the recognition that Origen is offering a thorough critique of Herod in *Comm. Matt.* 10.21–22, which includes the recurring theme of Herod's lawlessness in particular, this departure more likely than not reflects an attempt on Origen's part to depict Herod in violation of the Decalogue. After all, φονεύω occurs in both Exod 20:15 LXX (Exod 20:13 MT) and Deut 5:18 LXX (Deut 5:17 MT): "You shall not murder (οὐ φονεύσεις)." But, since Origen does not specifically invoke the Decalogue, this contention remains an informed guess. At minimum, however, Origen's word choice is evocative of the Decalogue. Cf. Matt 14:10: "He beheaded (ἀπεκεφάλισεν) John in prison."

[70] In this passage, Origen relates Luke 16:16 ("the law and the prophets [were] until John") to Matt 14:3 in this regard. Cf. Matt 11:13 ("For, all the prophets and the law until John were prophesying").

people so that even if this [the teaching] was hindered by the Jews, it would not reach the point of the execution of the believers, thinking to act according to the law.[71] (*Comm. Matt.* 10.21)

Heine's translation ("When Herod contrary to the law, destroyed [ἀναιρεθέντος] the last prophet, the king of the Jews was deprived [ἀφῃρέθη] of the authority to take a life") aptly conveys the political reversal that the participle ἀναιρεθέντος ("destroyed") and finite verb ἀφῃρέθη ("was deprived") signify. His rendering fails, however, to capture adequately that Origen is activating the language of ritualized violence to assert the political consequences of the severing of John's head.[72] A more fitting translation would draw out Origen's coarse phraseology: "When the last of the prophets *was executed* lawlessly by Herod, the king of the Jews was *cut off* from the authority to execute." Although John is the one who lost his head, Herod too underwent a type of beheading: the removal of his power to authorize executions (cf. Luke 23:6–12; John 18:31).

Origen, moreover, integrates "the Jews" (Ἰουδαῖοι) into the same consequence that Herod's execution of the Baptist incurred.[73] Origen makes this claim using language that again invokes the methodological procedure of beheading. Just as Herod "was cut off" (ἀφῃρέθη), so also the Jews "were cut off" (ἀφῃρέθησαν) from exercising the power to execute. In this respect, although John is the one physically executed, Origen negotiates his beheading of its symbolic potential by turning it on its head: in Origen's allegorical reasoning, John's literal beheading constitutes in truth the self-inflicted symbolic decapitation of Herod and the Jews.

Origen goes further than this, however, by speculating that the removal from the Jews of the power to execute was rooted in divine foreknowledge to enable the "spreading" of "the teaching of the Christ," while safeguarding Christ-followers ("believers") from the risk of death. Origen suggests the removal of power from the Jews was designed by God to protect Christ-followers.[74] The

---

[71] Heine, OECT.

[72] Parthenius (*Sufferings in Love* 8.9), for example, employs ἀφαιρέω to refer to the severing of a head from its body: καὶ τὴν κεφαλὴν αὐτῆς ἀφαιρεῖ ("And he cut off her head") [Lightfoot, LCL]). The same verb occurs in triple tradition material to refer to the "cutting off" of an ear (Matt 26:51//Mark 14:47//Luke 22:50).

[73] In other words, if Herod was deprived of the power to authorize executions, the Jewish populace at large was accordingly deprived of the avenue to approach Herod specifically to execute those they wanted dead. Hence, Origen goes on to say, Jesus was condemned to death by Pilate. The logic, in Origen's thought, is that Roman avenues of execution would not have been needed in Jesus' case if Jewish avenues had still been authorized. Cf. John 18:31.

[74] In grammatical terms, the genitive absolute construction—τῆς θείας παρασχούσης προνοίας τῇ τοῦ Χριστοῦ διδασκαλίᾳ ἐν τῷ λαῷ νομήν—seems to be indicating a causal circumstance ("*because* divine foresight allowed the teaching of the Christ spreading among the people") under which the main verb ἀφῃρέθησαν ("they [the Jews] were cut off") takes place, not merely a temporal circumstance ("*when* divine foresight allowed the teaching of the Christ spreading among the people").

protection of believers, ensured by divine foresight, implies that God assumed the worst of the Jews and passed a moral judgment on them. If their authority had been left in place, they *would* execute Christ-followers, erroneously "thinking" (δοκούσης) they acted "according to the law" (κατὰ νόμον).⁷⁵ For Origen, under this hypothetical scenario, the Jews' ostensibly lawful conduct mirrors Herod's, who executed "the last of the prophets" "contrary to the law." Origen's symbolic connection between Herod and the Jews has the cultural impact of negotiating the memory of John's beheading into a tradition that displays (1) the severed vitality of the Jews' political power to enact executions and, therefore, (2) divine oversight in protecting the spread of Christ-followers' pedagogy.

On this particular issue, Origen is pinpointing the immediate political consequences that the beheading of John had within Jewish circles in the first century. The removal of power from the Jews to execute perceived criminals was a phenomenon that protected Christ-followers from non-Christ-following Jews.⁷⁶ The moral legitimacy of these non-Christ-following Jews is put on dubious display. They are portrayed as predisposed to execute Christ-followers under the false presumption of lawful behavior; Origen aligns this portrayal with a divine perspective on the matter. Now, Origen does not explicitly map the moral configuration of these first-century Jews onto third-century non-Christian Jews. Nevertheless, for Origen to perpetuate a compressed configuration of "the Jews" that reduces their moral aptitude—and positions them as those whose power is fatal to "believers" if left unchecked—holds the capacity implicitly (1) to encode the same reductive ethical formulation onto Jews in his third-century social context, and likewise (2) to establish "believers" in the third century as those who are under the hostile threat from Jews. As B. Lincoln says, "*invocation* of an ancestor [is] simultaneously the *evocation* of a correlated social group."⁷⁷ Such a fusion of groups in the past with groups in the present contains the dangerous

---

⁷⁵ Origen's depiction of the Jews "thinking" their execution of Christ-following Jews would occur "according to the law" is an ironic indictment of their reasoning. The implication in Origen's rhetoric is that such hypothetical executions would in reality *not* be in accordance to the law (even if legally sanctioned by Jewish authority). The irony here parallels another instance we already alluded to in our analysis: Origen's characterization of the daughter's dance movements as "seemingly (δοκοῦντα) graceful" but in reality driven by "lawless (παρανόμου) reasoning" (*Comm. Matt.* 10.22).

⁷⁶ The present pericope indicates that the removal of this political authority occurred in the context of "the teaching of Christ" disseminating "among the [Jewish] people" (ἐν τῷ λαῷ). The purpose of the removal, then, was "so that" (ἵνα) Christ-following Jews—"believers" (τῶν πιστευόντων)—would not face the suppression of their ideology to the extent that they would be physically killed. On Origen's general use of the terms Ἰουδαῖος ("Jew"), Ἑβραῖος ("Hebrew"), and Ἰσραηλίτης ("Israelite"), see Nicholas de Lange, *Origen and the Jews: Studies in Jewish-Christian Relations in Third-Century Palestine*, UCOP 25 (Cambridge: Cambridge University Press, 1976), 29–33.

⁷⁷ Bruce Lincoln, *Discourse and the Construction of Society: Comparative Studies of Myth, Ritual, and Classification* (Oxford: Oxford University Press, 1989), 20 (italics original).

156   A Dangerous Parting

potential to aggravate social estrangements, animate conflict, and inscribe stereotypes and attitudes that legitimize conflict.

Although Origen does not explicitly construct such a cultural system here, in his wider discussion, however, he does expressly key the negotiated image of John's beheading to his present horizon, thereby explicitly connecting separate temporal realms of history. To this fusion of the horizons of the past and present we now turn.

Anti-Jewish Turns: Keying the Beheading to Third-Century Jews

Origen's symbolic understanding of John's beheading takes on anti-Jewish characteristics as he presses the tradition into the horizon of his present social context. As our above analysis demonstrated, the Herodian court functions as a symbol of "the Jews" (οἱ Ἰουδαῖοι)[78] while John's "head" (κεφαλή) symbolizes the presence of prophecy among the Jews. Origen's symbolic maneuvers have the cultural impact of refracting the memory of John's decapitation into a tradition that (1) showcases the Herodian court's—and by extension the Jews'—maltreatment of the prophets that results in the loss of prophecy among the Jews, and that (2) frames the severing of Jewish executive authority in sanctioning executions, which in turn enables the spread of "the teaching of the Christ." According to this schematic, Christ-followers are the beneficiaries of the Jews' self-inflicted laceration.

In our proceeding discussion, we will analyze the cultural impact of Origen keying John's beheading explicitly to his contemporary third-century context. Two interrelated anti-Jewish characteristics are perceptible in this keying maneuver. First, as contemporary Jews are made to reflect the Herodian court, the moral coloration of the Herodian court becomes emblematic of contemporary Jews. Origen transforms a violent incident specific to space and time into a trans-temporal cultural system that inscribes non-Christian Jews as killers of God's prophets and who do not understand true teaching.[79] Second, as contemporary Jews are made to reflect John's fragmented body, and as contemporary Christ-followers are made to reflect Jesus' crucified—yet non-fragmented—body, Origen allegorizes the mechanisms of John's beheading and Jesus' crucifixion into a cultural schematic that establishes the superior current status of gentile Christ-followers (who possess the gift of prophecy intact) to that of non-Christian Jews (who are a perpetually broken corpse without prophecy).[80]

---

[78]   Lupieri, "John the Gnostic," 325: "In Origen's view, Herod, as the king of the Jews, was a symbol for all of them."

[79]   On "the Jews" as killers of God's prophets in Origen's writings, see, e.g., *Cels.* 5.43; *Comm. Matt.* 10.18; 16.3. See also de Lange, *Origen and the Jews*, 76–81.

[80]   That John's death is brought into focus with the contested absence of prophecy among the Jews is not necessarily an anti-Jewish claim in itself. Some Jewish sources propagate the

In short, John's severed head operates as a cultural symbol on which the moral, philosophical, and charismatic superiority of gentile Christians vis-à-vis non-Christian Jews is etched. Four passages in *Comm. Matt.* 10.21–22 collectively illustrate these dynamics.

The first passage concerns the connection of the dance of Herodias' daughter in Matthew 14:6 and the loss of John's head. Our earlier analysis of her dance demonstrated that Origen's portrayal constitutes an ironic moral indictment of the daughter. Her "seemingly graceful movements" (τὰ δοκοῦντα εὔρυθμα κινήματα) prove rather to be (1) motivated by "lawless (παρανόμου) reasoning" and (2) the reason why "a prophetic head/source is no longer among the people" (μηκέτι εἶναι ἐν τῷ λαῷ κεφαλὴν προφητικήν) (*Comm. Matt.* 10.22).[81] The daughter is construed according to Origen's philosophical understanding of the Jews as dominated by false teaching.

Origen then proceeds to say, "And until now, I suppose, the seemingly lawful movements (τὰ δοκοῦντα κατὰ τὸν νόμον κινήματα) of the Jewish people (τοῦ λαοῦ τῶν Ἰουδαίων) turn out to be not anything other than Herodias' daughter" (*Comm. Matt.* 10.22). Origen activates his portrayal of Herodias' daughter in his present social context ("And until now"), extending the same ironic indictment of Herodias' dance "movements" to contemporaneous Jewish "movements." Thus, he compresses contemporary Jewish actions to "not anything other than Herodias' daughter." With these maneuvers, Origen draws a direct line between Herodias and third-century Jews. He inscribes the latter with the moral and philosophical incompetence of the former and closely interweaves the violent treatment of prophets/prophecy with the inability to listen to true teaching.[82] Origen thereby insinuates that Jews from the time of John's death to Origen's present time continue to facilitate the absence of prophecy among the Jewish people.[83] The underlying logic is that ongoing

---

idea of the absence of prophecy, even if only a temporary or punctuated absence. See Frederick E. Greenspahn, "Why Prophecy Ceased," *JBL* 108 (1989): 37–49. What makes assigning John temporal significance as the "last of the prophets" particularly anti-Jewish is that Origen positions this as a perpetually inferior charismatic status that bolsters the superior charismatic status of Christ-followers.

[81] As Heine (*Commentary of Origen*, 1:56, n. 161) suggests, Origen is playing on the word κεφαλή ("head" or "source") "since Herod had 'beheaded' John and sent his head to Herodias."

[82] Origen also invests the dinner guests with the moral/philosophical incompetence of the Jews. He writes: "And those celebrating his birthday recline and stand by with the wretched reasoning (λόγῳ μοχθηρῷ) that rules the Jews (Ἰουδαίων)" (*Comm. Matt.* 10.22).

[83] Cf. *Comm. Matt.* 16.3 (see Matt 16:20–21) where Origen claims that the Jews continue to crucify Jesus in Jerusalem: "But if, according to a certain way of signifying things, humans are the city, even now Jesus is delivered in Jerusalem (and by Jerusalem, I mean those people whose hopes are centred on this earthly place) to the Jews who claim to be serving God. And those who are high priests, as it were, and the scholars, who boast that they interpret the divine Scriptures, condemn Jesus to death by their evil speech against him. They are always

158   A Dangerous Parting

Jewish rejection of Christian teaching mimics antecedent Jewish treatment of the prophet. Origen makes this connection unequivocal in the next passage under consideration.

The second passage concerns the public presentation of John's severed head on a platter (Matt 14:11):

> Ἔτι δὲ ὅρα τὸν λαὸν παρ᾽ ᾧ καθαρὰ μὲν καὶ ἀκάθαρτα ἐξετάζεται βρώματα, καταφρονεῖται δὲ προφητεία ἐπὶ πίνακι ἀντὶ ὄψου προσαγομένη. Τὴν δὲ κεφαλὴν τῆς προφητείας Ἰουδαῖοι οὐκ ἔχουσι, τὸ κεφάλαιον πάσης προφητείας Χριστὸν Ἰησοῦν ἀρνούμενοι. (*Comm. Matt.* 10.22)

> But consider further the people who, on the one hand, examine food [to see whether it is] clean or unclean, but on the other hand, despise prophecy that is brought on a platter instead of prepared food. And the Jews do not have the source/head of prophecy, because they are denying the summation/head of all prophecy, Christ Jesus. (*Comm. Matt.* 10.22)

Origen's remarks here are striking. Matthew 14:3–12 identifies Herod's dinner guests only as "those reclining (τοὺς συνανακειμένους)" (Matt 14:9). The Matthean account does not identify them as Jews.[84] Nevertheless, Origen assumes their Jewish identity as they are "the people" (τὸν λαόν) who scrutinize their sustenance to observe if it is "clean" (καθαρά) or "unclean" (ἀκάθαρτα). Introducing the matter with the correlative conjunctions μέν ("on the one hand") and δέ ("but on the other hand"), Origen contrasts their concern for gastronomic purity with their disregard for prophecy: the severed prophetic head of John on a platter is the object of their contempt.

Significantly, Origen keys their contempt to contemporary Jewish rejection of Jesus. "The Jews (Ἰουδαῖοι) *do not have* (ἔχουσι [present tense]) the head (κεφαλήν) of prophecy, because they are denying the head (τὸ κεφάλαιον) of all prophecy, Christ Jesus." Origen activates in his present horizon the image of John's severed head from the past, rendering the image as a symbol that integrates contemporary Jewish rejection of Jesus into the imagery of John's severed head on a platter. Hence, Origen's phraseology

---

handing Jesus over to the gentiles, mocking him and his teaching among themselves, and tongue-lashing the worship of God through Jesus Christ. They themselves crucify him by their anathemas and their desire to destroy his teaching" (Heine, OECT).

[84]   Nor does the Gospel of Matthew identify Herod Antipas, Herodias, or Herodias' daughter as Jewish. See Matt 14:1, 3, 6, 9, 11. As we noted previously in this chapter, the Herodian dynasty's identity as Jewish was a matter of dispute from the first century onwards.

pivots on the repetition of "head" (κεφαλή) cognates.⁸⁵ The Jews' posture toward John and Jesus, therefore, is converged into a singular line of cultural discourse that makes their posture toward one figure reflective of their posture to the other.⁸⁶

While the first and second passages emphasize the Jews' current status as a people without the gift of prophecy, the third passage contrasts this absence with the presence of a greater gift among gentile Christians. The pericope in question follows this comparison between Herod and the Pharaoh of Genesis 40:20–23:

> Ἄδικος γὰρ μᾶλλον ἐκείνου τοῦ Φαραὼ ὁ Ἡρώδης καὶ γὰρ ὑπ' ἐκείνου μὲν ἐν γενεθλίῳ ἀρχισιτοποιὸς ἀναιρεῖται, ὑπὸ δὲ τούτου Ἰωάννης, οὗ μείζων ἐν γεννητοῖς γυναικῶν οὐδεὶς ἐγήγερται, περὶ οὗ ὁ σωτὴρ λέγει Ἀλλὰ τί ἐξελήλυθατε; προφήτην ἰδεῖν; ναὶ λέγω ὑμῖν, καὶ περισσότερον προφήτου. (*Comm. Matt.* 10.22)

> For, more unrighteous than that Pharaoh [was] Herod. For, by the former, on the one hand, the chief baker was executed on a birthday, but on the other hand, by the latter John [was executed], concerning whom "no one greater among those born of women has arisen," concerning whom the savior says: "But why did you go out? To see a prophet? Indeed, I say to you—and more than a prophet." (*Comm. Matt.* 10.22)

Using two relative clauses, Origen carefully describes John as an exceptional figure. The first relative clause resembles Matthew 11:11a//Luke 7:28a. The second relative clause is an allusion to Matthew 11:9//Luke 7:26 that bolsters John's identity not only as a prophet, but also as someone greater than a prophet. Instead of quoting Matthew 11:11b//Luke 7:28b ("But the least in the Kingdom of the Heavens/God is greater than he [John]") immediately after this present excerpt,⁸⁷ Origen constructs a contrast between the repercussion of John's beheading and the benefit of Jesus' crucifixion:

---

⁸⁵ The κεφαλή cognates are both fronted in their respective clause. A translation that reflects this word order would be thus: "*The head* of prophecy the Jews do not have, [because] *the head* of all prophecy, Christ Jesus, they deny."

⁸⁶ Likewise, Jerome in the late fourth century writes concerning Matt 14:11: "But down to the present day we discern in the head of the prophet John the fact that the Jews destroyed Christ, who is the head of the prophets" (*Comm. Matt.* 14.11 [Scheck, FC]).

⁸⁷ This latter logion has enabled some scholars to understand Matt 11:11b/Luke 7:28b as mitigating John the Baptist's prestige. See, e.g., James D. G. Dunn, *Christianity in the Making*, vol. 1: *Jesus Remembered* (Grand Rapids: Eerdmans, 2003), 451–52; Marcus, *John the Baptist in History and Theology*, 90–91. See also Martin Dibelius, *Die urchristliche Überlieferung von Johannes dem Täufer* (Göttingen: Vandenhoeck & Ruprecht, 1911), 13; David L. Turner, *Matthew*, BECNT (Grand Rapids: Baker Academic, 2008), 293.

160 A Dangerous Parting

> Ἀλλὰ εὐχαριστητέον τῷ θεῷ ὅτι, εἰ καὶ ἡ προφητικὴ ἀπὸ τοῦ λαοῦ ἦρται χάρις, ἡ πάσης ἐκείνης μείζων ἐξεχύθη εἰς τὰ ἔθνη διὰ τοῦ σωτῆρος ἡμῶν Ἰησοῦ, ὅς ἐγένετο ἐν νεκροῖς ἐλεύθερος. Ἐι γὰρ καὶ ἐσταυρώθη ἐξ ἀσθενείας, ἀλλὰ ζῇ ἐκ δυνάμεως θεοῦ. (*Comm. Matt.* 10.22)

> However, we must give thanks to God because, although the prophetic gift was taken away from the people, the [gift] greater than that [gift] entirely was poured out on the Gentiles through our savior Jesus, who became free among the dead. For although he was crucified in weakness, he lives in the power of God. (*Comm. Matt.* 10.22)

Origen symbolically charges the methods of John's death and Jesus' death by contrasting their respective outcomes. John's beheading is tantamount to the *loss* of the presence of prophecy among the Jews ("the prophetic gift was taken away [ἦρται] from the people"). Jesus' crucifixion, on the other hand, constitutes the *gain* of a superior gift for the gentiles ("the [gift] greater than that [gift] entirely was poured out [ἐξεχύθη] on the gentiles through our savior Jesus").[88]

The superior gift Origen alludes to is the outpouring of God's spirit in Acts 2:1-41. Peter's address to the crowd in Acts 2:17-18 twice specifies that the outpouring enables *prophesying*: "And in the last days it will be, God says, that I will pour out (ἐκχεῶ) of my spirit on all flesh and your sons and your daughters will prophesy (προφητεύσουσιν). . . . In those days I will pour out (ἐκχεῶ) of my spirit, and they [male and female slaves] will prophesy (προφητεύσουσιν)."[89] Whereas Acts 2:1-41 presents this outpouring of the spirit on Christ-following Galilean Jews in Jerusalem (and Diaspora Jews visiting Jerusalem), Origen describes the outpouring "on the gentiles" (εἰς τὰ ἔθνη).[90] He heightens the contrast between Jews and gentiles by fusing the past with his present social horizon: the outpouring is accomplished through the agency of "our (ἡμῶν) savior Jesus."

---

[88] Cf. Origen, *Comm. Matt.* 10.23, where Origen allegorizes Jesus' withdraw to the wilderness after John's beheading (Matt 14:13-14): "Jesus withdrew from the place where prophecy was plotted against and condemned. Now he withdraws to the place bereft of God among the nations, so that the Logos of God might be among the nations when the kingdom is taken from the Jews and given 'to a nation bringing forth its fruits'" (Heine, OECT).

[89] Cf. Joel 2:28-29 LXX, where the verb προφητεύω occurs once.

[90] The outpouring of the Holy Spirit on Christ-following Jews in Acts 2:1-4, followed by their speaking to Diaspora Jews "from every nation" in their respective languages (Acts 2:5-13), anticipates Luke's emphasis on the outreach to the gentiles. See Craig S. Keener, *Acts: An Exegetical Commentary*, vol. 1: *Introduction and 1:1-2:47* (Grand Rapids: Baker Academic, 2012), 780-837.

Origen harnesses the terminology of losing one's head in the act of decapitation[91] and the language of blood loss in the act of crucifixion[92] to assert the preeminent status of gentile Christians, who possess a superior gift than the gift that the Jews formerly possessed but no longer hold. In this respect, Origen weaponizes the degradation of John's beheading as a negative foil that sharpens the superiority of Jesus' crucifixion. By extension, Origen makes a degrading construction of Jewish identity an integral component of constructing Christian identity. Interestingly, therefore, although Origen can integrate the beheading and crucifixion into a cultural schematic that organizes non-Christian Jewish conduct, he can also, as we have observed here, sharply differentiate the impact of both violent incidents.

The final passage concerns the setting of John's decapitation "in prison" (Matt 14:10) and the status of the body of a beheaded person versus the body of a crucified person:

> Ἔτι δὲ πρόσχες ὅτι οὐ μετὰ παρρησίας, ἀλλὰ κρύφα καὶ ἐν φυλακῇ φονεύει τὸν Ἰωάννην ὁ Ἡρώδης· καὶ γὰρ οὐ μετὰ παρρησίας ἀρνεῖται ὁ νῦν Ἰουδαίων λαὸς τὰς προφητείας, δυνάμει δὲ καὶ ἐν κρυπτῷ αὐτὰς ἀρνεῖται καὶ ἐλέγχεται αὐταῖς ἀπιστῶν. Ὥσπερ γὰρ εἰ ἐπίστευον Μωσῇ, τῷ Ἰησοῦ ἐπίστευσαν ἄν, οὕτως εἰ ἐπίστευον τοῖς προφήταις, προσήκαντο ἄν τὸν προφητευόμενον. Ἀπιστεῦντες δὲ τούτῳ κἀκείνοις ἀπιστοῦσι καὶ ἀποτέμνουσιν ἐν φυλακῇ κατακλείσαντες τὸν λόγον τὸν προφητικόν, καὶ ἔχουσιν αὐτὸν νεκρὸν καὶ διαιρεθέντα καὶ μηδαμοῦ ὑγιῆ ἐπεὶ μὴ νοοῦσιν αὐτόν.

[91] Origen's word choice of ἦρται ("was taken away") is puzzling. On the one hand, its basic meaning of "take up/away" evokes the physicality of the method of John's death: his head is taken up and away from his body. On the other hand, the verb αἴρω is a *hapax legomenon* in *Comm. Matt.* 10.21–22. Not only does this word depart from Origen's preferred language in describing John's beheading/execution (ἀποκεφαλίζω, ἀφαιρέω, and ἀναιρέω), it is also the same word used in Matt 14:12 in reference to the removal of John's headless *body* for burial (so also Mark 6:29). Matthew 14:12, moreover, comprises the only occurrence of αἴρω in the Matthean account of John's death (so also in Mark 6:14–29). Origen's word choice, therefore, presents the interpreter with three general ways of understanding this saying: (1) as a reference to John's beheading proper, (2) as alluding to the removal of John's body for burial, or (3) a combination of both ideas and thus a reference to the totality of John's death. I prefer the third option because it makes the contrast with Jesus' death more pointed: John was beheaded and his body buried, whereas Jesus "was crucified" (ἐσταυρώθη) "yet lives" (ἀλλὰ ζῇ).

[92] Origen converges two images in this text. First, the verb ἐκχέω ("I pour out") alludes to the outpouring of God's spirit in Acts 2:1–41. Second, given (1) Origen's emphasis on John's beheading throughout *Comm. Matt.* 10.22, and (2) the explicit mention of Jesus' crucifixion in this passage (ἐσταυρώθη [he was crucified]), it is difficult not also to see in this saying an allusion to the image of Jesus' blood loss on the cross. Elsewhere, Origen utilizes ἐκχέω in reference to Jesus' "blood" (αἷμα) that "was poured out" at his crucifixion (*Cels.* 8.42; cf. 1 Clem. 7.4). Hence, my emphasis on Origen charging Jesus' crucifixion by stressing its outcome is intended to capture Origen's allegorical marriage of these two images in the passage.

162   A Dangerous Parting

> Ἀλλ' ἡμεῖς ὁλόκληρον ἔχομεν τὸν Ἰησοῦν, πληρωθείσης τῆς περὶ αὐτοῦ λεγούσης προφητείας, Ὀστοῦν αὐτοῦ οὐ συντριβήσεται. (*Comm. Matt.* 10.22)

> Consider further that not in openness but secretly and in prison Herod murdered John. For also, not in openness are the present Jewish people denying the prophecies, but in power and in secret they are denying them, and they are convicted by their disbelieving in them. For just as if they had believed Moses they would have believed Jesus, so also if they had believed the prophets, they would have accepted the one who was prophesied. And because they do not believe this one, they disbelieve those [prophets] and they behead [them], having locked up the prophetic word in prison. And they [the Jews] have it [the prophetic word] dead, divided, and not unbroken, because they do not understand it [the prophetic word]. But we [Christians] have Jesus whole, since the prophecy which says about him "A bone of him will not be broken" has been fulfilled. (*Comm. Matt.* 10.22)

This pericope contains several moving parts. Of principal importance is Origen's fusion of the horizons of the past and the present. He unequivocally manipulates the beheading in his present social framework ("the *present* Jewish people" [ὁ νῦν Ἰουδαίων λαός]), so that it is emblematic of contemporary Jewish denial of "the prophecies." For Origen, the manner and location of John's death—"not in openness but secretly and in prison" (οὐ μετὰ παρρησίας, ἀλλὰ κρύφα καὶ ἐν φυλακῇ)—signals the nature of the Jews' denial: "not in openness" (οὐ μετὰ παρρησίας) but rather "in power and in secret" (δυνάμει καὶ ἐν κρυπτῷ).[93]

One naturally asks: how do the Jews *secretly* reject "the prophecies" in Origen's reasoning? Origen is not suggesting that the Jews affirm prophecies in literal public settings but deny them in literal private ones. His next comments build on John 5:46 ("For if you had believed Moses, you would believe me") and provide an answer: the Jews' manifest unbelief in Jesus is an implicit (i.e., secret) denial of the prophets/prophecies. Because Origen envisages an essential link between the prophets and Jesus, patent unbelief in the latter inherently involves a covert denial of the former. Their denial of Jesus, moreover, constitutes their continued status as a people who behead the prophets.

The rest of the passage provides a bleak assessment of the "the present Jewish people." Origen contrasts the different statuses of John's and Jesus' bodies resulting from their violent deaths. The irreparable damage of a head divided

---

[93]   Cf. Caesarius of Arles, *Serm.* 218: "John remained in chains and in a prison. The law, too, was kept locked up in the minds of the Jews as though in places of condemnation, and spiritual understanding was restrained by the letter of the law as in a hidden, secret place" (Mueller, FC).

from its body makes John's death more degrading than Jesus' death, which left the latter's body fully intact.⁹⁴ However, Origen massages this portrayal into a picture of Jews and Christians writ large. The Jews "have" (ἔχουσιν [present tense]) the prophetic word "dead, divided, and not unbroken" (νεκρὸν καὶ διαιρεθέντα καὶ μηδαμοῦ ὑγιῆ). The Jews' dispossession of the gift of prophecy and understanding of true teaching is wrapped up in the singular image of John's fragmented body.⁹⁵

"We" (ἡμεῖς), however, "have (ἔχομεν [present tense]) Jesus whole (ὁλόκληρον)." In this respect, Origen does not so much negate the degradation of John's beheading so much as he harnesses it, reallocates it to underscore the austerity of the Jews, and thereby bolsters the preeminence of Christians. Lupieri's summary works well in this regard: "In cutting off John's head, the Jews separated the prophecy of God from their religious body: the Jews lie down, now, as a headless corpse, while the Christians can worship Jesus, the totality of revelation, of whom not even a bone had been broken!"⁹⁶

Final Remarks

Similar to the Gospel of Mark before them, the prominent and influential early Christian figures Justin Martyr and Origen both negotiate the degradation of John's decapitation to reflect the Herodian court's negative disposition toward prophets and prophecy. As we have argued, however, Justin and Origen further negotiate the image of John's severed head in anti-Jewish directions while activating the bodiless head in their present social frameworks. The dangerous upshot of this commemorative activity is that both authors thereby actively construct a culture of invisible violence. We now turn to offer some reflections on the signifance of these observations and the findings of this book as a whole.

---

⁹⁴ On Jesus' unbroken body, see John 19:31–37 (cf. Exod 12:46 LXX; Ps 33:21 LXX).

⁹⁵ Origen bases his evaluation of the Jews on the claim that "they do not understand it [the prophetic word] (μὴ νοοῦσιν αὐτόν)." With this assertion Origen comes full circle in his argument in this passage: (a) the Jews do not believe Jesus, nor as a corollary, the prophets, (b) the Jews behead the prophetic word, (c) the Jews have a headless prophetic word, because (d) the Jews do not understand the prophetic word. The progression of Origen's rhetoric reveals a close association between Jewish (a) unbelief in Jesus and (d) misunderstanding of the prophets. Thus, at work in this passage is akin to what de Lange, *Origen and the Jews*, 82, refers to as "Origen's principal complaint" against his Jewish contemporaries, namely, misunderstanding because of their adherence to a literalist understanding of scripture. Origen intimately links "Jewish rejection of Jesus" "with the literal interpretation of the law" (de Lange, *Origen and the Jews*, 83). See also Martens, *Origen and Scripture*, 107–60 (quotation, p. 107), who argues that Origen's "charge of literalism" was "profoundly doctrinal" and not a "procedural" criticism of Jewish exegesis.

⁹⁶ Lupieri, "John the Gnostic," 325.

Conclusion

Reading beyond Violence

Armed with the heuristic framework of social memory theory and a robust understanding of ancient ideologies of beheading, we have seen that John's severed head served as a vehicle of communication across space and time. In its earliest written verbalization (Mark), John's severed head, keyed to Jesus' crucifixion, formulated a cultural apparatus whereby John and Jesus are mutually exonerated as victims of violent deaths, and the Herodian court is made to reflect the Jewish and Roman leadership in opposition to Jesus. The textualized public request and display of John's decapitated head accentuated the loss of manliness of a local client-ruler of Rome. John's beheading, and the corpse abuse of his head being separated from its body's burial, moreover, not only ridiculed Herod Antipas for considering the impossible notion of a fragmented body returning to a fully embodied life on earth, but also enhanced Jesus' reputation as a healer (since Mark 6:16 can be read as if Antipas is considering the possibility that Jesus managed to revive the beheaded Immerser). In its subsequent first-century articulations, John's beheading continued to exonerate Jesus as a casualty of crucifixion (Matthew) and explicitly dispelled the idea that Jesus was the revived John the Baptist (Luke).

As John's head was localized in second- and third-century "Jewish-Christian relations," John's head became the locus of early "Christian" constructions of identity in relation to "Jews." Justin Martyr incorporated second-century Jews into a cultural schematic of selective Jewish history that configured the Jews as the killers of their prophets and messiah. As part of this schematic, John's beheading served to frame and legitimize the horrific conditions confronting Jews in the aftermath of the Bar Kokhba revolt—including the desolation of Judea, the burning of their villages to the ground, their expulsion from Jerusalem, and their status as refugees in the Diaspora. Justin also activated John's bodiless head on a platter in an internal Christian dispute to subvert the adoptionistic Christology of his Christian rivals by associating his rivals' position with Jewish ideology regarding the relationship between Elijah and the messiah.

For Origen, John's beheading provided a historical explanation for why first-century Jews apparently lost the political authority to execute criminals (a loss that Origen articulates as a symbolic decapitation). Origen casts this shift in authority, moreover, as a godsend for early Christ-followers, allowing them to spread the teachings of Jesus without the threat of political violence. In Origen's allegorical usage, John's severed head also served as a cultural frame of reference that (1) keyed the moral coloration of the Herodian court's treatment of a prophet to the pedagogical failure of third-century non-Christian Jews to understand true teaching regarding the messiah, and that (2) pictured the disintegration of the presence of the gift of prophecy among non-Christian Jews—a charismatic status that continues to characterize third-century Jews in Origen's social framework (non-Christian Jews are a beheaded cadaver in this regard).

The Present in the Past and the Past in the Present

It is not the case that the present conceptualizations of John the Baptist's bodiless head in the works of Justin Martyr and Origen merely run roughshod over and manipulate the past. To be sure, John's beheading *is* reworked in these authors to reflect their present social frameworks. Both Justin and Origen draw a direct line between Herod Antipas and contemporary Jews who do not follow Christ. John's head on a platter gets swept up into second-century debate regarding adoptionistic Christology and the notion of the messiah's preexistence. John's beheading is framed to legitimize the violent suffering of Jews in the post-Bar Kokhba era and to explain the perpetual absence of the gift of prophecy among non-Christian Jews. These are connections and claims that no singular gospel text makes, but are indicative of the power of the horizon of the present to remake the past in its image. Perception of the past is always under fluctuation because present frameworks of recollection are constantly shifting.

Simultaneously, however, we can still detect that the inherited past of John's beheading constrained the extent to which subsequent recipients creatively (I do not use this term as a compliment) adapted the tradition to meet their rhetorical agendas in their respective present. For example, the commemorative maneuver that we observed at work in the Synoptic Gospels—the *keying* of John's beheading to Jesus' crucifixion—established for future generations of Christ-followers a cultural system of aligning Jesus to the prophets of Jewish history and the Herodian court to those perceived to be in opposition to Jesus and the prophets. As differences between gentile Christ-followers and non-Christian Jews became more pronounced in the second and third centuries, this cultural system enabled Christians like Justin Martyr and Origen to map this schematic onto non-Christ-following Jews in their milieu even as they expanded it to assert the moral, pedagogical, and charismatic destitution of non-Christian Jews. The inherited past of John's beheading foreshadowing Jesus' crucifixion itself foreshadowed these expressions of Jewish and Christian difference. In this sense, the inherited past acted as a constraint on the adaptive capabilities of the present to manufacture an image of the past from scratch.

The Parting of the Ways

Etched onto the memory of John's severed head are localized expressions of the so-called parting of the ways, at least in restricted senses. Lieu describes the metaphor of parting as a "short-hand for speaking of the separation between Judaism and Christianity understood not as a T junction but as a Y junction—two channels separating from a common source."[1] Previous generations of scholars tended to view the destruction of the Jerusalem temple in 70 C.E. as the decisive moment in the apparent partition.[2] Others do not prefer to speak of Christianity and Judaism as individually bounded institutions, distinct from one another, until the fourth century.[3] Still others have voiced the idea of multiple partings and identified pressure points that served as major catalysts. Dunn, for example, set forth the idea of multiple partings (hence the pluralized title of his monograph) and argued that the end of the Bar Kokhba Revolt (c. 135 C.E.) serves as the crucial point when "Christian and Jew were clearly distinct and separate."[4] Dunn, therefore, recognized the separation as a lengthy and complex process, but he nevertheless postulated a point of no return, when the partition became irreversible.

Numerous factors, however, complicate the utility of the parting metaphor as a category to describe the intricacies of the ancient data regarding

---

[1] Judith Lieu, "'The Parting of the Ways': Theological Construct or Historical Reality," *JSNT* 56 (1994): 101.

[2] For examples, see those cited in Marcel Simon, *Verus Israel: A Study of the Relations between Christians and Jews in the Roman Empire AD 135–425*, trans. H. McKeating (Oxford: The Littman Library of Jewish Civilization, 1986), x.

[3] For examples, see those cited in Daniel Boyarin, "Semantic Differences; or, 'Judaism'/'Christianity,'" in *The Ways That Never Parted: Jews and Christians in Late Antiquity and the Early Middle Ages*, ed. Adam H. Becker and Annette Yoshiko Reed (Minneapolis: Fortress, 2007), 66, n. 4. See also Robert A. Kraft, "The Weighing of the Parts: Pivots and Pitfalls in the Study of Early Judaisms and Their Early Christian Offspring," in Becker and Reed, *Ways That Never Parted*, 87–94.

[4] James D. G. Dunn, *The Partings of the Ways between Christianity and Judaism and Their Significance for the Character of Christianity*, 2nd ed. (London: SCM, 2006), 318 (italics removed).

Jewish and Christian distinctions.⁵ One factor, for instance, is the recognition that alongside clear assertions of separation (by, e.g., Justin Martyr) are perceptible indications of continuous socioreligious interactions between Jews and Christians.⁶ Even in the fourth century—a century for which one scholar makes the claim that "it is quite obvious that the 'ways' . . . did indeed 'part'"⁷—vehement expressions of distinction can be indelibly interwoven with hints of intimate connectivity between Christians and Jews. In Chrysostom's efforts to dissuade Judaizing Christians from participating in Jewish festivals and fasts and from approaching Jews for healing, his vilification of Jews presupposes the lived reality of such close associations between Jews and Christians.⁸ Further, as Lieu notes, "in most cases we cannot know

---

⁵ For a recent and thorough overview of such factors, see Timothy A. Gabrielson, "Parting Ways or Rival Siblings? A Review and Analysis of Metaphors for the Separation of Jews and Christians in Antiquity," *CBR* 19 (2021): 178–204.

⁶ Paula Fredriksen, "What 'Parting of the Ways'? Jews, Gentiles, and the Ancient Mediterranean City," in Becker and Reed, *Ways That Never Parted*, 61.

⁷ Kraft, "Weighing of the Parts," 87.

⁸ Consider this excerpt from his eighth homily:

> Sit down and speak with him, but begin with another topic so that he does not suspect you came to set him straight. Then say, "Tell me, do you agree with the Jews who crucified Christ and who blaspheme him to this day and call him a transgressor of the law?" Surely he will not dare say—if he is a Christian, and even if he has been judaizing countless times—"I agree with the Jews." But he will cover his ears and say to you, "Of course not; hush up, man." When you have gotten him to agree to this, continue with the topic and say, "Tell me, how can you participate in their activities? How can you join in their feasts, or fast with them?" Next, accuse the Jews of ingratitude. Tell him of every transgression, which I have narrated to your charity in recent days, and which has been proven from the place, from the time, from the temple, and from the predictions of the prophets. Show him how the Jews do everything without purpose and in vain, that they will never return to their former way of life and that it is illegitimate to keep their former way of life outside of Jerusalem. . . . Tell him that Jewish fasting, just like circumcision, casts the one who fasts out of heaven even though he might have a thousand other good deeds. Tell him that we are Christians and are called Christians for this reason, that we obey only Christ, not that we run to his enemies. If some healing remedies are shown to you, and someone says that they are able to heal, and for this reason he *goes to the Jews*, expose their magical tricks, their spells, their amulets, their potions. The Jews appear incapable of healing in any other way; for they do not truly heal. Far from it! I'll go even further and say this: if they truly heal, it is better to die than run to the enemies of God and be healed in this way.

John Chrysostom, *Adv. Jud.* 8.5. Col. 934–935 (trans. Wayne A. Meeks and Robert L. Wilken, in *Jews and Christians in Antioch in the First Four Centuries of the Common Era* [Missoula, Mont.: Scholars Press, 1978], 115–16; italics added). On Chrysostom's rhetoric, see F. J. Elizabeth Boddens Hosang, "Attraction and Hatred. Relations between Jews and Christians in the Early Church," in *Violence in Ancient Christianity*, ed. Albert C. Geljon and Riemer Roukema, Supplements to *Vigiliae Christianae* 125 (Leiden: Brill, 2014), 102–3.

whether those involved would have adopted the label 'Jew' and/or 'Christian', or would have felt constrained to choose between them, while the labels that they may have been ascribed by others might be different again."[9] Thus, if one were to postulate a parting, for example, in the mid-second century, they would necessarily need to account for the apparent lived reality that some in the fifth century—who were construed as Christians by certain Christian writers—evidently participated in Jewish festivals and even sought out Jews for healing and input for interpreting Scripture.[10] Relatedly (and as a further complicating factor), if one were to postulate a post-Constantine parting in the fourth century, they would need to account for certain earlier pagan perceptions, such as Suetonius who can speak of "Christians" (*Christiani*) as following "a new (*novae*) and wicked superstition."[11]

What even just this limited tiptoeing into the data reveals is the limitations that the data casts on the historian trying to catch a glance at the nature of the connective and severed tissue between Jews and Christians in antiquity. Our hypotheses are conditioned by the privileged authors whose voices found durable form in texts and have survived to the present, and by the localized rhetorical aims of such texts that obscure the correspondence between argument and lived reality.[12] In light of this complexity, Lieu's comments strike me as quite reasonable:

[9] Judith M. Lieu, *Christian Identity in the Jewish and Graeco-Roman World* (Oxford: Oxford University Press, 2004), 305. See also John Gager, *The Origins of Anti-Semitism: Attitudes toward Judaism in Pagan and Christian Antiquity* (Oxford: Oxford University Press, 1985), 7: "The voice of the Judaizing Christians—those who saw no need to tie their acceptance of Christianity to a repudiation of Judaism—is scarcely heard at all. The conception of early Christian history as governed by a progressive de-Judaization is true only for the victorious minority whose position is reflected in the surviving literature. The New Testament and other extant Christian writings represent and reinforce the views of the ultimate winners."

[10] Similar to Chrysostom in the fourth century is Cyril of Jerusalem's polemics in the fifth century: "Now the Greeks plunder you with their smooth tongues, 'for honey distils from the lips of a strange woman,' while the circumcision lead you astray by means of the Holy Scriptures, which they wrest vilely, *if you go to them*. They study Scripture from childhood to old age, only to end their days in gross ignorance" (Cyril, *Catechetical Lectures*, 4.2 [Telfer, LCC; italics added]).

[11] Suetonius, *Nero* 16.2 (Rolfe, LCL).

[12] See also Adele Reinhartz, "A Fork in the Road or a Multi-Lane Highway? New Perspectives on the 'Parting of the Ways' Between Judaism and Christianity," in *The Changing Face of Judaism, Christianity and Other Greco-Roman Religions in Antiquity*, ed. Ian Henderson and Oegema Gerbern, Studien zu den Jüdischen Schriften aus hellenistisch-römischer Zeit 2 (Gütersloh: Gütersloher Verlagshaus, 2006), 287, who observes that conceptualizing the parting of the ways in terms of different theological belief systems "requires us to essentialize both religious systems, in order to judge which elements are central, which peripheral, and how one goes about determining the point of difference that requires us to define them as separate religions rather than variations on a theme."

> Both "Judaism" and "Christianity" have come to elude our conceptual grasp; we feel sure that they are there, and can quote those "others," outsiders, who were no less sure. How else are we to understand the *fiscus judaicus*, how else to make sense of the death, if not of the myriads of whom Eusebius speaks, at least of some who would not let go of their conviction about Jesus, as they understood it? Yet when we try to describe, when we seek to draw boundaries which will define our subject for us, we lack the tools, both conceptual and material. It seems to me equally justifiable to "construct" "Christianity" in opposition to "Judaism" at the moment when Jesus "cleansed the Temple," at least in the literary representation of that event, and to think of that separation only in the fourth century, stimulated by dramatic changes in access to power—and I could call to my defence advocates of both positions, no doubt determined by their own starting-points and definitional frameworks.[13]

In stating that John's dismembered body operated as the locus of localized expressions of Jewish and Christian difference, therefore, I do not thereby intend to solve the riddle of the parting of the ways (I am not convinced there is a tidy solution). Nor is it my aim to sidestep the aforementioned complexities and suggest a clean meta-level break at a specific moment between "Christianity" and "Judaism" that the metaphor of a singular "parting" might imply. Rather, by looking at how John's severed head was activated in early "Jewish-Christian relations," we can illustrate and augment some of the factors typically forwarded as complicating our comprehension of the parting.

Our analysis of John's beheading in the *Dialogue with Trypho* in the previous chapter resists conforming neatly to a parting conceptualization. We can, of course, observe that Justin creates a sharp rhetorical distance between "you (Jews)" and "us (Christians)" and incorporates the tradition of John's beheading into this structural gulf. We can also notice that the integration of John's severed head into an apparatus of Jewish maltreatment of the messiah and the prophets helps Justin legitimize the refugee status of non-Christ-following Jews in the aftermath of the second Jewish Revolt.[14] And finally, Justin clearly establishes an

---

[13] Judith Lieu, *Neither Jew Nor Greek? Constructing Early Christianity*, 2nd ed. (London: T&T Clark, 2016), 239. Likewise, idem, "'Parting of the Ways,'" 108. See also Daniel Boyarin, *Border Lines: The Partition of Judaeo-Christianity* (Philadelphia: University of Pennsylvania Press, 2004), 6–7: "But a partial answer to the paradox that, as early as the first century, Christians were, nevertheless, recognizable at least in some places as not-Jews (Tacitus, the *fiscus judaicus*, other evidence) is to note that whether or not there were Christianity and Judaism, there were, it seems, at least some Christians who were not Jews, and, of course, many Jews who were not Christians."

[14] In this vein, we can also observe that the Synoptic Gospels' commemorative maneuver to align the beheading and the crucifixion enabled this later construction of Jewish and Christian difference.

Conclusion   171

antithesis between Jewish christological assumptions and his own, with Jews like Trypho positing an anointing of the anointed one (the Christ) and Justin denying this. Justin sets forth a clear separation between the ethical makeup, existential experiences, and ideological components of non-Christ-following Jews and Christians. At the same time, the staging of Justin's discourse as a dialogue between a Jew and a Christian presumes a paradigm of ongoing socioreligious contact between Jews and Christians. As part of this staging, moreover, Justin (via Trypho) associates Jewish ideologies concerning the advent of the messiah with certain pockets of Christians who advocate an adoptionistic Christology. In other words, even as Justin discursively drives an ideological wedge between Justin-like Christians and Jews, he aligns Jews with other strands of Christian thinking. Lost in all of this are the autonomous expressions of identity by Jews and Justin's Christian opponents, as both groups' voices are animated in the *Dialogue with Trypho* by means of Justin's omnipotent pen.

Origen's harnessing of John's severed head represents the voice of an elite Christian intellectual, whose interpretation probably reflects his concentrated interactions with Jews in Caesarea Maritima in the early third century. As Heine avers, Origen's treatment of John's decapitation "rumbles with the undertones of the debate between the Church and the Synagogue."[15] But even so, we simply do not have direct access to how Jews in Caesarea evaluated the charismatic line he draws between Jews as those without the gift of prophecy *and* Christians as the possessors of a gift even greater than prophecy. Be that as it may, what is striking about Origen's construction of Jewish and Christian difference is that it amounts to a claim of diverging charismatic statuses of Jews and Christians. And this dissimilarity, moreover, is conceptualized by Origen as stemming from the enduring disparate conditions of John's beheaded body and Jesus' crucified body—the latter, crucified yet resurrected and whole; the former, beheaded and thus broken and unrevived. Here, Jewish and Christian difference is conceptualized as somatic difference. Reinhartz once convincingly argued that "while we can no longer claim that there was a single 'parting of the ways', nor can we, in my view, declare that the ways did not part at all in the first few centuries of the Common Era."[16] Origen, I think, would at least agree with the latter half of this sentiment: the ways parted as John's head parted its body.

The Dangerousness of Anti-Jewishness

Not only have we seen that John's severed head became a cultural frame of reference that certain early Christians harnessed to embody Jewish and Christian distinctions, it also came to embody difference in anti-Jewish ways. As we have

---

[15] Ronald E. Heine, *Origen: Scholarship in the Service of the Church* (Oxford: Oxford University Press, 2010), 227.
[16] Reinhartz, "A Fork in the Road or a Multi-Lane Highway?" 293.

argued in this book, the early reception history we have analyzed herein is characterized by a dangerous synchroneity. On the one hand, John's beheading served as the locus of identity construction, where the degradation of a victim who undergoes bodily violence is destabilized and redistributed. On the other hand, as John's beheading came to facilitate Jewish and Christian difference, it marked that difference in terms of moral, ideological, and charismatic qualities. In other words, as the degradation of John's beheading is contested and reallocated, the degrading gaze began to encompass the Jews writ large, allowing early Christian writers to capitalize on this inferiorization to allege their own moral, ideological, and charismatic supremacy.

I have specifically labeled these anti-Jewish maneuvers as dangerous for two reasons. The first is to acknowledge and fix our gaze squarely on anti-Jewishness as a "morality-attenuating process" that "weaken[s] erstwhile moral restraints against violence."[17] Both Justin and Origen integrate the keyed deaths of John and Jesus onto their present horizon, incorporating contemporary Jewish behavior into the ethical configurations of the opposition that John and Jesus face in the Synoptic Gospels' portrayals. They perpetuate the motif of non-Christian Jews as the killers of Christ and the prophets, essentializing their conduct. Both Justin and Origen, furthermore, make compressing Jewish qualities integral to configuring Christian identity—a pattern of thinking that has become routinized because of their lasting influence on subsequent generations.[18] Notions that Justin Martyr and Origen both voiced—e.g., that "Jews" killed prophets like Jesus and John the

---

[17] Lois Presser, *Inside Story: How Narratives Drive Mass Harm* (Oakland: University of California Press, 2018), 33, 32 (respectively).

[18] John T. Pawlikowski, "Anti-Judaism," in *A Dictionary of Jewish-Christian Relations*, ed. Edward Kessler and Neil Wenborn (Cambridge: Cambridge University Press, 2005), 19–20: "The most important and comprehensive anti-Judaic document was Justin Martyr's *Dialogue with Trypho*. It became a model for discussions about Judaism in the ancient Church and sowed the seeds for an anti-Judaic attitude that would come to dominate the thinking of the churches from the fourth to the twentieth century." See Boyarin, *Border Lines*, 11–13, who argues that "Judaism" as a bounded institution mainly came into existence as a needed Christian construct to erect Christian orthodoxy over and against heresy, hence the tendency of many early Christians to define heresy "with reference to *Judaism*" (p. 12). Joseph S. O'Leary, "The Recuperation of Judaism," in *Origeniana Sexta*, BETL 118 (Leuven: Leuven University Press, 1995), 378: "Anti-Judaism is a structural necessity of his [Origen's] thought, which systematizes the previous efforts to judge and recuperate Judaism and which in turn was inherited by all subsequent Christian theology." Already in the late fourth century we can observe the influence that Origen's anti-Jewish interpretation of John's beheading in the *Commentary on Matthew* had on Jerome in the latter's own *Commentary on Matthew*, which relied heavily on Origen's work. See, e.g., Jerome, *Comm. Matt.* 14.11. See also Paula Fredriksen and Oded Irshai, "Christian Anti-Judaism: Polemics and Policies," in *The Cambridge History of Judaism*, vol. 4: *The Late Roman-Rabbinic Period*, ed. Steven T. Katz (Cambridge: Cambridge University Press, 2006); Paula Fredriksen, "The Birth of Christianity and the Origins of Christian Anti-Judaism," in *Jesus, Judaism and*

Baptist—have fueled, authorized, justified, or animated (whether overtly or covertly, intentionally or unintentionally) indifference to acts of physical violence against Jews regularly throughout history, as is well known.[19] The inferiorization of Jews lowers the subject's ability and readiness to examine adverse Jewish experience. Violence, in this way, is encoded by invisible (invisible, at least, to the untrained eye that is not ready to examine the deep roots of violence) aspects of culture, ideological patterns, and identity.[20]

The second reason is to offer readers a heuristic suggestion on how to combat perpetuating anti-Jewishness (and the dangers implied therein) by contemplating the ethics *of* reading ancient texts. In view of our emphasis throughout this study of the procreative capability of the horizon of a given present to remake the inherited past in the image of the present, an essential component of dismantling the endurance of anti-Jewishness must be to resist any compulsion to read ancient configurations of non-Christian Jews as implicit or explicit descriptions of contemporary Jews. The anti-Jewish characteristics that we have analyzed in the reception of John's beheading in the works of Justin Martyr and Origen are selective, compressed, and enmeshed in localized polemic. They do not provide unmediated or objective description of the fullness or richness of contemporary Jewish life, let alone ancient Jewish vitality.[21]

Final Remarks

If this book is any indication, the future of John the Baptist research is ripe with potential. Our focus on the communicative impact of his severed head has shown that a focus on the body as a discursive conduit of society and culture can shed fresh perspective on the ancient conceptualizations of this enigmatic figure and, more broadly, on how we engage (sacred) texts and bring them forward in our variegated present social arrangements. From configuring the

---

Christian Anti-Judaism: Reading the New Testament after the Holocaust, ed. Paula Fredriksen and Adele Reinhartz (Louisville: Westminster John Knox, 2002), 8–30.

[19] In this book, we have thoroughly documented one such instance: Justin Martyr explicitly deploys the schematic of the Jews as the killers of John the Baptist and Jesus to legitimize the violent suffering of Jews after the Bar Kokhba revolt. See also Anders Gerdmar, *Roots of Theological Anti-Semitism: German Biblical Interpretation and the Jews, from Herder and Semler to Kittel and Bultmann*, Studies in Jewish History and Culture 20 (Leiden: Brill, 2009), 8, who demonstrates that "Anti-Judaism may be 'fertilised' and develop into anti-Semitism." Gerdmar detects an indelible link between anti-Judaism and anti-Semitism, with the former often acting as "a *praeparatio antisemitica*." Thus, although anti-Judaism is seemingly the more innocuous term in that it does not necessarily connote a stated hatred of Jews, it is no less dangerous due to its ability to facilitate hatred and violence.

[20] On the enculturation of violence, see especially Presser, *Inside Story*, 23–60.

[21] For further ideas on dismantling anti-Jewishness in contemporary contexts, see especially Amy-Jill Levine, *The Misunderstood Jew: The Church and the Scandal of the Jewish Jesus* (New York: HarperCollins, 2006), 215–26.

gendered vice of a local client-ruler of the Roman Empire and enhancing the prestige of a first-century Jewish miracle-worker to rationalizing the refugee status of postwar Jews and signifying what is absent in Jews but present in Christians, John's beheading channeled discourse specific to place and time. And in our reception, John's beheading is framed to highlight early developments of Christian anti-Jewish mechanisms of thinking in a bid to dismantle them. John's severed head continues to be a malleable substance in our collective memories. A head this slippery demands to be handled with care!

Bibliography

Abbreviations conform to the *SBL Handbook of Style*, 2nd ed.

Critical Biblical Texts

Aland, Barbara et al., eds. *Novum Testamentum Graece*. 28th ed. Stuttgart: Deutsche Bibelgesellschaft, 2012.

Elliger, K. and W. Rudolf, eds. *Biblia Hebraica Stuttgartensia*. Revised by A. Schenker. 5th ed. Stuttgart: Deutsche Bibelgesellschaft, 1997.

Rahlfs, Alfred, ed. *Septuaginta*: Editio altera. Revised by Robert Hanhart. Stuttgart: Deutsche Bibelgesellschaft, 2006.

Primary Texts

Ambrose. *Select Works and Letters*. Translated by Rev. H. De Romestin. NPNF² 10.

Appian. *Roman History*. Translated by Brian McGing and Horace White. 4 vols. LCL. Cambridge, Mass.: Harvard University Press, 1912–1913.

Asconius. *Commentaries on Speeches of Cicero*. Edited by R. G. Lewis. Translated by R. G. Lewis. Revised by Jill Harries, John Richardson, Christopher Smith, and Catherine Steel. Clarendon Ancient History Series. Oxford: Oxford University Press, 2006.

Augustine. *Sermons* (306–340A). Edited by John E. Rotelle. Translated by Edmund Hill. The Works of Saint Augustine: A Translation for the 21st Century 3/9. Hyde Park, N.Y.: New City Press, 1994.

Basil of Caesarea. *Letters*. Translated by Sister Agnes Clare Way. 2 vols. FC 28. Washington, D.C.: Catholic University of America Press, 1955.

Braund, Susanna Morton, ed. and trans. *Juvenal and Persius*. LCL 91. Cambridge, Mass.: Harvard University Press, 2004.

Caesarius of Arles. *Sermons*. Vol. 3. Translated by Sister Mary Magdeleine Mueller. FC 66. Washington, D.C.: Catholic University of America Press, 1973.

Calvin, John. *Commentary on a Harmony of the Evangelists, Matthew, Mark, and Luke*. Translated by Rev. William Pringle. Grand Rapids: Baker, 2005.
Charlesworth, James H., trans. "Psalm 151." *OTP* 2:612–15.
Chrysostom, John. *Homilies on the Gospel of St. Matthew*. Translated by Rev. Sir George Prevost. *NPNF*[1] 10.
Cicero. *On Duties*. Translated by Walter Miller. LCL 30. Cambridge, Mass.: Harvard University Press, 1913.
———. *The Verrine Orations*. Translated by L. H. G. Greenwood. 2 vols. LCL. Cambridge, Mass.: Harvard University Press, 1928–1935.
Dio Cassius. *Roman History*. Translated by Earnest Cary and Herbert B. Foster. 9 vols. LCL. Cambridge, Mass.: Harvard University Press, 1914–1927.
Diodorus Siculus. *Library of History*. Translated by Francis R. Walton et al. 12 vols. LCL. Cambridge, Mass.: Harvard University Press, 1933–1967.
Dionysius of Halicarnassus. *Roman Antiquities*. Translated by Earnest Cary. 7 vols. LCL. Cambridge, Mass.: Harvard University Press, 1937–1950.
Elliott, J. K., trans. *The Apocryphal New Testament: A Collection of Apocryphal Christian Literature in an English Translation Based on M. R. James*. Oxford: Clarendon, 1993.
Epictetus. *Discourses*. Translated by W. A. Oldfather. 2 vols. LCL. Cambridge, Mass.: Harvard University Press, 1925–1928.
Euripides. *Children of Heracles. Hippolytus. Andromache. Hecuba*. Translated by David Kovacs. LCL 484. Cambridge, Mass.: Harvard University Press, 1995.
Goodspeed, Edgar J., ed. *Die ältesten Apologeten*. Göttingen: Vandenhoeck & Ruprecht, 1914.
Herodian. *History of the Empire*. Translated by C. R. Whittaker. 2 vols. LCL. Cambridge, Mass.: Harvard University Press, 1969–1970.
Herodotus. *The Persian Wars*. Translated by A. D. Godley. 4 vols. LCL. Cambridge, Mass.: Harvard University Press, 1920–1925.
Hilary of Poitiers. *Commentary on Matthew*. Translated by D. H. Williams. FC 125. Washington, D.C.: Catholic University of America Press, 2012.
Homer. *Iliad*. Translated by A. T. Murray. 2 vols. LCL. Cambridge, Mass.: Harvard University Press, 1924–1925.
———. *Odyssey*. Translated by A. T. Murray. 2 vols. LCL. Cambridge, Mass.: Harvard University Press, 1919.
Isaac, E., trans. "1 Enoch." *OTP* 1:13–89.
Jerome. *Commentary on Matthew*. Translated by Thomas P. Scheck. FC 117. Washington, D.C.: Catholic University of America Press, 2008.
Josephus. *Flavius Josephus: Translation and Commentary*. Vol. 1B: *Judean War 2*. Translated and edited by Steve Mason. Leiden: Brill, 2008.
———. *Jewish Antiquities*. Translated by H. St. J. Thackeray et al. 9 vols. LCL. Cambridge, Mass.: Harvard University Press, 1930–1965.
———. *The Jewish War*. Translated by H. St. J. Thackeray. 3 vols. LCL. Cambridge, Mass.: Harvard University Press, 1927–1928.

———. *The Works of Flavius Josephus*. Translated by William Whiston. Peabody, Mass.: Hendrickson, 1987.

Justin Martyr. *Dialogue with Trypho*. Translated by Thomas B. Falls. FC 6. Washington, D.C.: Catholic University of America Press, 1948.

———. *Dialogue avec Tryphon: Édition critique, traduction, commentaire*. Edited and translated by Philippe Bobichon. 2 vols. Fribourg: Academic Press, 2003.

———. *Justin, Philosopher and Martyr: Apologies*. Edited and translated by Denis Minns and Paul Parvis. OECT. Oxford: Oxford University Press, 2009.

Lightfoot, J. L., trans. and ed. *Hellenistic Collection: Philitas. Alexander of Aetolia. Hermesianax. Euphorion. Parthenius*. LCL 508. Cambridge, Mass.: Harvard University Press, 2010.

Livy. *History of Rome*. Vol. 8: *Books 28–30*. Translated by Frank Gardner Moore. LCL. Cambridge, Mass.: Harvard University Press, 1949.

Lucan. *De Bello Civili. Book II*. Edited by Elaine Fantham. Cambridge Greek and Latin Classics. Cambridge: Cambridge University Press, 1992.

———. *The Civil War (Pharsalia)*. Translated by J. D. Duff. LCL 220. Cambridge, Mass.: Harvard University Press, 1928.

Lucian. *How to Write History. The Dipsads. Saturnalia. Herodotus or Aetion. Zeuxis or Antiochus. A Slip of the Tongue in Greeting. Apology for the "Salaried Posts in Great Houses." Harmonides. A Conversation with Hesiod. The Scythian or The Consul. Hermotimus or Concerning the Sects. To One Who Said "You're a Prometheus in Words." The Ship or The Wishes*. Translated by K. Kilburn. LCL 430. Cambridge, Mass.: Harvard University Press, 1959.

Martinez, Florentino Garcia, and Eibert J. C. Tigchelaar, eds. *The Dead Sea Scrolls: Study Edition*. 2 vols. Leiden: Brill, 1997.

Musurillo, Herbert, trans. *The Acts of the Christian Martyrs*. Oxford: Oxford University Press, 1972.

Neusner, Jacob, trans. *The Mishnah: A New Translation*. New Haven: Yale University Press, 1991.

Origen. *Commentaire sur l'Évangile selon Matthieu*. Vol. 1. *Livres 10–11*. Trans. Robert Girod. SC 162. Paris: Cerf, 1970.

———. *The Commentary of Origen on the Gospel of St Matthew*. Translated by Ronald E. Heine. 2 vols. OECT. Oxford: Oxford University Press, 2018.

———. *Homilies on Luke*. Translated by Joseph T. Lienhard. FC 94. Washington, D.C.: Catholic University of America Press, 1996.

Ovid. *Metamorphoses*. Translated by Frank Justus Miller. 2 vols. LCL. Cambridge, Mass.: Harvard University Press, 1916.

Page, Denys L., trans. *Select Papyri*. Vol. 3: *Poetry*. LCL 360. Cambridge, Mass.: Harvard University Press, 1941.

Philo. *On the Decalogue. On the Special Laws, Books 1–3*. Translated by F. H. Colson. LCL 320. Cambridge, Mass.: Harvard University Press, 1937.

———. *The Works of Philo: Complete and Unabridged*. Ed. and trans. Charles D. Yonge. Peabody, Mass.: Hendrickson, 1993.

Plato. *Laws*. Translated by R. G. Bury. LCL 192. Cambridge, Mass.: Harvard University Press, 1926.

———. *Republic*. Translated by Christopher Emlyn-Jones and William Preddy. 2 vols. LCL. Cambridge, Mass.: Harvard University Press, 2013.

Plutarch. *Lives*. Vol. 2: *Theseus and Romulus. Lycurgus and Numa. Solon and Publicola*. Translated by Bernadotte Perrin. LCL 46. Cambridge, Mass.: Harvard University Press, 1914.

———. *Lives*. Vol. 7: *Demosthenes and Cicero. Alexander and Caesar*. Translated by Bernadotte Perrin. LCL 99. Cambridge, Mass.: Harvard University Press, 1919.

———. *Lives*. Vol. 9: *Demetrius and Antony. Pyrrhus and Gaius Marius*. Translated by Bernadotte Perrin. LCL 101. Cambridge, Mass.: Harvard University Press, 1920.

———. *Lives*. Vol. 11: *Aratus. Artaxerxes. Galba. Otho. General Index*. Translated by Bernadotte Perrin. LCL 103. Cambridge, Mass.: Harvard University Press, 1926.

Polybius. *The Histories*. Translated by F. W. Paton and S. Douglas Olson. 6 vols. LCL. Cambridge, Mass.: Harvard University Press, 2010–2012.

Quintilian. *The Lesser Declamations*. Translated by D. R. Shackleton Bailey. 2 vols. LCL. Cambridge, Mass.: Harvard University Press, 2006.

Seneca. *Moral Essays*. Vol. 1: *De Providentia. De Constantia. De Ira. De Clementia*. Translated by John W. Basore. LCL 214. Cambridge, Mass.: Harvard University Press, 1928.

Silius Italicus. *Punica*. Translated by J. D. Duff. 2 vols. LCL. Cambridge, Mass.: Harvard University Press, 1934.

Suetonius. *Lives of the Caesars*. Translated by J. C. Rolfe. 2 vols. LCL. Cambridge, Mass.: Harvard University Press, 1914.

Tacitus. *Histories*. Translated by Clifford H. Moore. 2 vols. LCL. Cambridge, Mass.: Harvard University Press, 1925–1931.

Telfer, William, ed. *Cyril of Jerusalem and Nemesius of Emesa*. LCC. Louisville: Westminster John Knox, 2006.

Velleius Paterculus. *Compendium of Roman History. Res. Gestae Divi Augusti*. Translated by Frederick W. Shipley. LCL 152. Cambridge, Mass.: Harvard University Press, 1924.

Virgil. *Aeneid*. Translated by H. Rushton Fairclough. 2 vols. LCL. Cambridge, Mass.: Harvard University Press, 1916–1918.

Wise, Michael O., Martin Abegg, Jr., and Edward Cook, trans. *The Dead Sea Scrolls: A New Translation*. New York: HarperCollins, 1996.

Xenophon. *Cyropaedia*. Translated by Walter Miller. 2 vols. LCL. Cambridge, Mass.: Harvard University Press, 1914.

Secondary Texts

Adinolfi, Federico. "Gesù continuatore di Giovanni. Studio storico-esegetico sulla relazione tra Gesù di Nazaret e Giovanni il Battista." PhD thesis, University of Bologna, 2014.

Akiyama, Kengo. *The Love of Neighbour in Ancient Judaism: The Reception of Leviticus 19:18 in the Hebrew Bible, the Septuagint, the Book of Jubilees, the Dead Sea Scrolls, and the New Testament*. AGJU 105. Leiden: Brill, 2018.

Aldhouse-Green, Miranda. "Chaining and Shaming: Images of Defeat, From Llyn Cerrig Bach to Sarmitzegetusa." *OJA* 23 (2004): 319–40.

Allison, Dale C. *Constructing Jesus: Memory, Imagination, and History*. Grand Rapids: Baker Academic, 2010.

———. "The Continuity between John and Jesus." *JSHJ* 1 (2003): 6–27.

———. "How to Marginalize the Traditional Criteria of Authenticity." In Holmén and Porter, *Handbook for the Study of the Historical Jesus*, 1:3–30.

———. *Jesus of Nazareth: Millenarian Prophet*. Minneapolis: Fortress, 1998.

———. *Night Comes: Death, Imagination, and the Last Things*. Grand Rapids: Eerdmans, 2016.

———. *Studies in Matthew: Interpretation Past and Present*. Grand Rapids: Baker Academic, 2005.

Anderson, Janice Capel. "Feminist Criticism: The Dancing Daughter." In *Mark and Method: New Approaches in Biblical Studies*, edited by Janice Capel Anderson and Stephen D. Moore, 103–34. Minneapolis: Fortress, 1992.

———. *Matthew's Narrative Web: Over, and Over, and Over Again*. JSNTSup 91. Sheffield: JSOT Press, 1994.

Aplin, Max. "Was Jesus Ever a Disciple of John the Baptist? A Historical Study." PhD thesis, University of Edinburgh, 2011.

Aretxaga, Begoña. "Dirty Protest: Symbolic Overdetermination and Gender in Northern Ireland Ethnic Violence." *Ethos* 23 (1995): 123–48.

———. "Dirty Protest: Symbolic Overdetermination and Gender in Northern Ireland Ethnic Violence." In Scheper-Hughes and Bourgois, *Violence in War and Peace*, 244–52.

Asikainen, Susanna. *Jesus and Other Men: Ideal Masculinities in the Synoptic Gospels*. BibInt 159. Leiden: Brill, 2018.

Assmann, Aleida. "From Collective Violence to a Common Future: Four Models for Dealing with a Traumatic Past." In Modlinger and Sonntag, *Other People's Pain*, 43–62.

———. "To Remember or to Forget: Which Way Out of a Shared History of Violence?" In Assmann and Shortt, *Memory and Political Change*, 53–71.

Assmann, Aleida, and Linda Shortt. "Memory and Political Change: Introduction." In Assman and Shortt, *Memory and Political Change*, 1–14.

———, eds. *Memory and Political Change*. Palgrave Macmillan Memory Studies. Basingstoke: Palgrave Macmillan, 2012.

Assmann, Jan. "Communicative and Cultural Memory." In Erll and Nünning, *Cultural Memory Studies*, 109–18.

———. *Death and Salvation in Ancient Egypt*. Translated by David Lorton. Ithaca, N.Y.: Cornell University Press, 2005.

———. *Das kulturelle Gedächtnis. Schrift, Erinnerung und politische Identität in frühen Hochkulturen*. München: Beck, 1992.

———. *Moses the Egyptian: The Memory of Egypt in Western Monotheism.* Cambridge, Mass.: Harvard University Press, 1997.

———. *Religion and Cultural Memory.* Translated by Rodney Livingstone. Stanford: Stanford University Press, 2006.

Aune, David E. *Prophecy in Early Christianity and the Ancient Mediterranean World.* Eugene, Ore.: Wipf & Stock, 2003.

Aus, Roger. *Water into Wine and the Beheading of John the Baptist: Early Jewish-Christian Interpretation of Esther 1 in John 2.1–11 and Mark 6.17–29.* BJS 150. Atlanta: Scholars Press, 1988.

Backhaus, Knut. "Echoes from the Wilderness: The Historical John the Baptist." In Holmén and Porter, *Handbook for the Study of the Historical Jesus*, 2:1747–85.

———. *Die "Jüngerkreise" des Täufers Johannes: Eine Studie zu den religionsgeschichtlichen Ursprüngen des Christentums.* Paderborner Theologische Studien 19. Paderborn: Schöningh, 1991.

Badke, William B. "Was Jesus a Disciple of John?" *EvQ* 62 (1990): 195–204.

Baert, Barbara. *Caput Johannis in Disco (Essay on a Man's Head).* Translated by Irene Schaudies. Visualizing the Middle Ages 8. Leiden: Brill, 2012.

Barnard, L. W. *Justin Martyr: His Life and Thought.* Cambridge: Cambridge University Press, 1966.

Bartlett, Frederic C. *Remembering: A Study in Experimental and Social Psychology.* Cambridge: Cambridge University Press, 1932.

Bauckham, Richard. *The Fate of the Dead: Studies on the Jewish and Christian Apocalypses.* NovTSup 93. Leiden: Brill, 1998.

———. *Jesus and the Eyewitnesses: The Gospels as Eyewitness Testimony.* 2nd ed. Grand Rapids: Eerdmans, 2017.

Bauer, Walter, and F. W. Danker. *A Greek-English Lexicon of the New Testament and Other Early Christian Literature.* 3rd ed. Chicago: University of Chicago Press, 2000.

Beard, Mary. *Laughter in Ancient Rome: On Joking, Tickling, and Cracking Up.* Berkeley: University of California Press, 2014.

Becker, Adam H., and Annette Yoshiko Reed, eds. *The Ways That Never Parted: Jews and Christians in Late Antiquity and the Early Middle Ages.* Minneapolis: Fortress, 2007.

Becker, Jürgen. *Johannes der Täufer und Jesus von Nazareth.* BibSN 63. Neukirchen-Vluyn: Neukirchener Verlag, 1972.

Bell, Duncan. "Introduction: Violence and Memory." *Millennium: Journal of International Studies* 38 (2009): 345–60.

Berkowitz, Beth A. *Execution and Invention: Death Penalty Discourse in Early Rabbinic and Christian Cultures.* Oxford: Oxford University Press, 2006.

Bernier, Jonathan. *The Quest for the Historical Jesus after the Demise of Authenticity.* LNTS 540. London: T&T Clark, 2016.

Bernstein, Alan E. *The Formation of Hell: Death and Retribution in the Ancient and Early Christian Worlds.* London: UCL Press, 1993.

Betz, Otto. "Was John the Baptist an Essene?" *BRev* 6 (1990): 18–25.

Blomquist, Gregory L. "Patristic Reception of a Lukan Healing Account: A Contribution to a Socio-Rhetorical Response to Willi Braun's Feasting and Social Rhetoric in Luke 14." In *Healing in Religion and Society from Hippocrates to the Puritans*, edited by J. Kevin Coyle and Steven C. Muir, 105–34. Lewiston, N.Y.: Mellen, 1999.

Bockmuehl, Markus. "A Commentator's Approach to the 'Effective History' of Philippians." *JSNT* 60 (1995): 57–88.

———. *Seeing the Word: Refocusing New Testament Study*. STI. Grand Rapids: Baker Academic, 2006.

Boddens Hosang, F. J. Elizabeth. "Attraction and Hatred. Relations between Jews and Christians in the Early Church." In *Violence in Ancient Christianity*, edited by Albert C. Geljon and Riemer Roukema, 90–107. Supplements to *Vigiliae Christianae* 125. Leiden: Brill, 2014.

Bond, Helen K. *The First Biography of Jesus: Genre and Meaning in Mark's Gospel*. Grand Rapids: Eerdmans, 2020.

———. *Pontius Pilate in History and Interpretation*. SNTSMS 100. Cambridge: Cambridge University Press, 1998.

Boring, M. Eugene. *Mark: A Commentary*. NTL. Louisville: Westminster John Knox, 2006.

Bornkamm, Günther, Gerhard Barth, and Heinz Joachim Held. *Tradition and Interpretation in Matthew*. London: SCM, 1963.

Bourdieu, Pierre. *Masculine Domination*. Translated by Richard Nice. Cambridge: Polity, 2001.

Bourdieu, Pierre, and Loïc J. D. Wacquant. "Language, Gender, and Symbolic Violence." In *An Invitation to Reflexive Sociology*, 140–74. Chicago: University of Chicago Press, 1992.

Bovon, François. *Luke: A Commentary on the Gospel of Luke 1:1–9:50*. Hermeneia. Minneapolis: Fortress, 2002.

Boyarin, Daniel. *Border Lines: The Partition of Judaeo-Christianity*. Philadelphia: University of Pennsylvania Press, 2004.

———. "Semantic Differences; or, 'Judaism'/'Christianity.'" In Becker and Reed, *Ways That Never Parted*, 65–85.

Brandenburger, E. "σταυρός." *NIDNTT* 1:391–405.

Brown, Raymond E. *The Birth of the Messiah: A Commentary on the Infancy Narratives in Matthew and Luke*. Garden City, N.Y.: Doubleday, 1977.

Brown, Steven D., Matthew Allen, and Paula Reavey. "Remembering 7/7: The Collective Shaping of Survivors' Personal Memories of the 2005 London Bombing." In *Routledge International Handbook of Memory Studies*, edited by Anna Lisa Tota and Trever Hagen, 428–41. London: Routledge, 2016.

Brownlee, W. H. "A Comparison of the Covenanters of the Dead Sea Scrolls with Pre-Christian Jewish Sects." *BA* 13 (1950): 50–72.

———. "John the Baptist in the New Light of Ancient Scrolls." In *The Scrolls and the New Testament*, edited by Krister Stendahl, 33–53, 252–56. London: SCM, 1958.

Bryen, Ari Z. *Violence in Roman Egypt: A Study in Legal Interpretation*. Philadelphia: University of Pennsylvania Press, 2013.

Buckley-Zistel, Susanne. "Between Pragmatism, Coercion and Fear: Chosen Amnesia after the Rwandan Genocide." In Assmann and Shortt, *Memory and Political Change*, 72–88.

———. "Remembering to Forget: Chosen Amnesia as a Strategy for Local Co-Existence in Post-Genocide Rwanda." *Africa: Journal of the International African Institute* 76 (2006): 131–50.

Bull, Stephen. *Triumphant Rider: The Lancaster Roman Cavalry Tombstone*. Lancaster: Lancashire Museums, 2007.

Bultmann, Rudolf. *History of the Synoptic Tradition*. Translated by John Marsh. Oxford: Basil Blackwell, 1963.

Burridge, Richard A. *What Are the Gospels? A Comparison with Graeco-Roman Biography*. 3rd ed. Waco, Tex.: Baylor University Press, 2018.

Burr, Viv. "'Oh Spike You're Covered in Sexy Wounds!' The Erotic Significance of Wounding and Torture in Buffy the Vampire Slayer." In *Sex, Violence, and the Body: The Erotics of Wounding*, edited by Viv Burr and Jeff Hearn, 137–56. Basingstoke: Palgrave Macmillan, 2008.

Butler, Judith. *Gender Trouble: Feminism and the Subversion of Identity*. New York: Routledge, 1990.

Callon, Callie. *Reading Bodies: Physiognomy as a Strategy of Persuasion in Early Christian Discourse*, LNTS 597. London: T&T Clark, 2019.

Capps, Walter H. *Religious Studies: The Making of a Discipline*. Minneapolis: Fortress, 1995.

Carrigan, Tim, Bob (R. W.) Connell, and John Lee. "Toward a New Sociology of Masculinity." *Theory and Society* 14 (1985): 551–604.

Casey, Edward S. *Remembering: A Phenomenological Study*. Bloomington: Indiana University Press, 1987.

Casey, Maurice. *Jesus of Nazareth: An Independent Historian's Account of His Life and Teaching*. London: T&T Clark, 2010.

Castelli, Elizabeth A. *Martyrdom and Memory: Early Christian Culture Making*. New York: Columbia University Press, 2004.

Chapman, David W. *Ancient Jewish and Christian Perceptions of Crucifixion*. WUNT 224. Tübingen: Mohr Siebeck, 2008.

Chapman, David W., and Eckhard J. Schnabel. *The Trial and Crucifixion of Jesus*. WUNT 344. Tübingen: Mohr Siebeck, 2015.

Chilton, Bruce. "Friends and Enemies." In *The Cambridge Companion to Jesus*, edited by Markus Bockmuehl, 72–86. Cambridge: Cambridge University Press, 2001.

———. "John the Baptist." In *The Routledge Encyclopedia of the Historical Jesus*, edited by Craig A. Evans, 339–42. New York: Routledge, 2008.

———. "John the Baptist: His Immersion and His Death." In *Dimensions of Baptism: Biblical and Theological Studies*, edited by Stanley E. Porter and Anthony R. Cross, 25–44. JSNTSup 234. Sheffield: Sheffield Academic Press, 2002.

———. "John the Purifier." In *Jesus in Context: Temple, Purity, and Restoration*, edited by Bruce D. Chilton and Craig A. Evans, 203–20. Leiden: Brill, 1997.

———. "Justin and Israelite Prophecy." In Parvis and Foster, *Justin Martyr and His Worlds*, 77–87.

Coleman, Kathleen M. "Fatal Charades: Roman Executions Staged as Mythological Enactments." *JRS* 80 (1990).

Collins, Adela Yarbro. *Mark: A Commentary*. Hermeneia. Minneapolis: Fortress, 2007.

Collins, John J., and Daniel C. Harlow, eds. *The Eerdmans Dictionary of Early Judaism*. Grand Rapids: Eerdmans, 2010.

Collins, John J., et al. "Death, the Afterlife, and Other Last Things." In *Religions of the Ancient World: A Guide*, edited by Sarah Iles Johnston, 470–95. Cambridge, Mass.: Belknap Press, 2004.

Cone, James H. *The Cross and the Lynching Tree*. Maryknoll, N.Y.: Orbis Books, 2011.

Connell, R. W. *Masculinities*. 2nd ed. Berkeley: University of California Press, 2005.

Connell, R. W., and James W. Messerschmidt. "Hegemonic Masculinity: Rethinking the Concept." *Gender and Society* 19 (2005): 829–59.

Connerton, Paul. *How Societies Remember*. Cambridge: Cambridge University Press, 1989.

———. "Seven Types of Forgetting." *Memory Studies* 1 (2008): 59–71.

Conway, Colleen. *Behold the Man: Jesus and Greco-Roman Masculinity*. Oxford: Oxford University Press, 2008.

Conzelmann, Hans. *The Theology of St. Luke*. London: Faber & Faber, 1961.

Cook, John Granger. "Crucifixion and Burial." *NTS* 57 (2011): 193–213.

———. *Crucifixion in the Mediterranean World*. WUNT 327. Tübingen: Mohr Siebeck, 2014.

———. "Crucifixion as Spectacle in Roman Campania." *NovT* 54 (2012): 68–100.

———. "Envisioning Crucifixion: Light from Several Inscriptions and the Palatine Graffito." *NovT* 50 (2008): 262–85.

———. "Roman Crucifixions: From the Second Punic War to Constantine." *ZNW* 104 (2013): 1–32.

Cope, Lamar. "The Death of John the Baptist in the Gospel of Matthew; Or, the Case of the Confusing Conjunction." *CBQ* 38 (1976): 515–19.

Coser, Lewis A. "Introduction: Maurice Halbwachs 1877–1945." In *On Collective Memory*, by Maurice Halbwachs, 1–34.

Cranfield, C. E. B. *The Gospel According to Saint Mark*. CGTC. Cambridge: Cambridge University Press, 1959.

Crossan, John Dominic. *The Historical Jesus: The Life of a Mediterranean Jewish Peasant*. New York: Harper Collins, 1991.
Crossley, James G. *Cults, Martyrs, and Good Samaritans: Religion in Contemporary English Political Discourse*. London: Pluto, 2018.
———. "History from the Margins: The Death of John the Baptist." In *Writing History, Constructing Religion*, edited by James G. Crossley and Christian Karner, 147–61. Aldershot: Ashgate, 2005.
———. *Jesus and the Chaos of History: Redirecting the Life of the Historical Jesus*. Biblical Refigurations. Oxford: Oxford University Press, 2015.
Cubitt, Geoffrey. *History and Memory*. Manchester: Manchester University Press, 2007.
Culpepper, R. Alan. "Mark 6:17–29 in Its Narrative Context: Kingdoms in Conflict." In *Mark as Story: Retrospect and Prospect*, edited by Kelly R. Iverson and Christopher W. Skinner, 145–63. RBS 65. Atlanta: Society of Biblical Literature, 2011.
Daniélou, Jean. *The Dead Sea Scrolls and Primitive Christianity*. Baltimore: Helicon, 1958.
Dapaah, Daniel S. *The Relationship between John the Baptist and Jesus of Nazareth: A Critical Study*. Lanham, Md.: University Press of America, 2005.
Darr, John A. *Herod the Fox: Audience Criticism and Lukan Characterization*. JSNTSup 163. Sheffield: Sheffield Academic Press, 1998.
Davies, Douglas J. *A Brief History of Death*. Oxford: Blackwell, 2005.
Davies, William D., and Dale C. Allison. *A Critical and Exegetical Commentary on the Gospel According to Saint Matthew*. 3 vols. ICC. London: T&T Clark, 1988.
De Pina-Cabral, João. "Tamed Violence: Genital Symbolism in Portuguese Popular Culture." *Man* 28 (1993): 101–20.
Delorme, Jean. "John the Baptist's Head—The Word Perverted: A Reading of a Narrative (Mark 6:14–29)." *Semeia* 81 (1998): 115–29.
Dennert, Brian C. *John the Baptist and the Jewish Setting of Matthew*. WUNT 403. Tübingen: Mohr Siebeck, 2015.
Dennis, J. "Death of Jesus." *DJG*, 172–93.
Dibelius, Martin. *From Tradition to Gospel*. Translated by Bertram Lee Woolf. The Library of Theological Translations. Cambridge: James Clarke, 1971.
———. *Die urchristliche Überlieferung von Johannes dem Täufer*. Göttingen: Vandenhoeck & Ruprecht, 1911.
Dicken, Frank E. "Herod as Jesus' Executioner: Possibilities in Lukan Reception and Wirkungsgeschichte." In *Characters and Characterization in Luke-Acts*, edited by Frank E. Dicken and Julia A. Snyder, 199–211. LNTS 548. London: T&T Clark, 2016.
Dinkova-Bruun, Greti. "The Beheading of John the Baptist in Medieval Poetic Discourse." In *Decapitation and Sacrifice: Saint John's Head in Interdisciplinary Perspectives: Text, Object, Medium*, edited by Barbara Baert and Sophia Rochmes, 41–59. Leuven: Peeters, 2017.

Dobschütz, Ernst von. "Bible in the Church." In *Encyclopaedia of Religion and Ethics*, edited by James Hastings, 2:579–615. Edinburgh: T&T Clark, 1909.

Dogan, Kamil Hakan. "Decapitation and Dismemberment of the Corpse: A Matricide Case." *Journal of Forensic Science* 55 (2010): 542–45.

Dolce, Rita. *"Losing One's Head" in the Ancient Near East: Interpretation and Meaning of Decapitation*. London: Routledge, 2018.

Donahue, John R., and Daniel Harrington. *The Gospel of Mark*. SP. Collegeville, Minn.: Liturgical Press, 2002.

Douglas, Mary. *Natural Symbols: Explorations in Cosmology*. London: Barrie and Jenkins, 1973.

Drake, H. A., ed. *Violence in Late Antiquity: Perceptions and Practices*. Aldershot: Ashgate, 2006.

Dulk, Matthijs den. *Between Jews and Heretics: Refiguring Justin Martyr's Dialogue with Trypho*. London: Routledge, 2018.

Dunn, James D. G. *Christianity in the Making*. Vol. 1: *Jesus Remembered*. Grand Rapids: Eerdmans, 2003.

———. *The Partings of the Ways between Christianity and Judaism and Their Significance for the Character of Christianity*. 2nd ed. London: SCM, 2006.

Duran, Nicole Wilkinson. "Having Men for Dinner: Deadly Banquets and Biblical Women." *BTB* 35 (2005): 117–24.

———. "Return of the Disembodied or How John the Baptist Lost His Head." In *Reading Communities Reading Scripture: Essays in Honor of Daniel Patte*, edited by Gary A. Phillips and Nicole Wilkinson Duran, 277–91. Harrisburg, Penn.: Trinity Press International, 2002.

Eastman, David L. *The Ancient Martyrdom Accounts of Peter and Paul*. Atlanta: SBL Press, 2015.

Edmondson, J. C. "Dynamic Arenas: Gladiatorial Presentations in the City of Rome and the Construction of Roman Society during the Early Empire." In *Roman Theatre and Society*, edited by W. J. Slater, 69–112. Ann Arbor: University of Michigan Press, 1996.

Edwards, J. Christopher. *The Ransom Logion in Mark and Matthew*. WUNT 327. Tübingen: Mohr Siebeck, 2012.

Ehrlich, M. Avrum, ed. *Encyclopedia of the Jewish Diaspora: Origins, Experiences, and Culture*. Santa Barbara, Calif.: ABC-CLIO, 2009.

Elledge, C. D. *Resurrection of the Dead in Early Judaism: 200 BCE–CE 200*. Oxford: Oxford University Press, 2017.

Enslin, Morton Scott. "John and Jesus." *ZNW* 66 (1975): 1–18.

Erickson, Richard J. "The Jailing of John and the Baptism of Jesus: Luke 3:19–21." *JETS* 36 (1993): 455–66.

Erll, Astrid. "Cultural Memory Studies: An Introduction." In Erll and Nünning, *Cultural Memory Studies*, 1–15.

Erll, Astrid, and Ansgar Nünning, eds. *Cultural Memory Studies: An International and Interdisciplinary Handbook*. Media and Cultural Memory 8. Berlin: de Gruyter, 2008.

Ernst, Josef. *Das Evangelium nach Markus*. Regensburg: Verlag Friedrich Pustet, 1981.

———. *Johannes der Täufer: Interpretation, Geschichte, Wirkungsgeschichte*. BZNW 53. Berlin: de Gruyter, 1989.

Evans, Craig A. *Jesus and the Ossuaries: What Jewish Burial Practices Reveal about the Beginning of Christianity*. Waco, Tex.: Baylor University Press, 2003.

———. *Mark 8:27–16:20*. WBC 34B. Nashville: Thomas Nelson, 2000.

———. *Matthew*. New Cambridge Bible Commentary. Cambridge: Cambridge University Press, 2012.

Evans, Robert. *Reception History, Tradition and Biblical Interpretation: Gadamer and Jauss in Current Practice*. Scriptural Traces 4; LNTS 510. London: T&T Clark, 2014.

Fagan, Garrett G. "Urban Violence: Street, Forum, Bath, Circus, and Theater." In Riess and Fagan, *Topography of Violence in the Greco-Roman World*, 231–47.

———. "Violence in Roman Social Relations." In *The Oxford Handbook of Social Relations in the Roman World*, edited by Michael Peachin, 467–95. Oxford: Oxford University Press, 2011.

Farmer, Paul. "An Anthropology of Structural Violence." *Current Anthropology* 45 (2004): 305–25.

———. "On Suffering and Structural Violence." In Scheper-Hughes and Bourgois, *Violence in War and Peace*, 281–89.

———. "On Suffering and Structural Violence: A View from Below." *Daedalus* 125 (1996): 261–83.

———. "On Suffering and Structural Violence: A View from Below." *Race/Ethnicity: Multidisciplinary Global Contexts* 3 (2009): 11–28.

———. *Pathologies of Power: Health, Human Rights, and the New War on the Poor*. Berkeley: University of California Press, 2003.

Farris, Stephen. *The Hymns of Luke's Infancy Narratives: Their Origin, Meaning, and Significance*. JSNTSup 9. Sheffield: JSOT Press, 1993.

Fentress, James, and Chris Wickham. *Social Memory*. New Perspectives on the Past. Oxford: Blackwell, 1992.

Finney, Mark T. "Christ Crucified and the Inversion of Roman Imperial Ideology in 1 Corinthians." *BTB* 35 (2005): 20–33.

———. "Servile Supplicium: Shame and the Deuteronomic Curse—Crucifixion in Its Cultural Context." *BTB* 43 (2013): 124–34.

Fischer, Alexander Achilles. *Tod und Jenseits im Alten Orient und Alten Testament*. Neukirchen-Vluyn: Neukirchener Verlag, 2005.

Foote, Kenneth. "On the Edge of Memory: Uneasy Legacies of Dissent, Terror, and Violence in the American Landscape." *Social Science Quarterly* 97 (2016): 115–22.

Foster, Paul. "Memory, Orality, and the Fourth Gospel: Three Dead-Ends in Historical Jesus Research." *JSHJ* 10 (2012): 191–227.

Foucault, Michel. *Discipline and Punish: The Birth of the Prison*. Translated by Alan Sheridan. New York: Vintage, 1977.
Fowler, Robert. *Let the Reader Understand: Reader-Response Criticism and the Gospel of Mark*. Harrisburg, Penn.: Trinity Press International, 2001.
France, R. T. *The Gospel of Mark*. NIGTC. Grand Rapids: Eerdmans, 2002.
Fredriksen, Paula. "The Birth of Christianity and the Origins of Christian Anti-Judaism." In *Jesus, Judaism and Christian Anti-Judaism: Reading the New Testament after the Holocaust*, edited by Paula Fredriksen and Adele Reinhartz, 8–30. Louisville: Westminster John Knox, 2002.
———. *From Jesus to Christ: The Origins of the New Testament Images of Jesus*. New Haven: Yale University Press, 1988.
———. "What 'Parting of the Ways'? Jews, Gentiles, and the Ancient Mediterranean City." In Becker and Reed, *Ways That Never Parted*, 35–63.
Fredriksen, Paula, and Oded Irshai. "Christian Anti-Judaism: Polemics and Policies." In *The Cambridge History of Judaism*. Vol. 4: *The Late Roman-Rabbinic Period*, edited by Steven T. Katz, 977–1034. Cambridge: Cambridge University Press, 2006.
Freud, Sigmund. "An Autobiographical Study." In *The Freud Reader*, edited by Peter Gay, 3–41. London: Vintage, 1989.
Freyne, Seán. *The Jesus Movement and Its Expansion: Meaning and Mission*. Grand Rapids: Eerdmans, 2014.
Gabrielson, Timothy A. "Parting Ways or Rival Siblings? A Review and Analysis of Metaphors for the Separation of Jews and Christians in Antiquity." *CBR* 19 (2021): 178–204.
Gadamer, Hans-Georg. *Truth and Method*. Translated by Joel Weinsheimer and Donald G. Marshall. London: Bloomsbury Academic, 2013.
———. *Wahrheit und Methode*. Tübingen: Mohr Siebeck, 1990.
Gager, John. *The Origins of Anti-Semitism: Attitudes toward Judaism in Pagan and Christian Antiquity*. Oxford: Oxford University Press, 1985.
Garland, Robert. *The Greek Way of Death*. London: Duckworth, 1985.
Garnsey, Peter. "Why Penalties Become Harsher: The Roman Case, Late Republic to Fourth Century Empire." *Natural Law Forum* 143 (1968): 141–62.
Gelber, Mark H. "Literary Anti-Semitism." In Ehrlich, *Encyclopedia of the Jewish Diaspora*, 107–111.
Georgia, Allan T. "Translating the Triumph: Reading Mark's Crucifixion Narrative against a Roman Ritual of Power." *JSNT* 36 (2013): 17–38.
Gerdmar, Anders. *Roots of Theological Anti-Semitism: German Biblical Interpretation and the Jews, from Herder and Semler to Kittel and Bultmann*. Studies in Jewish History and Culture 20. Leiden: Brill, 2009.
Geyser, A. S. "The Youth of John the Baptist: A Deduction from the Break in the Parallel Account of the Lucan Infancy Story." *NovT* 1 (1956): 70–75.
Glancy, Jennifer A. "Unveiling Masculinity: The Construction of Gender in Mark 6:17–29." *BibInt* 2 (1994): 34–50.

Gnilka, Joachim. *Das Evangelium nach Markus*. 5th ed. 2 vols. EKK. Neukirchen-Vluyn: Neukirchener Verlag, 1998.

———. "Das Martyrium Johannes' des Täufers (Mk 6, 17–29)." In *Orientierung an Jesu: Zur Theologie der Synoptiker*, edited by P. Hoffmann, Norbert Brox, and Wilhelm Pesch, 78–92. Freiburg: Herder, 1973.

Goguel, Maurice. *Au seuil de l'Évangile: Jean-Baptiste*. Bibliothèque Historique 40. Paris: Payot, 1928.

Goodacre, Mark. "Mark, Elijah, the Baptist and Matthew: The Success of the First Intertextual Reading of Mark." In *Biblical Interpretation in Early Christian Gospels*, vol. 2: *Matthew*, edited by Tom Hatina, 73–84. LNTS 310. London: T&T Clark, 2008.

———. *The Synoptic Problem: A Way Through the Maze*. London: T&T Clark International, 2001.

Gould, Ezra P. *The Gospel According to St. Mark*. ICC. Edinburgh: T&T Clark, 1896.

Gourevitch, Philip. "We Wish to Inform You That Tomorrow We Will Be Killed with Our Families: Stories from Rwanda." In Scheper-Hughes and Bourgois, *Violence in War and Peace*, 136–42.

Graybill, Rhiannon. *Are We Not Men? Unstable Masculinity in the Hebrew Prophets*. Oxford: Oxford University Press, 2016.

Green, Joel B. "The Death of Jesus and the Ways of God: Jesus and the Gospels on Messianic Status and Shameful Suffering." *Int* 52 (1998): 24–37.

———. *The Gospel of Luke*. NICNT. Grand Rapids: Eerdmans, 1997.

Greenspahn, Frederick E. "Why Prophecy Ceased." *JBL* 108 (1989): 37–49.

Guelich, Robert A. *Mark 1–8:26*. WBC 34A. Dallas, Tex.: Word, 1989.

Gutchess, Angela H., and Maya Siegel. "Memory Specificity Across Cultures." In Assmann and Shortt, *Memory and Political Change*, 201–15.

Guyénot, Laurent. "A New Perspective on John the Baptist's Failure to Support Jesus." *Journal of Unification Studies* 1 (1997): 71–92.

Hagner, Donald A. *Matthew 14–28*. WBC 33B. Dallas, Tex.: Word, 1995.

Halbwachs, Maurice. *Les cadres sociaux de la mémoire*. Paris: Librarie Félix Alcan, 1925.

———. *On Collective Memory*. Edited and translated by Lewis A. Coser. Chicago: University of Chicago Press, 1992.

Hamm, Mark S. "Apocalyptic Violence: The Seduction of Terrorist Subcultures." *Theoretical Criminology* 8 (2004): 323–39.

Harries, Jill. "Violence, Victims, and the Legal Tradition in Late Antiquity." In Drake, *Violence in Late Antiquity*, 85–102.

Harrington, Daniel J. *The Gospel of Matthew*. SP. Collegeville, Minn.: Liturgical Press, 2007.

Hartmann, Michael. *Der Tod Johannes des Täufers: Eine exegetische und rezeptionsgeschichtliche Studie auf dem Hintergrund narrativer, intertextueller und kulturanthropologischer Zugänge*. SBB 45. Stuttgart: Verlag Katholisches Bibelwerk, 2001.

Hayter, Daniel W. "'How Are the Dead Raised?' The Bodily Nature of Resurrection in Second Temple Jewish Texts." In *The Body in Biblical, Christian, and Jewish Texts*, edited by Joan E. Taylor, 123–43. LSTS 85. London: T&T Clark, 2014.

Hebron, Carol. *Judas Iscariot: Damned or Redeemed? A Critical Examination of the Portrayal of Judas in Jesus Films (1902–2014)*. Scriptural Traces 4; LNTS 510. London: T&T Clark, 2016.

Heine, Ronald E. Introduction to *The Commentary of Origen on the Gospel of St Matthew*, 1–31. OECT. Oxford: Oxford University Press, 2018.

———. "Origen." In *The Routledge Companion to Early Christian Thought*, edited by D. Jeffrey Bingham, 188–203. London: Routledge, 2010.

———. *Origen: Scholarship in the Service of the Church*. Oxford: Oxford University Press, 2010.

Hengel, Martin. *Crucifixion in the Ancient World and the Folly of the Message of the Cross*. Philadelphia: Fortress, 1977.

Henry, Doug. "Violence and the Body: Somatic Expressions of Trauma and Vulnerability during War." *Medical Anthropology Quarterly* 20 (2006): 379–98.

Henten, Jan Willem van, and Friedrich Avemarie. *Martyrdom and Noble Death: Selected Texts from Graeco-Roman, Jewish and Christian Antiquity*. London: Routledge, 2002.

Herman, Judith, Nancy Scheper-Hughes, and Philippe Bourgois. "Trauma and Recovery: The Aftermath of Violence—From Domestic Abuse to Political Terror." In Scheper-Hughes and Bourgois, *Violence in War and Peace*, 368–71.

Hinard, François. "La male mort. Exécutions et statut du corps au moment de la première proscription." In *Du châtiment dans la cité. Supplices corporels et peine de mort dans le monde antique*, 295–311. Table ronde de Rome (9–11 novembre 1982). Rome: École Française de Rome, 1984.

Hinson, E. Glenn. "Justin Martyr." *ER* 7:5043–45.

Hoehner, Harold W. *Herod Antipas*. Grand Rapids: Zondervan, 1980.

Hoffeditz, David M., and Gary E. Yates. "Femme Fatale Redux: Intertextual Connection to the Elijah/Jezebel Narratives in Mark 6:14–29." *BBR* 15 (2005): 199–221.

Hollenbach, Paul W. "The Conversion of Jesus: From Jesus the Baptizer to Jesus the Healer." *ANRW* 2.25.1:196–219. Berlin: de Gruyter, 1982.

Holmén, Tom. "Crucifixion Hermeneutics in Judaism at the Time of Jesus." *JSHJ* 14 (2016): 197–222.

Holmén, Tom, and Stanley E. Porter, eds. *Handbook for the Study of the Historical Jesus*. 4 vols. Leiden: Brill, 2011.

Hölscher, Tonio. "Images of War in Greece and Rome: Between Military Practice, Public Memory, and Cultural Symbolism." *JRS* 93 (2003): 1–17.

Hooker, Morna. "Christology and Methodology." *NTS* 17 (1971): 480–87.

———. *The Gospel According to Saint Mark*. London: Black and Peabody, 1991.

———. "On Using the Wrong Tool." *Theology* 75 (1972): 570–81.

Hope, Valerie M. *Death in Ancient Rome: A Sourcebook*. London: Routledge, 2007.
Hopkins, Keith. *Death and Renewal*. Sociological Studies in Roman History 2. Cambridge: Cambridge University Press, 1983.
Horsley, Richard A., and John S. Hanson. *Bandits, Prophets and Messiahs: Popular Movements in the Time of Jesus*. Minneapolis: Winston, 1985.
Hübenthal, Sandra. "Gospel of Mark." In Keith, Bond, Jacobi, and Schröter, *Reception of Jesus in the First Three Centuries*, 1:41–72.
———. "Reading the Gospel of Mark as Collective Memory." In *Social Memory and Social Identity in the Study of Early Judaism and Early Christianity*, edited by Samuel Byrskog, Raimo Hakola, and Jutta Jokiranta, 69–87. NTOA/SUNT 116. Göttingen: Vandenhoeck & Ruprecht, 2016.
———. "Social and Cultural Memory in Biblical Exegesis: The Quest for an Adequate Application." In *Cultural Memory in Biblical Exegesis*, edited by Pernille Carstens, Trine Bjornung Hasselbach, and Niels Peter Lemche, 175–99. PHSC 17. Piscataway, N.J.: Gorgias Press, 2012.
Hurtado, Larry. "Greco-Roman Textuality and the Gospel of Mark: A Critical Assessment of Werner Kelber's *The Oral and the Written Gospel*." *BBR* 7 (1997): 91–106.
Ifill, Sherrilyn A. *On the Courthouse Lawn: Confronting the Legacy of Lynching in the Twenty-First Century*. Boston: Beacon, 2007.
Igartua, Juanjo, and Dario Paez. "Art and Remembering Traumatic Collective Events: The Case of the Spanish Civil War." In Pennebaker, Paez, and Rimé, *Collective Memory of Political Events*, 79–101.
Ilan, Tal. "Flavius Josephus and Biblical Women." In *The Bible and Women*, vol. 3.1: *Early Jewish Writings*, edited by Eileen Schuller and Marie-Theres Wacker, 167–85. Atlanta: SBL Press, 2017.
Iersel, Bas M. F. van. *Mark: A Reader-Response Commentary*. Translated by W. H. Bisscheroux. JSNTSup 164. Sheffield: Sheffield Academic Press, 1998.
Jack, Alison M. *The Prodigal Son in English and American Literature: Five Hundred Years of Literary Homecomings*. Biblical Refigurations. Oxford: Oxford University Press, 2019.
Jacobs, Janet. "Gender and Collective Memory: Women and Representation at Auschwitz." *Memory Studies* 1 (2008): 211–25.
———. "The Memorial at Srebrenica: Gender and the Social Meanings of Collective Memory in Bosnia-Herzegovina." *Memory Studies* 14 (2017): 423–39.
Janes, Regina. *Losing Our Heads: Beheadings in Literature and Culture*. New York: New York University Press, 2005.
———. "Why the Daughter of Herodias Must Dance (Mark 6.14–29)." *JSNT* 28 (2006): 443–67.
Jauss, Hans Robert. *Toward an Aesthetic of Reception*. Translated by Timothy Bahti. Minneapolis: University of Minnesota Press, 1982.

Jensen, Morton. *Herod Antipas in Galilee: The Literary and Archaeological Sources on the Reign of Herod Antipas and its Socio-Economic Impact on Galilee*. Tübingen: Mohr Siebeck, 2006.

Joynes, Christine E. "Changing Horizons: Reflections on a Decade at Oxford University's Centre for Reception History of the Bible." *JBRec* 1 (2014): 161–71.

———. "The Reception of the Bible and Its Significance." In *Scripture and Its Interpretation: A Global, Ecumenical Introduction to the Bible*, edited by Michael J. Gorman, 155–67. Grand Rapids: Baker Academic, 2017.

———. "The Sound of Silence: Interpreting Mark 16:1–8 through the Centuries." *Int* 65 (2011): 18–29.

Kansteiner, Wulf. "Finding Meaning in Memory: A Methodological Critique of Collective Memory Studies." *HistTh* 41 (2002): 179–97.

———. "Genocide Memory, Digital Cultures, and the Aesthetization of Violence." *Memory Studies* 7 (2014): 403–8.

Kansteiner, Wulf, and Harald Weilnböck. "Against the Concept of Cultural Trauma (or How I Learned to Love the Suffering of Others without the Help of Psychotherapy)." In *A Companion to Cultural Memory Studies*, edited by Astrid Erll and Ansgar Nünning, 229–40. Berlin: de Gruyter, 2010.

Karakolis, Christos. "Narrative Funktion und christologische Bedeutung der markinischen Erzählung vom Tod Johannes des Täufers (Mk 6:14–29)." *NovT* 52 (2010): 134–55.

Keener, Craig S. *Acts: An Exegetical Commentary*. Vol. 1: *Introduction and 1:1–2:47*. Grand Rapids: Baker Academic, 2012.

Keith, Chris. "The Competitive Textualization of the Jesus Tradition in John 20:30–31 and 21:24–25." *CBQ* 78 (2016): 321–37.

———. "Early Christian Book Culture and the Emergence of the First Written Gospel." In *Mark, Manuscripts, and Monotheism: Essays in Honor of Larry W. Hurtado*, edited by Chris Keith and Dieter T. Roth, 22–39. LNTS 528. London: T&T Clark, 2015.

———. *The Gospel as Manuscript: An Early History of the Jesus Tradition as Material Artifact*. Oxford: Oxford University Press, 2020.

———. *Jesus against the Scribal Elite: The Origins of the Conflict*. 2nd ed. London: T&T Clark, 2020.

———. *Jesus' Literacy: Scribal Culture and the Teacher from Galilee*. LNTS 413. London: T&T Clark, 2011.

———. "Prolegomena on the Textualization of Mark's Gospel: Manuscript Culture, the Extended Situation, and the Emergence of the Written Gospel." In Thatcher, *Memory and Identity in Ancient Judaism and Early Christianity*, 161–86.

———. "Social Memory Theory and Gospels Research: The First Decade (Part One)." *Early Christianity* 6 (2015): 354–76.

———. "Social Memory Theory and Gospels Research: The First Decade (Part Two)." *Early Christianity* 6 (2015): 517–42.

Keith, Chris, Helen K. Bond, Christine Jacobi, and Jens Schröter. Introduction to Keith, Bond, Jacobi, and Schröter, *Reception of Jesus in the First Three Centuries*, 1:xv–xxvii.

——, eds. *The Reception of Jesus in the First Three Centuries*. 3 vols. London: T&T Clark, 2020.

Kelber, Werner. *The Oral and Written Gospel: The Hermeneutics of Speaking and Writing in the Synoptic Tradition, Mark, Paul and Q*. Philadelphia: Fortress, 1983.

Kelhoffer, James A. *The Diet of John the Baptist: "Locusts and Wild Honey" in Synoptic and Patristic Interpretation*. WUNT 176. Tübingen: Mohr Siebeck, 2005.

Kertelge, Karl. *Markusevangelium*. NEchtB. Würzburg: Echter Verlag, 1994.

Keshgegian, Flora A. "Finding a Place Past Night: Armenian Genocidal Memory in Diaspora." In Stier and Landres, *Religion, Violence, Memory, and Place*, 100–112.

Kinman, Brent. "Luke's Exoneration of John the Baptist." *JTS* 44 (1993): 595–98.

Kirk, Alan. *Memory and the Jesus Tradition*. The Reception of Jesus in the First Three Centuries. London: T&T Clark, 2018.

——. "The Memory of Violence and the Death of Jesus in Q." In Kirk and Thatcher, *Memory, Tradition, and Text*, 191–206.

——. "Memory Theory and Jesus Research." In Holmén and Porter, *Handbook for the Study of the Historical Jesus*, 1:809–42.

——. "Social and Cultural Memory." In Kirk and Thatcher, *Memory, Tradition, and Text*, 1–24.

Kirk, Alan, and Tom Thatcher, eds. *Memory, Tradition, and Text: Uses of the Past in Early Christianity*. SemeiaSt 52. Atlanta: Society of Biblical Literature, 2005.

Klein, Ralph W. *1 Chronicles*. Hermeneia. Minneapolis: Fortress, 2006.

Kloppenborg, John S. *Christ's Associations: Connecting and Belonging in the Ancient City*. New Haven: Yale University Press, 2019.

——. "The Representation of Violence in the Synoptic Parables." In *Mark and Matthew I: Comparative Readings: Understanding the Earliest Gospels in Their First Century Settings*, edited by Eve-Marie Becker and Anders Runesson, 323–51. WUNT 271. Tübingen: Mohr Siebeck, 2011.

Klostermann, Erich. *Das Markusevangelium*. HNT. Tübingen: Mohr Siebeck, 1971.

Kraeling, Carl H. *John the Baptist*. New York: Scribner's Sons, 1951.

Kraemer, Ross S. "Implicating Herodias and Her Daughter in the Death of John the Baptizer: A (Christian) Theological Strategy?" *JBL* 125 (2006): 321–49.

Kraft, Robert A. "The Weighing of the Parts: Pivots and Pitfalls in the Study of Early Judaisms and Their Early Christian Offspring." In Becker and Reed, *Ways That Never Parted*, 87–94.

Kuhn, Heinz-Wolfgang. "Die Kreuzesstrafe während der frühen Kaiserzeit: Ihre Wirklichkeit und Wertung in der Umwelt des Urchristentums." *ANRW* 2.25.1. Berlin: de Gruyter, 1982.

Kyle, Donald G. *Spectacles of Death in Ancient Rome*. London: Routledge, 1998.

Landres, J. Shawn, and Oren Baruch Stier. Introduction to Stier and Landres, *Religion, Violence, Memory, and Place*, 1–12.

Lane, William L. *The Gospel According to Mark*. NICNT. Grand Rapids: Eerdmans, 1974.

Laneri, Nicola, ed. *Performing Death: Social Analyses of Funerary Traditions in the Ancient Near East and Mediterranean*. Chicago: Oriental Institute of the University of Chicago, 2007.

Lange, Nicholas de. *Origen and the Jews: Studies in Jewish-Christian Relations in Third-Century Palestine*. UCOP 25. Cambridge: Cambridge University Press, 1976.

Lawrence, Bruce B., and Aisha Karim. "General Introduction: Theorizing Violence in the Twenty-First Century." In *On Violence: A Reader*, edited by Bruce B. Lawrence and Aisha Karim, 1–15. Durham, N.C.: Duke University Press, 2007.

Le Donne, Anthony. *The Historiographical Jesus: Memory, Typology, and the Son of David*. Waco, Tex.: Baylor University Press, 2009.

———. "Memory, Commemoration and History in John 2:19–22: A Critique and Application of Social Memory." In *The Fourth Gospel in First-Century Media Culture*, edited by Anthony Le Donne and Tom Thatcher, 186–204. LNTS 426. London: T&T Clark, 2011.

———. "Theological Memory Distortion in the Jesus Tradition." In *Memory and Remembrance in the Bible and Antiquity*, edited by Stephen C. Barton, Loren T. Stuckenbruck, and Benjamin G. Wold, 163–77. WUNT 212. Tübingen: Mohr Siebeck, 2007.

Levin, Kevin M. "Black Bostonians Fought for Freedom from Slavery. Where Are the Statues That Tell Their Stories?" June 16, 2020. https://www.wbur.org/cognoscenti/2020/06/16/abraham-lincoln-statue-emancipation-memorial-kevin-m-levin.

Levine, Amy-Jill. *The Misunderstood Jew: The Church and the Scandal of the Jewish Jesus*. New York: HarperCollins, 2006.

Liddell, Henry George, Robert Scott, and Henry Stuart Jones. *A Greek-English Lexicon*. 9th ed. Oxford: Clarendon, 1996.

Lieu, Judith. *Christian Identity in the Jewish and Graeco-Roman World*. Oxford: Oxford University Press, 2004.

———. *Neither Jew Nor Greek? Constructing Early Christianity*. 2nd ed. London: T&T Clark, 2016.

———. "'The Parting of the Ways': Theological Construct or Historical Reality." *JSNT* 56 (1994): 101–19.

Lincoln, Bruce. *Discourse and the Construction of Society: Comparative Studies of Myth, Ritual, and Classification*. Oxford: Oxford University Press, 1989.

———. "Theses on Religion and Violence." *ISIM Review* 15 (2005): 12.

Lohmeyer, Ernst. *Das Evangelium des Markus*. Göttingen: Vandenhoeck & Ruprecht, 1967.

———. *Johannes der Täufer*. Göttingen: Vandenhoeck & Ruprecht, 1932.

Lupieri, Edmondo. "John the Baptist in New Testament Traditions and History." *ANRW* 2.26.1. Berlin: de Gruyter, 1992.

———. "John the Gnostic: The Figure of the Baptist in Origen and Heterodox Gnosticism." *StPatr* 19 (1989): 322–27.

Luz, Ulrich. "The Contribution of Reception History to a Theology of the New Testament." In *The Nature of New Testament Theology: Essays in Honour of Robert Morgan*, edited by Christopher Rowland and Christopher Tuckett, 123–34. Oxford: Blackwell, 2006.

———. *Das Evangelium Nach Matthäus*. 4 vols. EKKNT. Zürich/Neukirchen-Vluyn: Benziger/Neukirchener, 1985–2002.

———. *Matthew 8–20*. Hermeneia. Minneapolis: Fortress, 2001.

———. *Matthew in History: Interpretation, Influence, and Effects*. Minneapolis: Fortress, 1994.

Malamud, Martha. "Pompey's Head and Cato's Snakes." *CP* 98 (2003): 31–44.

Malina, Bruce J., and Richard L. Rohrbaugh. *Social-Science Commentary on the Synoptic Gospels*. Minneapolis: Fortress, 1992.

Malkki, Liisa H. *Purity and Exile: Violence, Memory, and National Cosmology among Hutu Refugees in Tanzania*. Chicago: University of Chicago Press, 1995.

Maloney, Frances J. *The Gospel of Mark: A Commentary*. Peabody, Mass.: Hendrickson, 2002.

Mann, C. S. *Mark*. AB. New York: Doubleday, 1986.

Manns, Frédéric. "Justin's Dialogue with Trypho." In *The Beginnings of Christianity*, edited by Jack Pastor and Menachem Mor, 359–78. Jerusalem: Yad Ben-Zvi Press, 2005.

Marcus, Joel. "Crucifixion as Parodic Exaltation." *JBL* 125 (2006): 73–87.

———. *John the Baptist in History and Theology*. Columbia: University of South Carolina Press, 2018.

———. *Mark 1–8: A New Translation with Introduction and Commentary*. AB 27. New York: Doubleday, 2000.

Marotta, Valerio. "St. Paul's Death: Roman Citizenship and Summa Supplicia." In *The Last Years of Paul: Essays from the Tarragona Conference, June 2013*, edited by Armand Puig i Tàrrech and John M. G. Barclay, 247–69. WUNT 352. Tübingen: Mohr Siebeck, 2015.

Marshall, I. Howard. *The Gospel of Luke: A Commentary on the Greek Text*. NIGTC. Exeter: Paternoster, 1978.

Martens, Peter W. *Origen and Scripture: The Contours of the Exegetical Life*. OECS. Oxford: Oxford University Press, 2012.

Martin, George R. R. *A Game of Thrones*. New York: Bantam Spectra, 1996.

Martínez, Roberto. *The Question of John the Baptist and Jesus' Indictment of the Religious Leaders: A Critical Analysis of Luke 7:18–35.* Cambridge: James Clarke, 2011.

Marxsen, Willi. *Mark the Evangelist: Studies on the Redaction History of the Gospel.* Translated by Roy A. Harrisville. Nashville: Abingdon, 1969.

Masciandaro, Nicola. "Non potest hoc corpus decollari: Beheading and the Impossible." In *Heads Will Roll: Decapitation in the Medieval and Early Modern Imagination,* edited by Lariss Tracy and Jeff Massey, 15–36. MRAT 7. Leiden: Brill, 2012.

McCane, Byron R. *Roll Back the Stone: Death and Burial in the World of Jesus.* Harrisburg, Penn.: Trinity Press International, 2003.

McDonald, J. I. H. "What Did You Go Out to See? John the Baptist, the Scrolls and Late Second Temple Judaism." In *The Dead Sea Scrolls in Their Historical Context,* edited by T. H. Lim, A. Graeme Auld, Larry W. Hurtado, and Alison Jack, 53–64. Edinburgh: T&T Clark, 2000.

McGuckin, John A., ed. *The Westminster Handbook to Origen.* Louisville: Westminster John Knox, 2004.

McManigal, Daniel W. *A Baptism of Judgment in the Fire of the Holy Spirit: John's Eschatological Proclamation in Matthew 3.* LNTS 595. London: T&T Clark, 2019.

McVann, Mark. "The 'Passion' of John the Baptist and Jesus before Pilate: Mark's Warnings about Kings and Governors." *BTB* 38 (2008): 152–57.

Meeks, Wayne A., and Robert L. Wilken. *Jews and Christians in Antioch in the First Four Centuries of the Common Era.* Missoula, Mont.: Scholars Press, 1978.

Meier, John P. *A Marginal Jew: Rethinking the Historical Jesus.* Vol. 2: *Mentor, Message, and Miracles.* ABRL. New York: Doubleday, 1994.

———. "John the Baptist in Josephus: Philology and Exegesis." *JBL* 111 (1992): 225–37.

Metcalf, Peter, and Richard Huntington. *Celebrations of Death: The Anthropology of Mortuary Ritual.* 2nd ed. Cambridge: Cambridge University Press, 1991.

Metzger, Bruce M. *A Textual Commentary on the Greek New Testament.* 2nd ed. Stuttgart: Deutsche Bibelgesellschaft, 1994.

Miller, Geoffrey D. "An Intercalation Revisited: Christology, Discipleship, and Dramatic Irony in Mark 6.6b–30." *JSNT* 35 (2012): 176–95.

Miller, Susan. *Women in Mark's Gospel.* JSNTSup 259. London: T&T Clark International, 2004.

Minns, Denis. "Justin Martyr." In *The Cambridge History of Philosophy in Late Antiquity,* edited by Lloyd P. Gerson, 258–69. Cambridge: Cambridge University Press, 2010.

Misztal, Barbara. *Theories of Social Remembering.* Maidenhead: Open University Press, 1990.

Modlinger, Martin, and Philipp Sonntag, eds. *Other People's Pain: Narratives of Trauma and the Question of Ethics*. Cultural History and Literary Imagination 18. Oxford: Peter Lang, 2011.

Montesanti, Stephanie R., and Wilfreda E. Thurston. "Mapping the Role of Structural and Interpersonal Violence in the Lives of Women: Implications for Public Health Interventions and Policy." *BMC Women's Health* 15, no. 100 (2015): 1–13.

Mor, Menahem. *The Second Jewish Revolt: The Bar Kokhba War, 132–136 CE*. BRLJ 50. Leiden: Brill, 2016.

Moss, Candida R. *Divine Bodies: Resurrecting Perfection in the New Testament and Early Christianity*. New Haven: Yale University Press, 2019.

Muir, Steven. "Vivid Imagery in Galatians 3:1—Roman Rhetoric, Street Announcing, Graffiti, and Crucifixions." *BTB* 44 (2014): 76–86.

Müller, Ulrich B. *Johannes der Täufer: Jüdischer Prophet und Wegbereiter Jesu*. Biblische Gestalten 6. Leipzig: Evangelische Verlagsanstalt, 2002.

Murnane, William J. "Taking It with You: The Problem of Death and Afterlife in Ancient Egypt." In Obayashi, *Death and Afterlife*, 35–48.

Murphy, Catherine M. *John the Baptist: Prophet of Purity for a New Age*. Collegeville, Minn.: Liturgical Press, 2003.

Murphy-O'Connor, Jerome. "John the Baptist and Jesus: History and Hypotheses." *NTS* 36 (1990): 361–66.

Nautin, Pierre. *Origène: sa vie et son oeuvre*. Paris: Beauchesne, 1977.

Neal, Arthur. *National Trauma and Collective Memory: Major Events in the American Century*. Armonk, N.Y.: Sharpe, 1998.

Neginsky, Rosina. *Salome: The Image of a Woman Who Never Was*. Newcastle upon Tyne: Cambridge Scholars Publishing, 2013.

Nicklas, Tobias, Friedrich V. Reiterer, and Joseph Verheyden, eds. *The Human Body in Death and Resurrection: Deuterocanonical and Cognate Literature Yearbook 2009*. Berlin: de Gruyter, 2009.

Nineham, D. E. *Saint Mark*. Harmondsworth: Penguin, 1963.

Nir, Rivka. *The First Christian Believer: In Search of John the Baptist*. New Testament Monographs 38. Sheffield: Sheffield Phoenix Press, 2019.

Nirenberg, David. *Anti-Judaism: The Western Tradition*. New York: W. W. Norton, 2013.

Nolland, John. *The Gospel of Matthew*. NIGTC. Grand Rapids: Eerdmans, 2005.

Nyström, David E. *The Apology of Justin Martyr: Literary Strategies and the Defence of Christianity*. WUNT 462. Tübingen: Mohr Siebeck, 2018.

Nytagodien, Ridwan, and Arthur Neal. "Collective Trauma, Apologies, and the Politics of Memory." *Journal of Human Rights* 3 (2004): 465–75.

Obayashi, Hiroshi, ed. *Death and Afterlife: Perspectives of World Religions*. Contributions to the Study of Religion 33. New York: Greenwood Press, 1992.

O'Brien, Kelli S. "The Curse of the Law (Galatians 3.13): Crucifixion, Persecution, and Deuteronomy 21.22–23." *JSNT* 29 (2006): 55–76.

O'Collins, Gerald G. "Crucifixion." *ABD* 1:1207–10.

Oden, Thomas C., and Christopher A. Hall, eds. *Mark*. ACCS. Downers Grove: InterVarsity Press, 1998.
O'Leary, Joseph S. "Judaism." In McGuckin, *Westminster Handbook to Origen*, 135–38.
———. "The Recuperation of Judaism." In *Origeniana Sexta*, edited by Gilles Dorival and Alain le Boulluec, 373–79. BETL 118. Leuven: Leuven University Press, 1995.
Olick, Jeffrey K. *In the House of the Hangman: The Agonies of German Defeat, 1943–1949*. Chicago: University of Chicago Press, 2005.
———. "Products, Processes, and Practices: A Non-Reificatory Approach to Collective Memory." *BTB* 36 (2006): 5–14.
Olick, Jeffrey K., and Daniel Levy. "Collective Memory and Cultural Constraint: Holocaust Myth and Rationality in German Politics." *American Sociological Review* 62 (1997): 921–36.
Olick, Jeffrey K., and Joyce Robins. "Social Memory Studies: From 'Collective Memory' to the Historical Sociology of Mnemonic Practices." *Annual Review of Sociology* 24 (1998): 105–40.
Olick, Jeffrey K., Vered Vinitzky-Seroussi, and Daniel Levy. Introduction to *The Collective Memory Reader*, edited by Jeffrey K. Olick, Vered Vinitzky-Seroussi, and Daniel Levy, 3–62. Oxford: Oxford University Press, 2011.
Oliver, William. "Cultural Racism and Structural Violence: Implications for African Americans." *Journal of Human Behavior in the Social Environment* 4 (2001): 1–26.
———. "Cultural Racism and Violence in African American Communities." In *Black Culture and Experience: Contemporary Issues*, edited by Venise T. Berry, Anita Fleming-Rife, and Ayo Dayo, 181–92. New York: Peter Lang, 2015.
Osgood, Josiah. "The Topography of Roman Assassination, 133 BCE–222 CE." In Riess and Fagan, *Topography of Violence in the Greco-Roman World*, 209–27.
Parker, Pierson. "Jesus, John the Baptist, and the Herods." *PRSt* 8 (1981): 4–11.
Parker, Robert. *Miasma: Pollution and Purification in Early Greek Religion*. Oxford: Clarendon Press, 1983.
Parris, David Paul. *Reception Theory and Biblical Hermeneutics*. Princeton Theological Monograph Series 107. Eugene, Ore.: Pickwick, 2009.
Parvis, Paul. "Justin Martyr." *ExpTim* 120 (2008): 53–61.
Parvis, Sara, and Paul Foster, eds. *Justin Martyr and His Worlds*. Minneapolis: Fortress, 2007.
Pawlikowski, John T. "Anti-Judaism." In *A Dictionary of Jewish-Christian Relations*, edited by Edward Kessler and Neil Wenborn, 19–21. Cambridge: Cambridge University Press, 2005.
Pellegrini, Silvia. *Elija—Wegbereiter des Gottessohnes: Eine textsemiotische Untersuchung im Markusevangelium*. Herders Biblische Studien 26. Freiburg: Herder, 2000.
Pennebaker, James W. Introduction to Pennebaker, Paez, and Rimé, *Collective Memory of Political Events*, vii–xi.

Pennebaker, James W., Dario Paez, and Bernard Rimé, eds. *Collective Memory of Political Events: Social Psychological Perspectives*. New York: Psychology Press, 1997.
Pesantubbee, Michelene E. "Wounded Knee: Site of Resistance and Recovery." In Stier and Landres, *Religion, Violence, Memory, and Place*, 75–88.
Pesch, Rudolf. *Das Markusevangelium*. Freiburg: Herder, 1984.
Pohl, Walter. "Perceptions of Barbarian Violence." In Drake, *Violence in Late Antiquity*, 15–26.
Popović, Mladen. "Bones, Bodies and Resurrection in the Dead Sea Scrolls." In Nicklas, Reiterer, and Verheyden, *Human Body in Death and Resurrection*, 221–42.
Porter, Martin. *Windows of the Soul: The Art of Physiognomy in European Culture 1470–1780*. Oxford: Oxford University Press, 2005.
Presser, Lois. *Inside Story: How Narratives Drive Mass Harm*. Oakland: University of California Press, 2018.
Prince, K. Stephen. *The Ballad of Robert Charles: Searching for the New Orleans Riot of 1900*. Chapel Hill: University of North Carolina Press, 2021.
———. "Remembering Robert Charles: Violence and Memory in Jim Crow New Orleans." *Journal of Southern History* 83 (2017): 297–328.
Pryor, John W. "John the Baptist and Jesus: Tradition and Text in John 3.25." *JSNT* 66 (1997): 15–26.
Radstone, Susannah, ed. *Memory and Methodology*. Oxford: Berg, 2000.
———. "Trauma Studies: Contexts, Politics, Ethics." In Modlinger and Sonntag, *Other People's Pain*, 63–90.
Räisänen, Heikki. "The Effective 'History' of the Bible: A Challenge to Biblical Scholarship?" *SJT* 45 (1992): 303–24.
Rajak, Tessa. *The Jewish Dialogue with Greece and Rome: Studies in Cultural and Social Interaction*. AGJU 48. Leiden: Brill, 2001.
Rawlinson, A. E. J. *St Mark*. London: Methuen, 1925.
Rawson, Beryl. *Children and Childhood in Roman Italy*. Oxford: Oxford University Press, 2003.
Reinhartz, Adele. "A Fork in the Road or a Multi-Lane Highway? New Perspectives on the 'Parting of the Ways' Between Judaism and Christianity." In *The Changing Face of Judaism, Christianity and Other Greco-Roman Religions in Antiquity*, edited by Ian Henderson and Oegema Gerbern, 280–95. Studien zu den Jüdischen Schriften aus hellenistisch-römischer Zeit 2. Gütersloh: Gütersloher Verlagshaus, 2006.
———. Review of *Judaism: The Genealogy of a Modern Notion*, by Daniel Boyarin. *Reading Religion*, 2018. http://www.readingreligion.org.
Reischer, Erica, and Kathryn S. Koo. "The Body Beautiful: Symbolism and Agency in the Social World." *Annual Review of Anthropology* 33 (2004): 297–317.
Reventlow, Henning Graf. *History of Biblical Interpretation*. Vol. 1: *From the Old Testament to Origen*. Translated by Leo G. Perdue. RBS 50. Atlanta: Society of Biblical Literature, 2009.

Ricoeur, Paul. "Memory—Forgetting—History." In *Meaning and Representation in History*, edited by Jörn Rüsen, 9–19. Oxford: Berghahn Books, 2006.

Riess, Werner. Introduction to Riess and Fagan, *Topography of Violence in the Greco-Roman World*, 1–16.

———. "Where to Kill in Classical Athens: Assassinations, Executions, and the Athenian Public Space." In Riess and Fagan, *Topography of Violence in the Greco-Roman World*, 77–112.

Riess, Werner, and Garrett G. Fagan, eds. *The Topography of Violence in the Greco-Roman World*. Ann Arbor: University of Michigan Press, 2016.

Rindos, Jaroslav. *He of Whom It Is Written: John the Baptist and Elijah in Luke*. ÖBS 38. Frankfurt am Main: Lang, 2010.

Robertson, Ritchie. "Varieties of Anti-Semitism." In Ehrlich, *Encyclopedia of the Jewish Diaspora*, 103–7. Santa Barbara, Calif.: ABC-CLIO, 2009.

Robinson, John A. T. *Twelve New Testament Studies*. SBT. London: SCM, 1962.

Rodríguez, Rafael. "Authenticating Criteria: The Use and Misuse of a Critical Method." *JSHJ* 7 (2009): 152–67.

———. "The Embarrassing Truth About Jesus: The Criterion of Embarrassment and the Failure of Historical Authenticity." In *Jesus, Criteria, and the Demise of Authenticity*, edited by Chris Keith and Anthony Le Donne, 132–51. London: T&T Clark, 2012.

———. *Structuring Early Christian Memory: Jesus in Tradition, Performance, and Text*. LNTS 407. London: T&T Clark, 2010.

Rollens, Sarah E. "The Anachronism of 'Early Christian Communities.'" In *Theorizing "Religion" in Antiquity*, edited by Nickolas Roubekas, 307–24. Studies in Ancient Religion and Culture. Sheffield: Equinox, 2019.

Rosaldo, Renato. "Grief and a Headhunter's Rage." In Scheper-Hughes and Bourgois, *Violence in War and Peace*, 150–56.

Rothschild, Clare K. *Baptist Traditions and Q*. Tübingen: Mohr Siebeck, 2005.

———. Review of *He of Whom It Is Written: John the Baptist and Elijah in Luke*, by Jaroslav Rindos. *RBL*, 2012. http://www.bookreviews.org.

Rowling, J. K. *Harry Potter and the Chamber of Secrets*. Illustrated by Jim Kay. London: Bloomsbury, 2016.

Samuelsson, Gunnar. *Crucifixion in Antiquity: An Inquiry into the Background and Significance of the New Testament Terminology of Crucifixion*. WUNT 310. Tübingen: Mohr Siebeck, 2011.

Sanders, E. P. *The Historical Figure of Jesus*. London: Penguin, 1993.

Scarry, Elaine. "The Body in Pain: The Making and Unmaking of the World." In Scheper-Hughes and Bourgois, *Violence in War and Peace*, 365–67.

Schenk, Wolfgang. "Gefangenschaft und Tod des Täufers Erwägungen zur Chronologie und ihren Konsequenzen." *NTS* 29 (1983): 453–83.

Scheper-Hughes, Nancy. *Death without Weeping: The Violence of Everyday Life in Brazil*. Berkeley: University of California Press, 1992.

Scheper-Hughes, Nancy, and Philippe Bourgois. "Introduction: Making Sense of Violence." In Scheper-Hughes and Bourgois, *Violence in War and Peace*, 1–31.

———, eds. *Violence in War and Peace: An Anthology*. Oxford: Blackwell, 2004.

Schnackenburg, Rudolf. *Das Evangelium nach Markus*. Düsseldorf: Patmos-Verlag, 1966.

Schöpflin, Karin. "The Revivification of the Dry Bones: Ezekiel 37:1–14." In Nicklas, Reiterer, and Verheyden, *Human Body in Death and Resurrection*, 67–85.

Schröter, Jens. *Erinnerung an Jesu Worte: Studien zur Rezeption der Logienüberlieferung in Markus, Q und Thomas*. WMANT 76. Neukirchen-Vluyn: Neukirchener Verlag, 1997.

———. *Jesus of Nazareth: Jew from Galilee, Savior of the World*. Translated by Wayne Coppins. Waco, Tex.: Baylor University Press, 2014.

Schudson, Michael. "The Present in the Past versus the Past in the Present." *Communication* 11 (1989): 105–13.

Schütz, Roland. *Johannes der Täufer*. ATANT 50. Zürich: Stuttgart, 1967.

Schwartz, Barry. *Abraham Lincoln and the Forge of National Memory*. Chicago: University of Chicago Press, 2000.

———. "Iconography and Collective Memory: Lincoln's Image in the American Mind." *Sociological Quarterly* 32 (1991): 301–19.

———. "The Social Context of Commemoration: A Study in Collective Memory." *Social Forces* 61 (1982): 374–402.

———. "Where There's Smoke, There's Fire: Memory and History." In Thatcher, *Memory and Identity in Ancient Judaism and Early Christianity*, 7–37.

Schweitzer, Frederick. "Persecution of Diaspora Jews: History of Jewish Persecution and Expulsion." In Ehrlich, *Encyclopedia of the Jewish Diaspora*, 95–103.

Schweizer, Eduard. *The Good News According to Mark*. Atlanta: John Knox, 1970.

Scobie, Charles H. *John the Baptist*. London: SCM, 1964.

Segal, Alan F. *Life after Death: A History of the Afterlife in Western Religion*. New York: Doubleday, 2004.

Sen, Amartya. *Identity and Violence: The Illusion of Destiny*. London: Penguin, 2006.

Shanks, Hershel. "Understanding the Dead Sea Scrolls." In *Was John the Baptist an Essene?* edited by Otto Betz, 205–16. New York: Random House, 1992.

Shedd, Nathan L. "John the Baptist." In the online *T&T Clark Jesus Library*, forthcoming.

———. Review of *The First Christian Believer: In Search of John the Baptist*, by Rivka Nir. *RBL*, 2020. http://www.sblcentral.org.

Shepherd, Tom. "The Narrative Function of Markan Intercalation." *NTS* 41 (1995): 522–40.

Simon, Marcel. *Verus Israel: A Study of the Relations between Christians and Jews in the Roman Empire AD 135–425*. Translated by H. McKeating. Oxford: Littman Library of Jewish Civilization, 1986.

Skarsaune, Oskar. *The Proof from Prophecy: A Study in Justin Martyr's Proof-Text Tradition: Text-Type, Provenance, Theological Profile*. Leiden: Brill, 1987.
Slusser, Michael. "Justin Scholarship: Trends and Trajectories." In Parvis and Foster, *Justin Martyr and His Worlds*, 13–21.
Smit, Peter-Ben. *Masculinity and the Bible: Surveys, Models, and Perspectives*. Leiden: Brill, 2017.
Smith, Abraham. "Tyranny Exposed: Mark's Typological Characterization of Herod Antipas (Mark 6:14–29)." *BibInt* 14 (2006): 259–93.
Snyder, Benjamin. *Ritual Purity and the Origin of John's Βάπτισμα Μετανοίας*. WUNT II. Tübingen: Mohr Siebeck, forthcoming 2021.
Sollertinsky, S. "The Death of St. John the Baptist." *JTS* 1 (1900): 507–28.
Stegemann, Hartmut. *The Library of Qumran: On the Essenes, Qumran, John the Baptist, and Jesus*. Grand Rapids: Eerdmans, 1998.
Stein, Robert H. *Mark*. BECNT. Grand Rapids: Baker Academic, 2008.
Steinmann, Jean. *Saint John the Baptist and the Desert Tradition*. Translated by Michael Boyes. London: Longmans, 1958.
Stichele, Caroline Vander. "The Head of John and Its Reception or How to Conceptualize 'Reception History.'" In *Reception History and Biblical Studies: Theory and Practice*, edited by Emma England and William John Lyons, 79–93. Scriptural Traces 6; LHBOTS 615. London: T&T Clark, 2015.
Stiebert, Johanna. *Fathers and Daughters in the Hebrew Bible*. Oxford: Oxford University Press, 2013.
Stier, Oren Baruch, and J. Shawn Landres, eds. *Religion, Violence, Memory, and Place*. Bloomington: Indiana University Press, 2006.
Stylianopoulos, Theodore. *Justin Martyr and the Mosaic Law*. SBLDS 20. Missoula, Mont.: SBL and Scholars Press, 1975.
Talbert, Charles H. *Matthew*. Paideia. Grand Rapids: Baker Academic, 2010.
Tatum, W. Barnes. *John the Baptist and Jesus: A Report of the Jesus Seminar*. Sonoma, Calif.: Polebridge, 1994.
Taylor, Joan E. *The Immerser: John the Baptist within Second Temple Judaism*. Grand Rapids: Eerdmans, 1997.
———. "John the Baptist." In Collins and Harlow, *Eerdmans Dictionary of Early Judaism*, 819–21.
———. "John the Baptist and the Essenes." *JJS* 47 (1996): 256–85.
———. *What Did Jesus Look Like?* London: T&T Clark, 2018.
Taylor, Joan E., and Federico Adinolfi. "John the Baptist and Jesus the Baptist: A Narrative Critical Approach." *JSHJ* 10 (2012): 247–84.
Taylor, Marion Ann, and Heather E. Weir, eds. *Women in the Story of Jesus: The Gospels through the Eyes of Nineteenth-Century Female Biblical Interpreters*. Grand Rapids: Eerdmans, 2016.
Taylor, Vincent. *The Formation of the Gospel Tradition*. London: Macmillan, 1933.
———. *The Gospel According to St Mark*. London: Macmillan, 1952.
Thatcher, Tom. "Preface: Keys, Frames, and the Problem of the Past." In Thatcher, *Memory and Identity in Ancient Judaism and Early Christianity*, 1–5.

———, ed. *Memory and Identity in Ancient Judaism and Early Christianity: A Conversation with Barry Schwartz*. SemeiaSt 78. Atlanta: SBL Press, 2014.

Theissen, Gerd. *The Gospels in Context: Social and Political History in the Synoptic Tradition*. Minneapolis: Fortress, 1991.

Theissen, Gerd, and Annette Merz. *The Historical Jesus: A Comprehensive Guide*. Translated by John Bowden. London: SCM, 1998.

Thiessen, Matthew. *Jesus and the Forces of Death: The Gospels' Portrayal of Ritual Impurity within First-Century Judaism*. Grand Rapids: Baker Academic, 2020.

Thomas, Joseph. *Le Mouvement Baptiste en Palestine et Syrie*. Gembloux: J. Duculot, 1935.

Thorne, Mark. "*Memoria Redux*: Memory in Lucan." In *Brill's Companion to Lucan*, edited by Paolo Asso. Leiden: Brill, 2011.

Tilly, Michael. *Johannes der Täufer und die Biographie der Propheten: Die synoptische Täuferüberlieferung und das jüdische Prophetenbild zur Zeit des Täufers*. BWANT 7. Stuttgart: Kohlhammer, 1994.

Tong, M. Andryael. "'Given as a Sign': Circumcision and Bodily Discourse in Late Antique Judaism and Christianity." PhD diss., Fordham University, 2019.

Toynbee, J. M. C. *Death and Burial in the Roman World*. Baltimore: Johns Hopkins University Press, 1971.

Trigg, Joseph W. *Origen*. ECF. London: Routledge, 1998.

Tucker, Katie. "'Whence This Severance of the Head?' The Osteology and Archaeology of Human Decapitation in Britain." PhD thesis, University of Winchester, 2012.

Turner, David L. *Matthew*. BECNT. Grand Rapids: Baker Academic, 2008.

Twelftree, Graham H. "Jesus the Baptist." *JSHJ* 7 (2009): 103–25.

Van Eickels, Klaus. "Gendered Violence: Castration and Blinding as Punishment for Treason in Normandy and Anglo-Norman England." *Gender History* 16 (2004): 588–602.

Van Hooff, A. J. L. *From Autothanasia to Suicide: Self-Killing in Classical Antiquity*. London: Routledge, 1990.

Vernant, Jean-Pierre. "La belle mort et le cadavre outragé." In *La mort, les morts dans les sociétés anciennes*, edited by Gherardo Gnoli and Jean-Pierre Vernant, 45–76. Paris: Éditions de la Maison des sciences de l'homme, 1990.

Vette, Nathanael, and Will Robinson. "Was John the Baptist Raised from the Dead? The Origins of Mark 6:14–29." *Biblical Annals* 9 (2019): 335–54.

Voisin, Jean-Louis. "Les Romains, chasseurs de têtes." In *Du châtiment dans la cité. Supplices corporels et peine de mort dans le monde antique*, 241–93. Table ronde de Rome (9–11 novembre 1982). Rome: École Française de Rome, 1984.

Voragine, Jacobus de. *The Golden Legend: Readings on the Saints*. Translated by William Granger Ryan. Princeton: Princeton University Press, 2012.

Watson, George, and Andrew Lintott. "Crucifixion." *OCD*, 396.

Wagner-Pacifici, Robin. "Memories in the Making: The Shape of Things That Went." *Qualitative Sociology* 19 (1996): 301–21.

Walsh, Robyn Faith. *The Origins of Early Christian Literature: Contextualizing the New Testament within Greco-Roman Literary Culture*. Cambridge: Cambridge University Press, 2021.

Watts, Dorothy. *Religion in Late Roman Britain: Forces of Change*. London: Routledge, 1998.

Webb, Robert. "John the Baptist and His Relationship to Jesus." In *Studying the Historical Jesus: Evaluations of the State of Current Research*, edited by Bruce Chilton and Craig A. Evans, 179–229. NTTS 19. Leiden: Brill, 1994.

———. *John the Baptizer and Prophet: A Socio-Historical Study*. JSNTSup 62. Sheffield: Sheffield Academic Press, 1991.

Wendel, Susan. "Interpreting the Descent of the Spirit: A Comparison of Justin's Dialogue with Trypho and Luke-Acts." In Parvis and Foster, *Justin Martyr and His Worlds*, 95–103.

———. *Scriptural Interpretation and Community Self-Definition in Luke-Acts and the Writings of Justin Martyr*. NovTSup 139. Leiden: Brill, 2011.

Wertsch, James V. "Deep Memory and Narrative Templates: Conservative Forces in Collective Memory." In Assmann and Shortt, *Memory and Political Change*, 173–85.

Wiedemann, Thomas. *Emperors and Gladiators*. London: Routledge, 1992.

Wilson, Brittany E. *Unmanly Men: Refigurations of Masculinity in Luke-Acts*. Oxford: Oxford University Press, 2015.

Wink, Walter. *John the Baptist in the Gospel Tradition*. SNTSMS 7. Cambridge: Cambridge University Press, 1968.

Winter, Jay. "Foreword: Rememberance as a Human Right." In Assmann and Shortt, *Memory and Political Change*, vii–xi.

Winter, Paul. "The Proto-Source of Luke I." *NovT* 1 (1956): 184–99.

Wise, Michael O. "Crucifixion." In Collins and Harlow, *Eerdmans Dictionary of Early Judaism*, 500–501.

Witherington, Ben. *The Gospel of Mark: A Socio-Rhetorical Commentary*. Grand Rapids: Eerdmans, 2001.

Yamasaki, Gary. *John the Baptist in Life and Death: Audience-Oriented Criticism of Matthew's Narrative*. JSNTSup 167. Sheffield: Sheffield Academic Press, 1998.

Young, James E. "The Stages of Memory at Ground Zero." In Stier and Landres, *Religion, Violence, Memory, and Place*, 214–34.

Zerubavel, Yael. *Recovered Roots: Collective Memory and the Making of Israeli National Tradition*. Chicago: University of Chicago Press, 1995.

Zimmermann, Martin. "Extreme Formen physischer Gewalt in der antiken Überlieferung." In *Extreme Formen von Gewalt in Bild und Text des Altertums*, edited by Martin Zimmermann, 155–92. Münchner Studien zur Alten Welt. München: Herbert Utz Verlag, 2009.

———. "Conclusion: Violence in Late Antiquity Reconsidered." In Drake, *Violence in Late Antiquity*, 343–58.

Žižek, Slavoj. *Violence: Six Sideways Reflections*. New York: Picador, 2008.

Index of Modern Authors

Adinolfi, Federico, 8n25
Akiyama, Kengo, 18n58
Aldhouse-Green, Miranda, 51, 65, 68, 70n61
Allison, Dale C., 8n25, 12n38, 13n43, 34, 34n43, 34n44, 76n82, 93n36, 99–100
Anderson, Janice C., 13n43, 93n36, 104n86
Aplin, Max, 8n25
Aretxaga, Begoña, 47, 52n138
Asikainen, Susanna, 65n30, 95n43, 106–8, 107n104, 116
Assmann, Aleida, 44n85, 45n92, 46n101, 48–50, 48n110, 48n113, 53n147
Assmann, Jan, 1, 31n31, 32, 32n33, 36, 37n53, 68n48
Aune, David E., 7n23
Aus, Roger, 10, 90n28, 91, 91n29, 119
Avemarie, Friedrich, 80n100

Backhaus, Knut, 8n25, 87n14
Badke, William B., 8n25
Baert, Barbara, 86n12, 88n20
Barnard, L. W., 130n3
Bartlett, Frederic C., 28
Bauckham, Richard, 33n38, 76n84
Beard, Mary, 2, 5–6, 81–82
Becker, Adam H., 167n3, 168n6
Becker, Jürgen, 8n25
Bell, Duncan, 50n122
Berkowitz, Beth A., 60–61, 64
Bernier, Jonathan, 34
Bernstein, Alan E., 73, 73n71, 124n161
Betz, Otto, 7n22
Blomquist, Gregory L., 18n58
Bockmuehl, Markus, 8n25, 17n54, 18, 18n59, 32
Boddens Hosang, F. J. Elizabeth, 168n8

Bond, Helen K., 17n55, 18n58, 50n124, 95n43
Boring, M. Eugene, 10n32
Bourdieu, Pierre, 39
Bourgois, Philippe, 38, 41n72, 42n77, 47n109, 49n119, 52n139
Bovon, François, 102
Boyarin, Daniel, 129n1, 136, 167n3, 170n13, 172n18
Brown, Raymond E., 7n21
Brown, Steven D., 20n68
Brownlee, W. H., 7n22
Bryen, Ari Z., 39n58
Buckley-Zistel, Susanne, 44, 45n94, 49
Bull, Stephen, 67–68
Bultmann, Rudolf, 11n32, 12n36, 129n1, 173n19
Burr, Viv, 51n132
Burridge, Richard A., 50n124
Butler, Judith, 107n101

Callon, Callie, 50n123, 50n125
Capps, Walter H., 17
Carrigan, Tim, 107n104
Casey, Edward S., 29
Casey, Maurice, 8n25, 91n29
Castelli, Elizabeth A., 80n100
Chapman, David W., 59n5
Chilton, Bruce, 8n25, 10, 135n22
Coleman, Kathleen M., 60–61, 78n95
Collins, Adela Yarbro, 12n38, 58n4, 87n16, 91n29, 104n86, 123n159
Collins, John J., 7n22, 59n5, 69n49
Cone, James H., 41n71, 55
Connell, R. W., 107n104
Connerton, Paul, 27n6, 48n113, 51–52

Index of Modern Authors

Conway, Colleen, 65n30, 106–7
Cook, John Granger, 59n5
Coser, Lewis A., 27n9, 28
Cranfield, C. E. B., 13n43, 58n4, 86n13, 91n29
Crossley, James G., 10n31, 12n38, 18n58, 90n27, 90n28, 99n63, 104n86, 105–6, 105n94, 110n110
Cubitt, Geoffrey, 27n6
Culpepper, R. Alan, 12n38, 97, 98n59, 119

Daniélou, Jean, 7n22
Dapaah, Daniel S., 8n25, 58n4
Darr, John A., 103
Davies, Douglas J., 69n51
Davies, William D., 12n38, 13n43, 93n36
Dennert, Brian C., 93n35, 100n68, 100n69, 101, 101n73, 101n74, 105, 118n147
Dennis, J., 59n5
De Pina-Cabral, João, 51n128
Dibelius, Martin, 10n32, 12n36, 94n37, 159n87
Dicken, Frank E., 144n48
Dinkova-Bruun, Greti, 86n12
Dobschütz, Ernst von, 18n58
Dogan, Kamil Hakan, 62n16
Dolce, Rita, 65n31
Donahue, John R., 58n4, 87, 104n86
Douglas, Mary, 51
Dulk, Matthijs den, 136
Dunn, James D. G., 7n24, 8n25, 159n87, 167
Duran, Nicole Wilkinson, 83, 99, 115–16

Eastman, David L., 77
Edmondson, J. C., 61n14
Edwards, J. Christopher, 18
Ehrlich, M. Avrum, 129n1
Elledge, C. D., 74n77, 75, 75n81
Enslin, Morton Scott, 8n25, 110n109
Erickson, Richard J., 101n75, 103n83, 103n84
Erll, Astrid, 27n6, 27n8, 32n33, 42n77
Ernst, Josef, 87n14, 87n15, 93n36
Evans, Craig A., 8n25, 10n30, 58n4, 61n11, 86n12, 100n69, 119n150
Evans, Robert, 18n58

Fagan, Garrett G., 57n2, 78n96, 79n96
Fantham, Elaine, 71n62
Farmer, Paul, 39, 39n60, 41
Farris, Stephen, 7n21
Fentress, James, 27n6, 27n8, 30n27

Fischer, Alexander Achilles, 68n48
Foote, Kenneth, 53n147
Foster, Paul, 33n38, 36, 130n3, 135n22
Fowler, Robert, 85, 85n3
France, R. T., 13n43, 58n4, 87n14, 93n36
Fredriksen, Paula, 131, 136n30, 168, 172n18
Freud, Sigmund, 54n150
Freyne, Seán, 89n25

Gabrielson, Timothy A., 168n5
Gadamer, Hans-Georg, 18n58, 25, 35, 37n53
Gager, John, 169n9
Garland, Robert, 69n49, 72–73
Garnsey, Peter, 60
Gelber, Mark H., 130n1
Gerdmar, Anders, 129n1, 173n19
Geyser, A. S., 7n21, 7n22
Glancy, Jennifer A., 104n86
Gnilka, Joachim, 10n31, 12, 19, 19n67, 58n4, 87n14
Goguel, Maurice, 8n25, 58n4, 125
Goodacre, Mark, 91n29, 93n35, 102n81
Gould, Ezra P., 88n21, 110n109
Gourevitch, Philip, 49n119
Graves, Alex, 57n3
Graybill, Rhiannon, 63n21
Green, Joel B., 102, 102n79
Greenspahn, Frederick E., 157n80
Guelich, Robert A., 58n4
Gutchess, Angela H., 46n101
Guyénot, Laurent, 8n25

Hagner, Donald A., 58n4
Halbwachs, Maurice, 27–28, 37n53, 54n150
Hall, Christopher A., 19, 115n134
Hamm, Mark S., 40n66, 53n147
Hanson, John S., 7n23
Harlow, Daniel C., 7n22, 59n5
Harries, Jill, 39n58
Harrington, Daniel J., 58n4, 87, 100n69, 101n73, 104n86
Hartmann, Michael, 19, 58n4, 65, 87, 92n34, 110n110, 116n137
Hayter, Daniel W., 75n81
Hebron, Carol, 18n58
Heine, Ronald E., 115n133, 147–48, 147n53, 148n59, 154, 157n81, 158n83, 160n88, 171
Hengel, Martin, 58n5, 59n5
Henry, Doug, 53, 55
Henten, Jan Willem van, 80n100
Herman, Judith, 42n77

Index of Modern Authors

Hinard, François, 71
Hinson, E. Glenn, 130n3
Hoehner, Harold W., 9n27, 9n28, 144n48, 145n59
Hoffeditz, David M., 10n32, 98n60
Hollenbach, Paul W., 8n25
Holmén, Tom, 30n28, 34n43
Hooker, Morna, 13n43, 34n41, 58n4, 93n36, 97n54, 116
Hope, Valerie M., 68n48, 71n66, 71n67
Hopkins, Keith, 68n49
Horsley, Richard A., 7n23
Hübenthal, Sandra, 25n3, 27n6, 30n28, 32n35, 33n39, 94n38, 94, 98, 98n55, 98n58
Huntington, Richard, 69
Hurtado, Larry, 30n29, 31n29

Iersel, Bas M. F. van, 119n150
Ifill, Sherrilyn A., 47
Igartua, Juanjo, 55n150
Ilan, Tal, 113n125
Irshai, Oded, 131, 136n30, 172n18

Jack, Alison M., 18n58
Jacobi, Christine, 17n55, 18n58
Jacobs, Janet, 29n19, 47, 54n150
Janes, Regina, 2, 57, 103n82, 104n86, 117
Jensen, Morton, 91n29
Joynes, Christine E., 18–19, 18n58

Kansteiner, Wulf, 38, 42n77, 45n94
Karakolis, Christos, 14n43, 97n54
Karim, Aisha, 39, 41, 43, 53n147, 55n153
Keener, Craig S., 160n90
Keith, Chris, 17, 18n58, 29n21, 30n29, 32n32, 32n34, 32n35, 33–35, 34n43, 34n44, 35n45, 35n47, 36n50, 37n53, 94n38
Kelber, Werner, 30n29
Kelhoffer, James A., 102n81
Kertelge, Karl, 58n4, 86n13
Keshgegian, Flora A., 42, 46
Kessler, Edward, 130n1, 172n18
Kinman, Brent, 103n83
Kirk, Alan, 30–32, 32n35, 33n39, 34n40, 42–43, 45, 48, 51n132
Klein, Ralph W., 72n68
Kloppenborg, John S., 15n46, 26, 26n4, 38n58, 66, 78
Klostermann, Erich, 58n4, 86
Koo, Kathryn S., 51, 51n129, 51n130

Kraeling, Carl H., 58n4
Kraemer, Ross S., 7n20, 10n29, 14n44, 15–16, 117–20
Kraft, Robert A., 167n3, 168n7
Kuhn, Heinz-Wolfgang, 59n5
Kyle, Donald G., 61n12, 61n14, 68n49, 69, 72, 77, 78n96, 80n101

Landres, J. Shawn, 42n75, 43n82, 47n109
Lane, William L., 13n43, 58n4, 61n11, 97n54
Laneri, Nicola, 68n48
Lange, Nicholas de, 155n76, 156n79, 163n95
Lawrence, Bruce B., 39, 41, 43, 53n147, 55n153
Le Donne, Anthony, 27n9, 29n20, 29n23, 34, 34n43, 34n44, 35n45, 35n47, 35n48, 48, 48n110
Lee, John, 107n104
Levin, Kevin M., 40n68
Levine, Amy-Jill, 173n21
Levy, Daniel, 17, 27n6, 27n8, 27n9, 30, 37n53, 38, 50n121
Lieu, Judith, 133n19, 167–70
Lincoln, Bruce, 16, 48, 155
Lohmeyer, Ernst, 7n24, 87n15, 93n35
Lupieri, Edmondo, 86n12, 118n144, 146n52, 149n64, 156, 163
Luz, Ulrich, 18–19, 36, 37n54

Malamud, Martha, 67, 78n93
Malina, Bruce J., 58n4, 86, 112n123
Malkki, Liisa H., 44, 51n132, 52–54
Maloney, Frances J., 58n4, 87n14, 120n153
Mann, C. S., 58n4, 86n14
Manns, Frédéric, 135n22
Marcus, Joel, 7n22, 9n28, 10n31, 11n32, 11n33, 13n43, 23, 89n26, 91n29, 98, 98n57, 103n82, 109n108, 110n109, 110n110, 114n131, 145n49, 159n87
Marotta, Valerio, 61n13
Marshall, I. Howard, 102n79
Martens, Peter W., 147n57, 163n95
Martínez, Roberto, 8n25
Marxsen, Willi, 13n43, 93n36
Masciandaro, Nicola, 121n155
McCane, Byron R., 69n49
McDonald, J. I. H., 7n22
McGuckin, John A., 147n53, 148n58
McManigal, Daniel W., 7n24
McVann, Mark, 13n43, 93n36
Meeks, Wayne A., 168n8

Meier, John P., 8n25, 11–12, 12n38, 17, 94n37
Merz, Annette, 9n27, 9n28
Messerschmidt, James W., 107n104
Metcalf, Peter, 69
Metzger, Bruce M., 119n152, 122
Miller, Geoffrey D., 96n47, 120n153
Miller, Susan, 95n43, 96n46, 105n86, 105n94, 106n97, 106n98, 109n108
Minns, Denis, 130n3, 131n4
Misztal, Barbara, 27n6, 46n100, 53n147, 54n150
Montesanti, Stephanie R., 41n72
Mor, Menahem, 131n5, 135n22
Moss, Candida R., 76n82
Muir, Steven, 18n58, 59n5
Müller, Ulrich B., 9n28
Murnane, William J., 69n52
Murphy, Catherine M., 10n32, 93n35, 104n86
Murphy-O'Connor, Jerome, 8n25
Musurillo, Herbert, 76n85

Nautin, Pierre, 147n53
Neal, Arthur, 43–47, 53n147, 54n148
Neginsky, Rosina, 19
Nineham, D. E., 58n4, 87n14
Nir, Rivka, 14n43, 89n23
Nirenberg, David, 136n25
Nolland, John, 87n19, 100, 110n110
Nünning, Ansgar, 27n6, 27n8, 32n33, 42n77
Nyström, David E., 130n3
Nytagodien, Ridwan, 44, 45n92, 45n94

Obayashi, Hiroshi, 69n49, 69n52
O'Collins, Gerald G., 59n5, 63
Oden, Thomas C., 19, 115n134
O'Leary, Joseph S., 148, 172n18
Olick, Jeffrey K., 17, 27n6, 27n7, 27n8, 27n9, 30, 33n39, 37n53, 38, 50n121
Oliver, William, 40–41, 40n68
Osgood, Josiah, 78n96

Paez, Dario, 21n71, 49n116, 55n150
Parker, Pierson, 8n25
Parker, Robert, 70
Parris, David Paul, 18n58
Parvis, Paul, 130n3, 131n4
Parvis, Sara, 130n3, 135n22
Pawlikowski, John T., 130n1, 172n18
Pellegrini, Silvia, 98n60, 118n147
Pennebaker, James W., 21, 49, 55n150
Pesantubbee, Michelene E., 43–45

Pesch, Rudolf, 10n31, 87n15
Pohl, Walter, 55
Popović, Mladen, 75n81
Porter, Martin, 50n123
Presser, Lois, 172, 173n20
Prince, K. Stephen, 55n153
Pryor, John W., 8n25

Radstone, Susannah, 27n6, 42n77
Räisänen, Heikki, 36
Rajak, Tessa, 135n22
Rawlinson, A. E. J., 13n43, 93
Rawson, Beryl, 112
Reed, Annette Yoshiko, 167n3, 168n6
Reinhartz, Adele, 129n1, 169n12, 171, 173n18
Reischer, Erica, 51, 51n129, 51n130
Reventlow, Henning Graf, 147n53
Ricoeur, Paul, 48n113
Riess, Werner, 47n2, 65, 78n96
Rindos, Jaroslav, 103n82
Robertson, Ritchie, 129n1
Robins, Joyce, 27n6, 27n7
Robinson, John A. T., 8n25
Robinson, Will, 120n154
Rodríguez, Rafael, 30n25, 33n39, 34
Rohrbaugh, Richard L., 58n4, 86, 112n123
Rollens, Sarah E., 31n30
Rosaldo, Renato, 42n77, 52n136
Rothschild, Clare K., 103n82
Rowling, J. K., 6n18

Samuelsson, Gunnar, 59n5
Sanders, E. P., 10, 89n26
Scarry, Elaine, 52
Schenk, Wolfgang, 9
Scheper-Hughes, Nancy, 38, 40, 41n72, 42n77, 47n109, 49n119, 52n139
Schnabel, Eckhard J., 59n5
Schnackenburg, Rudolf, 87n16
Schöpflin, Karin, 75n81
Schröter, Jens, 17n55, 18n58, 31n32, 34
Schudson, Michael, 28–29
Schütz, Roland, 58n4
Schwartz, Barry, 4, 14, 26n6, 28, 28n16, 29–30, 30n26, 31n30, 45n96, 46–47, 94
Schweitzer, Frederick, 129n1
Schweizer, Eduard, 13
Scobie, Charles H., 7n22, 8n25, 11n32, 110n109
Segal, Alan F., 68n48
Sen, Amartya, 42n76

Index of Modern Authors

Shanks, Hershel, 7n22
Shedd, Nathan L., 89n23, 94n41
Shepherd, Tom, 85n3
Shortt, Linda, 44n85, 45n92, 46n101, 48, 48n110, 50n121
Siegel, Maya, 46n101
Simon, Marcel, 167n2
Skarsaune, Oskar, 138n33, 146
Slusser, Michael, 130n3
Smit, Peter-Ben, 97n52
Smith, Abraham, 12n38, 96n46, 116n137
Snyder, Benjamin, 7n24
Snyder, Julia, 144n48
Stegemann, Hartmut, 7n22
Stein, Robert H., 58n4, 87n14, 94n42, 97n51, 119n150, 123n159
Steinmann, Jean, 58n4
Stichele, Caroline Vander, 19
Stiebert, Johanna, 110, 111n116
Stier, Oren Baruch, 42n75, 43n82, 47n109

Talbert, Charles H., 11n32
Taylor, Joan E., 7n22, 7n23, 7n24, 8n25, 9, 10n31, 50n124, 50n125, 58n4, 75n81, 88–90, 97n54, 105, 126
Taylor, Marion Ann, 13n40
Taylor, Vincent, 12n36
Thatcher, Tom, 28n15, 30n25, 30n29, 31, 35n48, 43n78, 45n94
Theissen, Gerd, 9n27, 9n28, 10n31, 94n37
Thiessen, Matthew, 85n3, 125
Thomas, Joseph, 87n14
Thorne, Mark, 71n63
Thurston, Wilfreda E., 41n72
Tilly, Michael, 7n23
Tong, M. Andryael, 51n126
Toynbee, J. M. C., 69n54
Trigg, Joseph W., 147, 147n53, 147n57
Tucker, Katie, 62n16
Turner, David L., 100n68, 159n87
Twelftree, Graham H., 8n25

Van Eickels, Klaus, 51
Vernant, Jean-Pierre, 70n57
Vette, Nathanael, 120n154
Vinitzky-Seroussi, Vered, 17, 27n6, 27n8, 27n9, 37n53, 38
Voisin, Jean-Louis, 67
Voragine, Jacobus de, 123n160

Wacquant, Loïc, 39n61
Wagner-Pacifici, Robin, 46
Walsh, Robyn Faith, 33n39

Watts, Dorothy, 62n16, 78n91, 124n160
Webb, Robert A., 7n23, 7n24, 8n25, 58n4, 89n26, 90n27, 93n35, 93n36, 97n54
Weilnböck, Harald, 42n77
Weir, Heather E., 13n40
Wenborn, Neil, 130n1, 172n18
Wendel, Susan, 133–35, 138n32
Wertsch, James V., 48n110, 53n147
Wickham, Chris, 27n6, 27n8, 30n27
Wiedemann, Thomas, 61n12
Wilken, Robert L., 168n8
Wilson, Brittany E., 65n30, 107n103
Wink, Walter, 13n43, 58n4, 93n35, 93n36, 97
Winter, Jay, 45n92
Winter, Paul, 7n21
Wise, Michael O., 59n5, 75n80
Witherington, Ben, 14n44, 58n4, 86n14, 117, 120

Yamasaki, Gary, 100n67
Yates, Gary E., 10n32, 98n60
Young, James E., 47n109

Zerubavel, Yael, 25, 30, 30n27
Zimmermann, Martin, 55, 63n21, 78
Žižek, Slavoj, 39–40, 43

Index of Primary Sources

1. Old Testament

Genesis
- 40:13 — 72n68
- 40:19 — 59n6, 63n18, 72n68, 72n69
- 40:20–23 — 159

Exodus
- 10:28 — 59n6
- 12:46 — 150n65, 163n94
- 20:3 — 98
- 20:12 — 113
- 20:13 — 153n69
- 34:14 — 98

Leviticus
- 18:6 — 111
- 18:16 — 88, 114n131
- 18:17 — 111
- 18:21 — 113n126
- 20:2 — 113n126
- 20:21 — 88, 114n131
- 21:1–9 — 68n49
- 21:10–15 — 68n49
- 26:40–41 — 133

Numbers
- 30:2 — 106

Deuteronomy
- 5:7 — 98
- 5:16 — 113
- 5:17 — 153n69
- 6:13–14 — 98
- 12:31 — 113n126
- 18:10 — 113n126
- 23:21–23 — 106n96
- 24:1–4 — 88
- 25:5–10 — 88n23, 114n131

Judges
- 7:25 — 59n6
- 11:29–40 — 113

1 Samuel
- 5:1–5 — 66
- 5:4 — 59n6, 66
- 17:51 — 59n6
- 17:54 — 59n6
- 18:25 — 59n6
- 25:2–39 — 115n134
- 31:1–13 — 72n68
- 31:8–9 — 59n6
- 31:9 — 59n6, 72n68

2 Samuel
- 4:1–12 — 59n6
- 20:10–22 — 59n6

1 Kings
- 16:29–33 — 98
- 17:2–6 — 98
- 17:17–24 — 74, 98, 102
- 18:17–19 — 98
- 19:2 — 98
- 19:4–9 — 98
- 19:10 — 133
- 19:19–21 — 98
- 21:25 — 98n60

2 Kings
- 1:8 — 93n35
- 1:10–14 — 102
- 2:1–15 — 123n159
- 4:18–37 — 74
- 4:34–35 — 98
- 6:31 — 59n6, 98n60
- 10:1–11 — 59n6

Index of Primary Sources 211

1 Chronicles
    10:1–14   72n68
    10:4   72n68
    10:9   72n68
    10:9–10   59n6
    10:10   72n68, 77n90

Esther
    2:4   91
    2:9   91
    2:14   91
    2:15   91
    2:17   91
    5:3   10, 91
    7:10   59n6

Psalms
    33:21   150n65

Proverbs
    7:11–12   105n92
    7:25–26   105
    8:1–3   105n92

Ecclesiastes
    5:5   106n96, 114n129

Isaiah
    7:14   134n20
    9:13   59n6
    11:1–3   138n32
    20:1–5   63n21
    57:5   132n16

Ezekiel
    37:1–10   75n81
    37:1–14   75, 75n81
    37:11–14   75n81

Daniel
    11:33   75
    12:2   75

Malachi
    1:10–12   133
    1:11   133
    3:1   93n35
    4:5–6   93n35

2. Septuagint (LXX)

Genesis
    19:8   110n110

Exodus
    10:28   59n6
    12:46   163n94
    20:15   153n69

Numbers
    30:3   105–6

Deuteronomy
    5:18   153n69

    25:5–6   89n23

1 Kingdoms
    17:51   59n6
    18:25   59n6
    31:1–13   72n68
    31:9   59n6
    31:10   77n90

2 Kingdoms
    4:1–12   59n6
    20:10–22   59n6

3 Kingdoms
    19:20   93n35

4 Kingdoms
    1:8   98, 103
    6:31   59n6
    10:1–11   59n6

1 Chronicles
    10:1–14   72n68
    10:9–10   59n6
    10:10   77n90

Esther
    1:21   91n30
    2:4   91n30
    2:9   91
    4:8   91
    4:11   91
    5:3   90–91
    5:6   90–91
    5:13   91n30
    7:2   90–91

Psalms
    33:21   163n94
    151:7   59n6

Job
    31:10   110n110

Joel
    2:28–29   160n89

Isaiah
    9:13   59n6
    29:14   133

3. New Testament

Matthew
    2:1–18   102n76
    2:16–18   144n48
    3:4   103
    5:12   102n76
    5:33–34   113
    5:37   113
    8:21–22   68n49
    11:7   89n25
    11:9   101, 159

212 Index of Primary Sources

11:11	101, 159, 159n87
11:12	9n28
11:12–15	142n40
11:13	153n70
11:15	101
11:17	152n67
14:1	91n29, 158n84
14:1–2	102, 142n41
14:1–12	12, 19, 83n2, 99–104, 101n74, 148
14:2	119, 123, 125n162
14:3	11n33, 100, 153n70
14:3–4	102n77
14:3–5	142n42
14:3–12	148, 158
14:5	13n39, 90n27, 100–101, 102n76, 105
14:6	11n33, 142n43, 151n66, 152, 157
14:8	85n5, 144
14:9	12n39, 85n6, 91n29, 100n68, 143n44, 144n48, 152n68, 158
14:10	85n7, 92, 148, 153n69, 161
14:11	86n8, 86n9, 86n10, 92, 96, 148, 158, 159n86
14:11–12	87n19, 148
14:12	86n11, 100, 143n45, 148, 161n91
14:13–14	160n88
16:20–21	157n83
17:9–13	101, 103, 143, 145
17:10	103n82, 145–46
17:12	145
17:12–13	101n74, 102n76
17:13	101, 101n75, 145
21:23–27	101n71
21:46	100–101
23:29–37	102n76
26:4	100
26:48	100
26:50	100
26:51	154n72
26:55	100
26:57	100
27:2	100
27:15–23	101n71
27:18–24	101n71
27:57	100
27:57–61	100

Mark

1:2–4	93n35
1:4–5	89
1:6	93n35, 98, 103
1:7	93n35, 98
1:9	89, 120
1:9–11	120
1:11	120
1:13	98
1:14	9n28, 92
1:16–20	98
1:23–28	125
1:40–41	96n46
1:40–45	125
3:19	92
3:20–35	85
3:35	96n46
5:1–21	125
5:21–24	16, 74, 98, 125, 126n165
5:21–43	85
5:25–34	125
5:35–43	74, 98, 125, 126n165
5:41	126
6:6–13	84–85, 97
6:14	9n28, 14, 16, 19n67, 85, 88, 91n29, 96, 109n108, 116–26, 118n147, 119n150, 119n152, 123n159
6:14–15	122
6:14–16	16, 102, 116–26
6:14–29	3, 13, 15, 19, 83–127, 144n48, 161n91
6:15	98, 122
6:16	14, 88, 109n108, 116–26, 118n147, 119n150, 119n152, 123n159
6:17	11, 85, 92, 97, 108
6:17–18	102n77
6:17–20	108n105, 142n42
6:17–29	3, 10, 83–127
6:18	95
6:18–19	88
6:19	90n27, 96n46, 100, 105–6
6:19–20	95
6:20	13n39, 21, 92, 94, 94n42, 100, 100n70, 105, 108–9, 109n108, 114, 116, 126
6:21	96, 96n45, 108n105, 116n137, 142n43
6:21–29	108n105
6:22	9, 11n33, 90–91, 91n29, 96, 96n46, 110–11, 110n110, 114–15, 126, 151n66
6:22–23	90–91, 108, 109n108
6:22–27	97
6:23	10, 90, 106, 115
6:24	3, 11n33, 85, 91, 106, 108

6:24–25	58n4, 105n86
6:24–27	22
6:24–28	87
6:24–29	124
6:25	3, 85, 91, 91n29, 96, 106n97, 108, 144
6:26	13n39, 91n29, 96, 96n46, 109n108, 115, 143n44, 152n68
6:26–27	92, 95
6:27	3, 85, 91n29, 96–97, 108
6:27–28	22, 88, 106
6:27–29	1n1, 86
6:28	3, 86, 97, 108, 109n107, 126
6:29	3, 86–87, 86n14, 92, 143n45, 161n91
6:30	85, 98n55
6:31–44	97
7:24–30	106n98
8:27	98
8:27–33	96n46
9:1–13	93n35
9:9–13	93n35, 97, 101, 103
9:11–13	93, 97n54, 103n82
9:12	97n54
9:13	93n35, 97, 98n55
9:30–32	96n46
9:31	92
9:34–35	96n46
10:32–34	96n46
10:33	92
10:35–44	96n46
10:45	97
10:51	96n46
11:12–25	85
11:18	95
12:12	92, 95
12:37	92
12:38–40	96n46
13:9	92, 97n48
13:11–12	92
14:1	85, 92, 96
14:1–11	85
14:1–15:47	96n46
14:3–9	106n98
14:10–11	92
14:11	96
14:18	92
14:21	92
14:36	96n46
14:41–42	92
14:44	92
14:46	92
14:47	154n72
14:49	92
14:53–72	85
14:55	96n44
14:71	106n96
15:1	92
15:2	97
15:6–32	85
15:9	95, 96n46, 97
15:10	92, 95
15:11	92, 96n46
15:12	95, 97
15:12–13	96n46
15:12–14	61n11
15:13–14	92
15:14	95
15:15	92, 95, 96n46
15:18	97
15:26	97
15:32	97
15:43–46	87n14
15:45	92
15:46	92
15:47	96n46
16:6	92

Luke

1:17	102, 103n82, 117n140
1:76	103
3:1	9n27
3:1–3	8–10, 89
3:2	103
3:19	11n33, 91n29
3:19–20	83n2, 99, 102n77, 103, 142n42
7:7–17	102
7:11–17	74
7:16	9n28
7:24	89n25
7:26	159
7:28	159, 159n87
7:32	152n67
9:1–6	102
9:7	91n29, 120, 120n154
9:7–9	83n2, 99–104, 142n41
9:9	102–3, 118, 120–21
9:10	102
9:18–22	102
9:51–56	102
9:59–60	68
13:31–33	102
16:16	142n40, 153n70
22:50	154n72
23:6–12	144n48, 154
23:7–11	102

John
- 1:21 — 93n35, 103n82
- 3:30 — 99n64
- 5:46 — 162
- 10:41 — 117n140
- 11:1–44 — 74
- 18:31 — 154, 154n73
- 19:1 — 47
- 19:31–37 — 163n94
- 19:36 — 150n65

Acts
- 2:1–4 — 160
- 2:1–41 — 160, 161n92
- 2:5–13 — 160n90
- 2:17–18 — 160
- 4:27 — 102
- 5:36 — 59n6
- 13:1 — 91n29
- 19:1–12 — 87n14

Philippians
- 2:5–11 — 56

Revelation
- 20:4 — 77n87

4. Old Testament Apocrypha

Judith
- 13–16 — 59n6
- 13:8 — 62n16
- 14:14–19 — 66
- 14:18 — 66
- 15:1–3 — 66
- 15:8–10 — 66
- 15:11 — 66
- 15:12 — 66
- 16:1–17 — 66
- 16:5 — 66
- 16:21 — 66

1 Maccabees
- 7:39–50 — 59n6
- 11:17 — 59n6
- 11:47 — 78n90

2 Maccabees
- 7:1–42 — 74
- 7:11 — 75
- 14:37–46 — 75
- 14:46 — 75
- 15:28–36 — 59n6
- 15:30–31 — 78n90
- 15:30–33 — 63n20, 72n69
- 15:33 — 78n90
- 15:35 — 78n90

Sirach
- 23:11 — 106n96, 114, 114n129

5. Old Testament Pseudepigrapha

1 Enoch
- 61:5 — 75

Psalm 151B (5ApocSyrPs 1b)
- 151B:2 — 66

6. Dead Sea Scrolls

4Q163 (4QIsaiah Pesher[c])
- frgs. 4–6 col. I 6 — 59, 72n68

4Q385 (4QPseudo-Ezekiel[a])
- in toto — 75n81

4Q521 (4Q Messianic Apocalypse)
- frg. 2 col. II 12 — 75

11Q5 (11QPsalms[a])
- col. XXI 11–18 — 105

7. Josephus

Jewish Antiquities
- 2.73 — 59n6
- 2.310 — 59n6
- 5.263–266 — 113n125
- 5.266 — 113
- 6.191 — 59n6
- 6.191–192 — 77n89
- 6.193–204 — 59n6
- 6.203–204 — 77n90
- 6.368–378 — 59n6, 72n68
- 6.374 — 63n18
- 7.47–49 — 67
- 7.50–52 — 80n102
- 9.125–131 — 72n68
- 9.127 — 78n90
- 14.9 — 145n49
- 14.381–385 — 144n48
- 14.448–450 — 59n6, 72n68
- 14.464 — 59n6, 72n68
- 15.8–9 — 59n6, 63n18
- 15.9–10 — 64
- 17.188 — 91n29
- 17.273–277 — 59n6, 79n97
- 18.36–38 — 89, 127
- 18.109 — 11n33
- 18.109–115 — 88
- 18.110 — 88n23
- 18.116 — 88n22
- 18.116–119 — 8–10, 9n28, 15n47, 83n2, 90n27, 99n64, 142n42, 145n50
- 18.118 — 90n27
- 18.119 — 88n22
- 18.136 — 11n33
- 18.136–137 — 9n26, 11, 11n33

Index of Primary Sources   215

18.241–256		91n29
18.289–304		106
20.97–99		59n6, 79n97, 90n27
20.117		59n6, 79n97

Jewish War

1.123	145n49
1.323–326	59n6
1.342–343	72n68
2.135	114
2.178–183	91n29
2.246	59n6, 63n19, 64, 77n89
6.360–362	59n6, 77n89

8. Philo

On the Decalogue

17.84	114

On Dreams

2.213	63n18

On the Life of Joseph

96	59n6
98	63n18

On the Special Laws

2.8	114

9. Babylonian Talmud

Sotah

10a	72n68

10. Mishnah

Bava Batra

8:5	113

Demai

2:3	114

Nedarim

9:1	113

Sanhedrin

7:3	63

11. Other Rabbinic Works

Esther Rabbah

7:10	59n6

12. Classical Works

Appian

Civil Wars

1.10.93	60n7, 64–65
3.26	60n7

Roman History

3.9.5	63n17

Callistratus

Justinian's *Digest*

48.19.28	63

Cicero

Against Verres

4.64.144	64n28

On Duties

3.25	112–13

Philippics

2.39–40	81n107

Dio Cassius

Roman History

49.2–3	60n7
49.22.6	63n18, 64n28
56.21.5	60n7
73.21.1	2, 5–6
73.21.1–2	2, 5–6
73.21.2	2, 5–6

Diodorus of Sicily

Library of History

36.4	63n17
38.8	63n17

Dionysius of Halicarnassus

Roman Antiquities

2.29	60n7, 77n89, 79n97
3.58.4	60n7, 63n17, 77n89
5.61.3	63n17
6.30.1–2	60n7, 77n89

Epictetus

Diatribes

1.1.19–20	62

Euphorion

Prose Fragments

194	60n7

Euripides

Andromache

173–180	111
410	60n7

Cyclops

399	60n7

Electra

813	60n7

Herodian

History of the Empire

1.15.1–15	1–2, 4–6
1.15.5–6	1–2
1.15.7	5, 6n17

Herodotus

Histories

7.238	60n7, 70n58, 72n68
8.21.3	63n18

Homer

Iliad

18.176–180	60n7, 70
18.177	77n90

Index of Primary Sources

22.337–343   68n49
23.65–74   69

Odyssey
11.41   73n71

Juvenal
Satires
3.254–267   70
3.264–267   70

Livy
History of Rome
2.5   63n17, 77n89, 79n97
3.9.3   60n7
4.10   79n97
28.29   79n99

Lucan
The Civil War
2.160–173   60n7
2.166–173   70–71

Ovid
Metamorphoses
4.765–785   60n7
5.103–106   78n91

Parthenius
Sufferings in Love
8.9   154n72

Petronius
Satyricon
71   69

Plato
Laws
8.838b   111
8.838b–c   112
Republic
5.461b–c   112

Plutarch
Lives: Antony
20   81–82
36   60n7, 63n18, 64n28
Lives: Artaxerxes
14   62n15
29   60n7
Lives: Brutus
52   114
Lives: Cicero
48.4   82n109
Lives: Crassus
33.4   116n137
Lives: Dion
57.2   60n7
Lives: Galba
27   66
27.2–4   60n7
28   71n65
Lives: Otho
2.3   60n7
Lives: Publicola
6.99   63n17
Moralia: Love Stories
3   60n7
Moralia: On Compliancy
4   60n7

Polybius
The Histories
1.7.11–12   60n7, 77n89
1.7.12   63n17, 79n97
8.21.3   63n18
11.27–30   73
11.29.9–13   73
11.29.10   73
11.30.2–3   73
11.30.4–5   73

Seneca (the Elder)
Controversiae
9.2.4   116n137

Seneca (the Younger)
Epistles
83.25   116n137
On Anger
1.6.4   63n21
2.5.3   80–81
2.5.4–5   80–81
2.5.5   67, 80–81

Sextus Empiricus
Outlines of Pyrrhonism
3.246   112n122

Silius Italicus
Punica
10.145–146   60n7

Suetonius
The Deified Augustus
13.2   72n69
Galba
20   71n65
Nero
16.2   169
49   71
49.4   60n7

Tacitus
Annals
14.64   60n7, 72n68
Histories
1.41   71n65
1.47   71

Index of Primary Sources   217

1.49	71n65
3.74	60n7, 63n20, 72n69

Valerius Maximus
Memorable Doings and Sayings

9.2.2	116n137

Velleius Paterculus
Compendium of Roman History

2.27.3	60n7
2.70.2–3	65n29
2.119.1–5	77n90

Virgil
Aeneid

2.557–558	65n35
6.327–328	69
6.440–476	73n76
6.445–446	73n76
6.450	73n76
6.623	112n122

Xenophon
Cyropaedia

5.1.10	111, 111n119

Memorabilia

4.4.19–23	111n114

13. Other Classical Works

Pauli Sententiae

5.17.2	63

14. Apostolic Fathers

1 Clement

7.4	161n92

15. New Testament Apocrypha, Pseudepigrapha and Related Works

Acts of Justin and His Companions

A.5	76–77

Apocalypse of Peter

4	76

Martyrdom of Paul

4	76–77

16. Other Early Christian Literature

Ambrose
Concerning Virgins

3.5.25–3.6.31	13n40

Augustine
Sermons

307.1	12n39, 99n64
308.1	105
308.1–2	115

Tractates on the Gospel of John

14.5.3	99n64

Basil
Letters

199.29	13n40, 45

Caesarius of Arles
Sermons

218	89n23, 162n93

Cyril
Catechetical Lectures

4.2	169n10

Eusebius
Ecclesiastical History

1.6	145n49
4.18.6	130

Hilary of Poitiers
Commentary on Matthew

14.7–8	12n39

Hippolytus
On the Antichrist

45	93n36

Jerome
Commentary on Matthew

14.3–4	89n23, 99n62
14.7	12n39
14.9	12n39
14.11	159n86, 172n18
14.13	148n63

John Chrysostom
Discourse against Judaizing Christians

8.5. col. 934–935	168n8

Homilies on Matthew

24.4	125n162
48	13n40
48.5	13n40
48.8	13n40

Justin Martyr
1 Apology

31	131
31.5	132n15
47–49	135
49.1–5	132n14

2 Apology

15.1	130n2

Dialogue with Trypho

1.3	130–31, 139n34
1.6	139n34
2–7	139n34
8–9	134n20
8.1–2	135n24, 139n34, 143
8.2–4	139n34
8.3–4	134n20

218 Index of Primary Sources

8.4	139n34, 140
10.1	134n20
10.4	134n20
11.5	133n18, 134
14.8	132, 142n28, 142n39
16	131
16.1	133
16.1–4	135
16.4	133
17.1	132
19.6	132
25.5	135
26.1	135n24, 143, 143n47
29.1	135
29.2	132, 135
31.1	142n38, 142n39
32.1	134n20, 142
32.1–2	142, 142n38, 142n39
32.2	132
32.5	132–33
35.2	134n21
35.8	136
36.1	139, 140n35, 142, 142n39
39.1	132–33
39.2	134n21
39.7	139, 140n35, 142
40.1–5	142
40.4	132n13
41.2–3	133
45.4	142n38
46.6	132, 132n16
46.7	135
47.1	134n20
47.3	134n21
48.1	137, 138n31
48.4	135n24, 143
49.1	136–40, 139n34, 146
49.2	139–40
49.3	142–44, 142n40, 143n46
49.3–5	140–47
49.4	109n107, 142–44, 142n43, 144n48, 146
49.5	142–43, 145–46
49.7	142
49.7–8	142–43
51.3	142n40
52.1	12n39
52.3	144n48, 145
54.1	152n38
54.2	138n31
69.1	143n46
69.7	142n38
72.3	132n13
77–78	144n48
77.1	134n20
82.1	132, 135, 135n24, 143, 143n46
87.1–2	138n32
87.3–88.2	138n32
87.4	143n46
88.2	142n40
103.3–4	144n48
108.3	135
110.2	142, 142n38
112.3	135n24, 143
112.5	132
120.4	142n38
120.5	132, 135n24, 143
120.6	130
121.3	142
123.6–9	134
125.5	134
133.1	132
133.6	132, 132n12
135.3	134
142.3	134n21

Origen
Against Celsus
5.43	156n79
8.42	161n92

Commentary on Matthew
10.18	156n79
10.21	89n23, 149–50, 152–54
10.21–22	23, 147–63, 153n69, 161n91
10.22	23, 115, 148–53, 148n61, 155, 157–60, 157n82, 161n92, 162
10.23	160n88
16.3	156n79, 157n83

Homilies on Luke
4.5	93n36

Tertullian
The Resurrection of the Flesh
32.1	76

17. Oxyrhynchus Papyri

22.2339
1.6	63n17
1.10–11	63n17

18. Inscriptions

Tombstone of Insus	67–68